A WIDE
NET OF
SOLIDARITY

RADICAL AMÉRICAS | *A series edited by Bruno Bosteels and Geo Maher*

ANNE
GARLAND
MAHLER

A WIDE
NET OF
SOLIDARITY

ANTIRACISM
AND ANTI-
IMPERIALISM
FROM THE
AMERICAS TO
THE GLOBE

DUKE UNIVERSITY PRESS | *Durham and London* | 2025

© 2025 DUKE UNIVERSITY PRESS
All rights reserved
Project Editor: Michael Trudeau
Designed by Matthew Tauch
Typeset in Arno Pro and Helvetica LT Std by
Westchester Publishing Services

Library of Congress Cataloging-in-Publication Data
Names: Mahler, Anne Garland, [date] author.
Title: A wide net of solidarity : antiracism and anti-imperialism
from the Americas to the Globe / Anne Garland Mahler.
Other titles: Anti-racism and anti-imperialism from the Americas
to the Globe | Radical Américas.
Description: Durham : Duke University Press, 2025. | Series:
Radical Américas | Includes bibliographical references and index.
Identifiers: LCCN 2024055525 (print)
LCCN 2024055526 (ebook)
ISBN 9781478032083 (paperback)
ISBN 9781478028819 (hardcover)
ISBN 9781478061038 (ebook)
Subjects: LCSH: Liga Antiimperialista de las Américas—
History. | Communist International—History. | Anti-imperialist
movements—Latin America—History. | Communism—Latin
America—History. | Racism against Black people—Latin
America—History. | Racism against Indigenous peoples—
Latin America—History.
Classification: LCC HX110.5.A6 M345 2025 (print) |
LCC HX110.5.A6 (ebook)
LC record available at https://lccn.loc.gov/2024055525
LC ebook record available at https://lccn.loc.gov/2024055526

Cover art: Tina Modotti, *Untitled (Sand)*, 1929.
© 2008 Christie's Images Limited.

FOR THE ACTIVISTS AND ARTISTS WHO INSPIRED
THIS BOOK ONE HUNDRED YEARS LATER

CONTENTS

ABBREVIATIONS

AAAIL	All-America Anti-Imperialist League
ANERC	Asociación de Nuevos Emigrados Revolucionarios Cubanos / Association of New Cuban Revolutionary Émigrés
ANLC	American Negro Labor Congress
APRA	Alianza Popular Revolucionaria Americana / American Popular Revolutionary Alliance
BC	Buró del Caribe / Caribbean Bureau
CNOC	Confederación Nacional Obrera de Cuba / Confederation of Cuban Workers
COMINTERN	Communist International
CPUSA	Communist Party of the United States of America
CSLA	Confederación Sindical Latino Americana / Confederation of Latin American Labor Unions
EDSN	Ejército Defensor de la Soberanía Nacional de Nicaragua / Army in Defense of the National Sovereignty of Nicaragua
FBI	Federal Bureau of Investigation
HPU	Haitian Patriotic Union
IC	Internacional Comunista / Communist International
IIAAF	International Imagination of Anti-National Anti-Imperialist Feelings
IRA	International Red Aid
ITUCNW	International Trade Union Committee of Negro Workers
LACO	League Against Colonial Oppression
LADLA	Liga Antimperialista de las Américas / Anti-Imperialist League of the Americas
LAI	League Against Imperialism and Colonial Rule and for National Independence
LCAEV	Liga de Comunidades Agrarias del Estado de Veracruz / Veracruz League of Agrarian Communities

LNC	Liga Nacional Campesina / National Peasant League
MAFUENIC	Manos Fuera de Nicaragua / Hands Off Nicaragua
NAACP	National Association for the Advancement of Colored People
OC	Oposición Comunista / Communist Opposition
OCMAL	Observatorio de Conflictos Mineros de América Latina / Observatory of Mining Conflicts of Latin America
PBL	Partido Bolchevique-Leninista / Bolshevik-Leninist Party
PCC	Partido Comunista Cubano / Cuban Communist Party
PCCR	Partido Comunista de Costa Rica / Costa Rican Communist Party
PCM	Partido Comunista Mexicano / Mexican Communist Party
PIC	Partido Independiente de Color / Independent Party of Color
PNPR	Partido Nacionalista de Puerto Rico / Puerto Rican Nationalist Party
POS	Partido Obrero Socialista / Mexican Socialist Party
PROFINTERN	Red International of Labor Unions
PRV	Partido Revolucionario Venezolano / Venezuelan Revolutionary Party
PSP	Partido Socialista Popular / Dominican Popular Socialist Party
SSA	Secretariado Sudamericano / South American Secretariat
TUEL	Trade Union Educational League
UNIA	United Negro Improvement Association
UP	Universidad Popular José Martí / José Martí Popular University
WP	Workers Party of America

INTRODUCTION

REDES

POLITICS AND AESTHETICS IN THE EXTRACTIVE ZONE

In the short film *Land of Friends* (2014) by Colombian American artist Carolina Caycedo, a fisherwoman and water rights activist repeatedly tosses out a fishing net while standing in the Suaza River (figure I.1). The film devotes more than a minute to this meditative gesture, representing the beginning of the artist's long-standing fascination with "the cast fishing net as an affective object."[1] In the final scene of this sequence, the fisherwoman (Zoila Ninco) pulls in an empty net before walking away defeated, introducing the film's focus on hydroelectric dams' detrimental impacts on local ecologies.[2] Caycedo has since incorporated the cast net into several projects about hydroelectric dams built for mining projects, including her impressive hanging sculptures that combine handmade nets and symbolic objects given to her by members of river communities. These *cosmotarrayas*—a neologism combining *cosmos* with *atarraya*, the Spanish term for "cast net"—imitate the conical shape of cast nets as they hang to dry from riverside trees.

Caycedo's attention to the act of casting a net in *Land of Friends* recalls the opening scene of the renowned Mexican film *Redes* (1936), a collaboration between directors Fred Zinneman and Emilio Gómez Muriel with photographer Paul Strand. *Redes* begins with a medium shot of the protagonist, Miro, standing in the ocean and holding a net. After he casts the net, a low-angle shot captures it spread out across the sky before it falls onto the camera (figures I.2 and I.3). After Miro pulls in only one fish, the film then cuts to panning shots of wooden shacks, tattered clothes on a line, and drying drag nets hanging from poles. These images introduce

I.1 Film still, *Land of Friends* (2014).

the setting: a fishing village in Veracruz. The village is controlled by a local businessman who, allied with a politician and holding a monopoly on the region's commercial fishing industry, underpays the local fishermen. The film's title, *Redes*, references the fishing nets owned by the businessman, but an alternative translation of *redes* refers to "networks." The film meditates on the affective connections necessary for the fishermen to take control of the means of production to free themselves from poverty. Like the film *Redes*, to which I will return, Caycedo's *cosmotarrayas* contain a parallel double meaning, referring both to fishing nets and to the "networks of solidarity and resistance in the fight for . . . social justice" where "the everyday gesture of casting a net is a political act that affirms the river as a common good."[3]

Caycedo is one of many artists in recent years whose work critiques mining and other extractive industries. This body of work has emerged alongside a surge in environmental social justice movements in Latin America and around the globe. These struggles carry ties across space and time, and they draw on longer histories of political organizing. *A Wide Net of Solidarity: Antiracism and Anti-Imperialism from the Americas to the Globe* situates these trends in contemporary activism within a longer history of struggle in the American continent and beyond by unearthing networks of activists and artists in the 1920s–30s and examining the insights of their vision for a "rebellious humanity" today.[4]

1.2 Film still, *Redes* (1936).

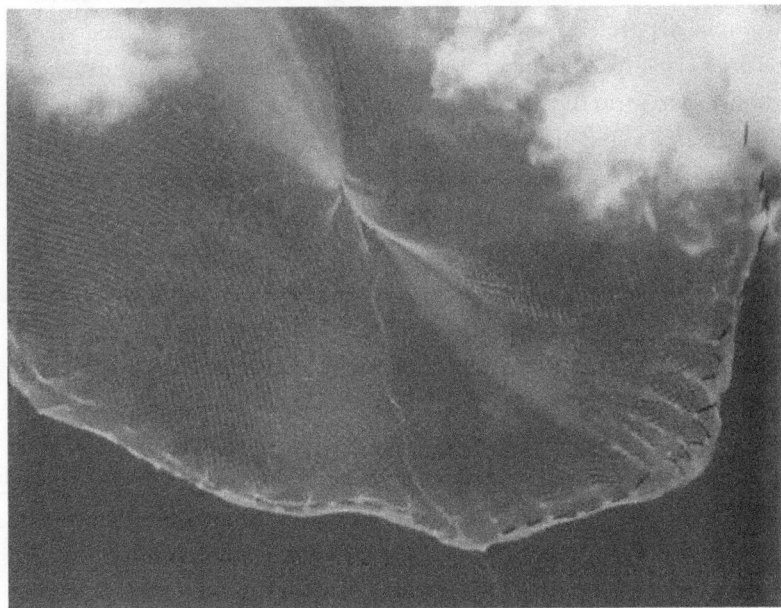

1.3 Film still, *Redes* (1936).

While this book touches on a broad set of organizations, individuals, and cultural production, at its core is the highly influential, but under-theorized, movement called the Anti-Imperialist League of the Americas (Liga Antimperialista de las Américas, LADLA). LADLA was founded in January 1925 in Mexico City but quickly grew to include fourteen national sections throughout the continent, and these national sections often over-saw additional subsections in local cities (including Spanish-speaking sections within the continental United States).[5] It joined urban trade unions, agrarian organizations, and cultural and artistic groups to combat US and European commercial and military expansion and eventually the rise of Depression-era nationalism. It directly linked its position of anti-imperialism to a critique of extractive and monocrop plantation econo-mies and to the related land dispossession and exploitation of Black, In-digenous, and immigrant populations. Through unifying the communities most affected by extractive projects into a transnational and multiracial political community, LADLA sought to forge an alternative relation among peoples across national, linguistic, and racial borders and to denaturalize the commodification of territories and resources.

Within two years of LADLA's founding, at the 1927 Congress Against Colonial Oppression and Imperialism and for National Independence in Brussels, LADLA members joined with 174 delegates from thirty-seven countries to form the global League Against Imperialism (LAI). In Brus-sels, the LAI would officially name LADLA as its Americas section.[6] There, LADLA activists interacted with Black activists from the United States and anticolonial leaders from Africa and Asia, like India's Jawaharlal Nehru and Senegal's Lamine Senghor. *A Wide Net of Solidarity* provides the first account of how these exchanges impacted debates in radical circles in the Americas, specifically regarding the subjects of Black and Indigenous leader-ship in political organizing, immigrant rights, racial policing, and links be-tween foreign intervention and internal forms of fascist governance. By connecting to issues in Africa, Asia, and the United States, LADLA devised a comparative approach to policing and racialized violence, particularly in extractive economies. With this lens, it theorized a relationship between labor exploitation, anti-blackness, and anti-immigrant sentiment in Latin American countries with high levels of Haitian and West Indian migrant labor, and it attempted to combat the rise of nativism in these contexts.

This book aims to situate LADLA in its rightful place among the most significant solidarity movements in the history of the American continent.

LADLA activists conceived of this movement in terms both practical and aesthetic, and several activist-artists shaped its core vision. If Caycedo, for example, seems to reference the cinematography of Paul Strand's *Redes* in her film, Strand himself drew inspiration from Tina Modotti, the Italian-born photographer based in Mexico City and one of LADLA's most active members. Modotti's 1929 photographs of drying drag nets, featured on the cover of this book, clearly reverberate in *Redes*. More importantly, Modotti's broader body of work, as I detail in the first chapter, attempted to capture aesthetically LADLA's worldview, visualizing an alternative social relation to extractive economies.

Beyond Modotti, several well-known artists, activists, and intellectuals counted among LADLA's core leadership in Mexico City. These included Mexican organizers Úrsulo Galván and Rafael Carrillo; Mexican visual artists Diego Rivera, Xavier Guerrero, and David Siqueiros; leaders of the Cuban anti-Machado resistance movement exiled in Mexico City, like Julio Antonio Mella and Sandalio Junco; Venezuelan activists Salvador de la Plaza and Gustavo Machado; and members of the so-called slackers from the United States who joined the Mexican Left when they evaded military conscription, like Manuel Gomez (aka Charles Francis Phillips) and Bertram and Ella Wolfe. Once LADLA joined the LAI in 1927, Swiss communist Fritz Sulzbachner (aka Federico Bach) became the LAI's representative in Mexico City. Bach was replaced in 1929 by the German economics professor Alfons Goldschmidt, who worked at the National Autonomous University of Mexico.[7] Although the members of LADLA's fourteen national sections would be too many to name here, they also included several poets and novelists, including Costa Rican author Carmen Lyra and Cuban writers Alejo Carpentier, Rubén Martínez Villena, Regino Pedroso, and Luis Felipe Rodríguez.

While it was partially funded by organizations with affiliations to the Communist International (1919–43), LADLA maintained an ideologically fluid vision based on the Comintern's "united-front" approach of the 1920s, joining a broad range of social classes and leftist ideologies behind a position of anti-imperialism.[8] Many of LADLA's central leaders belonged to communist parties and were heavily influenced by Marxism-Leninism, but they actively resisted labeling LADLA as a communist organization and intentionally propagated a flexible political platform. LADLA operated as a node in a broader network of leftist organizing and aimed to cast a wide net, bringing together varying perspectives, including those from anarcho-syndicalism and local traditions of anticolonial struggle.[9] LADLA's history challenges the proliferation of scholarship on Latin American communism, particularly Cuban and Mexican communism, by providing an alternative and more ideologically flexible perspective that gets buried in the predominant tendency to focus on the region's more orthodox communist parties.[10]

The networks studied in this book traverse a wide-ranging geography from Mexico City to Berlin, Brussels, Buenos Aires, Havana, Managua, Montevideo, Moscow, Santo Domingo, San Juan, and New York City. Its central actors include people born in Cuba, Costa Rica, the Dominican Republic, Italy, Mexico, Peru, the United States, and Venezuela. Tracing such a multinational constellation of individuals, held together around the shape of their shared political ideals, constitutes a core aim of this book. Some of the figures studied (like Afro-Cuban union organizer Sandalio Junco or African American miner Isaiah Hawkins) are little known. Despite the transnational sites of exchange in which these actors came into contact, their work is often kept separate in the scholarly record due to the linguistic and regional patterns through which we tend to organize scholarship. To tell the story of LADLA is to tell the story of these weavings—of ties at once political and artistic, and often romantic, erotic, or adversarial.

If LADLA's political project linked actors across national, linguistic, and racial borders, its artists' aesthetics also forged an entwined imagination. This study combines the analysis of personal papers, government records, speeches and resolutions, and trade union, Comintern, and anti-imperialist periodicals with related poetry, photography, illustrations, novels, and ephemera in both Spanish and English. The analysis of archival materials and rare newspapers alongside literary and artistic works reflects an understanding of cultural and artistic texts not as mere expressions of their historical reality but as works that help shape that reality. My training and experience in cultural studies and archival methods means an approach to archives that takes seriously the content of a political activist's letter and also the illustration on the letterhead and the poem enclosed within. Although the artists and activists discussed in these pages are frequently studied apart from one another, these individuals did not view their artistic and political realms as separate. This book, in turn, follows their lead.

A Wide Net of Solidarity ultimately argues that LADLA made three lasting contributions that are useful to social movements today. First, LADLA provides an early twentieth-century example of transnational political organizing across extractive economies, which it used to theorize the relationship between differing oppressions and to imagine a new global political community. Second, LADLA analyzed the relation (but not conflation) of differentiated experiences of capitalist exploitation suffered by Indigenous, Black, and immigrant communities. In doing so, it advanced a multiracial and hemispheric analysis of racialized capital accumulation. And third, LADLA serves as an important case study for thinking through the promises and limitations of transnational and multiracial solidarity movements.

LADLA FROM THE AMERICAS TO THE GLOBE

A Wide Net of Solidarity is the first book-length study of LADLA published in English. Because it uniquely brings together personal papers from LADLA's Latin American and US sections with LAI archives, it adds significantly to the historiography of LADLA and the LAI. The book moves in new directions by tracing LADLA's theoretical contributions, the broader debates that its members engaged, and the impact of its networks in interwar radical cultural production. The existing scholarship on LADLA, with which this study is closely engaged, has mostly framed it as a regional, Latin American organization with connections to the LAI and Comintern.[11] This includes the only prior book-length study of LADLA, Daniel Kersffeld's *Contra el imperio: Historia de la Liga Antimperialista de las Américas* (2013), which has been foundational to my understanding of the organization's inner workings and its place within Latin American leftist politics. The present study is indebted to Kersffeld's thorough and insightful work, to Ricardo Melgar Bao's painstaking digitization of LADLA's periodical, *El Libertador*, and to prior articles on LADLA's Continental Committee and individual national sections written by historians Barry Carr, Lazar Jeifets and Víctor Jeifets, Melgar Bao, Sandra Pujals, and Tony Wood.[12] I am also in conversation with studies of the internationalism of the Mexican Revolution, anti-imperialism in Mexico City, and interwar communism in Mexico and the Caribbean.[13]

Despite the regionalist framework through which LADLA has been understood, it was not a regional, Latin American organization. Rather, it had an explicitly hemispheric vision from the outset, maintaining an active section (and several subsections) in the United States and collaborating with US citizens, especially Jewish and Black activists. Through joining the LAI, LADLA's initially hemispheric vision would become more global in scope. By drawing on my research in special collections in Havana, Los Angeles, Mexico City, New York, and Palo Alto and in digital archives held

I.4 Salvador de la Plaza to Jaime N. Sager, March 10, 1926, box 1, BDW Papers.

in Amsterdam and Moscow, this study brings the personal papers of US activists into better conversation with Latin American and LAI archives.

LADLA was originally called the Pan-American Anti-Imperialist League but changed its name, within a few months of its founding, because of the association between US dominance and the project of "pan-Americanism." The symbolic importance of this name change is emblematized in the March 1926 letter from LADLA Continental Committee member Salvador de la Plaza to the head of the Puerto Rican section, in which Salvador de la Plaza scratched out the word "pan-Americana" and replaced it with the more appropriate phrase "de las Américas" (of the Americas) (figure I.4).[14] Whereas LADLA-US consistently translated the organization's name as the All-America Anti-Imperialist League (AAAIL), I use the more direct translation Anti-Imperialist League of the Americas, since it better captures the movement's hemispheric imagination.[15]

Emphasizing LADLA's transnational and hemispheric nature, this book joins a growing body of hemispheric Américas scholarship that approaches hemispheric studies from the perspectives of Caribbean and Latin American thinkers, practicing what Josefina Saldaña-Portillo calls "a hemispheric studies from below."[16] LADLA was founded in Mexico City and then expanded both northward and southward. Although LADLA is not yet a reference point for scholarship produced within the framework of hemispheric studies or transnational American studies, it modeled a hemispheric analysis and vision of political community that took Latin America and the Caribbean as its point of departure. LADLA activists would eventually expand their initially hemispheric connections with worker and minority struggles in the United States to embrace an interdependency and solidarity with anticolonial, anti-imperialist, and antiracist movements around the world. In this sense, recovering LADLA's vision offers a historiographical basis for interdisciplinary connections between hemispheric Américas scholarship and global comparatist models, like postcolonial studies and Global South studies.[17]

A closer look at LADLA's history challenges the Afro-Asian (and predominantly anglophone and francophone) lens through which global twentieth-century anticolonial politics are often understood.[18] Anticolonial history frames the 1966 Tricontinental Conference in Havana, Cuba, which founded the Organization of Solidarity with the Peoples of Africa, Asia, and Latin America (OSPAAAL), as the first time that Latin American activists entered into a global movement with a longer history in Afro-Asian anticolonialisms.[19] The prevailing narrative has positioned the 1955 Asian-African Bandung Conference as an origin point for the Afro-Asian People's Solidarity Organization (AAPSO), which Cuba later joined to form OSPAAAL, uniting Latin American anti-imperialist movements with prior Afro-Asian formations.[20] While this accounting from 1955 to 1966 is accurate, beginning this anticolonial history with the 1955 Bandung Conference elides the much longer history of Latin American engagement with Afro-Asian anticolonialisms through the LAI in the interwar years. In this sense, LADLA set an important precedent for the cold war networks studied in my previous book, *From the Tricontinental to the Global South: Race, Radicalism, and Transnational Solidarity* (Duke University Press, 2018).[21]

Although the 1927 Brussels Congress, which founded the LAI, is widely viewed as a precursor to the Bandung Conference, scholarship on the LAI tends to neglect LADLA's presence and contributions.[22] The scholarship of Michael Goebel, Daniel Kersffeld, and Thomas Lindner, each of whom has focused on Latin Americans' participation at the Brussels Congress, represents an important exception to this tendency.[23] Even so, scholarship on the LAI often either ignores LADLA entirely or presumes that the LAI created an anti-imperialist platform and network that eventually extended to the Americas.[24] In fact, the opposite is true since LADLA preceded the LAI by two years. When the LAI named LADLA as its Americas section, LADLA's already established sections became the LAI's connection to the American continent. That is, the LAI simply absorbed networks and political frameworks already created by LADLA.[25] Since existing scholarship on the LAI has focused on the history of Afro-Asian-European networks, it has reified the false impression that the 1966 Tricontinental Conference represented the first entry of Latin American movements onto a global stage.

A Wide Net of Solidarity is invested in recovering understudied histories of twentieth-century anticolonial and anti-imperialist internationalisms and in underscoring the often forgotten role of Latin American thinkers in these histories. Centering Latin American thinkers is important because two of the most well-trodden models of comparative analysis—postcolonial theory and world-systems analysis—emerged alongside each other in the 1970s in response to midcentury decolonization in Africa and Asia. These bodies of theory aimed to better understand global patterns of inequity through drawing parallels between the economic, political, and social circumstances of formerly colonized nations. Whereas Immanuel Wallerstein's world-systems analysis was concerned primarily with the economic continuities from the colony to the post-colony, postcolonial theory sought to address the enduring cultural and social legacies of colonialism after decolonization.[26] Both these comparative models focused mostly on the experience of European colonization in Africa and Asia, largely overlooking the Latin American context. The marginal position of Latin America within this scholarship has generated much debate about its relevance for addressing sociocultural relations following the nineteenth-century decolonization of Latin America as well as for addressing the role of twentieth-century US expansionism in the region.[27] These concerns led to the development of Latin American "decoloniality" theory in the 1990s.[28] Many have traced the roots of the comparative analysis found in world-systems and postcolonial theory to key moments of Afro-Asian anticolonial history, such as the 1927 Brussels Congress and 1955 Bandung Conference, even as scholars like Aijaz Ahmad have argued that academic assimilations of anticolonial politics share little ideologically with the movements that inspired them.[29] The role of intellectuals from the Americas, and especially from hispanophone and lusophone Latin America, is mostly sidelined in studies of the historical moments and movements that serve as the basis for these comparative analytics. In this sense, centering LADLA's involvement in the LAI helps reframe global twentieth-century anticolonial history, and thus the roots of these comparative frameworks, moving away from a focus on the enduring legacies of European colonialism in Africa and Asia.

Beyond shifting our understanding of the LAI and anticolonial movement history more broadly, *A Wide Net of Solidarity* intervenes in the recent proliferation of scholarship on global twentieth-century anticolonial writings and aesthetics that developed alongside anticolonial movements in the interwar and cold war periods.[30] As much of this scholarship on comparative anticolonial aesthetics (and closely related scholarship on the aesthetics of communist internationalism) elides Latin American writers and artists, this book represents my persistent insistence that the region has been at the heart of not only global twentieth-century anticolonial and anti-imperialist political movements but also their intersecting aesthetic forms.[31] Latin American–led anti-imperialist movements, like LADLA and OSPAAAL, do not simply illustrate the extension into the American continent of ideas that originated elsewhere. Rather, these movements represent sites of theoretical and cultural production that have had profound influence on political movements and aesthetics worldwide. *A Wide Net of Solidarity* helps reframe the history of twentieth-century Afro-Asian anticolonialisms to call attention to the contributions of intellectuals from the Americas, to understand how intellectuals from the Americas were influenced by anticolonial thinkers from elsewhere, and to suggest a rethinking of comparative models of analysis from the perspective of such histories.

If studies of twentieth-century anticolonial movements often overlook LADLA and Latin America more broadly, scholarship on twentieth-century Latin American radicalism tends to have a regional focus that does not situate these activists in the global, anticolonial milieus they inhabited. The scholarship on Latin Americans' engagement with the Comintern is an important exception, but this work is consistently framed within a narrative of global communism rather than the more ideologically fluid anticolonial politics found in Latin Americans' involvement from the LAI to OSPAAAL.[32] The tendency to apply a regionalist lens to Latin American radical politics is especially the case for the interwar period, which was characterized by the emergence of Latin America's regionalist ideologies. In response to post–World War I disillusionment with Western Europe and increasing US dominance, interwar Latin American writers and political figures defined the region through ideologies like *hispanoamericanismo, indoamericanismo, mestizaje,* and *indigenismo.* Many interwar Latin American intellectuals spent time in Western Europe, and these experiences influenced the distinctions they drew between European and Latin American contexts. Although there has long been a recognition of interwar Latin American cosmopolitanism in Europe, their anticolonial networks reaching Africa and Asia remain undertheorized and underexamined.

A closer look at LADLA shifts our understanding of interwar Latin American intellectual history. Contrary to the regionalist lens through which interwar Latin American political thought has been understood, LADLA members rejected interwar regionalisms for what I call a *hemispheric globalism,* wherein LADLA expanded on its initially hemispheric connections with worker and minority struggles in the United States to embrace an interdependency and solidarity with anticolonial, anti-imperialist, and antiracist movements around the world. While LADLA did not employ this term, I use *hemispheric globalism* to describe, first, an ideological tenet that self-determination for "oppressed, colonial, and semicolonial peoples" in Latin America could be achieved only through transnational alliances with similar struggles in the American continent and beyond, and, second, a practical strategy to foment systems of mutual support by facilitating communication between resistant movements across the American hemisphere and expanding those connections, through the LAI, to global horizons.[33]

There is a substantial body of scholarship on the relationship between aesthetics and politics in interwar Latin American literary and cultural production, and I am in close dialogue with that work.[34] Within Latin American literary studies the interwar period tends to be associated with regionalist literary genres, like the "identity essay," which described national culture and heritage. During this period appeared the "Spanish American regional novel," also called *novela de la tierra* (novel of the land).[35] These experimental socialist realist novels set in rural settings captured the region's unique essence and "autochthonous literary expression."[36] However, the proliferation of 1930s-40s Latin American proletarian novels that form the *novela de la tierra* genre directly engage the global questions central to LADLA, the LAI, and related organizations, like the Caribbean Bureau. Such novels are not the only example of links between LADLA's political project and literary aesthetics. For instance, the Afro-Chinese-Cuban poet Regino Pedroso is rarely read outside of Cuban studies, even though LADLA published his first book of poems, *Nosotros* (Us, 1933). *Nosotros* treats the very global subjects of anti-Blackness and immigrant labor that were central to the 1927 Brussels Congress and to the LAI. This book offers new readings of these and other texts within the transregional and multilingual political context in which they were produced.

CHAPTER SUMMARIES

A Wide Net of Solidarity is organized in two parts made up of a total of seven chapters, each of which emphasizes an individual, conference, or political organization as a site of hemispheric and global encounter. Across the book's arc, I trace transnational debates about Indigenous dispossession, Black and Indigenous labor, immigrant rights, racial policing, extractive capitalism, and solidarity politics during the interwar period. Although LADLA had sections throughout the American hemisphere, I zoom in on the region that LADLA framed as the Greater Caribbean since this is where LADLA was most active.

Rather than arranging the book chronologically, I have arranged it in two thematic parts, each of which follows a loose chronological order. The first part (chapters 1–4), "Weaving a Wide Net: Relational Solidarities and Hemispheric Globalism," maps LADLA's contributions and traces its evolving thinking on racial capitalism and political community, focused first on Indigenous communities and later expanded to Black and immigrant populations. The second part (chapters 5–7), "Knots in the Net: LADLA's Limits and Entanglements," turns to the limitations of LADLA's project and the lessons that these problems can teach us about transnational and multiracial solidarity politics today.

The first chapter, "A Photography of Relation: LADLA, Indigeneity, and Tina Modotti's Visual Language of Liberation," positions Modotti as a key node connecting the international community of activists that founded LADLA. Using Modotti's life and work in Mexico City as an anchor, this chapter tells the story of LADLA's multinational origins, especially focusing on the early influence of Indian anticolonialist Manabendra Nath Roy during his exile in Mexico City. It expands on this history by addressing how Modotti's work would engage LADLA's organizing across extractive economies and depict its focus on Indigenous communities. Using her photography, personal papers related to Modotti and other LADLA activists, LADLA's newspaper, *El Libertador*, and illustrations by Diego Rivera and Xavier Guerrero (Nahua artist-activist and Modotti's partner), "A Photography of Relation" studies how LADLA understood Indigenous communities' disproportionate experience of the most negative consequences of extractive capitalism. As I show, Modotti's work is overwhelmingly focused on the connections between subjects, and this chapter reinterprets her images of extractive and agricultural economies and of Indigenous agricultural workers, alongside LADLA's ideology, to argue that Modotti's "relational aesthetics" serve as an artistic expression of her political vision. Modotti's photography wrestles with the visual language needed for LADLA's effort and contains many of the same tensions and contradictions found within LADLA itself.

Building on LADLA's foundations in Mexico City, the second chapter, "Against Latin American Regionalisms: The 1927 Brussels Congress and LADLA's Hemispheric Globalism," examines the encounter between

LADLA organizers and African American, African, and Asian anticolonial intellectuals at the 1927 Brussels Congress. It argues that a closer look at LADLA's participation in the LAI shifts the traditional understanding of interwar Latin American regionalist ideologies, showing how LADLA members rejected these ideologies for a hemispheric globalism. If the Brussels Congress offered LADLA organizers the chance to see more clearly the connections between their struggles and those of colonial contexts in Africa and Asia, it also helped them draw deeper connections with non-Spanish-speaking communities that were closer geographically, like US Black activists and organizations from the francophone and anglophone Caribbeans. LADLA's global-mindedness enhanced its hemispheric connections and vice versa. The encounter with Black activists from francophone and anglophone contexts in Brussels influenced LADLA to eventually expand its initial focus on Indigenous movements to think more critically about Black and immigrant struggles in the Americas. It would also influence LADLA to theorize white supremacist and fascist ideologies as an integral part of imperialist domination.

The expansion of LADLA's vision at the Brussels Congress impacted the later positions held by Afro-Cuban LADLA secretary Sandalio Junco. The third chapter, "'Por la igualdad de todos los seres': Sandalio Junco's Afro–Latin American Perspective on Black, Immigrant, and Indigenous Struggles," follows Junco from Havana to the Soviet Union to Mexico City, positioning him as a pivotal, yet understudied, figure of Black radical thought. Although Junco was not present at the 1927 Brussels Congress, he would subsequently call into question a core assumption of its "Common Resolution on the Negro Question" regarding the supposed absence of anti-Black racism in many parts of Latin America. His arguments on this issue would become key for advancing anti-imperialist thought in Latin America, especially regarding the position of Black Latin American communities and Black immigrant labor.

From LADLA headquarters in Mexico City, Junco traveled in 1929 to two conferences in Buenos Aires and Montevideo where he exchanged ideas with African American organizer Isaiah Hawkins and renowned Peruvian intellectual José Carlos Mariátegui. The limited available scholarship on these conferences tends to recognize them for their contributions to an examination of Indigenous organizing through the interventions of Mariátegui.[37] However, it was in this same context that Junco presented a little-known yet foundational text of Black internationalism that analyzed the conditions faced by Black workers in the Americas. In his speech "The

Negro Question and the Proletarian Movement" and subsequent comments, Junco challenged Mariátegui's strict differentiation between Black and Indigenous experiences and rejected some of the conference participants' dismissal of the presence of anti-Black racism both among Latin American working classes and in Latin American societies more broadly. In contrast to these positions, Junco drew comparisons (but not equivalences) between Black Latin Americans' experiences of racialization and those of other racialized populations throughout the hemisphere, such as Indigenous peoples, US African Americans, and Haitian, West Indian, and Chinese migrant workers. Through these comparisons, he theorized the overlap between anti-Blackness and anti-immigrant sentiment faced by Black immigrant workers in Latin American contexts. Most important, Junco articulated an argument, from an Afro-Latin American position, for a Black internationalist politics situated between a race-based and a class-based subjectivity.

The fourth chapter, "Relational Poetics: LADLA-Cuba and Regino Pedroso's Afro-Chinese-Cuban Writings," examines LADLA's Cuban section and Junco's ongoing impact in Cuban anti-imperialist writings. It focuses on the work of Afro-Chinese-Cuban poet Regino Pedroso Aldama, who was an active member of LADLA's Cuban section. Pedroso would take up Junco's analysis of multiple oppressions and his pro-immigrant politics and significantly expand them. Similar to Junco's 1929 statements, Pedroso's poetry positions Black workers as exploited through an integrative relationship between race and class and is especially attentive to the experiences of immigrants, including Chinese immigrants. Beyond outlining the history of LADLA-Cuba, this chapter uses Pedroso's poetry as a case study for the nuanced visions of multiracial solidarities that emerged out of LADLA. Similar to the treatment of Modotti's photography, it takes seriously Pedroso's poetry as political discourse, especially considering that his poems often appeared in the pages of Masas, LADLA-Cuba's magazine.

The second part of this book considers the limitations of LADLA's project, providing a counterpoint to the emphasis thus far on its contributions. The fifth chapter, "Ethnic Impersonation and Masculine Erotics: James Sager / Jaime Nevares and LADLA–Puerto Rico," examines problems that can arise within a political project focused on bridging differences. It studies how solidarity discourses can obscure disparities and frame disparate experiences of oppression as interchangeable. This chapter tracks the history of LADLA's Puerto Rican section, relying on the personal papers of its founder, a Boston-born Jewish activist named James Sager. In his efforts to attract members of the Puerto Rican Nationalist Party to LADLA–Puerto Rico, Sager assumed the false identity of a man of Puerto Rican descent named Jaime Nevares. Many LADLA activists used aliases to avoid political persecution, but ethnic impersonation within the movement was unique to Sager and to Charles Francis Phillips, another US Jewish activist. Phillips, who sought exile in Mexico City to avoid conscription during World War I, became one of LADLA's founding members. On returning to the United States, where he directed LADLA-US, Phillips took the name Manuel Gomez (he dropped the accent in Gómez) to avoid detection by US authorities. While Phillips was claiming to be a Mexican American man in the United States, his LADLA colleagues in Mexico expressed frustration about the US section's limited financial contributions and Phillips's paternalistic meddling in which his communications falsely claimed to direct LADLA as a whole rather than just the US section.[38] LADLA's Continental Committee would eventually accuse Phillips of embezzling money, leading to his removal from his position.[39] The cases of ethnic impersonation by US activists studied in this chapter evince the disproportionate mobility of Sager and Phillips in comparison to their Latin American counterparts and suggest they made false equivalences between the conditions of Jewish minorities in the United States and those faced by their Latin American and US Latinx colleagues. These cases indicate the potential for LADLA's networked solidarities across difference to become entangled in overidentification and enmeshment.

Letters to James Sager reveal that he was, according to many, a strikingly handsome man, and this chapter includes an analysis of love letters sent to him by a Puerto Rican girlfriend. Sager's appearance is consistent with LADLA's leadership, dominated by young, often attractive, able-bodied individuals. While this movement consisted of a nationally and ethnically diverse group of people and focused on Indigenous, Black, and immigrant organizing, several of its core leaders' ease of travel through international borders was enabled through white, mestizo, and light-skin privilege. Moreover, as the individuals involved in LADLA circulated at political conferences and worked in close proximity, they often formed romantic and sexual relationships that were asymmetrical in terms of the individuals' level of access. This chapter sheds light on the history of the masculine erotics of the radical Left in the American hemisphere, considers how the affective politics of solidarity can veil rather than clarify differences in the way we experience the world, and highlights how solidarity movements have often been built through the mobility and connections afforded to a few key players.

While LADLA steadily grew across the American continent from 1925 to 1927, its growth exploded after January 1928 when it created its Manos Fuera de Nicaragua (MAFUENIC, Hands Off Nicaragua) campaign to support the insurgency of Augusto César Sandino. The sixth chapter, "Hands Off Nicaragua and the Sandino Fantasy: Navigating Nationalism, Internationalism, and Anti-fascism," studies how LADLA used this financial and propaganda campaign to tie together a range of different struggles under the banner of *sandinismo*. The Nicaraguan case helped LADLA solidify links between anti-imperialism, the fight against authoritarian dictatorships, and antifascism. It had particular success in unifying a Greater Caribbean movement (which included Central America and the coasts of Mexico, Colombia, and Venezuela) around the Sandinista cause. In this Greater Caribbean, LADLA used the Nicaraguan struggle to underline connections between the United Fruit Company's transnational holdings, the US government's actions in the Panama Canal zone, and the racial policing of labor by local authoritarian and fascist governments. These links were pivotal to LADLA's "united front" approach, which joined a broad coalition of social classes, and which LADLA maintained long after the Comintern shifted to its sectarian "class against class" platform.

Maintaining such unity represented a complicated effort that required merging LADLA's internationalist commitments with nationalist struggles. This commingling had significant implications for the region as leaders of its Nicaragua campaign would later attempt failed copycat revolts in Cuba and Venezuela. This chapter thus uses MAFUENIC to outline how LADLA understood the connections between anti-imperialist internationalism and nationalist struggles against authoritarian and fascist dictatorships as well as the complications it faced in balancing those commitments. It builds on existing historical scholarship on MAFUENIC, including its relationship to the 1929 Second LAI Congress in Frankfurt, but moves in new directions by focusing on the campaign's discursive and aesthetic aspects. Although LADLA presented an image of Sandino that perfectly harmonized all its positions, the real Sandino was more complicated. Such fantasy and projection around Sandino undergirded MAFUENIC and represented both the reason for its widespread expansion and its most severe shortcoming. MAFUENIC ultimately relied too heavily on the individual figure of Sandino, whose nationalist commitments did not align neatly with LADLA's fierce opposition to nativism and authoritarianism. The campaign contained a fundamental contradiction between a relational, transnational movement and a nationalist project centered around an individual male hero. While

MAFUENIC led to LADLA's rapid expansion, LADLA eventually collapsed due to the Mexican government's intense repression of LADLA organizers in the early 1930s. Nevertheless, the conflictual ideologies balanced in the campaign continue to play a central role in Latin American social movements to this day.

Due to a crackdown against radical elements in Mexico, much of LADLA's central leadership was deported or jailed. This led to the dissolution of its Continental Committee in Mexico City. However, some of LADLA's key leaders reconvened in the Comintern's Caribbean Bureau (Buró del Caribe, BC), established in 1931 in New York City. Because of the Comintern's "class against class" approach, which abandoned the broad alliances on which LADLA was based, the communist-controlled BC began to eclipse LADLA in influence in the early 1930s. During this sectarian period, which began in 1928, several of LADLA's core leaders, like Sandalio Junco and Diego Rivera, were ousted from their local communist parties for their non-orthodox positions. Despite these changes, the BC would continue much of LADLA's ideological project, especially by uniting movements across the Greater Caribbean through drawing parallels between extractive economies. In uniting these movements, the BC relied on networks initially forged through LADLA's MAFUENIC campaign.

Thus, the final chapter, "Remembering LADLA: The Caribbean Bureau and the Rise of Latin American Extractive Fictions," studies the BC's activities alongside the emergence of a set of 1930s–40s novels and short stories that take place in Latin American and Caribbean extractive economies, such as banana, sugar, tobacco, and rubber plantations, as well as oil fields. I refer to these works as *Latin American extractive fictions*. Unsurprisingly, Latin American extractive fictions were mostly written by writers with leftist politics, some with direct connections to LADLA. For example, Carmen Lyra, author of *Bananos y hombres* (*Bananas and Men*), became a member of LADLA–Costa Rica and led its MAFUENIC campaign.[40] Lyra published *Bananos y hombres* in 1931, the same year that she and other members of LADLA–Costa Rica founded the Costa Rican Communist Party, which fell under the BC's direction.[41] Using the case studies of Lyra's *Bananas y hombres*, the famed *Mamita Yunai* (1941) by Carlos Luis Fallas Sibaja (a prominent Costa Rican communist), *Marcos Antilla: Relatos de cañaveral* (Marcos Antilla: Tales from the canefield) (1932) by LADLA-Cuba member Luis Felipe Rodríguez, and especially focusing on the sugarcane novel *Over* (1939) by Dominican writer Ramón Marrero Aristy, this chapter considers how some interwar Latin American extractive fictions can be understood as meditations on LADLA's project and on the difficulties of forging transnational and transracial political collectivities. It sheds light on how the region's writers would come to understand, remember, and narrate LADLA's vision. Ultimately, it argues that these Latin American extractive fictions would draw on key elements of LADLA's worldview but obviate its furthest-reaching antiracist politics.

The BC ceased all activities by 1936 in the lead-up to the US-Soviet alliance in the Second World War. All national sections of LADLA closed around the same time, and the global LAI dissolved in 1937. Although many interwar Latin American extractive fictions are not widely read outside their immediate national and regional contexts, these works influenced the literary production of some of Latin America's most well-known writers. Works by Nobel Prize winners—like Pablo Neruda's "La United Fruit Co." (1950), the novels in Miguel Ángel Asturias's Banana Trilogy (1950–60), or the depiction of the 1928 United Fruit massacre of Colombian banana workers in Gabriel García Márquez's One Hundred Years of Solitude (1967)—clearly demonstrate the prolonged influence of these works on the writings of subsequent generations. These literary works provide perspective on how LADLA's history has been represented for broader consumption, what elements of its history have been remembered, and which of its key contributions have been forgotten along the way. Finally, the epilogue, "Twenty-First-Century Redes," explores how recent social movements against extractivism in the Americas rely heavily, if subconsciously, on LADLA's political vision for the hemisphere.

LADLA AND EXTRACTIVISM

The American continent today remains a hotbed of political thinking on extractivism, and LADLA's attempts to organize across extractive economies were ahead of its time. LADLA focused much of its critique on what it referred to as industrias extractivas (extractive industries), a phrase that dates in Latin America to the early twentieth century. In the first issue of El Libertador (March 1925), LADLA described the organization as an effort "to organize all the anti-imperialist forces of Latin America, to unify them in a continental unity, to ally them with natural allies that exist in Europe, in Asia, in Africa and WITHIN THE UNITED STATES ITSELF; to awaken the sleeping masses of workers and farmers, of Indigenous, mestizos, and whites that groan under the yoke of imperialism (since the master of our industries is the same Yankee capitalism, and a strike in the plantation or in the mines, in the refinery or the mill, in the salt or oil fields, is always a strike against the foreign master)."[42] Here, LADLA conceived of imperialism as a mechanism tied to extractive industries: plantations, mines, refineries, mills, salt production, and oil fields. What united LADLA's community of workers and farmers was their connection to this shared extractive geography. Fighting for one's labor rights within these industries represented a fight against their common "foreign master."

LADLA's reference to "extractive industries" was arguably a misnomer since the extraction of natural resources does not involve an industrial process of production.[43] "Extractivism," a term of more recent coinage, refers to the removal of large quantities of raw materials primarily for the purpose of export. Extractivism is not synonymous with the act of removing raw materials, but according to Eduardo Gudynas, it has three core characteristics: the removal of an extremely high volume of material, exportation of 50 percent or more of that material, and lack of accompanying industries to process it.[44] Maristella Svampa's definition includes these characteristics but adds an emphasis on the "vertiginous expansion of the borders of exploitation to new territories, which were previously considered unproductive or not valued by capital."[45] Extractivism ranges from open-pit mining and oil and energy industries to the construction of hydroelectric dams and overexploitation of fisheries and forests. It also includes large-scale monoculture agriculture, which is similarly high-volume and exported with little to no processing.

Critiques of extractive industries within Latin American political thought are generally associated with 1960s–70s dependency theory. LADLA anticipated these interventions by several decades, arguing that "extractive industries" and "the exploitation of the land" had profoundly negative consequences for Latin American societies.[46] LADLA claimed that reliance on an economic model based in resource extraction prevented the region from developing manufacturing, resulted in the poverty of communities forced to work in extractive industries and purchase imported products, threatened the national sovereignty of countries "that have the misfortune of possessing natural riches" and that are inundated by foreign investment capital, and required the cooperation of local "autocratic governments" friendly to foreign corporations.[47] Dependency theorists later referred to this condition as "subordinate dependence" on foreign capital and foreign manufacturing, leading to the perpetual "development of underdevelopment" in Latin America.[48]

These long-standing critiques of extractive industries in the region would undergird the pink tide Latin American governments that emerged at the turn of the twenty-first century and that arose alongside a boom in the prices of raw materials. Pink tide governments distanced themselves from the Washington Consensus, or the neoliberal model of austerity, privatization, and trade and finance liberalization that had dominated Latin American economics since the 1970s.[49] Instead, they practiced a "radical resource nationalism" (Riofrancos) or "progressive neo-extractivism" (Svampa), seeking to overcome long-standing relations of economic dependency through strategies like the nationalization and collective ownership of natural resources, use of extractive revenues to fund social welfare programs, and development of Latin American regional economic cooperation.[50] Even in conservative states, Latin America witnessed "the passage of the Washington Consensus, characterized by structural adjustment and the predominance of financial capital, to the *commodities consensus*, based on the large-scale export of primary goods, economic growth, and the expansion of consumption."[51] Since the commodities consensus left intact Latin America's subordinate position within the global division of labor, progressive governments sought to address poverty by capturing and redistributing profits generated by the export of raw materials.

The "progressive neo-extractivism" practiced by pink tide governments fostered a complex relationship with socio-environmental and Indigenous movements. Argentine sociologist Maristella Svampa has described this relationship as occurring in different phases. In the first phase, prior to 2008 and at the height of the commodity boom, the pink tide agenda largely aligned with Indigenous and ecological platforms. This was especially the case in Bolivia and Ecuador, which modeled "strong participatory processes . . . the construction of a plurinational state, indigenous autonomies, and the orientation to *Buen Vivir*" and recognition of the Rights of Nature.[52] The second phase, however, was characterized by extractive expansion through the creation of large-scale projects, like the Growth Acceleration Plan in Brazil, the Great Industrial Leap in Bolivia, or the beginning of open-pit mega-mining in Ecuador. This post-2008 expansion only intensified with the fall in raw materials' prices, prompting Latin American governments to increase extractive projects after 2013. The fall of raw materials' prices exposed inherent problems with funding social welfare programs through extractive economic growth models, which can exacerbate social inequities as these funds radically fluctuate with the commodities market.

The expansion of extractive projects led to an explosion of socio-environmental and territorial conflicts, especially involving *campesino* (farmer) and Indigenous groups since many of these projects are located in rural and Indigenous territories. Organizations like the Latin American Observatory of Environmental Conflicts and the Observatory of Mining Conflicts of Latin America (OCMAL) have documented these conflicts. As of August 2023, OCMAL documented 284 active mining conflicts affecting almost every country in the region.[53] Currently, Latin America is the most dangerous place in the world for environmental activists. In 2020, for instance, three-quarters of the 227 murders worldwide of these activists occurred within the region.[54]

Although progressive governments in Latin America waned amid a conservative backlash in the mid-2010s, they have become resurgent in the early 2020s. Experience of recent decades demonstrates that in the name of extractive revenues, both the region's progressive and neoliberal governments have attempted to roll back Indigenous rights of informed consultation and communal property and responded to territorial conflicts with violence. This has led many grassroots movements to critique progressive governments for corruption, authoritarianism, and failure to deliver on the demands of the very movements that put them in power. This has also contributed to the criminalization of environmental activism and to dangerous conditions faced by the region's *defensores de la tierra* (land defenders).

Alongside these critiques, a position of staunch "anti-extractivism" has emerged, which "rejects extraction entirely and envisions a post-extractive society" based on more harmonious relations between humans and nature.[55] The position of anti-extractivism is rooted in a "relational paradigm based on reciprocity, complementarity, and care" and draws from anti-capitalist, Indigenous, ecofeminist, antiracist, and environmental justice movements.[56] From the Colombian anti-dam activism featured in Caycedo's *Land of Friends* or the defense of the Rights of Nature by the Confederation of Indigenous Nationalities of Ecuador to protests at the Standing Rock Indian Reservation in the United States, recent socio-environmental movements throughout the American continent are predominantly led by Indigenous activists. Indigenous communities are not univocal, and some accept economic compensation for extractive projects or associate such projects with positive notions of development. However, overwhelmingly, it has been Indigenous activists who have put forth alternative visions to extractive capitalism, captured in terms like *sumak kawsay* in Quechua, *suma qamaña* in Aymara, *penker pujustin* in Shuar, or *ñande reko* in

Guaraní.[57] In Spanish, these concepts are often referred to in shorthand as *buen vivir* (good living), which envisions a socio-ecological relation based on "reciprocity, solidarity, concordance, interconnectedness, drawn from the Andean and Amazonian traditions."[58]

A parallel body of anti-extractivist scholarship has arisen, and researchers like Alberto Acosta, Gudynas, Svampa, and others directly oppose progressive governments' practice of the so-called extractive model and its accompanying environmental pollution, dependence on foreign capital, and destructive impacts on rural, Black, and Indigenous communities.[59] Critics of anti-extractivism characterize it as an unrealistic position of anti-development, pointing out that Latin America's progressive governments face a "cruel paradox" in needing to exploit natural resources to address historical inequities and improve the lives of poor and marginalized citizens.[60] While both sides of this debate agree that alternative forms of development would better serve marginalized communities in the long run, several attempts to advance such alternatives have been curtailed by external factors.[61] Marxists like Argentine sociologist Atilio Borón or former Bolivian Vice President Álvaro García-Linera have criticized some anti-extractivists for practicing an environmentalism void of anticapitalist critique. It is the capitalist mode of production that has caused our present ecological crisis, they argue, and "a *sumak kawsay* worthy of that name can only be so inasmuch as it is radically anti-capitalist."[62]

LADLA's critique of extractive industries anticipated key elements of both these progressive neo-extractivist and anti-extractivist positions. Although LADLA's critique of imperialism went beyond extractive capitalism and it did not view these two systems as synonymous, LADLA was an anti-imperialist organization that focused on organizing within, and theorizing the relationship between, extractive economies. LADLA necessarily directed its critique at foreign-owned corporations that dominated Latin American landholdings in the early twentieth century, and it would have differentiated between those corporations and national governments' use of resource extraction for self-determination. But even as it shared some commonalities with the progressive, neo-extractive position, LADLA was not a statist movement, and it linked its critique of extractive corporations to a rejection of populist nationalism and local, authoritarian governments.

Contemporary anti-extractivism has been characterized as distinct from prior "emancipatory visions in Latin America . . . which fused class analysis to a horizon of anti-imperial liberation" since, as Thea Riofrancos argues, it "centers the territories and communities directly affected by extractive projects."[63] Whereas Riofrancos frames contemporary anti-extractivism as quite different from earlier anti-imperialist projects, this framing in many ways aptly describes LADLA's vision. LADLA did not articulate its critique in environmental terms, but it did focus on the communities directly affected by extractivism, maintained that extractive industries led to an overreliance on foreign capital that perpetuated inequities, and looked to Indigenous organizing as key to a future ecosocial relation alternative to extractive capitalism. Thus, it provides an important historical backdrop to contemporary anti-extractive struggles.

LADLA AND RACIAL CAPITALISM

LADLA used phrases like "white terror" and "tropical fascism" to refer in shorthand to the ways that land dispossession, racism, and policing inhered in the logic of extractive capital. It reflected an understanding that extractivism has historically functioned in tandem with racial capitalism, which Jodi Melamed (following Ruth Wilson Gilmore) describes as a "technology of *antirelationality*" based on the "disjoining or deactivating of relations between human beings (and humans and nature) . . . needed for capitalist expropriation."[64] As LADLA constructed its political community across extractive economies, it prioritized agrarian populations as core to the anti-imperialist movement since these populations live in extractive regions and disproportionately experience its most negative consequences. In its early years, LADLA focused on Indigenous movements, but after the 1927 Brussels Congress, it expanded to address Black and immigrant struggles in the Americas. LADLA's initial focus on Indigenous communities is significant in that it anticipates contemporary critiques by Indigenous studies scholars of theories of racial capitalism for the way those theories center racial slavery and the process of proletarianization rather than the dispossession at the heart of settler colonialism.

LADLA provides an early twentieth-century example of hemispheric and multiracial organizing against racial capitalism. Although the term "racial capitalism" has become associated with Cedric Robinson, the concept has roots in 1970s South Africa, especially in the work of anthropologist Bernard Makhosezwe Magubane, and many other scholars have elucidated the relationship between racialization and capital accumulation.[65] Robinson reworked Marx's notion of primitive accumulation, referring to the process by which the privatization of land (enclosure of the commons) eventually creates a class of workers forced to enter the labor market (proletarianization), to better account for the role of racism in ordering internal relations among European peoples. Robinson argued that the violent process of primitive accumulation within Europe was facilitated by the racialization of some Europeans by others. As European capitalism expanded to other territories, it relied on racialization to legitimize dispossession and the superexploitation of enslaved labor. This interrelation between capital accumulation and racialization did not end with the abolishment of slavery, and racism continued to be used to extract greater value from wage labor. Robinson's work has served as a platform for a recent wave of innovative scholarship that both expands on and deviates from his theories.[66] This scholarship overwhelmingly studies the US context and a US intellectual genealogy. In studying LADLA, I aim to present earlier transnational thinking on racial capitalism, focusing especially on views that emerged from Spanish-speaking Latin America and in dialogue with African and Asian activists.

Although Robinson and Magubane's ideas largely echoed each other, Robinson ultimately arrived at different conclusions by using his reworking of primitive accumulation to argue for the insufficiency of Marxist class analysis for explaining racism. Since he believed that racism preceded capitalism, he contended that "racism is not extrinsic to capitalism; it does not merely exacerbate or justify class-based inequalities" and thus cannot be overthrown through anticapitalist struggle alone.[67] This aspect of his work has been the subject of significant critique, particularly from proponents of Black Marxism who acknowledge that the roots of racism precede capitalism but argue that racism in its present-day form must be understood through capitalist relations of production.[68] Similarly, some critics have argued that adding the modifier *racial* to *capitalism* is unnecessary since racial oppression results from "processes of class rule" within capitalism and thus is implied.[69]

Although LADLA did not use this terminology, I use racial capitalism here because it draws our attention to the intimate link between racialization and capital accumulation. Multiracial anticapitalist movements have a long track record of not being attentive enough to the voices of racialized peoples and to the ways that capitalism produces racial oppression. Experience has shown that recognizing capitalism as the root cause of various kinds of oppression is not sufficient. We must also understand how those oppressions are produced and experienced differentially. "Racial capitalism" speaks to the urgent need for multiracial, anticapitalist organizing that foregrounds issues facing racialized peoples, a kind of organizing that LADLA exemplified.

LADLA anticipated contemporary critiques by Indigenous studies scholars of the racial capitalism framework. For example, Glen Coulthard finds fault with Robinson's reliance on the concept of primitive accumulation because of how this concept frames violent dispossession as a mere stage in the development of capitalism rather than a process that remains ongoing for Indigenous peoples. Even if Marx later revised his more limiting and Eurocentric positions regarding colonial and semicolonial contexts, the very notion of a Marxist proletarian revolution and creation of a socialist state is facilitated in those contexts by the violent displacement of Indigenous peoples through settler colonialism.[70] Coulthard also questions the primacy of racial slavery and the category of labor in theories of racial capitalism since Indigenous struggles remain overwhelmingly focused on the question of land rather than labor rights.[71] Shona N. Jackson launches a similar critique, writing that a focus "on modern labor (even the development of a language of resistance within it) ultimately reflects an investment in an idea of time as progress (read development)" and the relegation of Indigenous peoples and their struggles to a precapitalist past that becomes replaced by wage labor.[72] Lisa Lowe writes, "Because ongoing settler projects of seizure, removal, and elimination are neither analogous to the history and afterlife of racial slavery, nor akin to the racialized exploitation of immigrant laborers, the discussion of settler colonialism cannot be simply folded into discussion of race without reckoning with its difference."[73] Lowe explains that it is more productive to think about "relation across differences rather than equivalence."[74] The dispossession of settler colonialism and the creation of a racialized labor force occur not in a sequential fashion but in a complex intertwined relation, or what Jodi Byrd has called a "cacophony" of colliding historical processes.[75]

Because of LADLA's efforts to bring together a broad range of social classes, it focused not only on industrial labor but also on agricultural communities, Indigenous farming collectives, and artist groups. LADLA viewed Indigenous dispossession as an ongoing process, calling for "the restoration of stolen lands."[76] As it expanded its project to better consider issues facing Black and immigrant populations, it provided an early theorization of racial capitalism that addressed the racialization of labor *and* accounted for the ongoing process of violent dispossession faced by Indigenous peoples. It framed Indigenous dispossession, anti-Black and anti-immigrant racism, and racial policing as core elements of extractive capitalism, wherein police and military enforce dispossession of resource-rich lands and racism is used to extract additional value from racialized labor. Importantly, these were posed not as processes that occur in a sequential fashion but as concomitant and interrelated processes that differentially impact different communities. Although scholarship on racial capitalism has largely focused on the racial oppression of Black peoples within the United States, LADLA provides a model for a *multiracial* analysis of racial capitalism within a *hemispheric* context. I find this energizing and useful, especially as LADLA's concerns remain relevant to political organizing today.

REDES AND RELATIONAL SOLIDARITIES

The history of extractivism in the Americas cannot be understood solely through mapping its geographies or changes to ecological life. Rather, as Macarena Gómez-Barris argues, the "extractive zone" also encapsulates a history of anti-Indigenous and anti-Black racial logics used to occupy resource-rich lands, dispossess communities, employ coerced and unsafe working conditions, and construct populations as barriers to capital flows. From monoculture plantations to mines, extractive capitalism is rooted in a value for the singular resource being extracted and in vertical perspectives that place humans over nature, the wealthy over the poor, and capital over all else.[77] Counterperspectives to the logic of extractive capital, as Gómez-Barris describes, seek to provide alternative visions to this singularity and verticality by rendering a "relational field of multiplicity."[78] Such alternative perspectives are central to my understanding of the views of LADLA's activists and artists.

If Indigenous communities stand at the forefront of socio-environmental struggles in the Americas today, these movements are also largely organized by women and have gained visibility through the use of mass communications technologies and far-reaching solidarity networks across national and linguistic boundaries.[79] From the *marea verde* (green tide) of feminist activism in Latin America to the Movement for Black Lives, the twenty-first century has marked a new era in both transnational solidarity politics and feminist organizing. Linking diverse struggles across a wide-ranging geography has been key to the expansion of these movements. Regarding the success of the *marea verde*, for example, scholar-activist Verónica Gago explains that it was the way that abortion rights demands were "woven together with other feminist struggles," including "the murders of female environmental and Indigenous activists in rural areas," that transformed a national, Argentine struggle for reproductive rights into a transnational feminist movement.[80] As these movements link critiques of different forms of capitalist, patriarchal, and environmental violence, they also envision alternative human and human-nonhuman relations: valuing horizontal over vertical organizational structures, emphasizing reciprocal political community over individual charismatic leaders, and forging new ways of understanding our connection to one another and to the planet.[81] These interwoven struggles draw on longer histories of political organizing, including LADLA.

LADLA resisted extractive capitalism through the practice of a politics and aesthetics of *redes* (nets / networks), meaning it used the transnational extractive zone as the site for theorizing the relation between oppressions and for imagining a new global political community. Here, I allude to the connections drawn in the 1936 Mexican film mentioned previously, in which *redes* references an Indigenous fishing tool, a tool of resource extraction used in large-scale commercial fishing, and the relations and affective networks needed to subvert the logics of extractive capitalism. I also reference the work of anthropologist Arturo Escobar, who does not translate the term *redes* in his *Territories of Difference: Place, Movements, Life, Redes* (2008) since "the Spanish redes, more than the English term networks commonly used to translate it, conveys more powerfully the idea that life and movements are ineluctably produced in and through relations in a dynamic fashion ('assemblages' would be a better translation)."[82]

By approaching LADLA through the framework of *redes*, strands interwoven and knotted, I emphasize the intimacies interlacing a diverse set of individuals across a geographically sprawling web of connections. LADLA had a central Continental Committee based in Mexico City, but this committee remained in constant flux since it was mostly composed of activists living in political exile who moved frequently across national borders. The directorship of its periodical, *El Libertador*, changed hands five times over a four-year period. LADLA's membership was heterogenous and its decision-making largely decentralized across the various national sections. This was so much the case that individual national sections continued to operate for several years after the 1929 dissolution of its Continental Committee.

It would not be a stretch to describe LADLA's organizational structure as similar to the "leaderless" (or "leader-full") social movements of our contemporary era that reject the authoritarian leanings of previous movements organized around singular, charismatic individuals.[83] In contrast to these contemporary "horizontalist" movements, LADLA took a more open posture toward collaboration with state governments, but similar to these movements, it did not aim to take state power nor to create a political party. LADLA described its para-institutional formation and networked structure as follows: "The League is no one—it belongs to everyone; veterans of the struggle and new fighters; organizations and individuals, unions and towns."[84] It characterized *El Libertador* similarly: "It is not the publication of any individual or intellectual, nor of all intellectuals together. Instead of a personal publication, it aims to be a movement's publication. The seed, sowed by all those and many more, now begins to sprout, and its fruit is 'organization.'"[85]

Despite this vision of collective leadership, horizontalist social movements (both then and now) do not lack power differentials. Although the primary strength of a weaving lies in the ties that bind together its fibers, some knots are thicker than others. In any network, there are nodes better connected to resources with stronger influence in deciding and applying the protocols for membership, as well as individuals with higher levels of mobility and access.[86] This is certainly true of LADLA. Despite the transnational and multiracial nature of the movement, the relative power of its individual activists had close links to the access afforded by each person's citizenship, race, gender, class background, able-bodiedness, linguistic expertise, and education. Exploring the limits of a project built on forging relation across difference, and the inequities that can become veiled within such solidarity discourses, represents one of this book's central concerns.

In seeking to understand how capitalism differentially impacted Indigenous, Black, and immigrant communities, LADLA modeled a form of *relational solidarity*. I use this concept, following prior theorizations of "relationality," to capture a vision of solidarity based on the relations (but not conflations) of differing forms of capitalist exploitation.[87] Although LADLA was more intent on building political affinities across racial divisions than it was concerned with gender or sexuality, it would be a mistake to attempt to describe LADLA's integrative thinking across differentiated experiences of oppression without the frameworks that Black and women-of-color feminists have provided to social movements since the early nineteenth century. Within this body of thought, I have chosen not to rely on the ubiquitous "intersectionality" framework, because I hope to better reference Black Marxist feminist thought, such as "super-exploitation" (Claudia Jones), "triple oppression" (Jones), "double jeopardy" (Frances

Beal), and "triple jeopardy" (Third World Women's Alliance).[88] As scholars like Delia Aguilar, Martha Giménez, and Barbara Foley have explained, these Marxist feminist positions are distinct from intersectionality, which frames sexism and racism as different systems of oppression rather than differing effects of the capitalist system.[89]

LADLA viewed capitalism as the root cause of diverse forms of exploitation, including anti-Black racism and Indigenous dispossession. If LADLA had given more thought to gender, and particularly to the experiences of women of color, it likely would have allied with the perspectives of Black Marxist feminists in maintaining that "superexploitation under capitalism lends content to racial and gender oppressions . . . and capitalism is constructed as the system that gives rise to the other two."[90] Alternatively, it is possible that LADLA would have nuanced the argument that "oppression is multiple and intersecting but its causes are not" by analyzing the root causes of patriarchy and racism differently.[91] Although LADLA activists participated in conferences and adjacent organizations that demanded equal pay for equal work and that discussed women's intensified labor exploitation and marginalization from labor unions, LADLA itself was resoundingly silent on the position of women within its movement. Despite this serious shortcoming, LADLA provides an early example of a movement that analyzed differential and integrated experiences of oppression under capitalism, and this contribution should be highlighted.

Solidarity movements can be powerful agents of change, moving beyond empathy and creating complicity and collaboration. Yet they are also characterized by a core problematic wherein bridging the struggles of diverse groups can risk flattening differences between them, leading to misinterpretations, overidentification, and enmeshment. Such a problem is central to LADLA's history and will be at the heart of the analyses developed in subsequent chapters. Terms like *relational solidarity*, "coalitional solidarity," and "thick solidarity" attempt to capture—as Roseann Liu and Savanna Shange have written—"a kind of solidarity" that recognizes a diversity of goals and that does not "gloss over difference, but rather pushes into the specificity, irreducibility, and incommensurability of racialized experiences."[92] On a similar note, Janet Jakobsen explains that the use of analogy to "show that one form of political oppression and or struggle is like another . . . may actually undercut, rather than enable, alliances among movements."[93] Analogies can simplistically frame "the relation between oppression to one of similarity," exploiting those whose experiences are "invoked as the stable ground" of that comparison.[94] Jakobsen calls instead for a politics of "relation" over analogy, in which "*both* likeness *and* difference could be the basis for connection and collaboration."[95] LADLA's focus on the relation between oppressions rather than their conflation is key to understanding its contributions to contemporary solidarity politics.

LADLA's interrogation of the relation between oppressions—its politics of *redes*—represents one of the key footholds that its history provides for social movements today. In my attention to the interconnected *redes* of LADLA's political project, I draw inspiration from Lisa Lowe's polysemantic use of "intimacies" in her study of the contact between enslaved and indentured laborers in the nineteenth-century Americas.[96] The intimacies that Lowe traces between four continents also represent historical intimacies, or connections between different historical moments of settler colonialism, slavery, and the introduction of indentured Chinese and Indian labor into the Americas. LADLA was deeply interested in these historical intimacies and sought to understand how prior colonial regimes overlapped with more recent imperialist forms.

LADLA can be described as a movement of *redes* in terms political, interpersonal, aesthetic, and historical. It formed political networks across a broad geography and over linguistic, ethnic, and racial borders. Those political networks were composed of webs of interpersonal relationships. Its aesthetics expressed a relational vision for a new global political community emerging out of extractive economies, and its ideology addressed historical links among different experiences of racial and capitalist oppression. The chapters that follow pull on these various threads. Ultimately, this book contends that future efforts to build transnational movements against extractive capitalism will require strong ties to the histories of similar movements that have come before them and necessitate as much attentiveness to those movements' errors as to their triumphs.

I WEAVING A WIDE NET

RELATIONAL SOLIDARITIES AND HEMISPHERIC GLOBALISM

ONE

A PHOTOGRAPHY OF RELATION

LADLA, INDIGENEITY, AND TINA MODOTTI'S VISUAL LANGUAGE OF LIBERATION

A photograph of a young man with his eyes closed fills a half page of the January 1930 *Labor Defender*, published by the International Labor Defense. The man's peaceful expression in the portrait, attributed to Italian-born photographer Tina Modotti, becomes unsettling when read with the statement below it—"This photo of Julio Mella was taken seven hours after his death"—informing the reader that the photo is of a corpse. The article, "Imperialism's Killers at Work," describes the deceased Mella as "one of the founders of the Communist Party of Cuba and the leader of the Anti-Imperialist Movement in Latin America" and characterizes his murder in Mexico City one year prior as a political assassination by Cuban President Gerardo Machado's regime. The blame for this political killing lies not only with Machado, the article argues, but also with the US government since Machado's persecution of his political opponents is backed by US economic interests. The Mexican government's recent deportation of Cuban labor organizer Sandalio Junco is just one example of how both Machado and Mexican President Portes Gil "obey the orders of one master—United States imperialism."[1]

In this brief article, the names of several of this book's key players—Julio Antonio Mella, Sandalio Junco, and Tina Modotti—appear within a few typeset lines of each other. The article quickly sketches a constellation of individuals drawn together in Mexico City around the shape of their shared political ideals. Tracing such constellations is a central aim of this study, and for this reason, the story told in these pages could begin with any one of these individuals. It could begin, for instance, with Junco, the Black Cuban baker turned trade union organizer who was living in exile in Mexico City when Mella was assassinated in 1929 and whose deportation is mentioned in the article. Junco worked in political organizing alongside Mella in both Havana and Mexico City, and after Mella's death, Junco replaced him as LADLA's general secretary. Tracing Junco's movements through archival and periodical sources—from Havana to Mexico City and later to Buenos Aires, Montevideo, Berlin, Moscow, and eventually back to Havana— initially led me to study LADLA, inspiring this book years later.

Junco's political globetrotting is one beginning to this story, but there are many other potential starting points. I choose to begin with the activities of the renowned Tina Modotti, the photographer, actress, model, and political activist who took the photograph of Mella's corpse. Mella, who was Modotti's lover, died at her side. Although Modotti was cleared of his murder within five days, the Mexican press painted her as an accomplice in the murder, which it characterized as a crime of passion rather than a political assassination.[2] The press caricatured her as a foreign femme fatale and exposed intimate details of her private life, including her sexual partners and descriptions of nude photographs found in her apartment.

Modotti worked with Mella and Junco in LADLA, and all three of these figures operated as key nodes in a hemispheric and eventually global network. To tell the story of that web of connections resists a clear beginning or endpoint. What united the individuals studied in this book is the expression of their beliefs through their participation in various political organizations, especially LADLA, the beating heart of this book.

TINA MODOTTI AS POLITICAL INTELLECTUAL

In a December 1929 photograph (figure 1.1) from the first solo exhibit of her work, held at the National Library in Mexico City, Tina Modotti stands, arms crossed, in front of a series of her photographs. The exhibit took place nearly a year after Mella's assassination and just two months before her arrest and deportation. Against the more familiar bright-eyed images of the artist, in this photograph Modotti seems subdued, her body language closed, and she has a somber expression that reads as impatience or fa-

1.1 Tina Modotti, Biblioteca Nacional, Ciudad de México (1929).

tigue.[3] The exhibit, billed as "The First Revolutionary Photographic Exhibition in Mexico" and held with free admission, had "overtones of a protest meeting rather than an artistic gathering."[4] It was advertised at workers' centers and union offices and culminated in an event with speeches by student leader Baltasar Dromundo and radical artist David Siqueiros.[5]

Behind Modotti hang a series of photographs taken in the seven years since her arrival in Mexico City. The subjects depicted include a hammer and sickle, a Veracruz worker unloading bananas from a truck, a woman holding a flag, hands on a shovel handle, scaffolding, stadium seats, a circus tent, and a typewriter owned by Mella. The images connect to one another through a thematic sequence usually understood as Modotti's documentation of the ideological and technological changes occurring in postrevolutionary Mexico. However, seen another way, these images also convey an attempt to visually express a radical project of liberation that reached far beyond Mexico's borders. Indeed, many of these images would become part of the iconography of twentieth-century radicalism around the globe.

In her exhibit, Modotti arranged the images in a loose pyramid, peaked by a lone photograph of the deceased Mella standing proud, jaw set, looking into the sun with a furrowed brow. This image, and other photographs that Modotti took of him, would become the basis for a host of works depicting

Mella, who remains one of Cuba's most celebrated heroes.[6] Modotti positions her assorted iterations of political struggle into a clear hierarchy where Mella's profile, already taken with a slightly low-angle shot, forces the viewer's eyes upward to observe him.[7]

Modotti, who died in 1942, has never lost her relevance. She is the subject of coffee-table photography books, the protagonist of the novel *Tinísima* (1992) by acclaimed Mexican writer Elena Poniatowska, a character played by actress Ashley Judd in Julie Taylor's *Frida* (2002), the protagonist of a proposed television miniseries, and more. This Modotti-inspired material culture often uses her photography simply as an illustration of her bohemian lifestyle and multiple love affairs with famous artists and political figures. Although her photography widely circulated in the 1920s, scholarship on Modotti's work did not appear until the 1980s and has since proliferated across several fields.[8] Latin Americanist scholars of visual culture frame Modotti as a proponent of "revolutionary photography" and as the first example of "critical photojournalism in Latin America," focusing on how her depiction of social inequalities differed from prior picturesque photographic representations of Mexico.[9] Scholars of photography and feminist art place Modotti within the larger movement of Mexican modernism and divide her work into an earlier abstract period versus a later politically themed period, with significantly more critical interest in the former.[10] Modotti also sporadically appears in histories of the Mexican Communist Party (Partido Comunista Mexicano, PCM) and the Communist International, but with little sustained interrogation of the nature of her activities. Individual works across these fields—especially those by Leonard Folgarait, Margaret Hooks, Rachel Kirby, and Stephanie J. Smith—do provide substantial details on Modotti's political activities, with a focus on her collaboration with the PCM and its periodical, *El Machete*.[11]

This chapter builds on this previous scholarship by broadening the attention from postrevolutionary Mexico and the PCM to consider in more depth the internationalist structures in which Modotti was involved. Of particular significance is Modotti's participation in LADLA, which aimed to form a hemispheric and multiracial political community and which eventually grew to include fourteen sections throughout Latin America and the United States. LADLA constructed its political community by drawing links between disparate communities in "extractive zones." I use this concept, following Macarena Gómez-Barris, to refer to the geographies of extractive capitalism, including changes to social and ecological life forged through the extraction of natural resources and the anti-Indigenous and anti-Black racial logics used to occupy resource-rich lands and dispossess communities. Studying feminist, queer, and primarily Indigenous perspectives as providing counterperspectives to the logic of extractive capital, Gómez-Barris has examined the alternative visions for a "network of relationality" that emerges from within the extractive zone.[12] Extractive capitalism is rooted in a visual regime, based on the verticality and singularity integral to monoculture economies, that "facilitates the reorganization of territories, populations, and plant and animal life into extractible data."[13] Alternative perspectives challenge this visual regime through presenting a "relational field of multiplicity" between humans, nonhuman animals, and inanimate life.[14] Although her privileging of Indigenous perspectives could easily collapse into romanticism or exoticism toward the "ecological native," Gómez-Barris reminds her readers that Indigenous communities around the world have long been "at the forefront of defending lands in regions that are continually extracted for their biodiversity."[15] Turning to Indigenous perspectives means looking to the perspectives of those who live in the extractive zone and disproportionately experience its most negative consequences.

Much like these alternative perspectives in the contemporary context, LADLA directly linked its critique of US imperialism to its critique of extractive economies and to the integrally related dispossession of land and exploitation of racialized labor. Because of its focus on these economies, LADLA centered Indigenous communities within its project. LADLA did not articulate its concerns through the lens of biodiversity, but because it envisioned a political network forged in a transnational extractive zone, it sought to forge an alternative relation among peoples across national, linguistic, and racial borders. Such multiplicity and relation are similarly at the heart of much of Modotti's work, and this chapter examines Modotti's photography—particularly her images of extractive and agricultural economies and Indigenous agricultural workers—alongside LADLA's ideology to argue that much of Modotti's work envisions a resistant political community within extractive economies. Modotti's photography is overwhelmingly focused on the connections between subjects, employing a "relational aesthetics" that serves as an artistic expression of her political vision.[16] The following pages use Modotti's time in Mexico City to tell the story of LADLA's multinational origins. In doing so, this chapter reinterprets Modotti's photography to show how her work wrestles with the visual language needed for LADLA's project and contains many of the same tensions and contradictions of LADLA itself.

Modotti's life as an activist and artist is often narrated through her relationship to famous men, where her choices are explained through her romantic encounters. Such a dominant narrative of her trajectory proceeds as follows: While working as a film actress in Los Angeles and married to artist Robo de Richey, Modotti had an affair with the couple's mutual friend, renowned photographer Edward Weston, through whom she became interested in photography. She later moved with Weston to Mexico City in 1923, where the couple met Diego Rivera, who introduced them to other Mexican artists and PCM members.[17] Although Modotti was surrounded by political radicals for several years, she did not become radicalized until after Weston returned to California and she began a relationship with communist Nahua artist Xavier Guerrero, under whose apparent "influence," as Leonard Folgarait writes, she "underwent a conversion into an active political being."[18] Then, through her involvement with the solidarity campaign against the execution of Italian-born workers Nicola Sacco and Bartolomeo Vanzetti, Modotti met Comintern representative Vittorio Vidali. According to Vidali, it was under his influence that in late 1927, "with Xavier Guerrero's encouragement, she took a definitive step towards political militancy and became a card-carrying member of the Mexican Communist Party."[19] After Guerrero left for Moscow to attend the International Lenin School, and while Modotti was collaborating more closely with the PCM newspaper, El Machete, in summer 1928, she fell in love with exiled Cuban activist Julio Antonio Mella. Mella, who had been instrumental in the creation of LADLA-Cuba, was now serving as general secretary of LADLA's Continental Committee in Mexico City. Modotti's political activities expanded significantly during her relationship with Mella.

Later, after Mella was assassinated and after Modotti was deported from Mexico and began a relationship with Vidali in 1930, she eventually abandoned her artistic practice and dedicated her life completely to political activities, especially to the International Red Aid (IRA), which assisted political prisoners. After six months in Berlin, the couple moved to Moscow, working for the IRA from 1930 to 1935 and spending time in Poland, France, and Spain.[20] Modotti ran an IRA center in Paris, through which she organized the International Women's Congress Against War and Fascism. In July 1936, she enlisted under the name María del Carmen Ruiz in the Republican Fifth Regiment in the Spanish Civil War, where she worked as a nurse and with the Spanish IRA newspaper, Ayuda.[21] In the lead-up to the defeat of the Spanish Republic, she fled to Paris, and then Modotti (alias

Carmen Ruiz Sánchez) and Vidali returned to Mexico, where she was given political asylum and remained active in the Anti-Fascist Alliance Giuseppe Garibaldi.[22] In January 1942, at forty-six years of age, she died of heart failure, according to her death certificate, and was buried in Mexico City.[23]

Although this story's dates and details are accurate, the predominant tendency to focus on male influence in narratives of Modotti's political trajectory falls short of fully recognizing her as a political intellectual and artist in her own right. One of the more comprehensive studies, Margaret Hooks's *Tina Modotti: Photographer and Revolutionary* (1993), provides substantial details on her political activities and helps undermine this narrative. Hooks acknowledges that as early as 1924, Modotti was likely responsible for translations of Italian antifascist articles published in *El Machete*. However, even Hooks writes that in Modotti's early years in Mexico she "became influenced by the muralists' communist ideas and ideals. But Modotti was not a political theorist and was seemingly naïve about the ideological debates taking place among Communists at the time." Following this statement, Hooks concedes that Modotti was involved in "campaigns to free political prisoners" and to "promote international liberation movements," an involvement that would call into question her apparent naïveté regarding the ideological debates in which she was engaged.[24] Similarly, although Folgarait notes that as early as her relationship with Richey in Los Angeles the couple's inner circle was made up of anarchists, he also writes, "There is no previous suggestion of Modotti's involvement in any form of politics. . . . At this point, she showed no awareness or interest in the radical political activity in Mexico."[25]

Many narratives of Modotti's life acknowledge her working-class and immigrant background, but the relevance of this background to her politics often gets lost in the tendency to focus on her changing political consciousness in relation to her male lovers.[26] Growing up in Italy, Modotti worked as a child laborer in a textile factory, and later she worked as a seamstress in San Francisco.[27] Before her brief career as a Hollywood actress, she performed in theater productions in the Italian quarters of San Francisco, leading to her discovery for film roles.[28] Additionally, she was not the only person in her family involved in politically radical organizations. Her brother, Benvenuto, eventually led the Italian anti-fascist group Rivendicazione.[29] It is highly likely that Modotti's own experiences as a working-class immigrant led her to hold political beliefs sympathetic with social justice politics and that she was informed (rather than naïve) about these positions.

Although Modotti did not officially join the PCM until 1927 and certainly became more politically engaged over time, I have identified a photograph (discussed later in this chapter) that indicates that Modotti was closely involved in the PCM from as early as 1925, two years before she became romantically involved with Guerrero and three years before she met Mella. While I acknowledge that lovers influence one another and that Modotti's viewpoints developed and matured over time, it should also be assumed that her relationships were as much a product of her own political interests as the other way around. Modotti must be treated seriously as a political intellectual and artist, at least as seriously as her male counterparts have been treated up to this point.

THE MULTINATIONAL ORIGINS OF THE ANTI-IMPERIALIST LEAGUE OF THE AMERICAS

Modotti, to whom this chapter will return shortly, was involved in LADLA from its inception in 1925, but the organization's roots can be traced back further, to the Comintern's first forays into Mexico. LADLA could be said to have many beginnings, including previous generations of labor movements in Mexico. However, its most direct history overlaps with the PCM's origins in the Mexican Socialist Party, founded in 1918, and particularly the activities of Indian nationalist Manabendra Nath Roy, or M. N. Roy (a pseudonym for Narendra Nath Bhattacharya), within that party.[30] Such transnational roots are consistent with the comparatist perspective at LADLA's core, which bridged its analysis of Latin American contexts with experiences of colonial oppression around the globe. Although M.N. Roy is a well-known figure in histories of the Communist International, the Mexican years of his biography bear repeating, since they shed light on the multinational exchanges that eventually led to LADLA's creation.[31]

In April 1917, Roy crossed the US border into Mexico.[32] He had spent the last year in the United States, attempting to arrange an arms deal with the German consulate to transfer weapons to the Indian independence movement. This was the last step of a global journey in search of weapons and funding, which Roy began in 1915 and which took him from India to Indonesia, Japan, Korea, China, and finally the United States. When the US government declared war against Germany in April 1917 and began pursuing Indian nationalists with German affiliations, Roy was arrested but jumped bail and fled to Mexico with his American wife, Evelyn Trent.[33]

Roy's decision to travel to Mexico was not mere coincidence. Revolutionary Mexico was observed closely by leftists around the world in the 1910s, and the Mexican Revolution served as "the foremost example of revolutionary politics" for anticolonial Indian radicals in the United States.[34] Living in Mexico City would transform how Roy understood the Indian nationalist movement. There, he realized that "national independence was not the cure for all the evils of any country." In Mexico and throughout the former Spanish colonies, independence had not eliminated the socioeconomic and racial hierarchies of the former colonial society. The struggle to radically overturn these entrenched social inequities motivated the Mexican Revolution, still underway when Roy arrived. In articles on the Indian independence movement that Roy published in subsequent years in the Mexican newspaper *El Pueblo*, he argued that "the poverty of the Indian masses was the result of economic exploitation by British imperialism *and* native feudalism. The liberation of the Indian masses, therefore, required not only the overthrow of British imperialism but subversion of the feudal-patriarchal order which constituted the social foundation of the foreign political rule. The corollary was that India needed a social revolution not mere national independence."[35] Roy's firsthand witnessing of the Mexican Revolution helped him arrive at this nuanced perspective and deepened his thinking on the roots of oppressive social structures.

While inequities from the Spanish colonial system continued after independence, with the 1898 Spanish-American War the United States introduced a new imperial project for the American hemisphere. In contrast to traditional European forms of colonial expansion, which relied on occupation of territory and installation of a colonial ruling bureaucracy, the US imperial project was more focused on economic than territorial control.[36] This would inspire Vladimir Lenin's theorization of a new form of power in *Imperialism: The Highest Stage of Capitalism* (1917), published the same year as Roy's arrival in Mexico, in which imperialist nations—through cooperation between state military, banks, and national industry—rival one another for economic control of territories.

In Mexico, Roy was witnessing a struggle to shift a system of US economic domination facilitated through the cooperation of a domestic elite. After the United States entered World War I in 1917 and the Wilson administration began pressuring the Mexican government to alter its neutral position, Mexican critiques of its northern neighbor sharpened.[37] These tensions in US-Mexico relations not only influenced Roy to rethink the anticolonial struggle in India, where national independence would not necessarily destabilize internal hierarchies, but also to call for an end to "North American tutelage" in Mexico and for the foundation of a Latin American League to counter the US-dominated project of pan-Americanism.[38]

Roy's published essays helped introduce him to several Mexico City leftists, including Adolfo Santibáñez, a lawyer specializing in workers' cases and the leader of the newly founded Mexican Socialist Party (Partido Obrero Socialista, POS).[39] Roy began attending POS meetings, which initially attracted only about twenty members. He helped draft a party resolution demanding independence for India to be distributed to other socialist parties in Latin America.[40] At one meeting, Roy met a US citizen named Charles Francis Phillips, a Jewish antiwar activist born in New York City who came to Mexico along with other American "slackers" to avoid military conscription.[41] Phillips used several aliases over the course of his life but mostly became known as Manuel Gomez.[42] Manuel Gomez, whose troubling ethnic impersonation as a Mexican American is analyzed in depth in chapter 5, would become central to LADLA's later formation.

Meanwhile, across the globe, another revolution was taking place in Russia that would lead to the establishment of the Third International—or Communist International (Comintern, 1919–43)—in Moscow. Facing the disintegration of Europe's world order, the Comintern aimed to build a global movement to overthrow capitalism and replace it with collective ownership of property and means of production. At its inaugural conference in March 1919, Comintern representatives resolved to act on Lenin's theories on the interdependent relationship between capitalism and imperialism by organizing communist parties in non-European countries. The Comintern intended to put pressure on the global capitalist economy at its peripheries. At the conference's conclusion, Lenin charged specific Bolshevik emissaries to travel to various locations around the globe to persuade potential sympathizers to join the Comintern by establishing communist parties and identifying delegates to attend the Comintern's Second Congress, planned to take place in 1920.[43]

The Comintern viewed Mexico as a strategic location for communist organizing. Not only had the Mexican Revolution preceded the Bolshevik Revolution by several years, but Mexico had geographic and economic proximity to the United States.[44] Mikhail Markovich Borodin, a Bolshevik who lived in political exile in the United States before returning to Russia after the 1917 October Revolution, was appointed to establish communist parties in the United States and Mexico. Conveniently, communist sentiment was growing in Mexico, and in August 1919, the POS sent a telegram of greetings to the US Communist Party, expressing its intention to name delegates to the Comintern.[45]

Shortly after Borodin's arrival in Mexico in October 1919, he met Phillips, who introduced him to Roy and POS members. Borodin moved into Roy's house, and the two became friends.[46] Although the POS had already turned toward communism prior to Borodin's arrival, Roy described his many conversations with Borodin as motivating him to shed any last attachments to the cultural nationalism with which he had begun his political activities. Roy, in turn, influenced Borodin's understanding of anticolonial struggles.[47] In November 1919, the POS decided to formally affiliate with the Comintern, changing its name to the Mexican Communist Party (PCM), and Borodin christened the new party as the Comintern's official Latin American Bureau.[48] Roy, Evelyn Trent, and Phillips (none of whom were Mexican) were selected to represent Mexico at the Comintern's Second Congress. Whether their selection occurred through PCM deliberation or at Borodin's invitation is unclear.[49] At the Second Congress, Roy was listed as a delegate from India and then as a delegate from Mexico under the alias Roberto Allen. As Daniela Spenser writes, "As Roy came to occupy a prominent role as representative of the East, Phillips took his place as the representative from Mexico."[50]

At the Comintern's Second Congress (figure 1.2), several developments took place that laid the foundation for LADLA. First, Roy presented his theses that capitalism in metropolitan centers relied on profits produced through colonial holdings. Revolution in the colonies, he argued, was necessary for the overthrow of capitalism in the metropoles, thus reversing the primacy of the European industrial proletariat in the Comintern's vision and turning on its head Lenin's thesis that revolution in the metropole was required to foment revolution in the colonies.[51] In essence, Roy emphasized liberation movements in colonial contexts as the linchpin of worldwide anticapitalist revolution. He argued for a "non-capitalist path of development," stating that countries that maintained communal forms of property could develop into socialist societies more quickly.[52]

Although Lenin defended his position that the revolutionary vanguard would be located in the industrial West, he compromised with Roy on their other point of disagreement regarding alliances with bourgeois nationalist movements in colonial contexts. Lenin believed that in the less industrially developed countries, communists needed to ally with nationalist movements even if these movements were led by the bourgeoisie. Roy countered that a small elite dominated many nationalist movements. Building

1.2 Delegates from Second Comintern Congress, Moscow 1920. Roy in center with Phillips to immediate left. Lenin in front, hands in pockets. CS Papers, box 3, folder 7.

on his comparatist understanding of Mexico and India, Roy argued that the Comintern should focus on class struggle in the colonies and support bourgeois democratic revolution only when accompanied by land reform and other signs of a more complete class-based revolution.[53]

In his memoir, Roy recalls the challenge of opposing Lenin, a charismatic leader seventeen years his senior. According to Roy, Lenin and other European Comintern leaders had only a superficial understanding of how power dynamics operated in colonial and semicolonial contexts. They did not understand that the people in India (or Mexico) who promoted capitalism and those who exploited feudal social relationships were one and the same. The class distinctions drafted on northern European experience and based on the sequence of feudal, capitalist, and socialist modes of production did not map neatly onto colonial contexts. For the oppressed masses in the colonized world to ally with the native elite meant to ally with their oppressors. In the final thesis, a compromise was found that limited communist support only to nationalist parties deemed "revolutionary" that did not hinder communist activity. Although ambiguously formulated, this change came in response to Roy's critique and would become central to LADLA's broadly conceived political collective.[54]

Beyond this exchange between Roy and Lenin regarding the best approach for joining nationalist and class struggles, Phillips had a private meeting with Lenin where they discussed Mexico's strategic position in the Western Hemisphere and the importance of focusing PCM efforts on recruiting speakers of Indigenous languages.[55] Both the integrated thesis on alliances with national movements and this focus on recruiting Indigenous leadership would become important for LADLA's later vision.

Roy and Phillips's interventions at the congress confirmed the perception that Mexico had a favorable climate for communist organizing in the American hemisphere. Roy was asked to stay in Moscow for the next few years. Eventually, Roy became the liaison between the Comintern's Eastern Secretariat and the League Against Imperialism (LAI), meaning that Roy represented LADLA's connection (through membership in the LAI) to Moscow.[56] Whereas Roy stayed in Moscow, the Comintern charged Phillips, the Italian American Louis Fraina, and Japanese communist Sen Katayama with returning to Mexico to continue supporting the PCM.[57] Their time in Mexico was short-lived due to the Mexican government's crackdown on foreign activists in May 1921.[58] In November 1921, Phillips, who had been deported to Guatemala, snuck back into Mexico under the alias Manuel Gomez and continued working underground, but by spring 1922, he believed he had been discovered and got a tourist visa to the United States.[59] Once there, he began organizing in Chicago through the Workers Party (WP), the legal name used by the Communist Party of America from 1921 to 1929.[60] In Chicago, Phillips was known as Comrade Manuel Gomez and thought to be a Mexican expatriate.

At the end of 1924, the WP sent union organizer Jack Johnstone to Mexico City to help organize protests against the Fourth Congress of the Pan-American Federation of Labor, which the WP viewed as the American Federation of Labor's effort to dominate the Latin American labor movement and isolate it from communist influence. Johnstone wrote a report regarding the potential for WP and PCM collaboration in creating a Pan-American Anti-Imperialist League, which would function as an alternative to the Pan-American Federation of Labor.[61] This league, which would have sections throughout Latin America that could cooperate with a section in the United States, was founded shortly afterward, in January 1925.[62] In March 1925, in order to shed associations between "pan-Americanism" and US dominance, it changed its name to the Anti-Imperialist League of the Americas (LADLA).

From its inception, LADLA was not conceived as a communist organization but aimed to have a broader reach to "Latin American patriotic

1.3 LADLA logo by Guerrero. *El Libertador* leaflet, box 3, BDW Papers.

societies, National Liberation movements, student groups, labor unions and working class fraternal organizations, peasant leagues and communists and other political parties."[63] Even so, its leadership in Mexico City overlapped significantly with the 1925 PCM Central Committee.[64] A few key members (all in their twenties and early thirties)—Xavier Guerrero, Úrsulo Galván, Bertram Wolfe, Ella Wolfe, and Rafael Carrillo—took responsibility for launching LADLA and early issues of its periodical, *El Libertador*.

Xavier Guerrero served as administrator of *El Libertador* from its founding until April 1926, and signed communications as LADLA's secretary. He provided all illustrations for early issues of *El Libertador*, which he signed as "Indio" (Indian). His illustrations included LADLA's logo—which appeared on the organization's letterhead and the periodical's masthead—of an Indigenous man breaking chains that descend from northern skyscrapers over the Latin American countries that appear on the map beneath his feet (figure 1.3)[65] Guerrero, the son of a master housepainter and commercial muralist, joined the PCM in the early 1920s along with a group of young artists from the Union of Technical Workers, Painters, and Sculptors. This union's publication, *El Machete*, became the PCM's unofficial publication until its formal adoption in May 1925.[66] In addition to illustrations that Guerrero created for *El Libertador*, he illustrated the first seven issues of *El Machete* and designed its logo as well.[67]

Another early influence on LADLA was the charismatic Úrsulo Galván Reyes, who served as director of *El Libertador*. Galván, the son of landless farmers, began organizing with agrarian committees in Veracruz in 1920 and became an early member of the PCM's Veracruz chapter. In 1923, he helped found the Veracruz League of Agrarian Communities (Liga de Comunidades Agrarias del Estado de Veracruz, LCAEV) and traveled to Moscow for the First Congress of the Peasant International, where he shared a stage with Ho Chi Minh.[68] In 1926, the LCAEV joined other agrarian organizations to become the National Peasant League, led by Galván. This was the most radical farmers' organization in Mexico at this time, calling for the creation of *ejidos*—land farmed communally with state support—as its minimal program and for the full socialization of land as its maximum goal.[69]

Bertram Wolfe served as *El Libertador*'s initial editor.[70] Wolfe and his wife, Ella Goldberg Wolfe—both Jewish US citizens and original members of the Communist Party of America—arrived in Mexico in 1923 and joined the PCM.[71] Bertram obtained the initial funding for *El Libertador* from Stanislav Pestovsky, Soviet ambassador to Mexico, but by June 1925, Bertram was deported, and Ella Wolfe followed him to the United States shortly afterward.[72] The couple stayed involved with LADLA, however, serving as liaisons to the WP.[73]

Finally, despite efforts to present LADLA and the PCM as separate organizations, correspondence between Ella Wolfe and PCM secretary Rafael Carrillo reveals that Carrillo remained closely connected to LADLA in its early years.[74] As a teenager, Carrillo emerged as a leader in union and communist youth organizing and traveled with Galván to Moscow in 1923. When Carrillo returned to Mexico amid the military uprising led by Adolfo de la Huerta, Carrillo joined Galván's forces to support the federal government against the rebellion. After the rebellion was suppressed, the PCM elected Carrillo as its new general secretary.[75]

These individuals—Guerrero, Galván, the Wolfes, and Carrillo—had major influence in LADLA's establishment. In April 1925, shortly after the publication of *El Libertador*'s first issue, Manuel Gomez, the new secretary of LADLA's US section, returned to Mexico City as WP representative to the PCM's Third National Congress. Gomez's visit had the explicit aim of advancing the collaborative organization of LADLA.[76]

Tina Modotti was already in Mexico City by this point, having moved there in July 1923. Again, the accepted narrative holds that, although Modotti associated with PCM members, she did not formally affiliate with the PCM or become radicalized until 1927 through her relationship with

1.4 Tercer Congreso del Partido Comunista de México (1925), CS Papers, box 3, folder 7.

Guerrero.[77] However, in a photograph (figure 1.4) from Gomez's April 1925 visit to Mexico City, where he traveled to support the creation of LADLA, Gomez sits in the center, surrounded by key PCM leaders, including Guerrero, the Wolfes, and Carrillo. Although Modotti's name does not appear under the photo in Gomez's memoir nor in the archival collection that holds this photo, and although the photo was taken two years before Modotti reportedly joined the PCM, seated to the right of Gomez (on his left), with her arm touching his, is none other than Modotti herself.[78]

Despite the erasure of Modotti's name from the archive, this portrait stages a set of relations wherein Modotti's proximity to Gomez, as the guest of honor, frames her centrality to the organizational process of establishing LADLA. The portrait's framing of relations in connection to Gomez suggests that the other men's institutional significance may have been defined as much by Modotti's proximity to them as by their proximity to her. To attribute Modotti's radicalization to Guerrero (first row, farthest to left) or to Mella or Vidali (who do not appear in the photo) is to flatten the complexities of this reciprocity.

In August 1925, a few months after this photograph was taken, Carrillo and Guerrero wrote to LADLA-US secretary Gomez to clarify a number of issues. They argued that LADLA's headquarters and leadership should remain in Mexico since "the residence in the United States of the League's leadership would awaken very bad suspicions by our movement."[79] They also requested that "the American secretariat fulfill its agreements contracted with the Mexican secretariat, regarding the maintenance of 'Libertador,' the League's publication. Today, it has only complied with this promise one time."[80] The question of the location of LADLA's headquarters (as well as the problem of securing WP funding) would remain an ongoing point of contention between the Mexico City leadership and Gomez.[81] Although LADLA continued to publish *El Libertador* after Wolfe's deportation, Carrillo continuously wrote to the Wolfes, asking them to advocate for WP monetary support. In September 1925, Guerrero had to borrow money to keep the journal afloat, and during a five-month period in late 1925, *El Libertador* was, as Carrillo put it, "muerto" (dead) due to financial difficulties.[82]

LADLA received a new boost of energy with the February 1926 arrival in Mexico City of Julio Antonio Mella, leader of LADLA-Cuba, founded in June 1925. Several members of LADLA-Cuba joined Mella in Mexico City in the coming months, seeking asylum from Cuban President Gerardo Machado's repressive government. This group, which included several Venezuelan exiles, including Salvador de la Plaza, who took over Guerrero's role as administrator of *El Libertador*, formed a "comité continental" (Continental Committee) based in Mexico City under Mella's leadership with representation from the various national sections.[83] Although funding remained a problem, the Continental Committee attempted to resolve the question of the headquarters once and for all. Mella wrote to Gomez, instructing him to clarify in his communications that he served merely as general secretary of LADLA-US, not the organization as a whole.[84] Mella served as LADLA's general secretary in Mexico City from 1926 until his assassination in 1929.

After establishing the first three sections in Mexico, Cuba, and the United States, LADLA expanded significantly. By December 1926, it reported fourteen national sections in Argentina, Brazil, Colombia, Cuba, the Dominican Republic, Ecuador, El Salvador, Honduras, Mexico, Peru, Puerto Rico, Uruguay, Venezuela, and the continental United States.[85] The writers of *El Libertador* asserted that while the publication would focus primarily on the American hemisphere, it would report on movements around the world. Petroleum workers in Tampico, Mexico, for example, must "seek out alliances with petroleum workers from Europe, Asia, and

South America, since the capital of Standard and Royal Dutch Shell is international."[86] A strike against these companies, "in order to be effective, must become international."[87] Connecting workers' movements in Latin America with internationalist labor structures, especially the Red International of Labor Unions, was among LADLA's core goals.

LADLA expanded on this global vision through the organization's participation in the Congress Against Colonial Oppression and Imperialism and for National Independence, held in Brussels in February 1927, which established the larger umbrella organization, the League Against Imperialism (LAI).[88] In a July 1927 article published shortly after the Brussels Congress in *América Libre: Revista Revolucionaria Americana* (Free America: American revolutionary magazine), a publication affiliated with LADLA-Cuba, Diego Rivera (who was director of *El Libertador* from August 1927 to November 1928) acknowledged strong anti-US sentiment among Latin American workers. He argued that a semicapitalist relationship existed between US and Mexican labor in which Mexican workers extracted primary materials for manufacture by US workers.[89] Within US-owned multinational companies, he explained, an increase in salary for US employees directly translated as depressed salaries in Mexico. Rivera argued that this dynamic could be found in all industrial countries, and he compared it to the relationship between British and Indian labor. Importantly, in identifying these divisions, he did not mobilize an attack against all US citizens but insisted on the importance of fomenting greater class consciousness that would transcend the US-Mexico border.

Because of LADLA's efforts to bridge national, geographic, and linguistic divisions, it maintained an ideological openness to any group that viewed itself as anti-imperialist. The second issue of *El Libertador* (May 1925) explained that LADLA included "unions; farmworker and Indigenous leagues; political parties of workers and farmers that fight against capitalism and imperialism; student, cultural, and intellectual groups that have participated or shown their desire to participate in our struggle; anti-imperialist revolutionary juntas—like that of Santo Domingo and Venezuela."[90] LADLA aimed to balance internationalist and nationalist positions by arguing that national independence for "oppressed, colonial, and semicolonial peoples" could be achieved only through the mutual support provided by internationalism.[91] The formation of the larger LAI would reflect similar ideological fluidity, accommodating nationalist and noncommunist movements from colonial territories and often resisting oversight and pressure from Moscow.[92]

In addition to LADLA's geographical and ideological openness, it held an explicit stance of antiracism rooted in the belief that agrarian laborers formed the base of the anti-imperialist struggle. In its early years, LADLA's vision for a multiracial, political community focused on Indigenous agrarian populations. Although LADLA later expanded this vision to Black and immigrant communities, Modotti's photography would have most resonance with the organization's initial focus on Indigenous agrarian workers.

LADLA'S POLITICAL VISION AND MODOTTI'S RELATIONAL AESTHETICS

Modotti found in postrevolutionary Mexico a context that opened new spaces for women to participate in politics and to have roles in the postrevolutionary state. However, even as official discourse reimagined women as "teachers, comrades, and revolutionaries," women were "still represented as 'helpers'" and not political leaders.[93] Within male-dominated organizations like LADLA, it can be challenging to pinpoint the precise responsibilities and leadership roles held by women like Modotti.[94] Modotti participated in several communist-affiliated organizations at once, including the PCM, LADLA, IRA, and Red International of Labor Unions. Although Modotti appears as the only woman listed among LADLA's international collaborators, the individuals on the masthead of El Libertador were all men.[95] LADLA member José Fernández Anaya recalled that in the organization's early days, Modotti gave a brief talk on Italian fascism during a meeting and was presented to those in attendance as "an anti-fascist fighter."[96] Periodicals, testimony, and letters reveal that Modotti collected money at meetings, raised and donated funds, provided translations, and used her apartment as a meeting site for activists.[97] In her only official political position while in Mexico, Modotti was eventually appointed (by Vidali) to head the IRA's Mexican section, beginning around 1928, and she joined the editorial board of the IRA newspaper, Mella.[98] This allowed her to take on a more visible role, particularly in supporting antifascism in Italy and in protesting Mella's 1929 assassination.[99] To reconstruct Modotti's political life is to bring together many small details found across multinational archives. When combined, these details demonstrate Modotti's extensive political activities in Mexico. Even so, because of her gender and perhaps also by personal choice, she mostly occupied supporting roles, such as translation and fundraising.[100]

Modotti's photographs of meetings and protests document and instantiate some of her political participation, including within LADLA. We know, for example, that she attended a 1928 meeting of LADLA's highly successful Manos Fuera de Nicaragua (Hands Off Nicaragua, MAFUENIC) campaign, because she took a photograph of the meeting held at LADLA headquarters. Fernández Anaya, who appears in the photograph, remembers accompanying Modotti as she petitioned wealthy Mexicans and government officials to fund the campaign, which supported Augusto César Sandino's army in Nicaragua.[101] She took yet another photograph of the MAFUENIC committee when it received an American flag reportedly captured by Sandino's troops, and the photo was then published in *El Libertador*.[102] When Modotti was eventually deported from Mexico, it was the umbrella organization LAI (under which LADLA represented its Americas section) that received her in Berlin.[103] The PCM, LADLA, and the LAI played a central role in the international circulation of Modotti's famous profile of Mella, which became a rallying cry against his assassination and against Machado's dictatorship in Cuba.[104] Through the global distribution of Mella's photograph, Modotti played a key role in the creation of the trope of the eroticized male Latin American revolutionary subject, a trope that later became identified with the midcentury image of Che Guevara.

Although Modotti gave Mella's portrait pride of place in her 1929 exhibit (figure 1.1), she also provided her viewer with a proliferation of radical vocabularies alternative to this image of the charismatic male leader. As she explained in the essay accompanying her exhibit, she did not like for her work to be considered "artistic," because she wanted to distance herself from "the majority of photographers" who "still seek 'artistic' effects, imitating other mediums of graphic expression."[105] In describing her work this way, she seemed to refer to how she, Weston, and contemporaries like Paul Strand defined themselves against pictorialist photography, which mimicked impressionist paintings through painting brushstrokes over the photograph. Instead, these artists produced what became known as straight photography, a modernist, high-contrast style focused on the abstract, geometric structure of subjects, which intended to make visible (rather than hide) that the image was made with a camera. Yet even as Modotti did not want her work to be associated with "artistic effects," she clearly wanted to be taken seriously as an artist who, as she wrote, uses "the camera as a tool just as the painter does his brushes."[106] Throughout her time in Mexico, Modotti photographed a range of subjects: scaffolding, calla lilies, telegraph wires, sugar cane, doors and arches, laundry drying, muralists as they painted, portraits of friends and clients, and more. As she attended political meetings around the country and took photos for publication in leftist newspapers, she captured other things, like workers loading bananas onto a ship, a man carrying a beam, fishing nets, or hands in the act of washing clothes or doing agricultural labor.

Mexican Folkways editor Frances Toor wrote about Modotti's 1929 exhibit: "One has but to look at these photographs to realize that there has been a great change in the photographer herself with respect to interests and values—from the purely esthetic to the esthetic as expressed in the homely but significant phenomena of everyday life, with their implied social significance."[107] Toor expressed a perspective consistent with contemporary critics' tendency to divide Modotti's work into an earlier period, focused on aestheticism and divorced from politics, and a later period, more representational and political. This division clouds the political perspective undergirding Modotti's entire corpus.

Although Modotti clearly showed a progression in the way she understood the relationship between photography and issues of "social significance," her more "esthetic" works also demonstrate her integrated vision of artistic and social concerns. In one of the most significant contributions to the critical analysis of Modotti's work, Carol Armstrong reads Modotti's still-life and abstract photography against the work of her mentor and lover Edward Weston. She compares the multiplicity of Modotti's *Roses* (1924) (figure 1.5), with its layering and indistinct boundaries—or its "petalled pluralism"—to the black-and-white singularity of Weston's photography, such as in his shell series (figure 1.6).[108] She uses this contrast as a framework for reading several of Modotti's works in dialogue and contradistinction to Weston. For instance, she analyzes "the gray zones," textures and shadows, and warps and bends of Modotti's *Cloth Folds* (1924) in contrast to the tautly stretched fabric and full black-and-white range of Weston's *Circus Tent* (1924). Modotti's emphasis on the gray zones and indeterminacy between subjects serves as a counterpoint to Weston's singular male gaze. Modotti's work represents, as Armstrong writes, "the 'negative, the underside, the reverse' of Weston's sublimated 'phallomorphism' . . . a counterformalism to oppose his formalism, with its 'predominance of the visual, and of the discrimination and individualization of form,' a haptics to contravene his optics."[109]

Taking Armstrong's lead, I propose that we understand Modotti's work not just as an intervention into an artistic world that Weston dominated but also as an intervention into the mostly male international political

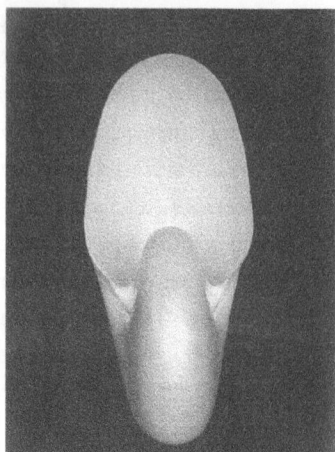

1.5 Tina Modotti, *Roses* (1924).

1.6 Edward Weston, *Nautilus* (1927). Collection Center for Creative Photography © Center for Creative Photography, Arizona Board of Regents.

community in which she was enveloped. In particular, Modotti's photography engages the core ideas of LADLA as it attempted to create a multinational and multiracial political community across extractive economies. From *Sugar Cane* (1929) to *Corn* (1929) to the *Loading Bananas, Veracruz* series (1927–29) to *Fishermen Mending Nets* (1927), agricultural and extractive economies remain a repeated theme of Modotti's work. Nowhere is this more evident than in the photographs she took of the work of Indian nationalist and agronomist Pandurang Khankhoje, who, as a political exile beginning in 1924, established Mexico's thirty-three Free Schools of Agriculture. The schools were created in collaboration with agrarian leader Úrsulo Galván, the first director of LADLA's *El Libertador*. Influenced by his personal experience of the Indian famine in 1896–97, Khankhoje developed high-yielding drought- and disease-resistant forms of wheat and corn to support self-determination for Mexican Indigenous farmers. He brought together "the *swadeshi* principles of radical Indian anticolonialism" with radical Mexican agrarianism to present agricultural models alternative to the exploitation of extractive labor.[110]

Modotti became the official photographer for the Free Schools of Agriculture and provided photographic illustrations for Khankhoje's books on plant genetics, including his *Nuevas variedades de maíz* (New varieties

1.7 Tina Modotti, *Cross-Section of Maize Granada* (1928). Courtesy of Savitry Sawhney.

of corn). Modotti captured images of Khankhoje in the fields with Indigenous farmers who studied at the Free Schools of Agriculture and photographed the hybrid varieties of corn that Khankhoje developed through crossbreeding. For instance, he developed *maíz granada*, which contains more kernels than common corn. In addition to its external kernels, each ear produces internal kernels whose interlocking structure replaces a cob. This lack of uniformity in the kernels, as Khankhoje explained in *Nuevas variedades de maíz*, allows for higher yield. Modotti photographed the different varieties of corn developed by Khankhoje, including a cross-section of *maíz granada* that displayed its interior kernels, its curved shape, and the varying shape and color of the kernels that darken as they reach the tip of the ear (figure 1.7). Although the ears of corn are fully contained within the frame in *Cross-Section of Maize Granada*, which exhibits the objective gaze of a scientific dissection, this photograph is one of several in *Nuevas variedades de maíz* that, when viewed in their totality, draw a relationship between agricultural diversity and the promise of self-determination for Indigenous peoples.

Modotti's photographs of Khankhoje's projects make up a small portion of her many works focused on agricultural economies. Much like the "petalled pluralism" of *Roses*—viewed by Armstrong as a direct response to Weston—many of Modotti's images of agricultural production challenge the visual regime of singularity fundamental to monoculture, extractive

1.8 Tina Modotti, *Corn* (1929). **1.9** Tina Modotti, *Workers Parade* (1926).

economies. Whereas Modotti's photographs in *Nuevas variedades de maíz* underscore the value of diversity and variability, *Corn* (1929) (figure 1.8) parallels the multiplicity of *Roses* in its overlapping shadows and layering of leaves that exceed the boundaries of the frame.

Many of Modotti's works on themes other than agricultural production, like *Workers Parade* (1926), *Meeting of Campesinos* (1927), *Oaxacan Market Scene* (ca. 1926–29), *Telephone Wires* (1925), and *Glasses* (1924), also emphasize multiplicity and layering and take the relation between subjects as their central focal point. For example, her first explicitly political photograph, *Workers Parade* (figure 1.9), taken at a 1926 May Day demonstration, is a high-angle shot of a mass of nearly indistinguishable men in identical sombreros.[111] The image depicts the subjects' relation to one another and—with the slight blur of the photograph—their movement together as a unit.[112] The repeated motif of the sombreros is visually similar to the compositional choices of much of her other work. That is, we can consider her apparently apolitical work as communicating a similar proto-political vision for an alternative social ecology that becomes more pronounced in her more overtly politically themed photography. As suggested by *Workers Parade*, to which I will return shortly, Modotti's visual representation of LADLA's notion of political community would also address the organization's focus on Indigenous communities.

LADLA'S FOCUS ON INDIGENOUS COMMUNITIES

LADLA's vision for a multiracial community was especially concerned with alliances with Indigenous populations within rural regions most impacted by extractive industries. The early leadership of both Nahua artist Guerrero and agrarian leader Galván largely drove this focus on Indigenous organizing. In the article "The Indian as the Base of the Anti-Imperialist Struggle," written by Bertram Wolfe and published in *El Libertador* in July 1925, Wolfe argued that until more Indigenous activists "enter into the struggle, the anti-imperialist movement is condemned to remain a mere literary tendency among intellectuals, a sterile struggle of pamphlets and books denouncing Yankee imperialism in the name of the 'Spanish race,' which does not constitute the race that numerically predominates in the countries most subjected to said imperialism."[113] The pervasiveness of US domination in much of Latin America, Wolfe claimed, was precisely because of the oppression of Indigenous workers by a domestic white and mestizo oligarchy. Wolfe called for LADLA to reach out to Indigenous leaders, who could use their linguistic and cultural expertise to organize anti-imperialist leagues among Indigenous, agrarian communities.

Whereas Wolfe characterized Indigenous peoples as "the base of the anti-imperialist struggle" in the Americas, Diego Rivera later seemed to expand this idea to encompass the globe. In Rivera's cover illustration (figure 1.10) for the June 1927 issue of *El Libertador*, which reported on the Brussels Congress, workers of multiple races gather behind a wall. Beneath the wall—whose square stones may allude to the Incan walls of Sacsayhuamán, in Cusco, Peru—is what appears to be a Quechua man wearing an Andean *chullo* hat with a chevron pattern. He is flanked by two bearded men holding weapons and wearing top hats with the insignia of British and US flags. The illustration could suggest multiple interpretations.[114] The Quechua man, who appears to strain under a weight, may be holding up the wall to protect those behind him. Alternatively, the world's peoples—including farmers (sickles), industrial workers (hammers), and intellectuals (pens)—may be coming to his aid by breaking down the wall. Above the drawing appear the words "The Anti-Imperialist Congress of Brussels," suggesting the Quechua man at the base of the wall as "the base of the anti-imperialist struggle" and the LAI's global project. The struggle for Indigenous rights, Rivera seems to suggest, is fundamental to a multiracial labor-based, anti-imperialist project across the globe.

1.10 Diego Rivera, cover, *El Libertador* (June 1, 1927), Centro INAH Morelos.

Rivera's illustration of the 1927 Brussels Congress and LADLA's focus on Indigenous communities occurred within the broader context of interwar *indigenismo*, a range of "intellectual movements, government programs, and aesthetic projects" that placed Indigenous cultures at the heart of Mexican national identity.[115] *Indigenismo* provided the Mexican revolutionary state with its origin myth that upheld pre-Columbian, Indigenous societies as untainted by European colonialism while often portraying contemporary Indigenous populations as needing modernization and incorporation into the nation. Although *indigenista* positions varied, many mestizo Mexican intellectuals viewed *indigenismo* as representing a step toward the assimilation of Indigenous peoples into dominant Mexican society rather than support for Indigenous political and cultural autonomy. In general, *indigenista* intellectuals were preoccupied with the nation, its articulation and cohesion, rather than with solidarity with semiautonomous Indigenous communities at odds with national formation.[116]

Since LADLA focused on transnational political organizing, it had little investment in questions of Mexican national identity. It criticized *indigenismo* for creating utopian representations of ancient Indigenous civilizations that ignored the practical realities faced by living Indigenous peoples. It also critiqued the parallel discourse of *mestizaje*, promoted by former Secretary of Education José Vasconcelos, which celebrated the cultural and genetic mixing of peoples of Hispanic and Indigenous descent into an imagined mestizo racial synthesis shared across the region. Instead, LADLA argued that a Latin American mestizo elite participated in the exploitation of Indigenous peoples. It differentiated between mestizo and Indigenous experiences in Mexico and throughout the region and posed Indigenous leaders as partners in an anti-imperialist movement that frequently conflicted with national integration projects.

Diego Rivera's work—including the Chapingo murals, which featured a prodigious nude of Modotti—played a key role in the visual depiction of the Mexican state's encounter with Indigenous communities. Rivera's interest in Mexico's Indigenous populations largely aligned with LADLA in that he advocated for their rights to land and natural resources and believed that Indigenous communities should not be expected to assimilate to access these rights.[117] Even so, he has also been criticized for idyllic portrayals of classless, Indigenous societies.[118] As I will explain, Modotti's photography would interrogate this particular aspect of Rivera's work, especially his portrayal of Indigenous women.

Rivera held a particular fascination with the matriarchal culture of the Tehuanas (Zapotec women from Tehuantepec, Oaxaca). He painted Tehuanas repeatedly, frequently as nudes in Edenic jungles, emphasizing their beauty and sensuality. Such depictions appear in Rivera's Chapingo murals, which include a massive fresco representing the Virgin Earth for which Modotti modeled. These depictions of Tehuanas resonated with photographs taken by nineteenth-century photographers, such as William Henry Jackson or Charles B. Waite, who captured images of Tehuanas as they bathed.[119] Jackson and Waite counted among several US photographers commissioned by railroad and steamship lines to photograph engineering and modernization projects of the repressive administration of Mexican President Porfirio Díaz (1876–80, 1884–1911). Their photography, which mostly focused on railroads, dams, and other engineering feats, "appeared in the guise of tourist views" since the images were intended to stimulate external investment and tourism.[120] Their photographs of Tehuanas contain a similarly exoticizing gaze, in which the women's bodies are framed as available for racialized and sexual consumption within a landscape poised for foreign investment and extraction. Although Rivera certainly opposed such political views, his images of Tehuanas rely on similar exoticizing tropes.

From Rivera's paintings, especially of full-figured Tehuanas, Rivera developed a homogenous, universalized Indigenous type that would appear across his work. Although his illustration of the Brussels Congress (figure 1.10) did not incorporate his familiar depictions of Tehuanas, the Quechua man in the foreground plays a similarly universalized role, standing in for Indigenous peoples everywhere. Such a generalized depiction is indicative of one of LADLA's central problems in that, despite Wolfe's call for diversification of leadership and despite evidence of engagement with Indigenous communities through the National Peasant League, LADLA's central leadership remained primarily white and mestizo. Modotti would use her photography not only to examine this problem but also, through her own representations of Tehuanas, to question the masculine category of labor envisioned by LADLA's overwhelmingly male activists.

INDIGENEITY IN MODOTTI'S PHOTOGRAPHY OF RELATION

As Modotti's photography visually represented much of LADLA's ideology, it responded to the limiting construction of Indigenous communities within LADLA and also within the indigenista movement. Modotti's *Workers Parade* (figure 1.9) mirrors the relational multiplicity depicted in *Roses* and *Corn*. In *Workers Parade*, Modotti takes the photo from behind, emphasizing the subjects' nearly identical clothing and identity as a group.[121] The *charro*-style sombrero and the *sarapes* over two of the men's shoulders mark the indigeneity of the marching men, who demand resources from a state that upholds them as the cultural heart of the nation while simultaneously marginalizing them.[122] The uniformity of the marching men could be read as a visual depiction of the assimilating discourse of the Mexican state that aims to convert diverse Indigenous communities into a singular *campesino* (farmer) class. However, Modotti inverts the mestizo state's discourse by pushing the non-sombrero-wearing subject, walking on the sidewalk in a dark hat, to the margins of the frame. Similarly, although *Workers Parade* could be seen to participate in the Indigenous everyman type

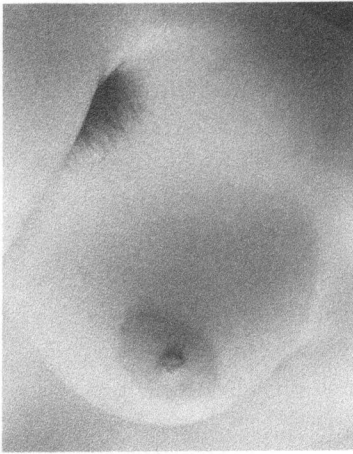

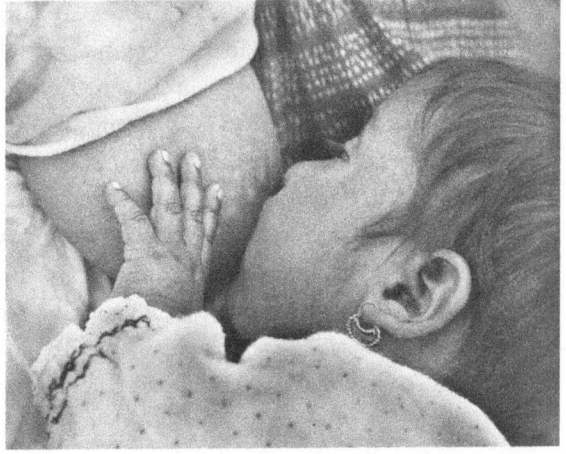

1.11 Edward Weston, *Nude* (1935). Collection Center for Creative Photography
© Center for Creative Photography, Arizona Board of Regents.

1.12 Tina Modotti, *Baby Nursing* (1926–27).

popularized by Rivera, the image also captures people in movement in the
street. They are not fixed in a mythological, Edenic setting far from the
centers of power but rather occupy the center of public life. Rather than
being relegated to an idyllic past or to a margin in need of integration, these
Indigenous men remain in motion in the present at the center of the frame.

Modotti's commitment to LADLA's vision for a multiracial political
community and its focus on Indigenous workers, as well as her response
to the limitations of this vision, becomes most clear in her photographs
of Indigenous women, and especially in her 1929 series of Tehuanas. I
understand these particular photographs as furthering LADLA's focus on
Indigenous labor while responding to three male-dominated worlds in
which Modotti was immersed. These worlds include LADLA and adjacent
political communities; the Mexican art world, led by Rivera; and the field
of modernist photography, dominated by Weston.

Weston's work repeatedly cropped and decontextualized Modotti's and
other women's bodies, studying the women's breasts or hands (figure 1.11).
Modotti's version of this technique, however, would show dark-skinned
women's hands in the act of washing clothes or doing other work, thus
rethinking and challenging the overwhelming masculine category of
labor conceived by organizations like LADLA or the PCM.[123] The cropped
breast in Modotti's photography is consistently used to depict Indigenous

women nursing (figure 1.12), an image that threatens to overstate women's roles as mothers but that also emphasizes the continuity of Indigenous peoples in the face of assimilationist projects. In comparison to Rivera's sensuous depiction of Indigenous women's bodies, Modotti's work highlights the biological function of breasts over the breast as an object of male desire. And in Modotti's images of the nursing breast appears yet another example of what Armstrong calls "the difficulty of 'distinguishing what is touching from what is touched'" in Modotti's work.[124] Modotti's examination of the relation between subjects destabilizes the singular masculinist and sexualizing gaze in a way similar to her destabilization of the singular visual regime of extraction through her depictions of multiplicity.

Modotti's photographs of Tehuanas focus on their labor, including the labor of motherhood: carrying heavy baskets in bare feet while holding a child on one hip, or carrying a baby, the folds of the baby's back pressed against the mother's arm. The familiar Tehuana bather is, in Modotti's work, an old woman with her back turned looking after bathing children. While Modotti's photographs often do not escape a distanced, observational gaze, the women she photographs are not depicted as sensuous beauties lying around naked in a jungle-like setting, available for racialized and sexual consumption. They are busy working and running their households, seemingly uninterested in the camera.[125] Alternatively, in some cases, the images break from the position of distant observer, and the women look directly at the camera and smile confidently. These shots are taken at eye level, neither elevating nor reducing their subjects. They are presented, as Sarah Lowe writes, "with sober matter-of-factness, as if to say, here is the proletariat of the proletariat."[126] In contrast to *Workers Parade*, the women are not depicted en masse; they are individuals, most of their faces visible in each shot. Modotti's images of Tehuanas unsettle both Weston's and Rivera's preoccupation with the female form and push LADLA's emphasis on Indigenous labor to contemplate the role of women, especially Indigenous women, in its political project.

These images fit within a larger trend in Modotti's work in depicting interconnectivity, which I read as central to her political aesthetics.[127] Although the focus on relation in her depiction of Indigenous women could be read as an *indigenista* representation of Indigenous communities as pre-Marxist, classless societies, there is little mythology or idealism in this series of photographs. The focus remains on the practical life of women, not their idealization.

1.13 Tina Modotti, *Julio Antonio Mella* (1928).

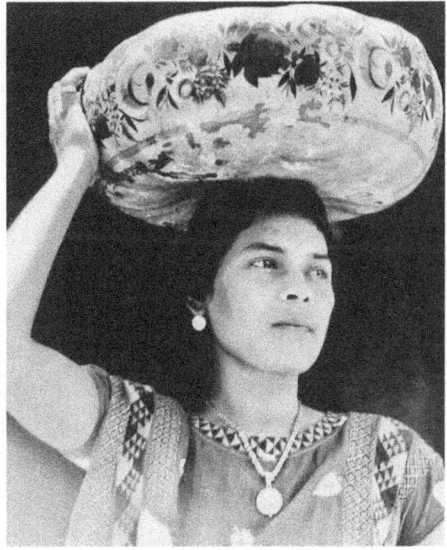

1.14 Tina Modotti, *Mujer de Tehuantepec* (1929).

The photograph that comes closest to such idealism is, interestingly, the one most similar to Modotti's famous photo of Mella, who was serving as LADLA's general secretary at the time of his death. Modotti visited Tehuantepec shortly after Mella's assassination and the subsequent trial. She traveled there alone to escape the media's depiction of her as the Italian femme fatale in a supposed murderous love triangle that ended in Mella's murder. During her stay in Tehuantepec, she photographed women almost exclusively.[128] She took many images of women balancing their painted *xicalpextles* (gourd containers) on their heads. Most of these were snapshots, but in one widely recognized portrait—*Mujer de Tehuantepec*—a Tehuana wearing an intricately woven huipil and balancing a *xicalpextle* with her right arm holds her chin high and looks to her left (figure 1.14). The image has a composition similar to that of Mella's portrait (figure 1.13), a medium close-up taken with a slight low angle of a subject whose face and shoulders turn toward the light on the right side of the frame. Of all Modotti's images of Tehuana, this is the closest to an idealized *indigenista* trope.[129] However, considering this image in direct conversation with Mella's profile and its political uses suggests a different interpretation.

In *Mujer de Tehuantepec*, Modotti revises the vision of radicalism she put forth in her portrait of Mella. Here, the heroic radical subject is presented as an Indigenous woman, who is decidedly not Mella. She is not the unfettered, young, white male intellectual looking into his bright future. Rather, she is a young, working Indigenous woman, her face framed by the strong arm balancing her labor on her head. *Mujer de Tehuantepec* signifies Modotti's self-conscious response to her portrait of Mella, and the two portraits together provide a window onto an artist wrestling with questions that resist clear answers.

Looking closely at Modotti's work alongside her political participation reveals a vision, which LADLA would circulate broadly, for a labor-based project and networked relation across extractive economies. Modotti appears to advance that vision further by drawing attention to its limitations. Her work questions the central direction of this project by white and mestizo, male activists and seems to push for a deeper commitment to Indigenous leadership that would center, rather than ignore, Indigenous women.

Modotti's representation of Indigenous women sheds light on her commitment to LADLA's politics of relational solidarity. Modotti's camera sought to capture a recognition and complicity with the burden of others that does not idealize the other and that acknowledges how their burden and experience is different from one's own. Importantly, Modotti seems to acknowledge that in building political community across difference, there are abundant opportunities for misunderstanding, mistranslation, and misinterpretation. Forging such intimacies and connections is not a smooth process but, as Modotti suggests, is one that is best visualized in the gray zones, in the indeterminate spaces, and between the folds.

TWO

AGAINST LATIN AMERICAN REGIONALISMS

THE 1927 BRUSSELS CONGRESS AND LADLA'S HEMISPHERIC GLOBALISM

In the Palais d'Egmont in Brussels, Belgium, the members of the General Council of the newly formed League Against Imperialism and Colonial Rule and for National Independence (LAI) crowded together for a photograph (figure 2.1). They were just a few of the 170 delegates from thirty-seven countries at the Congress Against Colonial Oppression and Imperialism and for National Independence, held February 10–15, 1927.[1] In this photograph appear several of the twentieth century's foremost anticolonial activists, like the German organizer of the conference Willi Münzenberg; Japanese communist Sen Katayama; Mohammad Hatta, later vice president of Indonesia; Senegalese anticolonial activist Lamine Senghor; and German women's rights activist Helene Stöcker, to name a few.[2] Sitting with a pile of papers on his lap is Indian independence leader Jawaharlal Nehru. Although their presence frequently goes unmentioned, several Latin Americans stand in the back row: Cuban activist and LADLA general secretary Julio Antonio Mella; Mexican intellectual José Vasconcelos; Italian Argentine communist Victorio Codovilla; and the non–Latin American US citizen Manuel Gomez, representing LADLA-US. These and other Latin Americans participated in the discussions in Brussels and subsequent LAI

2.1 General Council, Brussels Congress, 1927. *Das Flammenzeichen* (1927).

meetings. LADLA, designated in Brussels as the LAI's Americas section, was particularly well represented.[3] However, since most scholarship on the LAI focuses on the history of Afro-Asian collaborations, it has tended to neglect LADLA's involvement.[4]

This chapter revisits the 1927 Brussels Congress to better understand how intellectuals from the Americas were influenced by anticolonial thinkers from elsewhere and to underline the role of Latin American thinkers in the LAI's global history. The 1927 Brussels Congress is recognized for its unprecedented historical significance. It is often described as the forerunner to the 1955 Bandung Conference of African and Asian nations, frequently cited as a foundational moment for the development of postcolonial thought.[5] Centering LADLA's involvement in the LAI helps reframe this early history of postcolonial thought, which has overwhelmingly focused on the enduring legacies of European colonialism in Africa and Asia.[6]

If studies of the LAI often overlook LADLA's involvement, scholarship on Latin American radicalism, with some important exceptions, tends to have a regional focus that does not frame these activists in the global milieus that they inhabited.[7] This is especially the case regarding the interwar period, characterized by the emergence of Latin America's regionalist ideologies. In response to post–World War I disillusionment with Western Europe and the increasing dominance of the United States, interwar Latin American writers and political figures defined Latin America through regionalist ideologies like *hispanoamericanismo, indoamericanismo, mestizaje,* and *indigenismo.* Many interwar Latin American intellectuals spent time in Western Europe, and these experiences influenced the distinctions they drew between European and Latin American contexts. However, although interwar Latin American cosmopolitanisms in Europe have long been recognized, transnational networks reaching Africa and Asia remain undertheorized.

An exemplar of this problem appears in the depiction of the Brussels Congress in the novel *Recurso del método* (Reasons of State) (1974) by renowned Cuban author and former LADLA-Cuba member Alejo Carpentier. *Recurso del método* depicts a grassroots interwar struggle against a dictatorship in an unidentified Latin American country. A young man simply called "the Student," who leads the agitation, is responsible for publishing a communist-leaning paper called *Liberation* and is affiliated with the "Anti-Imperialist League of the Americas."[8] Thus, the novel contains a direct reference to LADLA. Toward the end of the novel, and after the fall of the country's dictatorship, the Student travels to Europe to attend the Brussels Congress. On his way to Brussels, he boards a train with various conference delegates, including Julio Antonio Mella and Jawaharlal Nehru. Nehru, who sits next to a window in the corner, begins to survey the papers piled on his lap, a description strikingly similar to Nehru's image in the photo of the LAI General Council (figure 2.1). Mella turns to the Student to ask questions about the political situation in the Student's country, drawing comparisons to his own struggle against the Gerardo Machado regime in Cuba. The two exchange their speeches and reports for the congress. As they pass coal mines, Nehru, who has been quiet and "absorbed in his own thoughts, hidden behind wide open eyes," throughout the exchange, suddenly says, "Cool, cool." With his Indian English pronunciation, the two Latin Americans do not know if he is referring to being cold (since the cabin is frigid) or to the coal mines outside. Nehru, whom Carpentier repeatedly refers to as "the Indian," then continues "sleeping with his eyes open" until the train arrives in Brussels.[9]

In an illuminating reading of Carpentier's novel, Magalí Armillas-Tiseyra interprets this moment as a commentary on "the challenges to transnational solidarity, where language stands for actual linguistic differences as well as possible historical and ideological divergences. These problems are not resolved; instead, they signal a refusal to idealize utopian alternatives."[10] Whereas the two Latin Americans exchange papers and ideas, Nehru's experience and words remain untranslatable to them, which Armillas-Tiseyra reads as "the novel's demurral from triumphant transnational political utopianism."[11] Although I agree with this reading of Carpentier's reticence toward utopianism, I take a less generous position toward his representation of the global exchange that occurred in Brussels. Carpentier's novel identifies some things that these three characters have in common: their "shabby" suitcases and their presence in the "second-class" train car, which is "excessively cold for these men from hot climates."[12] But these commonalities are overtly superficial. In the more substantive historical and ideological realms, Carpentier clearly reads the Brussels moment through the familiar lens of interwar Latin American regionalist exceptionalism, emphasizing the region's unique cultural and historical position over its connections with other contexts. In its brief representation of Nehru, the novel goes so far as to estrange and orientalize Nehru, and through synecdoche, it estranges other non–Latin American delegates at the congress as well. Carpentier's representation flattens the complexities of the encounter in Brussels between Latin Americans and anticolonial intellectuals from elsewhere, like Nehru.

It is not just in novels that an insistence on the region's exceptionalism is used to erase Latin Americans' full participation in the historic moment of the Brussels Congress. Michael Goebel has characterized Latin Americans' participation as representing a failure to "enhance mutual understanding between Latin Americans and the anticolonialists from Asia and Africa."[13] Goebel's understanding, however, draws from the perspectives of a few prominent Latin American congress participants, especially José Vasconcelos.[14] As I will argue, LADLA, representing over one-third of Latin American delegates, differed sharply from Vasconcelos's perspectives. Similarly, Vijay Prashad describes the Brussels Congress as follows:

> The collaboration between the African, Arab, and Asian regional formations had a much greater intensity than the contacts they had with the Latin Americans. This was for several reasons. First, the Latin American states had attained formal independence from Spain and Portugal in the early nineteenth century so they did not share the contemporary experience of colonial domination. . . . The distinctions between the Americas and elsewhere in terms of their colonial heritage became less pronounced over time as both zones understood how global capital subjected them. Yet this did not lead to organizational ties before the Cold War. Second, the Latin American states lived in an alternative imperial orbit. Their target was not Old Europe but the New Yankee, and

in this they differed greatly from most of Africa and Asia (except for the Philippines). Additionally, their colonial orbit gave them Spanish as their lingua franca (except for Brazil and the Dutch colonies) whereas most of the anticolonial leaders from Africa and Asia spoke English or French. . . . The worlds of the Latin Americans did not cross frequently with those of the Afro-Asians.[15]

As Prashad points out, Latin America's history of nineteenth-century decolonization and subsequent encounters with US empire did make the region's history distinct from that of Africa or Asia. Additionally, as the official languages of the conference were English and French (with some speeches translated into German), the language barrier could have marginalized some of the Spanish-speaking Latin Americans. Problems also arose in the quality of some translations.[16] Even so, Mella spoke English from birth with his Irish-born mother (Mella's father also spoke fluent English and French) and spent significant time in the United States, and many other Latin American delegates spoke English or French as well.[17] I would argue that Prashad's point is a better explanation of the disciplinary and linguistic divisions that have sidelined Spanish-speaking Latin America in the historiography of the LAI and in global twentieth-century anticolonial history than it is of the realities of the congress itself.

The photo referenced previously pushes against the linguistic and regional boundaries that define our academic disciplines and that have framed our understanding of this historical moment. The group, which has spent days together listening to one another's speeches, debating, and talking over meals, has clearly developed a sense of camaraderie. Hands are held, and arms are draped over shoulders. Some, on the other hand, look uncomfortable and distracted. This is not an image of a utopian community, as Carpentier would remind us, but it is an image of transnational and translinguistic exchange. The Latin American delegates, of whom those that appear in the photo are a fraction of those in attendance, do not stand apart in their own regional enclave; they influenced and were influenced by these conversations.

A closer look at LADLA's participation in Brussels shifts our understanding of interwar Latin American intellectual history. Contrary to the regionalist lens through which Latin American participation in the Brussels Congress has been understood, this chapter argues that LADLA members rejected interwar regionalisms for what I describe as a *hemispheric globalism*, wherein LADLA expanded on its initially hemispheric connections with US worker and minority struggles to embrace interdependency with anti-imperialist movements around the world.[18] During the Brussels Congress, LADLA began to clearly differentiate its platform from Latin American regionalisms, including the perspectives of two of the foremost thinkers of such regionalist ideologies: Vasconcelos and Víctor Raúl Haya de la Torre.

If the conference offered LADLA organizers the chance to see more clearly the connections between their struggles and those of other colonial contexts, it also helped them draw connections with non-Spanish-speaking communities that were closer geographically, like African Americans and activists from the francophone and anglophone Caribbeans. LADLA's global perspective enhanced its hemispheric connections and vice versa. The encounters in Brussels began a process of expanding LADLA's initial focus on Indigenous struggles to think more critically about Black communities in the Americas. This influenced LADLA's eventual theorization of white supremacy as an integral part of imperialist domination, which became a defining aspect of LADLA's worldview.

THE 1927 BRUSSELS CONGRESS, SETTING THE SCENE

A few months after LADLA's formation in Mexico City, German communist Willi Münzenberg organized in Berlin the committee Against Cruelties in Syria in response to the 1925 French bombing of Damascus.[19] This committee later became the broader League Against Colonial Oppression (LACO), which charged Münzenberg, Indian nationalist Virendranath Chattopadhyaya, and Hungarian Luis Otto Gibarti with organizing the Congress Against Colonial Oppression and Imperialism and for National Independence.[20] They formed an Executive Committee, which included LADLA leaders Mella and Gomez, to assist with congress invitations.[21] The congress was largely funded through the Workers International Relief, a Comintern-affiliated organization formed by Münzenberg, and the Comintern had significant influence over the conference agenda.[22] Even so, the organizers insisted on the LAI's independence from the Comintern, and many of the delegations had no affiliation with communism.[23] The government of Plutarco Elías Calles in Mexico also contributed funds through its ambassador to Germany, Ramón de Negri, as well as a statement to be read at the congress against US designs on Mexican petroleum.[24]

The congress was organized into six sessions over three days, with the final day dedicated to establishing the LAI, "a permanent worldwide organization linking up all forces against imperialism and colonial oppression."[25] Throughout the congress, statistics and maps of colonial holdings and photographs of executed anticolonial activists were displayed around the palace halls.[26] Latin American delegates spoke mostly on the panel dedicated to cooperation between nationalist movements in "oppressed countries" and labor and anti-imperialist movements in "imperialist countries."[27]

The congress's final resolution stated that the delegations agreed to establish the LAI and invited affiliation of any organization or individual fighting against capitalist imperialism, for nationalist independence, or for equal rights of all races, classes, and peoples. This flexible and open stance was consistent with the Comintern's united-front approach of the 1920s, which sought to ally with "bourgeois nationalist movements in the colonies as a means to encourage anti-imperialist revolution first, and class revolution later," bringing together "socialists, communists, trade unionists, civil liberties reformers, pacifists, Pan-Africanists, and anticolonial nationalists."[28] For the internationalists from the colonies who participated in the LAI, their commitment to such fluid solidarities with one another would endure beyond the Comintern's 1928 decision to abandon alliances with nationalists.[29]

Congress delegates elected a General Council, including Mella and Gomez, which then elected a smaller Executive Committee with authority to make decisions on the LAI's behalf. General Council and Executive Committee members were charged with organizing agitation and propaganda campaigns in each of their countries. Member organizations committed to pay an annual contribution to the LAI, which the LAI would use to assist with these organizing campaigns. In the circumstance of imperialist violence or war, the executive committee would communicate with member organizations to organize universal mass action.[30] The delegates penned several resolutions, including one on Latin America, and approved a "declaration of support" with the program of the Puerto Rican Nationalist Party (Partido Nacionalista de Puerto Rico, PNPR).[31] LADLA published the Latin America resolution in El Libertador, as well as an additional resolution by the LAI Executive Committee naming LADLA as its Americas section.[32]

Although several other Latin American organizations attended, LADLA had the largest representation (eight of twenty-three Latin American delegates in the program).[33] Beyond Gomez and Mella, who also represented the Panamanian and Colombian sections, LADLA delegates included Leonardo Fernández Sánchez, a Venezuelan representing LADLA-Cuba, and Gustavo Machado, a Venezuelan representing LADLA-Nicaragua, among others. Because each organization paid for its delegates' travel, some did not send delegates but asked trusted individuals already planning to attend to serve as proxy. The delegation for the PNPR, for example, did not include any Puerto Ricans, and one of their proxy delegates (Vasconcelos) never mentioned Puerto Rico during his speech in Brussels.[34]

Regarding this cross-representation, Goebel writes, "Since the conference obliged Spanish Americans from one country to speak on behalf of another country, it rallied them on a shared platform of 'Latin' Americanism, anti-imperialism, and Yankee-baiting, which were their main hallmarks in Brussels. . . . The LAI conference thus reinforced Latin American regionalism on the basis of a shared anti-imperialism."[35] Indeed, the fact that a single delegate like Mella could represent multiple LADLA national sections demonstrates the extent to which LADLA drew parallels across national boundaries at the risk of erasing differences between these contexts. Yet even as LADLA delegates traced connections between Latin American countries, LADLA's anti-imperialist perspective took shape in dialogue with—and in contrast to—Latin America's interwar regionalist ideologies. LADLA sought, for example, to provide a vision different from *hispanoamericanismo*, which rejected US influence through an identification with Spain. Instead, it critiqued any form of colonial power, including Spanish holdings in Morocco. LADLA also did not base its movement in the cultural ideology of *mestizaje*, which celebrated the cultural and genetic mixing of peoples of Hispanic and Indigenous descent into an imagined mestizo racial identity shared across the region. Additionally, although LADLA centered Indigenous struggles, it dismissed *indigenismo*, which frequently interpellated Indigenous subjects for the purpose of national assimilation, and denounced essentializing views of Indigenous communities as precursors to communist societies.

The 1927 Brussels Congress served to solidify and deepen LADLA's rejection of Latin American regionalisms in favor of hemispheric globalism, wherein LADLA expanded on its hemispheric connections with US struggles by insisting on interdependency with anti-imperialist movements around the globe. While LADLA did not employ the term *hemispheric globalism*, I use it to describe, first, an ideological belief that self-determination for "oppressed, colonial, and semi-colonial peoples" in Latin America could be achieved only through alliances with similar struggles in the American hemisphere and around the world, and, second, a practical strategy to foment systems of mutual support by facilitating communication between resistant movements across the American hemisphere and by expanding those connections, through the LAI, to global horizons.[36] Following the Brussels Congress, LADLA stated its position of hemispheric globalism repeatedly in its propaganda materials. In one example, an article in *El Libertador* delineating LADLA delegates' planned contributions to the 1929 Second LAI Congress in Frankfurt stated that "existing among many thinkers of Latin America . . . is an overly nationalist concept. . . . The members of LADLA are perhaps the only ones who understand that it is not necessary to limit the struggle to Latin America; rather, the imperious necessity exists to unite not only with the anti-imperialist forces of our Continent, but also with those of the whole world."[37] The 1927 Brussels Congress played an important role in shaping this perspective, because it was there that LADLA began to clearly differentiate its platform from Latin American regionalist ideologies, including the perspectives of two of the foremost thinkers of Latin American regionalisms—Vasconcelos and Haya de la Torre.

Despite differences between LADLA and some other Latin American organizations present, the "Resolutions on Latin America"—a document signed by all Latin American delegates—built on LADLA's unique political platform. It began by tracing how US imperialism had largely replaced British imperialism in the region, taking control of primary resources and means of production. This economic domination paved the way for political domination, and through investments and loans, the United States created debtor governments in Latin America that threatened national sovereignty.

The resolution divided Latin America in its relationship to US imperialism into four sectors: (1) the Caribbean islands, Mexico, Central America, and Panama, where the United States had economic and military interests; (2) Venezuela, Colombia, Peru, and Bolivia, where the US government supported despotic regimes for economic gain; (3) Argentina, Uruguay, and Chile, where British imperialism conserved its influence and where industrial capitalism was the most established; and (4) Brazil, which had its own unique conditions that were left undescribed.

The document explicitly referenced China, stating that "the base of the struggle against imperialism is found in the worker and peasant masses, which, like in China, can oppose the pressure of imperialist power through large collective movements, boycott, and also with weapons."[38] But even as the resolution identified workers and peasants as the base of the anti-imperialist struggle, true to the flexible stance of LADLA and the LAI, it argued that "it is necessary that all progressive elements take an interest in this struggle: intellectuals, students, and the middle class, also affected economically and politically by the penetration of imperialism."[39]

Three elements of the "Resolutions on Latin America" draw my attention. The first, which has been commented on by several scholars, is the signatures of the Peruvians Víctor Raúl Haya de la Torre and Eudocio Ravines Pérez, both members of the newly founded American Popular Revolutionary Alliance (Alianza Popular Revolucionaria Americana, APRA) and the only delegates to sign the resolution "with reservations."[40] The second, which has been discussed but begs deeper analysis, is the discussion of Black communities in the resolution.[41] This resolution was later reprinted in El Libertador, representing the first time that LADLA's periodical mentioned Black peoples. The third, which is closely tied to the second, is the presence of two signatures by members of the conference's Committee on the Negro Question: Carlos Deambrosis Martins and Richard B. Moore.

These three elements of the resolution, I argue, are integrally related. Haya de la Torre's "reservations" signal how the Brussels Congress was decisive in a rift within the Latin American Left in which LADLA differentiated itself from other Latin American regionalist visions. The congress offered LADLA organizers the opportunity to develop connections with movements in other contexts, including nearby non-Spanish-speaking communities. This encounter influenced LADLA to begin to expand its focus on Indigenous movements to consider the significance of Black labor and theorize the fight against anti-Black racism as inherent to the anti-imperialist struggle.

LADLA'S HEMISPHERIC GLOBALISM

The Brussels Congress helped broaden LADLA's vision from the Americas to the globe. Comparing LADLA's positions with those of Vasconcelos and Haya de la Torre sheds light on how LADLA's hemispheric globalism differed from Latin America's interwar regionalist anti-imperialisms. Several LADLA delegates and affiliates gave speeches in Brussels. Mella and LADLA-Cuba delegate Leonardo Fernández Sánchez, for example, presented the paper "Cuba: Yankee Factory," which detailed US domination in Cuba.[42] LADLA-US secretary Gomez gave a lengthy speech on US imperialism in Latin America and the Pacific.[43] Carlos Quijano described how "the struggle against imperialism in Latin America is now being led in a united way thanks to the Anti-Imperialist League in America" and how the Brussels Congress offered the framework to unite these efforts with a global movement.[44]

Venezuelan activist Salvador de la Plaza traveled to the Brussels Congress from Mexico, where he was living in exile and directing *El Libertador*. A few months later, in December 1927, he returned to Brussels to deliver LADLA's Continental Committee report to the LAI General Council. Therein, he described how although Latin American nations had long been independent from Spain, "that independence was fictional for workers" since Spanish domination was simply passed to the elite, *criollo* class.[45] He then described the mid-nineteenth-century penetration of British capital through loans to Latin American governments and subsequent expansion of the US economy into Latin American markets through military occupations. US expansion, De la Plaza described, was done "in search of primary materials and cheap manual labor from Indigenous people" such that the anti-imperialist struggle must simultaneously be a movement for national liberation, control of national resources, and a workers' movement focused on Indigenous rights.[46]

As explained in chapter 1, this vision of a transnational movement emerging from an extractive zone that centers Indigenous struggles would be LADLA's unifying philosophy, and in his speech, De la Plaza succinctly communicated its framework. Before the General Council, he argued for the importance of Latin America within the global anti-imperialist movement since it formed the base of the US economy. As De la Plaza's speech demonstrates, the LAI gave Latin Americans a platform to explain their regional context and emphasize why that context mattered globally. LADLA delegates brought to the LAI direct experience with US imperialism and a nuanced understanding of how it overlapped with, and differed from, the region's prior encounters with European colonialisms.

De la Plaza claimed that the increasing violence of US expansion in the region had led to a rapid increase in anti-imperialist activity, boasting that in only three years LADLA had developed sections in every country of the continent and that its membership had already passed two million. While these numbers were dubious, LADLA had indeed grown rapidly. By December 1926, it included fourteen sections: Argentina, Brazil, Colombia, Cuba, the Dominican Republic, Ecuador, El Salvador, Honduras, Mexico, Peru, Puerto Rico, Uruguay, Venezuela, and the continental United States.[47] Maintaining a US section was important since, as Diego Rivera explained in his report to the LAI General Council, the Latin American working class must understand "its absolute economic dependence on the foreign economy" and that the local ruling classes "employed by dictators are nothing more than servants to imperialist capitalism."[48] For this reason, workers should struggle for "their true national independence," which would imply liberation from local elites, and which "is not possible without an intimate connection and joint action with the revolutionary proletariat of the United States."[49]

This decidedly hemispheric project, which embraced an alliance with US workers, was always intended to have a global scope. As the first issue of *El Libertador* described, Latin American workers would ally with US workers to form "a single anti-imperialist continental movement" that will then "eventually perhaps save Europe, Asia, and Africa as well."[50] However, despite this global vision from its inception, in practice LADLA had been a mostly hemispheric project, operating autonomously from similar movements on other continents. This would change with the Brussels Congress and LADLA's incorporation into the LAI's global community.

The Brussels Congress and the LAI's formation would significantly broaden LADLA's vision from the Americas to the globe. At the same time, it exposed and deepened fissures within the Latin American Left and revealed differences between LADLA's views and other Latin American anti-imperialisms. In order to understand how LADLA's unique position of hemispheric globalism differed from some of the Latin American regionalisms in circulation at that time, we can compare LADLA's positions to those of Vasconcelos.

Because Vasconcelos's speech in Brussels is the only speech by a Latin American conserved in the LAI Archive in Amsterdam, Vasconcelos's perspectives have been misconstrued as representative of all Latin American delegates.[51] However, LADLA delegates had markedly different views than Vasconcelos, who is perhaps best known for his notion of the "cosmic race" that defined Spanish-speaking Latin America through a history of racial mixing. While seemingly an antiracist rejection of Anglo-centric white supremacism, Vasconcelos's "cosmic race" has been widely criticized for its eugenicist advocacy for the erasure of Indigenous peoples and for relying on biological notions of race to argue for the benefits of *mestizaje*.

Although never intimately involved in LADLA, Vasconcelos was an early friend of the organization.[52] But after the Brussels Congress, LADLA published articles critiquing Vasconcelos, reminding its readers that he had never been a member. Some have understood this derision as originating from Vasconcelos's opposition to Mexican President Calles, who financially supported the congress (although LADLA claimed that Calles had not paid for their delegates' attendance). However, the discord between LADLA and Vasconcelos should also be understood through their differing positions toward Latin American regionalist thinking. Vasconcelos began his speech in Brussels by explaining that he would speak in English since "it was decided in Committee that only two languages should be used in the Congress."[53] Although he was "one of those ardent defenders of the Spanish language as the main link of our race," when he heard British and US workers collaborating, he decided that "if there are still people who use the English language to speak of Liberty, then Latin Americans can use it to express their soul." In this opening section, Vasconcelos expressed the region's opposition to imperialism by defining Latin America as a singular "race" linked through the Spanish language. His speech combined his vision for a cosmic race with a Hispanist allegiance to the Spanish language, conveying an image of Latin American anti-imperialists as Spanish-speaking mestizos. This differed significantly from LADLA's multilingual vision of hemispheric globalism and focus on Indigenous struggles.

Vasconcelos argued that political divisions represented the biggest challenge for Latin American anti-imperialism and explained that the organization he represented (PNPR) "has given me instructions to make it clear they are not communists." This is "because we in Latin America feel we are entitled to settle our problems in our own manner. We are not blind followers of any creed. . . . We claim the right to be absolutely independent." Vasconcelos took a fiercely regionalist position that differed from LADLA's communist leanings and its vision of mutual interdependence between regional struggles and those around the globe. In his rejection of communism in favor of home-grown self-determination, Vasconcelos's ideas coincided with the perspective of Haya de la Torre, who will be addressed shortly.

Vasconcelos closed his speech, which harped on Latin American difference, by stating, "Remember, friends . . . that Latin America is not only our country but also your country, the country of every man, no matter what race or colour, the country of the future and the home of all men." This statement is undoubtedly an inclusive one that sought to build bridges. Yet those familiar with Vasconcelos's writings may also see in this final comment an allusion to his view that mestizos would come to represent the future of humanity, a eugenicist and assimilationist vision that sought to erase ethnic difference.

LADLA'S NAVIGATION OF NATIONALISM AND COMMUNISM

Most scholarly discussion of Latin Americans' participation at the congress has focused on yet another divide between LADLA's Mella and Haya de la Torre, who led APRA—one of "Latin America's longest-lived populist parties"—from 1926 until his death in 1979.[54] This has been characterized as a division between Mella's hard-line communist alignment with Moscow versus Haya's regional and nationalist vision that viewed communism as a foreign import.[55] As Goebel has insightfully argued, such a split "cannot be explained but through interaction, via Brussels, with China," as it was heavily influenced by the nationalist-communist split in China that erupted in April 1927.[56] This division between nationalist- and communist-leaning positions, Rafael Rojas argues, has characterized leftist politics in Latin America ever since.[57]

While helpful for understanding two major trends in Latin American leftism, the characterization of the disagreement between Mella and Haya as a stark ideological division between communists and nationalists is, in my view, exaggerated. Both Mella and Haya translated Marxism to Latin American contexts in slightly different ways. As the two battled through articles and pamphlets, both took more extreme positions, differentiating themselves more strongly. Because of the scant scholarly attention devoted to LADLA, it may appear that Mella's positions directly overlapped with LADLA's, but in truth, he took narrower positions. In fact, much of APRA's platform was a slight revision of LADLA's program. Specifically, APRA's commitments to anti-imperialism, internationalism, a united front that included intellectuals and artists, and a focus on Indigenous struggles all drew from LADLA. In recovering the history of LADLA, we recover the history of an elided ideological middle ground that sought to navigate between these two historical positions.[58]

Haya, a student and labor leader in Peru, first met Mella, then president of the University of Havana's student federation, in 1923 when Haya visited Cuba for two weeks after he was deported by Peruvian dictator Augusto Leguía.[59] Shortly thereafter, Mella expanded his leadership from student activism to struggles for workers' rights and Cuba's national sovereignty, helping to establish the José Martí Popular University (UP), LADLA-Cuba, the Cuban Anticlerical Foundation, and the Cuban Communist Party (PCC).[60] The PCC and LADLA-Cuba memberships had some overlap, but as the PCC would later point out, LADLA-Cuba was not a proletarian organization and had a more ideologically diverse membership. When Mella and other PCC members were jailed by the Machado government in November 1925 for "terrorist activities," Mella followed in Haya's footsteps by staging an eighteen-day hunger strike.[61]

During the hunger strike, LADLA-Cuba organized an international solidarity campaign, using its publication *Venezuela Libre* and its international connections to call for Mella's release.[62] *Venezuela Libre* published a statement that Mella wrote from his Havana jail cell called "Toward an American International," which argued for the unification of the continent's anti-imperialist forces.[63] Mella's essay repeated much of LADLA's platform and called for other organizations to join LADLA in its anti-imperialist struggle. The hunger strike would cause problems for Mella after his release when he was put on trial by the PCC for failing to consult beforehand with party leadership or the other twelve jailed members, who remained imprisoned for three more weeks.[64] Mella claimed that he had indeed reached out to PCC leadership, but when he did not receive a reply, he consulted with affiliate organizations, like LADLA-Cuba.

In the trial, PCC leadership reminded Mella that although LADLA-Cuba and the UP were affiliate organizations, neither could be considered communist or even proletarian in nature. As part of the PCC's questioning of Mella's commitment to Marxism, they questioned his frequent references to Cuban independence leader José Martí. Mella explained that he drew from Lenin's thesis on the colonial question in his understanding that "anti-imperialist bourgeois revolutionaries (students, intellectuals, and other sectors) should be utilized, albeit controlled by the communists, for anti-imperialist campaigns that support the emancipation of the proletariat from the major economic empires."[65] This understanding, he explained, also aligned with LADLA's position. So when he referred to "Martí's Cuba" in his writings, he did not endorse a bourgeois, post-independence Cuban republic but rather the program of Martí's Cuban Revolutionary Party, which collaborated with anarchists and socialists in its anticolonial mission.[66] As LADLA-Cuba's secretary, Mella presented himself in this exchange as an anti-imperialist who was fighting for Cuba's national self-determination and who believed that true independence necessarily implied the liberation of the working classes.

Despite Mella's efforts to defend himself, the PCC sentenced him harshly in January 1926, banning him from political activities for three months and from PCC activity for two years, and publicly reprimanding him in the communist press. Under heightened scrutiny from the Machado government and the PCC, and facing a disciplinary action at the University of Havana that threatened to re-imprison him, Mella left Havana for Mexico City, arriving in February 1926.[67] There, he was embraced by LADLA leadership, which immediately named him to the Continental Committee, and he also joined the Mexican Communist Party (PCM).[68]

Later, on January 28, 1927 (days before the Brussels Congress), the Comintern weighed in on the PCC's judgment of Mella. It recognized Mella's fault in practicing individualism but argued that the disciplinary action the PCC had applied was too strict, that the PCC had lost the opportunity to connect with the masses mobilized by Mella's hunger strike, and that the PCC had alienated LADLA-Cuba. The Comintern had also decided to formally incorporate the PCC, but on the condition that it reestablish a relationship with LADLA-Cuba and readmit Mella into the party.[69]

This context is important for understanding the rigid position that Mella took in his disagreements with Haya de la Torre. At the Brussels Congress, Mella was on the cusp of having his name cleared by the Comintern. He was awaiting readmittance into the PCC and was meeting Comintern colleagues in Brussels who were likely familiar with his case of indiscipline. For example, initially "the Italian-Argentine communist Vittorio Codovilla and other congress participants with traction in Moscow skirted the communist Mella, branding him a 'petit bourgeois,' and instead courted the non-communist Haya."[70] Mella had something to prove, and perhaps for this reason he took a more dogmatic stance that did not align perfectly with LADLA's more flexible positions, nor with his own prior writings, nor with the views that he expressed in his PCC trial.[71]

Haya was involved in LADLA in Mexico City, writing articles for *El Libertador* as early as July 1925, but by the time Mella arrived in Mexico City in February 1926, Haya had already left for Europe.[72] Although APRA's official history claims that Haya founded APRA in Mexico City in May 1924 (six months before LADLA's founding), it was actually founded by a group of Peruvians living in Paris when Haya traveled there in September 1926. A second cell was formed by Peruvian exiles in Buenos Aires in 1927, and eventually additional cells formed in Havana, La Paz, and Mexico City.[73] When Haya arrived at the Brussels Congress, APRA was five months old and did not yet have a base in Mexico. APRA did not appear among the organizations listed in the Brussels program; Haya was listed as a representative for LADLA's sections in Panama, Nicaragua, and Peru.[74]

Mella claimed that Haya did not make his differences from LADLA known until the congress itself.[75] Haya agreed to sign the Latin American resolution "with reservations," a move that Mella interpreted as resulting from Haya's frustration that the congress did not recognize APRA as the "only anti-imperialist organization in Latin America."[76] Haya and APRA took Mella by surprise in Brussels, and it would have been difficult for Mella to have known much about APRA at that time. Only two months earlier, Haya had published his first public statement on APRA, called "¿Qué es el APRA?" (What is APRA?) in Britain's Labour Monthly. There he described APRA's program, where the influence of LADLA's anti-imperialist vision is obvious. In fact, although APRA has not necessarily been understood in this way, I maintain that APRA's vision represented a slight revision of LADLA's platform and should be understood as one of the most lasting examples of LADLA's understudied legacy. Haya's insistence on APRA being unique, despite its overt borrowing of LADLA's positions, angered Mella and LADLA organizers.

Although Haya critiqued hispanoamericanismo, he coincided with Vasconcelos in dismissing communism as "exotic and oriental in Latin America" and instead claimed that he based APRA's continental vision on the anticolonial legacies of the region, like those of Simón Bolívar and José Martí.[77] Latin America, Haya argued, should not look to Europe for its political models but rather to its own traditions, especially the Mexican Revolution.[78] Mella did not reject communism, but he made a very similar argument during his PCC trial for the importance of relying on Latin America's nationalist revolutions.

Because of Haya's insistence on home-grown ideologies, it could be tempting to overstate the disagreement between LADLA and APRA as a stark ideological division between communists and nationalists, but the reality is more complicated. LADLA and APRA translated Marxism to Latin American contexts in different ways, and LADLA was not a hard-line communist organization since it bridged a range of ideologies under the banner of anti-imperialism. Moreover, APRA had broad influences, taking direct inspiration from Chinese nationalism and calling itself, after the Chinese Nationalist Party, the "Guomindang of Latin America."[79]

In the months following the Brussels Congress, a slew of anti-APRA articles appeared in the PCM's El Machete and in El Libertador, culminating in Mella's April 1928 pamphlet ¿Qué es el ARPA? (What is ARPA?), in which Mella intentionally changed the acronym to ARPA, meaning "harp."[80] While these works consistently claimed that APRA had a dismally small membership, the persistent attention to APRA would suggest that its influence was growing. Mella critiqued APRA for its Latin American exceptionalism and for targeting only US imperialism rather than all colonial and imperial powers. He found impractical APRA's efforts to form a "continental party" and dismissed the idea—touted by APRA—that LADLA "did not articulate a political program" because it had no intention of creating a continental political party.[81]

Mella argued that when APRA called for Latin American political unity without specifying the social classes it intended to unify, it endorsed the misleading regional identity politics practiced by Vasconcelos and others and risked calling for nationalization without socialization of resources. As Mella explained at his PCC trial, he was not opposed to collaboration with bourgeois nationalism, but only if the end goal was ending the domination of the exploited. Like APRA's call for a *frente único* (united front) against imperialism, Mella similarly supported a united front if it was led by and centered exploited peoples.[82] This was an important distinction that mirrored LADLA's call for "true" national independence, which included liberation from class dominance.

Mella also accused Haya of being internationalist only when it was convenient, pointing to Haya's tendency to draw inspiration from China while practicing a *chinismo anti-chino* (anti-Chinese Chinese-ism) since Haya supported the establishment of anti-Chinese committees in Mexican provinces.[83] This position, Mella wrote, mirrored the position toward Chinese immigrants taken by "Yankee patriots" and the KKK and paralleled the US government's treatment of Mexican workers who "find themselves obligated" to immigrate there.[84]

All these arguments more or less aligned with LADLA. However, in Mella's critique of Haya's vision of a united front that did not necessarily center workers' struggles, Mella took a more orthodox position than LADLA. He disagreed with APRA's characterization of intellectuals as intellectual workers who form a social base for political struggle. Although Mella recognized that some intellectuals could be revolutionary, he claimed that they are "almost always allies of reactionary national capitalism or instruments and servants of imperialism."[85] This statement diverged from LADLA, where intellectuals and artists played a central role and which took an explicit stance of inclusion toward "student, cultural, and intellectual groups that have participated or demonstrated their desire to participate in our struggle."[86]

On a different note, Mella agreed with APRA's focus on Indigenous communities but critiqued APRA's view of Indigenous cultures as originating a pre-Marxist communism. Mella's position here mirrored LADLA's critique of such essentializing viewpoints. However, Mella went so far as to insist that the oppression of Indigenous peoples was a purely economic issue. This position differed significantly from LADLA's more integrated approach to a class-based struggle that would underscore the role of Indigenous workers as an agrarian class exploited through racial and economic means.[87]

Mella ended his pamphlet *¿Qué es el ARPA?* with a call "to solidify the united front of all classes oppressed by imperialism in the Anti-Imperialist League of the Americas and to cooperate, on an international scale, with the Brussels Congress, genuine representative of all the revolutionary movements of the world."[88] But even as Mella drew a firm distinction between APRA and LADLA's adherence to the tenets of the Brussels Congress, it is important to recognize the many points these organizations had in common and that LADLA occupied a middle ground between orthodox communism and more regionalist and nationalist tendencies.

Due to these divisions within the Latin American Left, the August 1927 issue of *El Libertador* printed a block on the back page that succinctly articulated its positions: "NO it is not sectarian / YES it accepts all progressive creeds; NO it does not hate the US people / YES it fights against Yankee imperialism; NO it is not a continental political party / YES it contributes to the unity of America; NO it is not a 'Bolshevik' entity; YES it defends the USSR against imperialisms; NO it does not have ties to governments / YES it cooperates with all anti-imperialist work."[89] Here, LADLA differentiated itself from a continental political party like APRA and responded to accusations that it received orders from either Moscow or the Calles government. It emphasized its hemispheric perspective, in which the US people were potential allies, and situated this hemispheric alliance as one decidedly against US imperialism. By the second LAI congress in 1929, LADLA would name its opposition to APRA and other regionalist ideologies in the congress's Latin American resolution, which called activists to combat APRA and "all kinds of demagogic confucianism (pan-Indianism, regionalism, etc.)."[90]

The Brussels Congress solidified LADLA's differentiation from Latin American regionalisms and deepened its commitment to hemispheric globalism. It was also in Brussels that LADLA organizers met with members of the Committee on the Negro Question. These interactions, and LADLA's openness toward non-Spanish-speaking communities, influenced LADLA to begin expanding its focus from Indigenous to Black communities in the

Americas. A move away from Latin American regionalism, in this sense, allowed LADLA to move beyond the familiar trappings of Latin American racial exceptionalism, which relegates anti-Black racism to the United States.

LADLA'S TURN TOWARD BLACK COMMUNITIES

In 1927, LADLA did not yet have a strong grasp of anti-Black racism in Latin America. However, the LAI encounter in Brussels helped push LADLA activists to take Black voices seriously, beginning a dialogue within LADLA about this issue. This dialogue would be advanced especially by Afro-Cuban activist Sandalio Junco, who became LADLA's general secretary in 1929 and is discussed in depth in the next chapter.

Minkah Makalani has characterized the Brussels Congress as playing a significant role in the history of twentieth-century Black internationalisms, writing that "black Communists believed they had a venue where they could pursue the internationalist politics that continued to elude them even within the international communist movement."[91] The LAI's more flexible program provided a space for Black internationalist organizing that attracted Black radicals from a range of leftist ideologies. For example, although he was unable to attend because of the many postponements of the congress, William Pickens, the field secretary of the National Association for the Advancement of Colored People (NAACP), was only approved to attend after W. E. B. Du Bois met with congress organizers in Berlin and wrote a report assuring the NAACP that liberals would have a voice equal to that of communists. The decision to convene the International Conference of Negro Workers occurred at the LAI's second congress in Frankfurt in 1929, leading to the establishment of the International Trade Union Committee for Negro Workers, led by George Padmore, which focused on connecting Black workers in the United States, Caribbean, and Africa.[92]

The Committee on the Negro Question in Brussels was chaired by Lamine Senghor (Committee for the Defense of the Negro Race) with Richard B. Moore (American Negro Labor Congress) as secretary. Other members included Josiah T. Gumede (African National Congress), Max Clainville-Bloncourt and Camille Saint-Jacques (Intercolonial Union), Carlos Deambrosis Martins (Haitian Patriotic Union), Narcisse Danaë (Committee for the Defense of the Negro Race), and James La Guma (South African Non-European Trade Union Federation).[93] Several schol-

2.2 Committee on the Negro Question, 1927. Brussels, Institut Fondamental d'Afrique Noire.

ars have assumed that Deambrosis Martins (Haitian Patriotic Union) was Haitian and of African descent.[94] However, Deambrosis Martins (figure 2.2, second from left) was a white Uruguayan living in France.[95] This repeated, albeit understandable, error speaks again to the need to better understand Latin Americans' participation in the LAI. Deambrosis Martins had contact with the Haitian Patriotic Union, giving a detailed speech on its behalf about the 1915 US invasion of Haiti and its aftermath.[96] Significantly, no Black delegates from hispanophone or lusophone Latin America attended the congress. Even so, the committee's interventions would have a clear impact on LADLA.

The so-called Negro Question was discussed on the fifth day. Several members gave speeches and Moore, as committee reporter, presented the "Common Resolution on the Negro Question" along with an introduction. Moore emphasized that "the fight against imperialism is first of all an incessant struggle against imperialistic ideology. We must fight fascism, the Ku-Klux-Klan, chauvinism, and the doctrine of the supremacy of the white race."[97]

The interventions by the Committee on the Negro Question influenced LADLA. The Congress's "Resolutions on Latin America" addressed

US imperialism in Haiti and included signatures of two individuals from this committee, Deambrosis Martins and Moore. Although the resolutions were written by Latin American delegates who were not exclusively LADLA members, these resolutions, reprinted in *El Libertador* in June 1927, largely repeated LADLA's platform in framing Indigenous communities as disproportionately experiencing the violence of imperialist extractive industries. Yet in a way different from previous iterations of this position, the resolution argued that "imperialist penetration in these countries has exacerbated the inequality faced by Indigenous and Black peoples, because of the concentration of land, since Black and Indigenous people constitute the vast majority of the agrarian population."[98] This resolution signals the beginning of LADLA's redefinition of its program to include anti-Black racism as a central part of imperialist domination, identifying both Indigenous and Black communities as key to the anti-imperialist struggle.

As discussed in the book's introduction, contemporary theories of racial capitalism have been critiqued for relegating Indigenous peoples to a precapitalist past that becomes replaced by wage labor.[99] LADLA's program, however, was predominantly focused not on the category of labor but rather on "the concentration of land" and the "agrarian population." Because LADLA began with a focus on the impact of extractive economies on Indigenous communities and then expanded from there, it could not overlook the interrelation between ongoing Indigenous dispossession and racialized labor, and thus it made a unique and significant contribution to theorizing racial capitalism from a multiracial perspective. By framing Indigenous and Black agrarian populations as the base of anti-imperialism, LADLA would eventually take a further-reaching stance of antiracism than the Comintern, which sought to incorporate (but not center) these populations into a struggle of primarily industrial labor.

Whereas LADLA had always identified US workers as potential allies, this resolution recognized that "the oppressed races are also our allies with the United States itself."[100] Moore's signature on the resolution made clear that African Americans from the United States could be important collaborators in LADLA's project, and Moore became an active member of LADLA-US. Additionally, the resolution included the signatures of Deambrosis Martins and Andrew Almazan, representatives of the Haitian Patriotic Union (HPU) and League of Haitian Human Rights. Although neither of these men was Haitian, LADLA would indeed develop a relationship with the HPU. In an article about the Brussels Congress in *El Libertador* in August 1927, a photo of HPU founding members appeared alongside an announcement that the group had joined LADLA. This relationship would continue to develop, particularly through HPU leader Joseph Jolibois fils, who spent time with the Continental Committee in Mexico City and wrote several articles for *El Libertador*.[101]

Alongside the "Resolutions on Latin America," *El Libertador* printed "The Common Resolution on the Negro Question," accompanied by a photograph of Lamine Senghor delivering his speech. The resolution argued that the wealth of Western countries was developed through the slave trade and European expansion and that African Americans' rights are consistently denied in the United States. "That very power" that oppresses Black people within the United States, it stated, has now occupied Haiti and other Caribbean nations.

The resolution then included a curious statement regarding Spanish-speaking Latin America: "In Latin America, Negroes suffer no special oppression. The cordial relations resulting from the social and political equality in the races in these countries prove that there is no inherent antagonism between them."[102] This statement was not necessarily due to the influence of the Latin American delegates since the resolution was based on a 1926 UNIA resolution that contained a very similar claim.[103]

Importantly, I have found that when this resolution was reprinted in Spanish in *El Libertador*, LADLA editors made revisions in the section that discussed Latin America, adding text to the original that offered Cuba and Panama as exceptions. The revised version in Spanish stated: "In Latin America, except in Cuba, Black people do not suffer the yoke of any special oppression. (In Panama, the Yankee intervention has transplanted the United States' barbaric customs against Black people, and this is the same origin of social inequalities in Cuba.) Social and political equality, as well as the cordial relations between different races in other countries in Latin America, prove that no natural antagonism exists between them."[104] While LADLA's version recognized the existence of anti-Black oppression in Latin America, it claimed that it appeared only in Cuba and Panama and attributed it to US influence.

This simplistic understanding reflects LADLA's nascent theorizing on race relations in Latin America in 1927 as well as the absence of Spanish-speaking Black Latin American delegates in Brussels. Despite this, the Committee on the Negro Question raised issues that became vital for LADLA moving forward. The "Common Resolution on the Negro Question" made five recommendations, including organizing Black workers, fighting "imperialist ideology: Chauvinism, fascism, kukluxism, and race prejudice," "admission of the workers of all races into all unions on the basis of equality," organizing Black liberation movements, and establishing unity with other "suppressed peoples and classes for the fight against world imperialism."[105]

Although in 1927 LADLA wrongly attributed anti-Black racism only to the influence of imperialist powers, the "Common Resolution on the Negro Question" articulated a relationship between imperialism and white supremacism and identified how this ideology negatively impacted Black representation within anti-imperialist organizations. In the coming years, LADLA not only recognized how imperialist extractive industries affected Black communities in the Americas but also incorporated a fight against white supremacism into its platform.

Individual members of the Committee on the Negro Question influenced LADLA as well. For example, in response to Senghor's death in November 1927, *El Libertador* published an article with Senghor's photo from the Brussels Congress. It praised his speech at the congress as one that "unmasked French imperialism with courage and truth" and promised to publish the pamphlet he wrote while in prison.[106]

The relationship between Latin America and ideas put forth by the Committee on the Negro Question would be advanced especially through the later interventions of Afro-Cuban activist Sandalio Junco, who became LADLA's general secretary in Mexico City after Mella's 1929 assassination. Junco would reject the claim that anti-Black racism was only due to US influence and would attempt to shed light on this problem within Latin American leftist organizations. His specifically Afro–Latin American approach to the "Negro Question" will be the focus of the next chapter.

CONCLUSION

Studying LADLA reframes the global history of the LAI, which was foundational to the development of postcolonial thought and which has been largely understood through Afro-Asian exchanges. Through bringing the personal papers of LADLA's US activists into dialogue with materials from its Latin American sections and the LAI Archive, this chapter has argued that studying LADLA shifts prior scholarly understandings of Latin American intellectual history from the interwar period, known for its regionalist ideologies. LADLA activists rejected interwar regionalisms, like those espoused by Vasconcelos and Haya de la Torre, in favor of what I have called hemispheric globalism, an ideological and practical interdependency with anti-imperialist movements in the United States and around the world. Moreover, through a sustained analysis of the "Resolutions on Latin America" and "Common Resolution on the Negro Question," this chapter claims that the encounter between LADLA and LAI activists in Brussels influenced LADLA to begin to expand its initial focus on Indigenous struggles toward Black communities. This would lead LADLA to eventually offer an early theorization of racial capitalism that questioned the trappings of Latin American racial exceptionalism.

THREE

"POR LA IGUALDAD DE TODOS LOS SERES"

SANDALIO JUNCO'S AFRO–LATIN AMERICAN PERSPECTIVE ON BLACK, IMMIGRANT, AND INDIGENOUS STRUGGLES

Vale, entonces, decir: una lucha activa y sistemática por la igualdad de todos los seres. —SANDALIO JUNCO

In the novel *Tinísima* (1992) by renowned Mexican writer Elena Ponia-towska, the protagonist Tina Modotti is released from jail after being falsely accused of conspiring to murder her lover, Julio Antonio Mella. After her release, she makes a print of the last living photograph she took of Mella two days before his death. In the photo, a smiling Mella is surrounded by members of the "Committee for the Defense of the Proletariat," includ-ing Mexican artist David Siqueiros, Cuban tobacco union organizer Ale-jandro Barreiro Olivera, and Cuban bakers' union leader Sandalio Junco.[1] Junco, in particular, appears several times in the early chapters of the novel, which—typical of Poniatowksa's signature blend of journalism and fiction—is based on her ten years of research. Junco appears, for example, as one of the workers imprisoned with Mella in Havana during Mella's 1925 hunger strike. Then, in a chapter that takes place in Mexico, Junco and two other Cubans receive Mella's corpse after the autopsy. "Among those that wait for the corpse," Poniatowska writes, "Sandalio Junco stands out for being Black," a line conspicuously removed from the 2006 English translation of the novel.[2] At Mella's funeral procession, Junco leads the protest chants, and finally, after Modotti prints the photograph, Junco disappears altogether from the over-six-hundred-page novel.

Such scant appearances of the Afro-Cuban Sandalio Junco Camellón (1894–1942) are typical of his depiction in accounts (fictional and scholarly) of the interwar Latin American Left, in which Junco functions as an accessory to narratives focused on more famous figures, like Mella. Junco, who emerged as a labor leader through the Cuban bakers' union, did have a close relationship with Mella. They were imprisoned together during Mella's hunger strike, and later Junco worked with Mella and other Cubans during his exile in Mexico to form the Association of New Cuban Revolutionary Émigrés (Asociación de Nuevos Emigrados Revolucionarios Cubanos, ANERC) (figure 3.1).[3] The two collaborated in LADLA's Continental Committee, and when Mella was assassinated in 1929, Junco replaced him as LADLA's general secretary. Years later, after the PCC expelled Junco, he wrote a manifesto (1934) that criticized the PCC's hypocrisy for upholding Mella as a revolutionary leader post mortem. When Mella was alive, Junco pointed out, the PCC "vilified him in Mexico and expelled him in Cuba."[4] Mella was "besieged by the same people who now try to deify him," and this was the same organization, Junco reminded his reader, that eventually expelled Junco.[5]

Junco made a compelling point about the PCC's hypocrisy regarding whom it celebrated and whom it ignored, and his point remains as relevant today as it was then. Today's Cuba celebrates Mella as one of the country's prominent communist heroes. A town in the province of Santiago de Cuba bears Mella's name, a memorial holding his ashes sits in front of the University of Havana, and his face appears on stamps, on the 1,000-peso bill, and in murals beside the iconic figures of Che Guevara and Camilo Cienfuegos. Sandalio Junco, on the other hand, remains occluded and, with the exception of a few scholarly publications, expelled from the history of Cuban communism and the history of the Latin American Left more broadly.

Both Junco and Mella were integral to LADLA's Continental Committee. As discussed in chapter 1, LADLA focused its critique of imperialism on the role of extractive industries. For this reason, it veered from a traditional Marxist focus on industrial labor by arguing that agrarian populations formed the base of the anti-imperialist struggle. Initially, it argued that extractive capitalism had a disproportionately negative impact on

3.1 Members of ANERC in Mexico City, 1928. Junco is seated, second from right. Mella stands in center, back row. Mella and Cairo Ballester, *Mella: 100 años.*

Indigenous communities. Then, due to the influence of Black participants at the 1927 Brussels Congress, as detailed in chapter 2, LADLA expanded its claim to argue that "Black and Indigenous people constitute the vast majority of the agrarian population."[6] Because LADLA began its movement with a focus on Indigenous communities, it theorized the violent process of land dispossession through an enduring relation to racialized labor exploitation. LADLA's platform recognized Indigenous dispossession and anti-Black and anti-Indigenous racism as integral to the occupation of resource-rich lands and to the enforcement of coerced and unsafe working conditions. In this sense, LADLA took an antiracist stance that was further-reaching than the Comintern's platform, which sought to incorporate Black and Indigenous peoples into a struggle of primarily industrial labor. As a united-front movement, which intended to join artists, activists, workers, and intellectuals, LADLA provided an ideologically flexible space that allowed for a more explicitly antiracist politics to emerge.

Although LADLA made a major contribution to theorizing racial capitalism, it too had clear shortcomings. LADLA framed the transnational extractive economy within a longer history of settler colonialism and the enslavement of Black and Indigenous peoples in the Americas. However, even though it recognized the role of anti-Black racism in imperialist expansion and eventually became fiercely opposed to "white terror," it initially treated anti-Black racism as a completely foreign import to Latin America, where "Yankee intervention has transplanted the United States' barbaric customs against Black people."[7] This position, articulated in the "Common Resolution on the Negro Question" at the 1927 Brussels Congress, failed to acknowledge the legacy of African slavery in Latin America as well as the region's long struggle for Black liberation. The limitations of LADLA's 1927 positions continue to have important implications for the contemporary Latin American Left, where Indigenous movements often predominate in the region's conceptualizations of racial and ethnic minorities.

In studies of the formation of both the Latin American Left and the Black radical tradition more broadly, Black Latin Americans are often elided. This chapter thus seeks to position Afro-Cuban activist Sandalio Junco as a central figure of Black radical thought in the Americas, situating his interventions within LADLA's broader history and the connections that its activists made with Black activists at the 1927 Brussels Congress. Although Junco did not attend the Brussels Congress, he would later question a central assumption of its "Common Resolution on the Negro Question" regarding the supposed relative absence of anti-Black racism in Latin America. His interventions on this issue would become paramount for advancing anti-imperialist thought in Latin America, especially regarding the position of Black Latin American and immigrant labor within the movement.

Specifically, this chapter focuses on Junco's contributions to the discussion of the so-called Negro and Indigenous Questions, as well as his perspectives on immigrant labor, at the founding conference of the Confederation of Latin American Labor Unions (Confederación Sindical Latino Americana, CSLA) in Montevideo and the First Latin American Communist Conference in Buenos Aires. In May–June 1929, only a few months after Mella's murder, Junco traveled to these conferences from his exile in Mexico City, where he was serving as LADLA's general secretary. He traveled with other activists living in Mexico City, some of whom were also LADLA members. Related scholarship tends to recognize these two conferences for their contributions to an examination of Indigenous rights through the interventions of Peruvian philosopher José Carlos Mariátegui. However, it was in this same context where Junco presented a little-known yet foundational text of Black internationalism that provided an analysis of the conditions faced by Black peoples in the Americas. In this speech, "The Negro Question and the Proletarian Movement," and his subsequent comments, Junco attempted to nuance Mariátegui's strict differentiation between Black and Indigenous experiences and rejected some of the conference participants' dismissal of the presence of anti-Black racism both among the Latin American working classes and in Latin American societies more broadly.[8] In contrast to these positions, Junco drew comparisons (but not equivalences) between Black Latin Americans' experiences of racialization and those of other racialized populations throughout the hemisphere, such as Indigenous peoples, US African Americans, and Haitian, West Indian, and Chinese migrant workers. Through these comparisons, he theorized the overlap between antiblackness and anti-immigrant sentiment especially faced by Black immigrant workers in Latin American contexts. Most important, Junco articulated an argument, from an Afro–Latin American position, for a Black internationalist politics situated between a race-based subjectivity and a class-based one.

Often referred to simply as the debate on the Negro Question, the relationship between Black American activists and communist internationalism in the interwar years has been widely studied. Scholarship on this subject tends to focus on the Black Belt thesis in the US South, the Scottsboro Boys case, and the leadership of US and anglophone Caribbean intellectuals.[9] Yet the role of this particular debate in shaping Latin American political thought often goes unrecognized, albeit with some significant exceptions.[10] For example, Hakim Adi's overview of the transnational development of the Negro Question in the United States, South Africa, Britain, and Britain's colonies in Africa and the Caribbean briefly mentions that this issue was discussed in "South America." However, Adi does not mention Junco's speeches, the corresponding resolution, or the historic 1929 conferences.[11] Likewise, Marc Becker's detailed discussion of the 1929 Latin American Communist Conference, which focuses on Mariátegui's comments on the Indigenous Question, does not address Junco's participation in the discussion, in which Junco responded directly to Mariátegui.[12]

As Margaret Stevens—one of the scholars who has dedicated significant study to Junco—describes, recent scholarship on Black radicalism has moved away from the "tendency to theorize twentieth-century black radicalism as a 'tradition' of 'great men.'" This tendency, she writes, "dismisses the role of black workers as a class and also the collective organizations through which they mobilized forces and grew in consciousness—often alongside non-black comrades."[13] Such a move away from narratives of "great men" is unquestionably necessary, particularly as scholars produce histories that better recognize the contributions of Black women to this intellectual tradition. Even so, despite the fact that Junco was the most recognizable Black leader in the PCC at one time, because of his affiliations with Trotskyism he remains underrepresented (and sometimes belittled) in Cuban communist historiography.[14] Moreover, in the field of Afro–Latin American history, Junco's contributions are occluded. In one obvious example, Junco does not appear among the two thousand articles on Afro–Latin Americans in Franklin W. Knight and Henry Louis Gates Jr.'s *Dictionary of Caribbean and Afro–Latin American Bibliography* (2016). Similarly, he does not appear in the collection of Cuban antiracist writings, *Antología cubana del pensamiento antirracista* (2015), edited by renowned scholar of Afro-Cuban history Tomás Fernández Robaina. Junco does appear more frequently and in a more positive light in scholarship on Cuban labor history and Cuban Trotskyism.[15]

In many of the conversations and organizations in which Junco participated, he was the only Black person in the room. This alone is significant, and yet the continued scholarly emphasis on the voices of his white and mestizo colleagues—like Mella and Mariátegui—deprives us of Junco's insights. From his writings, Junco reveals himself as a brilliant thinker, certainly on par with his more famous comrades, and someone who comfortably navigated Marxist theory and the history of the African diaspora. Junco must be recognized for the Black radical leader and intellectual that he was, even as we grasp the broader multiracial collectives, like LADLA, in which he participated. This chapter thus presents Junco's comments, his speech "The Negro Question and the Proletarian Movement," and the resulting "Resolution on the Question of Negro Workers" as foundational texts of Black American radicalism articulated from a specifically Afro–Latin American subjectivity.[16]

Trade union and communist periodicals, scholarship on Trotskyism in Latin America, and the papers of the organizations in which Junco was involved reveal him as a highly experienced organizer integrated into workers' rights and anti-imperialist networks in the Americas and around the globe. He has been described as "a powerful orator with a magnetic personality," and he was well known among those—like Cyril Briggs, James W. Ford, and George Padmore—who feature prominently in anglophone studies of Black communism.[17] For example, *The Negro Worker*, edited by Padmore, characterized Junco as "one of the ablest trade union leaders."[18] Since Junco was a member of the American Negro Labor Congress (ANLC), several articles about his political persecution appeared in the ANLC's publication, *The Liberator*, edited by Briggs, which described Junco as a "Cuban negro revolutionary leader."[19] From December 1929 to January 1930, the ANLC, LADLA, and International Labor Defense organized protests and fundraising in the United States and Mexico to fight Junco's extradition from Mexico to Cuba, using those funds to send him to Germany instead.[20] His contributions to the 1929 conferences remain consistent with his long-term commitment to critiquing and reforming the Marxist Left from within. Before turning to an in-depth discussion of his contributions to thinking the Negro Question through an Afro–Latin American lens, I first provide a brief outline of the political trajectory of this activist-intellectual.

SANDALIO JUNCO: A BRIEF INTRODUCTION

According to his tourist visa from a two-week visit to Miami, Junco was born in Havana, Cuba, in 1894, shortly before the eruption of the Cuban War of Independence. He was short in stature (five foot four), with black hair and brown eyes, and his race was listed as "African."[21] Junco was politically active from a young age and made his way in labor organizing through the Havana bakers' union.[22] He was drawn to editorial work, and in 1923 he served as director of *El Productor*, the periodical for both the bakers' union and the Union of Confectioners and Pastry Chefs.[23] He became a founding member of the PCC and, as mentioned previously, was incarcerated along with Mella and other PCC organizers in 1925.[24] Over the next few years, Junco became the international secretary of the Confederation of Cuban Workers (Confederación Nacional Obrera de Cuba, CNOC) and a PCC leader.[25] He represented the CNOC at a meeting of Latin American labor unions in Moscow in April 1928. In the context of widespread persecution of communists under the Machado dictatorship, police detained Junco upon his return to Cuba.[26] Shortly after this incident, at thirty-four years of age, Junco went into exile in Mexico.[27]

Junco led an active political life during his four years of exile in Mexico City, where he lived in the working-class Doctores neighborhood.[28] Like Modotti and Mella, he was involved simultaneously in several organizations, in which he sometimes used the aliases Juárez and Hernández Suárez. He and other Cuban exiles founded ANERC, and he joined the PCM. He served as CSLA Caribbean secretary and, after Mella's assassination, as LADLA's general secretary.[29] In early 1930, he was arrested in

Mexico because of his "activities in the Mexican trade union movement and in anti-imperialist work."[30] He was arrested alongside Cuban organizer Alejandro Barreiros Olivera, and the administration of Mexican President Portes Gil intended to extradite Junco and Barreiros to Cuba.[31] LADLA immediately notified the ANLC and International Labor Defense of Junco's arrest and impending deportation. The ANLC's National Council sent a telegram to the Portes Gil administration demanding Junco's release, and "instructions were also sent to all ANLC branches to hold protest mass meetings in their territory against the proposed deportation of Junco, and to raise money for their defense." As the ANLC's *The Liberator* explained to its readership, Junco's deportation would likely be a death sentence, as "the Cuban dictator particularly hates Junco because of his activities in organizing the Cuban Negro workers and the Haitian workers in Cuba."[32] LADLA and the International Labor Defense also organized protests in the United States and Mexico in support of Junco. These protests succeeded in pressuring the Mexican government to send Junco to Germany instead, using money raised by participating organizations.[33]

Upon his deportation and under the radar of the US and Cuban authorities, Junco traveled from Germany to the Soviet Union, where he attended the International Lenin School and worked with the Cuban activist and writer Rubén Martínez Villena in the Red International of Labor Unions (Profintern).[34] He was in close contact with the Spanish politician and Profintern leader Andrés Nin, who had joined the Trotskyist Left Opposition. Through his employment in the Profintern from 1930 to 1932, Junco served on the international committee of the International Trade Union Committee of Negro Workers (ITUCNW). During his time in Moscow, he suffered ill health and spent a brief period in a sanatorium.[35]

When Junco returned to Cuba in January 1932, the PCC assigned him to local labor organizing, working specifically with bakers and Black workers.[36] Junco also resumed leadership in Cuban labor unions, becoming a leader in the Workers' Federation of Havana.[37] While in Cuba, he would marry and have three sons.[38] From May to July 1932, Junco was detained and imprisoned for political activities. Although he began organizing the Communist Opposition (Oposición Comunista, OC), a Trotskyist fringe group within the PCC, upon his arrival, the OC was not officially consolidated until August 1932, after his release from prison.[39] With the OC's consolidation, in 1932 Junco wrote a memorandum to the Comintern criticizing its analysis of the Cuban political context. He argued that in comparison to other postcolonial contexts, Cuba was not subject to an alliance between a landed oligarchy and an imperial power since Cuba's three wars of independence had largely destabilized its feudal landlord class. He also insisted on the importance of incorporating the Cuban middle class into labor organizing since in Cuba, he claimed, it represented more of a bureaucratic class than a traditional European bourgeoisie. In response, in September 1932, the PCC expelled Junco and his opposition group.[40]

While Junco's OC aligned with Trotsky's International Left Opposition, its membership was unorthodox, representing a left coalition with strong ties to labor unions.[41] The OC, which in 1933 became the Bolshevik-Leninist Party (Partido Bolchevique-Leninista, PBL), strongly opposed the communists' negotiation between those involved in the 1933 general strike and Machado, when the threat of US invasion led communist organizers to ultimately protect the very Machado government they had long opposed.[42] After Machado was forced to step down, the PBL endorsed the pro-labor government of Cuban politician Ramón Grau San Martín, both during his short presidency (1933–34) and after his ouster, when Fulgencio Batista installed Carlos Mendieta as president. Following the collapse of the Grau government, the PBL joined the political party Joven Cuba, and together they became the Cuban Revolutionary Party (Auténtico), or the party of former President Grau San Martín.

Around this time, in January 1934, Junco wrote an extensive response to what he described as "a national and international insult and slander campaign" directed at him over the two years since his PCC expulsion.[43] He described his detractors as careerist bureaucrats disconnected from workers' movements who were threatened by what they deemed an "intellectualized worker" who refused to simply follow orders.[44] Junco fiercely criticized the 1933 pact between Machado and the PCC, in which the PCC ordered an end to the strike that was ignored, Junco said, by the more revolutionary workers' organizations. He concluded by expressing his disagreement with the Stalinist strategy of "socialism in one country" and called for the "true workers" to take back control of workers' organizations from bureaucrats.[45]

In March 1935, the PBL and Joven Cuba organized a general strike that failed due to violent repression by the Mendieta-Batista regime.[46] This failed general strike resulted in a crisis in the Cuban labor movement followed by a major shift in PCC policy, in which it began to seek alliances with other labor and antifascist groups like the PBL in accordance with the Comintern's new "popular front" line. Batista legalized the PCC, and the communists began working to unify the labor movement under their leadership. As part of this effort to create a new centralized Cuban labor organization, communist, Auténtico (including Junco), and independent trade union leaders traveled to Mexico City for the founding conference of the Confederation of Latin American Workers in September 1938.[47]

Despite the unification of the labor movement under the newly created Confederation of Cuban Workers (Confederación de Trabajadores de Cuba), tensions remained between these factions in subsequent years. On May 8, 1942, Junco was scheduled to give a speech at an homage to Joven Cuba's leader Antonio Guiteras, who had been assassinated in 1935 by the Mendieta-Batista regime. As Junco walked up to the microphone, a group of men stormed the hall and began firing at the platform, firing sixty shots in total and killing Junco and two others.[48] While no one ever faced charges for his murder, it has often been attributed to the PCC, which had engaged in a character assassination of Junco in the weeks leading up to his death.[49]

I provide this limited, patchworked background on Junco's life to demonstrate his ideological trajectory. When he traveled from Mexico to Uruguay in May 1929 to participate at the CSLA founding conference and then crossed the Río de la Plata for the First Latin American Communist Conference in Buenos Aires in June of that same year, he had not yet turned toward an oppositional Trotskyism. However, at this time, he was serving as LADLA's general secretary. LADLA, as an ideologically flexible organization, tended to attract activists like Junco, Mella, and Diego Rivera, who were invested in broadly defined alliances, who subscribed to Trotsky's notion of worldwide revolution, and who bristled under more ideologically rigid communist leadership.[50] While Junco had not yet developed an oppositional relationship to the PCC, his statements at the two 1929 conferences reveal that he rooted his perspectives in his own experiences and in Cuba's revolutionary and syndicalist traditions. From those experiences, he critiqued the misapplication of theories conceived in Moscow to Latin American contexts. Moreover, consistent with LADLA's positions but pushing them even further, he was already challenging his colleagues to engage in a deeper and more nuanced internationalism, one that foregrounded especially the fight against anti-Black racism.

THE NEGRO QUESTION IN CONTEXT

Although Junco did not attend the 1927 Brussels Congress, "The Common Resolution on the Negro Question," created in Brussels, provided the context for many of his comments. More broadly, his interventions must be understood within the context of American Black radicals' relationship to the Comintern. If the Comintern, as Robin D. G. Kelley writes, "proved more sympathetic and sensitive to the racial nature of American class struggle" than the previous Second International (founded in Paris in 1889), "it is largely because black folk made it so."[51] Indeed, it was the growing influence of Black self-determination organizations like Cyril Briggs's African Blood Brotherhood and Marcus Garvey's United Negro Improvement Association that pushed the Comintern and affiliated organizations to engage Black struggles.

Lenin's proposal for a union of socialist republics that allowed national minorities the right to secede provided the basis for his later proposal to recognize colonies as oppressed nations. In 1920, in conversation with M. N. Roy, Lenin wrote the "Theses on the National and Colonial Questions," which called on communist parties to support "revolutionary movements among the dependent nations and those without equal rights (e.g. Ireland, and among American Negroes), and in the colonies."[52] This vision of self-determination resonated with Black radicals. Even so, a Comintern strategy around Black organizing did not formally begin until the Fourth World Congress in Moscow on November 25, 1922, when it was introduced through speeches by Jamaican American and Harlem Renaissance writer Claude McKay and the Suriname-born activist and WP representative Otto Huiswoud.[53] Their speeches introduced the "Thesis on the Negro Question" composed by the Comintern's Negro Commission, which had formed in the same year.

The Negro Commission's "Thesis on the Negro Question" pointed to the dependence of post–World War I capitalist accumulation on European expansion into the African continent and argued that the "Negro race" was essential to the destruction of capitalist power. It claimed that Moscow should do everything in its ability to help Comintern delegates from countries with large Black populations organize Black workers and forge multiracial alliances.[54] McKay and Huiswoud's speeches couched this endeavor in the various challenges that must be considered. Huiswoud argued that the Second International had been primarily focused on white workers, sidestepping the possibility of communist organizing in the colonial world and ignoring completely the Negro Question. The Negro Question, he claimed, is fundamental to "the Colonial question," or the Comintern's efforts to link freedom struggles in the colonies with working-class struggles in the metropoles. Because the Third International posited itself as "an International of the workers of the world," it should make every effort to unite colonized and nonwhite workers to the proletarian revolution.[55] Because of their large numbers, he suggested, outreach to Black Americans has enormous potential for fomenting broader revolt.

Huiswoud's speech carefully navigated the Comintern's class-before-race rhetoric. He defined the subjugation of US Black people as "fundamentally an economic problem," yet he also argued that Black workers' poor conditions were intensified by racism on the part of the white workers. This prejudice was not simply based on labor competition between Black and white workers but was largely due to the history of slavery and the racist ideologies that historically upheld that institution. These "psychological factors," he argued, must be taken into account in any consideration of the organization of Black and white workers together.[56]

McKay echoed Huiswoud's positions. However, he delivered a more pointed critique of the Comintern's commitment to racial justice, and especially of the WP, saying that "there is a great element of prejudice among the socialists and communists of America" and that in order to achieve unity among Black and white workers in the United States, communists must address racism within their own ranks.[57] Their speeches and the accompanying "Thesis on the Negro Question" traced a link between Black peoples and other racially oppressed populations, argued for Black activists as vanguards in a global struggle, and called for a revolutionary strategy that would foreground the issue of racial inequality and discrimination.[58] Importantly, the "Thesis on the Negro Question" recognized that its concerns extended to Black populations in Spanish-speaking Latin America, and specifically in Central America and the Caribbean. Some of the rhetoric from this thesis would resonate in the later work of the Committee on the Negro Question at the 1927 Brussels Congress, discussed in the previous chapter. The "Common Resolution on the Negro Question," along with Lamine Senghor's speech in Brussels, largely echoed McKay and Huiswoud, especially emphasizing the vanguard position of Black people in the anticapitalist struggle. However, this document would limit its discussion of Latin America to a brief, uninformed statement that "in Latin America, Negroes suffer no special oppression."[59]

At the 1928 Sixth World Congress, the Comintern's Negro Commission became two separate but collaborating Black-led organizations affiliated with the Comintern and Profintern. The Profintern's Negro Bureau would become the International Trade Union Committee of Negro Workers (ITUCNW)—led first by US communist James W. Ford and then, beginning in 1931, by the Trinidadian George Padmore.[60] Through these organizations, the Comintern began to focus on a more radical position of Black self-determination in the United States, South Africa, and Cuba. Promoted by US Black communist Harry Haywood and South Africa's James La Guma, the Comintern's Negro Commission asserted "the right of negroes to exercise governmental authority in the entire territory of the Black Belt, as well as to decide upon the relations between their territory and other nations."[61] This Black Belt thesis—usually cited in relation to African Americans in the Black Belt counties of the US South but also used regarding Cuba's Oriente province—supported self-determination for areas with majority Black populations up to and including self-government.[62] While the idea of self-determination was generally accepted by Black communists in the Americas in the theoretical sense, the notion that the Black Belt of the US South or eastern Cuba should seek independence and govern itself as a nation was critiqued by many Black communists as a radical theory conceived outside the local context. Notably, Junco's PBL strongly opposed Black self-determination for Cuba's Oriente province, characterizing this position as irresponsible since it would place Black workers at high risk of violent repression.[63] More successful than this thesis, however, were Black communist organizations' well-known campaigns on behalf of the Scottsboro Boys, the nine African American youths imprisoned in Scottsboro, Alabama, on false charges of raping two white women, which helped unite antiracist activists around the globe.

As the Comintern's 1928 Sixth World Congress represented a significant advancement for the growth of Black communism, it also marked a moment when the Comintern increased its activities in Latin America. Victorio Codovilla, an Italian Argentine, established the Comintern's South American Secretariat in Buenos Aires in 1926, and following the 1928 Sixth Congress in Moscow, the Latin American delegates used the South American Secretariat's biweekly newspaper, *La Correspondencia Sudamericana* (South American correspondence), to organize the 1929 First Latin American Communist Conference in Buenos Aires. Almost simultaneously, the delegates (including Junco) in attendance at the April 1928 Moscow meeting of Latin American labor unions resolved to hold the 1929 CSLA founding conference in Montevideo.[64] This conference would be organized by the biweekly CSLA newspaper, *El Trabajador Latinoamericano* (The Latin American worker), published out of Montevideo. Although these two conferences were planned by different organizations—the CSLA and the South American Secretariat—collaboration occurred between them, and many delegates attended both conferences. At both meetings, in response to the debates around the Negro Question at the 1927 Brussels Congress and at the 1928 Sixth Congress in Moscow, the strategy of Black and especially Indigenous self-determination became a topic of heated debate. As I will trace, Junco's voice arose as central to these discussions.

THE INDIGENOUS AND NEGRO QUESTIONS AT THE 1929 MONTEVIDEO CSLA CONFERENCE

In the months leading up to the May 1929 Montevideo conference, advertisements appeared in *El Trabajador Latinoamericano* inviting trade union representatives from across the continent to attend the CSLA's founding meeting. In its January–February 1929 issue, the editors included a preparatory questionnaire for delegates with detailed inquiries regarding the status of the national economy and trade union movement, quantity of immigrants, and working conditions of women and children, among other issues.[65] Ultimately, delegates from fifteen Latin American countries, the United States, France, and the Soviet Union attended, with Miguel Contreras, an Argentine, acting as general secretary.[66]

The opening session began before a packed audience at the Teatro Albeniz. From photographs of the event, the room was filled with mostly men, and the list of delegates named not a single woman even though the conference agenda included a planned discussion on the role of women in labor organizing. Toward the end of the opening session, "a numerous delegation of proletariat women from Montevideo donated a flag to the CSLA," which was received by David Siqueiros, the Mexican artist and activist who served with Junco on the CSLA General Counsel and who helped organize the Montevideo conference.[67] Despite the apparently limited participation of women, the conference produced a forward-thinking resolution calling for equal pay for equal work, maternity leaves, lactation rooms, and childcare for working mothers.[68]

Contreras delivered the opening speech, outlining the conference's goals. He described foreign exploitation of Latin American natural resources and appalling labor conditions for most Latin American workers. He explained that the continental reach of especially US-owned companies required a continental response from labor unions and suggested that the 1928 Colombian banana workers' strike against the United Fruit Company failed because it was not planned alongside strikes against the same company in Mexico and Panama.[69] One of the conference's primary goals was the unification of the CSLA with the Trade Union Educational League (TUEL) in the United States, which together would coordinate "workers from both Americas."[70] Contreras emphasized that the organization of agrarian communities was of primary importance to this continental approach since these communities made up the vast majority of Latin America's working masses.[71]

In many ways, Contreras's arguments mirrored the positions that LADLA had taken since 1925. Indeed, in his conference report on imperialism, Siqueiros called for the CSLA to align with the LAI, and LADLA's *El Libertador* (July 1929) applauded the CSLA's founding and announced the two organizations' direct cooperation.[72] Like in LADLA's platform, agrarian communities and their integral relationship to Indigenous and Black populations became a core focus of the conference.

The commissions over the following days were organized thematically. Junco spoke briefly at the opening session on "Antillean workers' difficult life conditions and of the necessity for workers' unity," but his more sustained interventions came during the eleventh and twelfth sessions, which dealt with the subjects of Indigenous and Black communities, particularly through his direct response to Peruvian intellectual José Carlos Mariátegui.[73] Mariátegui, who was widely known in Latin America by this point and whose terminal illness prevented his attendance, contributed an essay, "The Indigenous Question," to be read by his representative, Julio Portocarrero.[74] Mariátegui and Haya de la Torre had cofounded the González Prada Popular University in Peru, and when Haya was exiled in 1924, Mariátegui took over his editorship of the journal *Claridad*.[75] Then, in 1926, Mariátegui founded the internationally circulated cultural magazine *Amauta*, which had a Marxist framework and an intended orientation toward Indigenous literary and artistic expression. In June 1927, after a "strongly anti-imperialist issue of *Amauta*" and after the interception of a letter to Mariátegui from Haya, Mariátegui was briefly arrested and *Amauta* was temporarily shut down.[76] Newspapers throughout the region reported on these events, and Mariátegui wrote letters to left-leaning publications abroad criticizing the Peruvian government.[77] Although Mariátegui joined Haya de la Torre's APRA for a brief period, he broke with the group in April 1928 over its transformation into a political party.[78] In response, he and other colleagues founded the Socialist Party of Peru.[79] The group never founded a Peruvian section of LADLA since it would have been illegal under the Augusto Leguía government and since they already conceived of the Socialist Party of Peru as a broad-based, united-front organization.[80] Although LADLA reported a Peruvian section, it must have been limited to Peruvian exiles in Mexico City. Despite this, *Amauta* frequently featured articles about the broader LAI, and Mariátegui's articles and advertisements for *Amauta* appeared in LADLA-Cuba's *América Libre*.[81]

The Socialist Party of Peru received invitations to attend both the CSLA conference in Montevideo and the First Latin American Communist Conference in Buenos Aires.[82] The group sent five delegates under Julio Portocarrero to the Montevideo meeting and sent Dr. Hugo Pesce and Portocarrero to Buenos Aires. Mariátegui wrote essays to be delivered at both conferences.[83]

Mariátegui's essay delivered in Montevideo, "The Indigenous Question," focused on the Peruvian context. He said that "90% of the indigenous population" in Peru worked in a "semi-feudal" agricultural system of large landowners.[84] Textile factories in Cuzco similarly relied on the exploitation of Indigenous labor and on the feudal agricultural system. While the mining industry operated on a salary system, this industry subjected workers to unsafe conditions, ignored labor laws, and forbade workers from unionizing.[85] Mariátegui dismissed the stereotype of passivity that was often attributed to Indigenous peoples, reminding his interlocutors of the long history of Indigenous insurrection. He provided examples of recent "revolutionary" organizing around Indigenous rights in Peru, such as the Comité Pro-Derecho Indígena Tahuantinsuyo and the Federación Obrera Regional Indígena.[86] He argued that these organizations, primarily founded by non-Indigenous intellectuals, effectively collaborated with Indigenous leadership and supported Indigenous-led organizing efforts, which remained ongoing despite government repression.

Mariátegui defined the primary problem facing Indigenous peoples as one of access to land and argued that land reform should become a focus of trade union movements. He also emphasized the need to cultivate relationships with Indigenous workers already involved in unions in urban areas. These individuals, fluent in Indigenous languages, could play an important role in organizing efforts in more rural areas. They should hold leadership positions in coordinated efforts to defend communal property rights, protect Indigenous peoples' rights against police brutality, and organize libraries, study groups, and workers' publications in Indigenous communities. Although he argued that the problems facing Indigenous peoples were fundamentally social and economic, he believed that race and ethnicity played a significant role both in the exploitation of Indigenous communities and in the centrality of Indigenous leaders in organizing within their

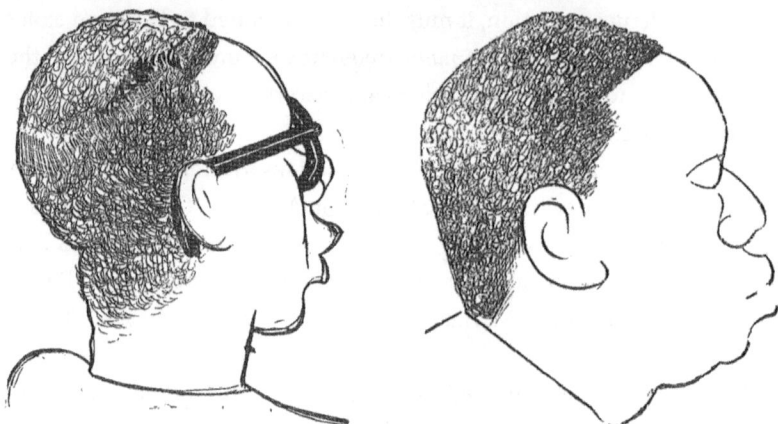

3.2 Drawing of Isaiah Hawkins at CSLA conference by David Siqueiros. CSLA, *Bajo la bandera*, 135.

3.3 Drawing of Sandalio Junco at CSLA conference by David Siqueiros. CSLA, *Bajo la bandera*, 171.

own communities. In the ensuing discussion with the audience, Junco responded to Mariátegui by suggesting that Black people faced many of the same issues and argued that, although an economic problem, this "also has the characteristics of a racial problem" since Black laborers enjoy many fewer rights than their white counterparts.[87]

The following session, opened by Isaiah Hawkins (figure 3.2), a Black miner from Pittsburgh and TUEL delegate from the US National Miners' Union, focused on the Negro Question. Hawkins described in detail the circumstances of US Black workers and called for a continental approach to supporting Black organizing.[88] In this session, Junco (figure 3.3) delivered his speech, "The Negro Question and the Proletarian Movement." This speech and the corresponding "Resolution on the Question of Black Workers," based on Junco's comments, presented a much broader continental analysis of the exploitation of Black workers in comparison to Mariátegui's analysis of Indigenous labor. In this speech, Junco responded to the limitations of the Brussels resolution by insisting on the existence of anti-Black racism in Latin America and by calling out racism specifically among Latin American workers. He did not direct his critique of anti-Black racism in Latin America only toward white and mestizo Latin Americans but also addressed discrimination by native-born Black workers toward Haitian and West Indian immigrant workers. Most significantly, he emphasized the necessity for Black workers to articulate an integrated class- and race-based transnational political subjectivity and to recognize their experiences as united with, yet distinct from, the experiences of their white and mestizo counterparts. He would further develop this argument in a 1930 article in *El Trabajador Latinoamericano*, discussed later in this chapter, where, seemingly in response to disagreements that arose at the 1929 conferences, he insisted much more emphatically on the importance of race-based organizing for Black workers.

Junco began his speech by commenting that this was the first time a Latin American workers' conference "of this importance" sought to address issues facing Black workers; for this reason, the CSLA would be seen by "the continent's Black proletariat" as "the greatest champion and defender of its rights and demands." Junco's speech drew connections between the experiences of Black Latin Americans and those of other racialized communities. He followed up on Mariátegui's essay by emphasizing that issues facing Black workers across the continent have "many similarities with those of the Indigenous. The Black and the Indigenous are two races equally oppressed and humiliated by capitalism and are the two largest sectors that have formed the bulk of the continental proletariat."[89]

He then laid out a brief history of the transatlantic slave trade, since this history was "not very well-known among workers," and outlined the vast expanse of the African diaspora in Latin America.[90] Describing the social structure that scholars would later call racial capitalism, Junco argued that the direct descendants of enslaved Africans in the Americas now "endure the most terrible and humiliating conditions in the dens of modern, capitalist exploitation." He listed all Latin American countries containing large Afro-descendant populations and emphasized that he had personally seen "a considerable number of Black people" in Argentina and Uruguay. The "quantity and range of those of the Black race throughout our entire continent already demonstrate the importance of the matter under discussion," he stated.[91]

Moving from this historical background to the state of contemporary Black labor, he began not in Latin America but by detailing the conditions of the Jim Crow South. He drew parallels to prior comments by Isaiah Hawkins describing segregation in the US South, lynching, and inferior working conditions faced by US Black workers. However, rather than falling back on the language of the Brussels resolution, which suggested that such oppression only existed in Latin America in areas of US occupation, he instead compared the situation in the US South to that in his home country, Cuba. He explained that the post-independence Cuban republic did not follow through on its promises to Black Cubans who fought in Cuba's wars of independence, and he especially condemned the 1912 Morúa Law, which prohibited race-based political organizing in Cuba.[92] Junco also pointed to racial discrimination in hiring practices and in highly skilled professions and critiqued the Cuban bourgeoisie for negating the existence of racial discrimination and denying their own "hatred and disdain toward Black people."[93] The US and Cuban cases, he argued, were indicative of the problems faced by Black people throughout the continent. Junco insisted that anti-Black racism represented a problem throughout Latin America and an intrinsic part of the region's dominant cultures, dismissing thus the familiar notion from the Brussels resolution that it was a mere US import.

Black immigrant workers from Haiti and the West Indies, whose employment by US-owned companies Junco presented as a form of modern-day slavery, faced especially dire circumstances. Junco's reflections on immigrant labor were situated within his own Cuban context, where a boom in the sugar industry, driven by rising prices during World War I, attracted immigrants from throughout the Caribbean to work in Cuba. By the late 1920s, the economic crisis that became the Great Depression impacted sugar prices, placing immigrant workers in an especially vulnerable position. Since the recruitment of Haitian and West Indian immigrants was tied to the US sugar industry, a nativist and anti-imperialist discourse arose that was expressed through antiblackness and especially through anti-Haitianism. While the repatriation of immigrant workers began under President Gerardo Machado, it would culminate in the 50 Percent Law under President Ramón Grau San Martín's "Cuba for the Cubans" policies.[94] The 50 Percent Law, which ordered that 50 percent of all companies' employees must be native Cuban, attempted to respond to native-born Cuban workers' discontent with the mass importation of Jamaican and Haitian agricultural workers and the common practice in the tobacco industry of choosing Spanish immigrants as apprentices. This nativist policy found particular support among the unemployed and working poor, including many Afro-Cubans.[95]

In Cuba, the communists and CNOC, which included many immigrant workers among its ranks, strongly opposed the 50 Percent Law.[96] Ironically, considering Junco's pro-immigrant statements in 1929, Junco's own PBL would endorse Grau San Martín's government, which was responsible for the law, in 1933–34. However, as Gary Tennant writes, the PBL viewed the Grau San Martín administration not necessarily "as an ally but as an inevitable phase in the development of the revolution."[97] Although it endorsed Grau San Martín, the PBL opposed the 50 Percent Law since it "represented the government's attempt to 'Cubanise' the working class and destroy its organisations by pitting the native Cuban workers against the foreign ones."[98] Junco himself wrote a biting critique of this law in a December 1933 issue of *El Obrero Panadero* (The bread worker), the Havana bakers' union periodical.[99]

In 1929 in Montevideo, Junco was absolutely clear in his condemnation of nativism among the working classes, pointing out and critiquing the intersection of anti-immigrant sentiment with antiblackness. "The imperialists and national bourgeoisies," he argued, encourage "hatred by natives, including by Black native workers, toward Jamaican and Haitian workers, as occurs in Cuba, Panama, Colombia, Guatemala."[100] In its broader extractive zone, US companies and complicit national bourgeoisies use nativism to divide and conquer workers, drumming up racial hatred even among Black citizens toward their Black immigrant coworkers. Workers' organizations need to better address the exploitation of Black immigrant workers.

Citing Jacinto Chacón Castrellón, a Panamanian delegate, Junco related two instances witnessed by Chacón during his employment on North American ships. In the first, Chacón was thrown out of an establishment in New Orleans because one of the members of his party was Black. In another, upon leaving Puerto Cortes, Honduras, a stowaway who was Black was discovered on Chacón's ship. When the stowaway resisted being shackled, the US captain ordered him locked in the coal room, where he became extremely overheated. According to Chacón's account, the sailors could hear his frantic cries and begged that he be freed. When his cries stopped, they believed the man had been released, only to realize that he had been burned alive. Despite the efforts of those present, the captain faced no criminal charges.

Through relating this secondhand account, Junco suggested that the disregard for Black life and impunity toward anti-Black violence extended the length of the continent, bridging New Orleans, Honduras, and Cuba and traveling through the ships that connected the territories of US-owned corporations. Jim Crow racism extended throughout "Yankeeland and its territories," presenting thus a transnational system of anti-Black violence and exploitation fomented through US imperialism.[101] However, despite his rhetorical employment of this gruesome image to express the relationship between US corporations and the transnational nature of anti-Black violence, Junco's statements did not externalize blame only to the United States. Anti-Black racism, like anti-Indigenous racism, Junco claimed, are foundational elements of bourgeois, capitalist society in Latin America: "These are the conditions in which the Black race suffers, and above all, the form in which Black workers are treated and mistreated by capitalism. Add to all this the additional problem that bourgeois and imperialist education instills in children a dismal concept and feeling of hatred and disdain for Black people—as everywhere it does with Indigenous people—and our colleagues will have a more complete idea of the terrible situation for Black workers."

Junco's speech did not fall into the trap—for which some interwar communist propaganda could be criticized—of harping on Black victimization while eliding the history of Black militancy. Rather, aligning with Mariátegui's comments on Indigenous workers, Junco reminded his interlocutors of the long tradition of Black resistance on the continent, which he situated within the region's history of class struggle: "The history of class struggle on our continent includes countless uprising and rebellions by Black people against slavery." Black people took part in all the region's independence struggles and "instinctively placed the issue of their liberation on the forefront of these social and political struggles." He described the Haitian Revolution as an agrarian revolution, claiming that this fact had been occluded by a dominant narrative focused on "demonstrations of the savagery of Blacks against whites." Instead, he encouraged his interlocutors to understand this violence as fundamentally a struggle against feudalism: "All these struggles were against feudal lords, whatever color they were."[102] Junco then referred to the founding of the "Black republic of Palmares," the largest *quilombo* (maroon community) in Brazil.[103] He claimed that when the Portuguese eventually defeated this republic, many of its inhabitants preferred to commit suicide rather than return to slavery. He argued that these two examples, Haiti and Palmares, prove that "Black workers have known how to rebel, just like all oppressed peoples on the Continent, against their oppressors, against enslaving and feudal rulers."[104]

By describing the Haitian Revolution as an agrarian workers' revolution, Junco's statements anticipated by almost ten years the core argument of C. L. R. James's renowned *The Black Jacobins* (1938).[105] Even so, his emphasis on the Haitian Revolution as a labor struggle that transcended race risked underplaying its direct challenge to the racist ideologies undergirding slavery. By harping on the example of courageous Black militants who committed suicide rather than submit to enslavement, Junco suggested a false association between enslavement and passivity. Yet even with these problems in Junco's rhetoric, it is important to remember that Junco spoke to an almost completely white and mestizo audience that likely made little to no connection between the continent's history of labor movements and its history of Black resistance. His speech directly challenged his audience's understanding of class struggle, and in so doing, he undermined a dominant narrative that conceived of labor struggles in the region through white and mestizo industrial workers. He aimed to reframe his interlocutors' understanding of the region's history so that they could comprehend not only how their own struggles had been shaped by Black activists but also how Black leadership was necessary for their contemporary goals.

Articulating a communist critique against "negro reformism," Junco rejected Garveyism and its proposal for Black Americans to form a new Black republic in Africa. He described it as a Zionism concerned only with a bourgeois class, rather than with offering concrete solutions to Black workers, and as a position allied with US imperial interests in Africa.[106] However, his critique of Garveyism did not lead him simply to embrace the purely class-based perspective of many of his fellow communists.[107] Echoing McKay and Huiswoud, he called for an outreach campaign to Black American workers and for the education of white, mestizo, and native-born Black workers on the subject of anti-Black racism, especially toward Haitians and West Indians. All unions, he argued, should open their doors not only to native-born Black workers but also to Black immigrants. He critiqued the perspective of syndicalist movements in the Caribbean that focused their efforts on ending immigrant labor rather than finding ways to organize with immigrant workers, and he provided examples of how immigrant labor organizing had been accomplished successfully on Cuban sugar plantations.[108]

Black workers should not have to take sole responsibility for leading this outreach, he argued. Junco directly enlisted the help of his audience, mentioning that he arrived in Uruguay on a British ship that had 150 Black crew members working sixteen-to-eighteen-hour days shoveling coal. Trade unions in the Río de la Plata should engage these workers, he said, adding that the world's most important revolutionary organizations had already taken a stand on this issue and that a new international committee of Black workers (ITUCNW) had formed within the Profintern. He recommended that the CSLA follow suit by adopting a resolution that would communicate with the "millions and millions of Black proletarians who are waiting to fight with workers of all races and colors for the shared emancipation from all the yokes that have oppressed them for centuries."[109]

In pushing for outreach to this transnational Black proletariat, Junco articulated a Black internationalist position situated between a commitment to either a race-based or a purely class-based subjectivity. He stated, "We should go and demonstrate to them that as a race and as a class that is economically, socially, and politically oppressed, from one end of the continent to the other, by both the imperialists and the native bourgeoisie—which includes the complicity of certain wealthy Black people who play the game—they will not achieve their full and effective liberation without entering the terrain of open struggle for their immediate and political vindication against imperialism and against all the exploiters, whatever their color or their origin may be."[110] Junco claimed that the CSLA must develop its movement in a way that would address the integrated relationship between race and class in order to reach Black workers. While he expressed suspicion toward purely race-based political ideologies that overlooked the complicity of the Black elite and he insisted that oppression could come in any color, his critique of race-based ideologies did not imply that issues facing Black peoples could necessarily be resolved through a purely class-based analysis. Rather, he understood these oppressions through a complex relation, arguing that Black Americans should be understood both as part of a larger oppressed class and as part of an oppressed racial category.

Junco was undoubtedly successful in communicating his positions in Montevideo. As evidence, the CSLA adopted the "Resolution on the Question of Black Workers," which drew heavily from Junco's comments and which described Black workers through a "double condition as proletarians and as members of a race that the white bourgeoisie and imperialists continue to oppress."[111] In contrast to the Brussels resolution, the CSLA resolution stated that Black workers suffer unequal conditions "in Cuba, Panama, in all Central American countries, and even—with very little variation—in South America."[112] The resolution addressed the circumstances of Black immigrant workers and called on all unions to fight with and on behalf of Black peoples. It included seven concrete actions that should be taken, including supporting and sustaining Black-led struggles when they arise. However, while the resolution clearly reflected Junco's positions, the debate a month later in Buenos Aires suggests that it would not be enough to change some of his comrades' entrenched views. Junco would have to make his arguments even more forcefully at the First Latin American Communist Conference the following month. There, he would differentiate his positions more stridently from Mariátegui's analysis of the Indigenous Question and from a more decidedly class-based approach.

CONTINUING THE DEBATE AT THE 1929 FIRST
LATIN AMERICAN COMMUNIST CONFERENCE

A few days after the CSLA conference in Montevideo, many of the delegates crossed the Río de la Plata to attend the First Latin American Communist Conference in June 1929 in Buenos Aires. This conference drew thirty-eight delegates from communist parties throughout Latin America, and Junco attended as PCC representative under the pseudonym Juárez.

The Buenos Aires conference dedicated a session to LADLA and the broader LAI. William Simons, who was a New York descendant of Jewish immigrants and who had been among the "slackers" in Mexico between 1918 and 1921, spoke on behalf of LADLA-US.[113] He laid out the relationship that LADLA sections should have with trade unions and communist parties: As "mass organizations" based around the "united front," LADLA sections should work most closely with "masses employed by the imperialist industries" and seek the involvement of trade union and communist organizers.[114] However, LADLA should not intervene in the inner workings of trade unions, which must maintain their class identity, nor should membership come predominantly from communist parties. LADLA sections needed to unite a broader range of classes and leftist ideologies behind a position of anti-imperialism, a feat accomplished more effectively by some sections than others. He said the US and Latin American sections should communicate more frequently with one another since it was only on arriving in Argentina that Simons had learned of an ongoing strike there against General Motors.[115] He mentioned that the Uruguayan section in particular needed to improve its outreach to agricultural communities and to women, and he urged LADLA sections throughout the Americas to form deeper ties to LAI sections in "any colony or semi-colony around the world."[116]

The Spanish-born Argentine activist Paulino González Alberdi spoke next on behalf of the Grupo Izquierda (Left Group) from LADLA-Argentina. The Grupo Izquierda, a faction of communists and workers within LADLA-Argentina, formed in July 1927 in protest of the section's leadership, which it found conservative and ineffective. The group aimed "to do whatever possible to save the League . . . so that the League could be what it should be: a powerful anti-imperialist mass organization that, without sectarian exclusions or restrictions, without preventions against any ideology, carries out a united front against imperialism."[117]

González Alberdi acknowledged the various accomplishments of LADLA's Continental Committee in Mexico City.[118] However, he argued that all

LADLA sections could do more to ally with workers' campaigns against the abuses of foreign companies.[119] While he recognized that LADLA sections communicated with LAI headquarters in Berlin and with the Continental Committee in Mexico City, he urged them to have better contact with one another and encouraged the Continental Committee to improve its communications with national sections. Members of the Brazilian, Venezuelan, and Panamanian sections responded to these comments, agreeing with most points made. Simons ended the discussion by reiterating that all present should join in the work of LADLA in their home country and that the discussion should continue at the second LAI congress, coming up the next month in July 1929.

In addition to this attention to LADLA and the LAI, the conference also devoted a session to the Negro and Indigenous Questions. The conversation in Buenos Aires focused primarily on the issue of self-determination and formation of Black and Indigenous republics. Though Mariátegui was unable to attend, he sent three position papers, including "The Question of Race in Latin America," to be read by his representative, Dr. Hugo Pesce (the Peruvian physician who later introduced Che Guevara to Marxism while Guevara worked at Pesce's leprosarium in 1951).[120] This paper took a more comparatist approach to the Indigenous Question than Mariátegui's CSLA paper and expanded to consider racial discrimination more broadly. In this essay, Mariátegui explained that by referring to the "Indigenous Question," he referred to the "feudal exploitation of natives on agrarian property," and he argued that political organizing related to this question should focus on land reform.[121] He categorically rejected any notion of inferior and superior races and the eugenicist belief, popular at the time among some *indigenista* intellectuals, that racial mixing would present a solution to inequities faced by Indigenous peoples. This ideology of *mestizaje* and cultural redemption through assimilation, he argued, only served to facilitate the conditions for further resource extraction. He explained that poverty faced by Indigenous communities derived not from racial inferiority but from economic inequality and the long history of colonial feudalism. The elite's racism toward Indigenous peoples prevented national unity, further facilitating imperialist penetration.[122] To reach Indigenous communities, he argued, communist parties must stand behind Indigenous organizers. Yet even as Mariátegui recognized that the Indigenous Question had to be partly analyzed through the social categories of race and ethnicity, he insisted the deeper issue was a social and economic one that could only be addressed through class struggle. For this reason, he dismissed as misguided the Comintern proposal for a republic of Quechua and Aymara in the South American Andes, claiming that this would only result in a "bourgeois Indigenous State with all the internal and external contradictions of bourgeois states."[123]

While Mariátegui argued for the importance of Indigenous peoples within a larger class struggle, in his rejection of Indigenous nationalism and self-determination Mariátegui went so far as to dismiss the viability of any ethnicity-based organizing for Indigenous communities and ended up defending a more orthodox Marxist position than even Moscow was promoting at this moment. Mariátegui has been celebrated for his innovative ideas on land reform and economic justice for Indigenous peoples and for theorizing a rural, peasant-based movement that adapted Marxist theory to the concrete realities of Peru rather than following the Comintern's centralized attempts to export revolutionary models.[124] However, it must also be said that Mariátegui, as an *indigenista* intellectual, was not Indigenous but speaking on behalf of Indigenous peoples. As Marc Becker writes, "During the debates in Buenos Aires apparently no one considered consulting with Indians as to their views on establishing an independent native republic or even bringing them into the discussion."[125]

Mariátegui's comments on Black communities at the Buenos Aires conference were even more troublesome. In contrast to Junco's insistence on the long history of Black resistance on the continent, Mariátegui claimed that Black people were brought to the Americas to allow colonists to increase their power over Indigenous peoples and that they "passively filled their colonialist function. Harshly exploited themselves, they reinforced the oppression of the Indigenous race."[126] He argued that the Indigenous Question was more tied to land rights and that because Black people spoke the colonial language and did not have the same historical ties to the land, "they almost do not have any of their own traditions."[127] Seemingly oblivious to the anti-Black prejudice inherent in his comments and likely unaware of Junco's arguments from the month before, he claimed that "Black people in Latin America do not suffer the same disdain as in the United States" and that anti-Black prejudice was nonexistent among working classes. He argued that racial prejudice and discrimination in employment was not a problem for Afro–Latin Americans, a contention later repeated by Brazilian delegate Leoncio Basbaum, and he reiterated the position from the Brussels resolution that, in contrast to the United States, "in Latin America, in general, the Negro Question does not take on a noticeable racial character."[128] Mariátegui then used this argument to further sustain that "the race question" is an economic and social problem that must be combatted with class struggle.[129]

Unsurprisingly, the person who spoke out most strongly against these comments was Sandalio Junco. Junco responded by affirming that anti-Black racism did indeed exist in all countries of Latin America despite its frequent denial by Latin American representatives of communist parties. He emphasized this fact several times, listing the names of all Latin American countries, including Mariátegui's Peru, where Black people faced discrimination. Rather than creating a stark contrast with US race relations, Junco stated that although Black Latin Americans had de jure equality, in reality they experienced "a grating inequality, that tends to be equal to the treatment that Blacks in North America receive."[130] In Cuba, for example, despite the state's proclamations of legal equality, Black Cubans consistently faced discrimination in employment and only certain jobs were reserved for them. His authority on this subject, he explained, came from his own experiences of discrimination, since the bakers' union he directed was fighting to force bakeries to hire Black Cubans. In the ensuing discussion, the white Cuban delegate Alejandro Barreiro Oliveira concurred with Junco and rejected Basbaum's argument that anti-Black prejudice existed only among the bourgeoisie and was absent among workers.

Junco again pointed to Cuba's Morúa Law, but this time, perhaps because he was speaking under a pseudonym, his comments were more radical. He discussed how Cuba's Partido Independiente de Color (Independent Party of Color, PIC) protested this law in 1912, and how the Cuban government responded by massacring thousands of Black Cubans. He claimed that the PIC's resistance was easily repressed, because the PIC represented a primarily Black professional class disconnected from Black industrial and agricultural workers: "If the majority had intervened, perhaps we would have witnessed a reproduction of the memorable events of Haiti."[131] By imagining what could have occurred in 1912 if Black working classes had been more involved, Junco seemed to suggest a future vision for Black revolution in Cuba led by Black working classes. Significantly, Junco diverged from the Comintern line and did not limit this vision to Cuba's majority-Black Oriente province but hinted at Black governance for the entire country.

He subtly rejected Mariátegui's claim that Black people had participated in reinforcing Indigenous oppression, saying rather that enslaved Africans "suffered the same condition of servitude that previously the Indigenous had suffered."[132] He again returned to the subject of Black immigrant workers on US-owned plantations in Cuba and Central America, comparing their conditions to a form of enslavement. Whereas Junco had begun his statements in Montevideo by focusing on racial terror in the US South and then expanding to make comparisons to Latin America, in Buenos Aires he took the reverse tactic. Perhaps because of his colleagues' repeated externalization of anti-Black racism to the United States, he began by addressing the existence of this issue throughout Latin America. Only at the very end of his speech did he recognize that "this problem does not just belong to Latin America but is also quite acute in North America." He concluded his comments by urging his listeners to struggle not only on behalf of Black people in Latin America but also for those in the United States, calling ultimately for "an active and systematic struggle for the equality of all beings."[133]

Most of the discussion that followed the speeches by Mariátegui and Junco focused on the question of national self-determination. The Young Communist International representative Zacharij Mijailovich Rabinovich warned that recognizing the classed nature of the oppression of agrarian workers should not result in a negation of the "national nature" of Indigenous struggles nor in a reductive understanding of Indigenous self-determination movements as simply class struggles.[134] He urged the Peruvian delegates to support the right of Indigenous peoples to self-determination and independence from the bourgeois state and to abandon "fetishism with current borders between Latin American countries."[135] Delegates from Bolivia, Argentina, Mexico, Peru, Venezuela, and El Salvador weighed in, with most supporting a strategy of Indigenous self-determination and others calling for Indigenous land rights within already established national boundaries. Hugo Pesce (Mariátegui's representative) took issue with the Venezuelan delegate Ricardo Arturo Martínez's naïve suggestion that a national Indigenous state would necessarily lack class divisions. In his counterargument, Pesce again took the most orthodox position, rejecting Indigenous national self-determination entirely and saying that "it is necessary to keep the racial question in mind, but it must be subject to the question of class."[136] While there was lively debate around Indigenous self-determination, delegates paid little attention to Black self-determination and seemed unsure of whether this question could actually apply to Black Latin Americans.

When Junco spoke up again, he did not address national self-determination for Black peoples but called attention to the overwhelming focus of the conversation on Indigenous communities and silence on the subject of immigration. Adding to his earlier comments on Black immigrants, and true to his call for "equality of all beings," he returned to a brief comment made by the Guatemalan delegate about Chinese immigration in Latin America. In Cuba, Junco explained, Chinese immigrants had played an active role in the independence struggles and remained a powerful force in Cuban politics. They represented a significant portion of the population in Mexico as well. "The lack of a serious study on this immigration question is due to a shortcoming of our agenda," he said, suggesting that one of the conference sessions should have focused on immigrant populations.[137] Siqueiros added that strong anti-Chinese sentiment existed at almost all levels of Mexican society, and efforts to foster advocacy for Chinese laborers in workers' organizations had been largely unsuccessful. While the discussion of Chinese immigrants went little further, this issue, along with Junco's broadly inclusive and pro-immigrant vision for "equality of all beings," became a key platform for some activists in LADLA-Cuba, discussed in the next chapter.

The delegations did not come to an agreement on the Negro and Indigenous Questions, especially on the issue of national self-determination, leading La Correspondencia Sudamericana to publish one analysis that synthesized delegates' various comments and described two potential resolutions to be discussed at the next continental conference, an event that would never take place. The published analysis argued that, despite the perspective of many communists, race is a complex and relevant problem in Latin America and Indigenous and Black Latin Americans form a central base of production and are important to class struggle in the region. One of the resolutions called specifically for Indigenous national self-determination and expressed support for a view of Black Latin Americans as an oppressed nation. Importantly, echoing Junco, this resolution condemned government legislation that restricted immigration to protect national workers, calling rather for the "revolutionary proletariat" to "unite all the exploited of diverse races in the struggle against imperialism."[138] The other did not advocate for self-determination; reflecting one of Junco's interventions, it called on Latin American communist parties to revise their indifferent attitudes toward racial inequities and seek alliances with Indigenous and Black people.

Following these historic conferences, Junco continued to develop his positions, in which he did not necessarily advocate for self-determination but rather urged the importance of integrated class-conscious and race-based organizing. This argument appears, for example, in his article "The Latin American Black Proletariat and the Conference in London," published in El Trabajador Latinoamericano in July 1930.[139] Junco wrote the essay in the lead-up to the ITUCNW's First International Conference of Negro Workers in 1930, which he explained was begun as an LAI initiative, and which was initially planned for London but eventually held in Hamburg, Germany. He again claimed that racial inequity exists in all Latin American countries and that the bourgeoisie hides and denies this fact through the practice of racial tokenism. While he recognized the suffering of all Latin American workers, he argued that the oppression faced by Black peoples was especially brutal and had become so naturalized that it was widely accepted: "The humiliation, disdain and insult to which the negro is subjected is every day more naturalized such that it begins to produce no indignation and to continue being accepted."[140] He again critiqued "a true slave trafficking" practiced by US sugar and fruit industries.[141]

In this article, however, Junco took his argument a step further. Rather than focusing his critique primarily on anti-Black racism within the Latin American working classes, he expanded to consider a lack of race consciousness specifically among Black workers. He argued that the Latin American Black working class has a tendency to think of itself only in terms of class but "it has to demonstrate also that it has an understanding of all of its obligations and that it will be incorporated into the struggle of its brothers from the African and Antillean colonies, raising the banner of its demands as a race."[142] In this iteration of his argument, Junco made a more forceful claim for the need for Black Latin American workers to recognize themselves as belonging not only to an oppressed class but also to a transnational race-based community and to understand "that which is his doubly exploited condition, as a race and as a class."[143] He proposed a political position situated between a purely race-based ideology and a wholly class-based one, and articulated this position from the complexity of his own experience as an Afro–Latin American. In contrast to US and West Indian intellectuals—like Ford, Huiswoud, McKay, and Padmore— who are better known for their contributions to the Negro Question, Junco faced a different and arguably more complex dilemma. He similarly had to address the problems of racial discrimination among the working classes, but he also had to contend with the widely accepted narrative that anti-Black racial discrimination did not exist in Latin America. Moreover, he had to consider the difficulties of outreach to Black Latin Americans who did not necessarily view their conditions of subjugation through a race-based lens and thus did not necessarily identify with the Black internationalist organizations that reached out to them. Junco's writings on the Negro Question navigate all these complexities of the Latin American context, making a significant contribution to the integrated theorizing of race and class from a specifically Afro–Latin American lens and using this analysis to think through relations with forms of oppression experienced by Indigenous and immigrant populations.

THE LEGACY OF SANDALIO JUNCO AND THE NEGRO QUESTION IN LATIN AMERICA

Junco's 1929 interventions on race in Latin America had a significant impact. For one, in the months after these conferences, Mariátegui himself would nuance some of his positions. In December 1929, for example, he published an article in the Peruvian newspaper *Mundial* that sought to differentiate Black internationalist politics from the bourgeois cosmopolitan movements that tended to exoticize Black culture, arguing that European artistic fascination with Black cultural forms represented simply another— albeit artistic—exploitation of Black labor.[144] The article celebrated Black internationalists' contributions in the Comintern and condemned Garveyism. While Mariátegui directed his critique at Europe and not necessarily Latin America, this critique could easily apply to the hispanophone Caribbean *negrista* movement, which was becoming popular at the time especially among leftist artists and intellectuals, and which tended to celebrate Black cultural forms while reproducing stereotypical representations.

Following the 1929 conferences, the organization that would develop the most comprehensive discussion on the Negro Question was the ITUCNW, which hosted the 1930 First International Conference of Negro Workers in Germany. Junco expressed optimism that this conference would draw significant Black Latin American participation.[145] However, as Holger Weiss has argued, the ITUCNW existed primarily as a propaganda organization through its publication, *The Negro Worker*.[146] Despite Junco's hopes, *The Negro Worker* focused on Africa, the United States, and the anglophone and francophone Caribbeans, with Spanish-speaking Latin America largely absent from its pages.

However, Junco's argument especially for outreach to immigrant workers became a central focus for LADLA-Cuba, studied in the next chapter, and for the Comintern's Caribbean Bureau, founded in 1931 in New York City by Cuban, Venezuelan, and Puerto Rican communists. Although the PCC expelled Junco in 1932, the Comintern's Caribbean Bureau responded to Junco's and others' calls to work to better incorporate Black workers, including Black immigrant workers, and to foment unity among exploited populations in the broader Caribbean basin. The Caribbean Bureau, discussed in chapter 7, was short-lived (1931–36). And in the lead-up to the Second World War, the Soviet Union "began to backpedal on black liberation" as it allied with colonial powers to fight fascism.[147]

Nonetheless, Junco's discussion of the so-called Negro Question in the Americas continues to have relevance today. In the US context, the Movement for Black Lives has paid increasing attention to relations between anti-immigrant racism and antiblackness, theorizing links between trade liberalization, corporate profiteering from the prison industrial complex, and militarized policing that oppresses African Americans and immigrants alike.[148] Sandalio Junco is an early theorist of these seemingly contemporary ideas. Junco's contributions also continue to have relevance in the Latin American context, where in the 1990s and early 2000s Latin American leftist governments instituted a wave of multicultural constitutional reforms intended to recognize Indigenous cultural and economic rights, shifting from singular national identities based on assimilation toward a conceptualization of national populations as ethnically, culturally, and racially diverse.[149] Although the extent of gains made has depended on individual contexts, overall these reforms were directed at Indigenous groups, and peoples of African descent were largely ignored.[150] The United Nations' International Decade for Peoples of African Descent (2015–2024) had important influence in Latin America even as Indigenous movements continued to predominate in the region's conceptualizations of racial and ethnic minorities. In some cases, Afro-descendants have been able to use these multicultural reforms for their own gain—through strategies that recall Junco's comparison of the Indigenous Question to the Negro Question—in what Peter Wade calls an attempt to "indianize" claims to land rights, such as Black communities' claims to territory on Colombia's Pacific coast.[151] As many of these multicultural reforms were instituted by the *marea rosada* (pink tide) leftist governments, we might then see a link between the elision of Junco's ideas and other Afro–Latin Americans' voices in scholarship on Latin American leftism and the elision of Afro-descendant communities in the policies of the contemporary Latin American Left.

This chapter has represented a partial response to these problems by reviving Junco's contributions and resituating him as a key theorist of the

Afro–Latin American experience, issues faced by Black immigrant labor in Latin America, and intersections between antiracism and class struggle. Junco provides a model for relational solidarities, focused on the intertwined relationships between historical processes of exploitation that differentially impact different communities. Junco's interrogation of the relation between oppressions is perhaps his most lasting contribution.

FOUR

RELATIONAL POETICS

LADLA-CUBA AND REGINO PEDROSO'S AFRO-CHINESE-CUBAN WRITINGS

In May 1934, Afro-Cuban physician Dr. Martín Castellanos published an article entitled "A Little Something on the Negro Question" in *Masas*, published by LADLA-Cuba.[1] Castellanos, active in the PCC and LADLA-Cuba, argued that the dominant classes use racial prejudice to divide workers, employing certain token Black leaders as accomplices in suppressing labor movements. As an example, he named Martín Morúa Delgado, who played a central role in repressing the Partido Independiente de Color (Independent Party of Color, PIC) in 1912 by introducing a bill—the Morúa Law—that banned political parties organized around race or class. Alongside Morúa, he also named Afro-Cuban politicians Juan Gualberto Gómez and Generoso Campos Marquetti because of their lack of support for the PIC. In 1929, Sandalio Junco made a very similar critique of the Morúa Law in his groundbreaking speeches on the Negro Question. Despite the initial similarities of this article to Junco's statements, Castellanos then added Junco as an example of a Black leader who functions in this same role "within the proletariat."[2]

As detailed in the previous chapter, the PCC expelled Junco in 1932 shortly after his return to Cuba because of his unorthodox views. At the time of Castellanos's article, Junco led a Trotskyist opposition group, the Bolshevik-Leninist Party (PBL). Castellanos viewed Junco as a traitor to communist and anti-imperialist movements. However, in addition to Castellanos's critique of the Morúa Law, he and Junco shared several other political positions, especially a condemnation of nativist racism against Haitian and West Indian workers. Notably, in contrast to Junco's nuanced vision for a Black political subjectivity based in Black workers' "doubly exploited condition, as a race and as a class," Castellanos's article argued for a more rigid class-based analysis.[3] His article asked the rhetorical question, "Does the oppression of the Negro respond to the color of his skin or the curl of his hair?" to which it answered, "Clearly anyone can see that it does not."[4] As evidence, he pointed to the exploitation of white Cuban workers and to countries where white people occupy roles of both oppressor and oppressed. Castellanos then attributed anti-Black racism in Cuba to the importation of racial terror, such as lynchings, from the United States. Junco had similarly faulted US imperialism, but he intentionally avoided externalizing blame and argued that anti-Black racism was a foundational component of capitalist societies in Latin America.

Castellanos diverged from Junco in other ways as well, especially in developing the theory of self-determination in Cuba's "Black Belt of Oriente," where Black Cubans "are the majority."[5] This vision for Black self-determination, he explained, did not contradict his class-over-race analysis since self-determination for Oriente represented "a class struggle that takes a national form."[6] Castellanos's positions aligned with the PCC party line in the mid-1930s, but the PCC would also expel Castellanos in 1937 for "his individualistic and divisive conduct" and for his stronger commitment to Black struggles than to the PCC.[7]

Castellanos is one of several LADLA activists who eventually became persona non grata in his local communist party. Although expulsion from the communist party sometimes resulted in expulsion from LADLA, LADLA was intended as a united-front organization that joined artists and intellectuals with nationalist struggles and workers' movements. Whether considering the cases of Castellanos, Junco, Mella, or Rivera, LADLA attracted activists interested in broad leftist coalitions and in thinking about how to bridge race-based and class-based activism, meaning LADLA's ideological flexibility appealed to irreverent communists who did not always align with orthodox positions. As examined in the previous chapter, Junco's 1929 vision represents the furthest-reaching conception by any of LADLA's leadership of a broad-based, anti-imperialist solidarity politics that bridged racial justice, anticapitalist, and workers' rights movements. Although LADLA-Cuba (and members like Castellanos) sided with the

PCC in expelling Junco, Junco's vision continued to have clear resonance within LADLA-Cuba after his departure.

This chapter studies Junco's ongoing impact through examining the work of yet another LADLA activist, Afro-Chinese-Cuban poet Regino Pedroso Aldama (1896–1983). Pedroso, an active member of LADLA-Cuba, would expand on Junco's pro-immigrant politics and integrated analysis of differentiated experiences of capitalist oppression. Similar to the first chapter's treatment of Modotti's photography, this chapter takes seriously Pedroso's poetry as political discourse, especially considering that he often published his poetry in LADLA-Cuba's *Masas*. Whereas the journalistic articles in *Masas* tended to express positions more similar to Castellanos's class-over-race analysis, Pedroso's poetry, published in these same pages, provides an alternative perspective that positions Black workers as exploited through an integrative relationship between race and class and that is especially attentive to the experiences of immigrant workers, including Chinese immigrant workers. As I will argue, Junco's ongoing influence on intellectuals like Pedroso, even after his PCC expulsion, challenges the dominant narrative of the history of Cuban communist thought and its relationship to race-based organizing.

Pedroso, an autodidact, was born to an Afro-Cuban mother and a Chinese father who came to Cuba as an indentured laborer on an eight-year contract during the so-called coolie trade, which ended in 1874 (final contracts expired in 1883).[8] When Pedroso was still a child, his father returned to Canton, where he died shortly afterward, leaving Pedroso's mother with six children in Cuba.[9] Pedroso dropped out of school at age eight, and at thirteen he started working on railroads, on sugar plantations, and in sugar mills.[10] He began writing at seventeen to cope with his mother's death.[11] At twenty-three, he moved to Havana, where he worked as a carpenter, mechanic, and blacksmith, as well as for the American Steel Company.[12] In Havana he made his way into leftist literary circles, like the avant-garde Grupo Minorista. He began publishing his first poems, several of which were introduced by LADLA-Cuba member and well-known writer Rubén Martínez Villena, in the literary sections of Cuban newspapers.[13]

By 1928, Pedroso was involved in leftist politics and soon worked on the editorial team for LADLA-Cuba's *Masas* and for the leftist publications *Ahora* and *La Palabra*.[14] Due to his collaboration with LADLA-Cuba, he was condemned in February 1935 to serve a six-month prison sentence for "seditious propaganda."[15] Later, in 1938 and under less repressive political circumstances, Pedroso received the National Poetry Prize from Cuba's secretary of education. After the Cuban Revolution, he was named cultural ambassador to Mexico and later to China.[16]

Despite his prestigious position in postrevolutionary Cuba, Pedroso's poetry remains relatively understudied, especially in comparison to his contemporary Nicolás Guillén. Pedroso is mostly read within the framework of *afrocubanismo*, the literary and artistic movement in 1920s–40s Cuba through which mostly white Cuban writers ventriloquized blackness in an effort to celebrate national cultural forms.[17] Pedroso is read alongside the few Afro-Cuban poets who participated in this movement, like Guillén and Marcelino Arozarena, as exemplary of Black protest poetry that contrasted with white writers' imitations of Black culture.[18] Literary scholars recognize Pedroso for introducing "social poetry" to Cuba and have characterized his work as representing a "transnational anti-imperialist perspective against racial and class exploitation."[19] However, this scholarship focuses less on Pedroso's political commitments, instead addressing how his work challenges dominant notions of *cubanía* (Cubanness) and critiques the *afrocubanismo* movement. Recent scholarship also reads Pedroso alongside other Asian writers in Latin America and examines his orientalist representations of Chinese culture.[20] These scholars read Pedroso's work within the context of "self-orientalism," in which he strategically appropriates stereotypes of Chinese culture to construct a heterogenous alternative to dominant notions of Cuban identity.

This chapter expands on prior readings by examining more carefully Pedroso's political affiliations, especially with LADLA-Cuba, and considering the insights this context provides for reading his poetry. We can better understand Pedroso's social poetry, including works first published in *Masas*, by reading these poems in dialogue with LADLA's political platform. For example, when Pedroso appropriates orientalism, he not only reframes national identity, as previously argued. Rather, in line with LADLA's hemispheric globalism, discussed in chapter 2, he also rejects interwar Latin American regionalisms that resisted comparisons to African and Asian contexts.

Pedroso's work incorporated many of LADLA-Cuba's positions, including its critique of anti-Black and anti-immigrant racism. However, as this chapter will show, Pedroso's poetry also recuperated some of Junco's earlier 1929 interventions, including a more integrated analysis of race and class exploitation and a focus on Chinese immigrant workers. Like LADLA artist Tina Modotti, Pedroso's poetry exhibits a politics and poetics of *redes*, a relational aesthetics that takes a transnational extractive zone as the site for imagining a new global political community. Such aesthetics are characterized by an emphasis on the relation between oppressions, multiracial intimacies across difference, and ecosocial relationships alternative to those of extractive capitalism. Through these aesthetics, Pedroso illuminates a vision for political community among exploited peoples across national and racial lines.

A BRIEF HISTORY OF LADLA-CUBA

Nicolás Guillén described Regino Pedroso's work in three phases: an initial "artificial" phase, "social poetry," and a "Chinese" period.[21] These phases map onto Pedroso's political engagements, and his "social poetry" appeared alongside the height of his anti-imperialist activities. To better understand the politics behind Pedroso's social poetry, it is necessary to provide background on the formation of LADLA-Cuba—the first LADLA section established outside of Mexico and the United States—and Pedroso's involvement with it.

LADLA-Cuba emerged from Cuba's long history of anticolonial and anti-imperialist organizing, including its three independence wars (1868–98). In the early 1920s, Cuban student activist and workers' organizations planned anti-imperialist actions primarily through the José Martí Popular University (UP), organized by student leader Julio Antonio Mella at the University of Havana. In early 1925, shortly after LADLA's founding in Mexico City, Mella received an invitation for an article contribution from Úrsulo Galván, director of *El Libertador* in Mexico City.[22] Around this time, Galván also sent an invitation for the constitution of a Cuban section of LADLA.[23] Mella responded to Galván's query in a letter published in *El Libertador* (May 1925), where he said he was working to set up LADLA-Cuba.[24]

LADLA-Cuba, the longest-lasting of LADLA's sections and one of the most active, was founded shortly afterward, in July 1925, not long after Cuban President Gerardo Machado took office.[25] Representatives from student and workers' organizations attended the founding meeting, as did José Wong, of the "delegation from the Chinese Nationalist Party, the Kuomintang," who presented a statement on British and Japanese colonialism in China.[26] José Wong (Wong Tao-Bai or Huang Tao-Bai) arrived in Cuba from China in the 1920s and was among many Chinese Cubans involved in the Cuban branch of the Chinese Nationalist Party, which at that time had formed a coalition with the Chinese Communist Party.[27] Wong was eventually executed by the Machado regime in 1930, becoming "Cuba's best known Chinese revolutionary martyr."[28]

LADLA-Cuba's founding group wrote a manifesto explaining the need for the organization and delineating its future projects. The manifesto, published in several Cuban periodicals as well as in *El Libertador* (August 1925), framed LADLA-Cuba's struggle not within the ideology of communism but as a continuation of Cuba's independence struggles.[29] However, even as the manifesto relied on a longer history of Cuban anti-colonial organizing, it stated that LADLA-Cuba's creation was not motivated by nationalism. It pointed to the Kuomintang representative as evidence of LADLA-Cuba's internationalist vision and asserted that it aimed to join with anti-imperialist struggles around the world, including within the United States.[30]

At LADLA-Cuba's July 1925 meeting, Venezuelan activist Salvador de la Plaza presided and Mella was named "organizing secretary."[31] Soon after, LADLA-Cuba began planning its Great International Anti-Imperialist Rally to take place in August 1925.[32] Mella reached out to various organizations to invite them to join. In a letter to an unnamed Afro-Cuban organization, Mella acknowledged that despite the Cuban government's Martí-inspired rhetoric of "with all for all," "the reality is very different" for Black Cubans, "who do not have the same rights as the white man."[33] He encouraged the group to attend the rally and to join LADLA-Cuba, which he argued would fight on behalf of Black Cubans.[34]

At the rally, attendees ratified statements of solidarity with striking workers in Guantánamo and against the regimes of Juan Vicente Gómez in Venezuela, Augusto B. Leguía in Peru, and Bautista Saavedra Mallea in Bolivia. The Cuban section followed LADLA's general platform in calling for the "withdrawal of all US troops from Latin American soil and from the colonies of the Pacific," including in Haiti, the Dominican Republic, and Nicaragua; the independence of Puerto Rico and the Philippines; abrogation of the Platt Amendment; internationalization of the Panama Canal; nationalization of natural resources and basic industries; and repudiation of the Monroe Doctrine. It specifically called for "restrictive action in Latin America against the tendencies toward imperialistic monopoly" of companies like National City Bank, J. P. Morgan and Co., Standard Oil, United Fruit, Firestone Rubber, and others. This platform did not focus exclusively on Latin America, also demanding an end to the privileges of diplomatic immunity enjoyed by foreign governments in Africa and Asia, advocating for "the complete abolition of economic, political, and social discrimination against the Negroes in the United States," and calling for "solidarity with the struggles of the oppressed peoples in all parts of the world (China, India, Syria, Egypt, etc.)."[35]

While not explicitly advertised as LADLA-Cuba's periodical, *Venezuela Libre: Órgano Revolucionario Latinoamericano* (Free Venezuela: Revolutionary Latin American organ), established four years prior in protest of Gómez, functioned in this capacity in the early years.[36] LADLA-Cuba's headquarters shared the same street address as the *Venezuela Libre* editorial department and printing press, and LADLA-Cuba member José Zacarías Tallet worked as *Venezuela Libre*'s managing director.[37] The publication's title referenced the Venezuelans who sought political exile in Cuba prior to Gerardo Machado's election.[38] Two of them, Gustavo Machado and Salvador de la Plaza, would eventually leave for Mexico City, where they joined LADLA's Continental Committee.[39] *Venezuela Libre* published statements from LADLA headquarters in Mexico City, and LADLA-Cuba members frequently published in its pages.[40]

During Mella's 1925 imprisonment, he published an essay in *Venezuela Libre* written from jail. This essay called for the founding of an "American International" and discussed LADLA.[41] LADLA-Cuba's executive committee also released a statement declaring that Mella's imprisonment would not diminish its actions since "this institution, beyond making up thousands of supporters in this Republic, is continental. Our alarm sets in motion the proletariat and the conscious youth in all of America and joined to our voice of protest are those of twenty republics, vigilant guardians of their sovereignty."[42] Repression of LADLA-Cuba's leaders, the statement claimed, would not negatively impact the widespread dissemination of the organization's message since it belonged to LADLA's broader, continental network.

When Mella left for Mexico in January 1926 along with Salvador de la Plaza, Cuban activist Jorge Vivó replaced Mella as LADLA-Cuba's organizing secretary and Venezuelan expat Gustavo Machado became its "secretary of the exterior."[43] However, Machado would also soon leave Cuba for Mexico City. A few months later, in October 1926, Cuban writer and activist Rubén Martínez Villena reorganized LADLA-Cuba under his leadership and called a meeting of LADLA-Cuba with the UP to discuss preparations for representation at the 1927 Brussels Congress.[44] In April 1927, under Villena's directorship, *Venezuela Libre*, which had ceased publication, was revived under the new name *América Libre: Revista Revolucionaria Americana* (Free America: American revolutionary magazine).[45] Its first issue explained that the earlier *Venezuela Libre*, "despite its name, never reduced its interests nor its actions to one single country" and similarly intended to "fight in America for the liberation of its people and against capitalist imperialism" and express its "continental American" intentions.[46] The name change represented an attempt to simply "call things by their name."[47] Likely due to the threat of political persecution, *América Libre* did not explicitly state its affiliation to LADLA-Cuba. However, from its inception, *América Libre* published articles on the Brussels Congress, and it included advertisements for *El Libertador*, articles by Rivera and Mella, and statements from LADLA's Continental Committee and Colombian section.[48]

Collaborators on *América Libre* included the artist Eduardo Abela, who provided illustrations, and notable activists Sarah Pascual and Raúl Roa García, among others.[49] However, *América Libre* was short-lived. Villena was hospitalized with a lung infection in June 1927, and the following month, Machado outlawed the publication. Villena edited its fourth and final issue from his hospital bed.[50] After that point, it is unclear whether Villena continued to organize LADLA-Cuba activities underground. In April 1930, Villena left Cuba for the Soviet Union, where he worked closely with both Sandalio Junco and Tina Modotti.[51]

According to a September 1933 statement by LADLA-Cuba, José Zacarías Tallet, one of the original founders, reorganized it illicitly in 1930, and for three years the organization continued to coordinate protests and propaganda.[52] After the collapse of the Machado government in August 1933, LADLA-Cuba returned to legality, and Cuban intellectual Juan Marinello took on its leadership. The newly reconstituted LADLA-Cuba announced that it had "entered a stage of maximum activity," organizing in September 1933 both a demonstration in Havana's Central Park against foreign intervention and a United Front Against Imperialism Conference in Havana's National Theater.[53] It began publishing its new journal, *Masas*, in May 1934. For the first time, the masthead officially listed the journal as the monthly magazine of the "Cuban Anti-Imperialist League."[54]

The platform of the new LADLA-Cuba shared many similarities with its previous iteration. However, this time, it took a much stronger stance against anti-Black racism, critiquing the exclusion of Black workers in foreign-owned industries and stating its opposition to notions of racial inferiority used to exploit Black workers.[55] Most issues of *Masas* contained at least one article about the Negro Question or about Black self-determination. Many of these articles were authored anonymously, but they were likely written by Dr. Martín Castellanos, discussed at the beginning of this chapter. Some articles argued that Cuba's Oriente province constituted a Black nation since Afro-Cuban culture continued to define this region despite anti-Black repression. Other articles critiqued anti-Black and anti-immigrant racism in Cuba's 50 Percent Law under the administration of President Ramón Grau San Martín.

These articles appeared in a particular context in which, as discussed in chapter 3, a boom in the sugar industry, driven by rising prices during World War I, attracted immigrants from throughout the Caribbean to work in Cuba. Between 1917 and 1931, three hundred thousand Haitians, Jamaicans, and other Caribbean laborers arrived in Cuba.[56] The importation of Chinese labor into Cuba, which had ended in 1874, was reinitiated at this time, doubling Cuba's Chinese population between 1919 and 1931.[57] In the 1920s, the economic crisis that became the Great Depression deeply impacted sugar prices, placing immigrant workers in an especially vulnerable position. Since the recruitment of Haitian and West Indian immigrants was tied to the US sugar industry, a nativist and anti-imperialist discourse arose in Cuba that was often expressed through anti-blackness and especially through anti-Haitianism. As Alejandro de la Fuente writes, the employment practices of the sugar companies fomented this nativism through promoting "open hostility through a policy of ethnically based distribution of employment . . . as well as by using foreign labor to break native workers' resistance or vice versa."[58] These companies often used Chinese contract labor to end workers' strikes. Anti-immigrant nativism in 1920s–30s Cuba, which sometimes erupted in violence, was also directed toward Chinese immigrants.[59]

The repatriation of immigrant workers, which began under Machado, culminated in the "1934 Nationalization of Labor Decree that mandated that 50 percent of all employees in industry, commerce, and agriculture have Cuban nationality," passed under President Ramón Grau San Martín's "Cuba for the Cubans" policies.[60] This 50 Percent Law attempted to respond to discontent among Cuban workers regarding the importation of Jamaican and Haitian agricultural workers, the common practice in the tobacco industry of choosing Spaniards over Cubans as apprentices, and the predominance of Spaniards and Chinese in commerce. Although the PCC and LADLA-Cuba strongly opposed the 50 Percent Law, this nativist policy found significant support among the unemployed and working poor, including many Afro-Cubans.[61]

From as early as December 1925, LADLA-Cuba maintained that "Cuba should be for the Cubans," but it made clear that "this does not mean hatred of the foreigner; it means hatred of foreign capital."[62] In its later iteration, LADLA-Cuba's *Masas* articulated strong opposition to the 50 Percent Law and argued for the support of all Black workers, regardless of citizenship. It critiqued protectionist positions as misguided and argued for complete economic overhaul, stating that "only with the total fall of the colonial economic regime can Black people find equality and the right to work."[63]

LADLA-Cuba and the PCC understood the importance of organizing with immigrant labor—especially field workers in the sugar industry—for the success of the larger labor movement. To do so, however, they would have to challenge "the narrow nationalism which encouraged blaming immigrants for widespread unemployment and other economic problems."[64] According to De la Fuente, to create a unified labor movement of native and immigrant workers, the workers' movement "had to forge a new, cross-national identity based on what they had in common: class."[65] The "nonracialized class identity" that was forged during this period would form the basis for the eventual "emergence of class as the most important point of reference in Cuban politics."[66]

The articles on the Negro Question that appeared in *Masas* largely align with De la Fuente's analysis since these articles demonstrate that LADLA-Cuba echoed the PCC's "nonracialized class" discourse. Whereas resonances of Junco's 1929 discussion of the Negro Question can be found in LADLA-Cuba's strong support of Black immigrants, Junco's analysis of the relationship between race and class exploitation seems to have been abandoned by LADLA-Cuba after his PCC expulsion. In his 1929 intervention, Junco had discussed not only Black immigrant populations but also Chinese immigrant communities. Although LADLA-Cuba was highly attentive to Black immigrant communities, it tended to overlook discrimination faced by Chinese.[67]

Despite this, the Afro-Chinese-Cuban poet Regino Pedroso, who began his involvement with LADLA-Cuba in 1930 and was listed on the masthead of *Masas* as a core part of its editorial team, would revive and expand some of Junco's contributions.[68] Pedroso was one of several poets published in *Masas*.[69] He had a sustained collaboration with LADLA-Cuba, which would have influenced his worldview in the mid-1930s. The remainder of this chapter reads some of Pedroso's social poetry, including poems published in *Masas* as well as his best-known work, *Nosotros*, within the framework of LADLA-Cuba's political platform. I examine how Pedroso incorporated many of the organization's positions into his poetry, including its critique of anti-Black and anti-immigrant racism. However, I also argue that Pedroso's poetry recuperated some of Junco's 1929 interventions, including a more integrated analysis of differentiated experiences of oppression, as well as a more pointed focus on Chinese immigrant workers. In Pedroso's poetry, we see resonances not only of Junco's positions but also of LADLA's hemispheric globalism as well as its ideological and aesthetic vision for a political community emerging out of a transnational extractive zone. Framing Pedroso as a political thinker reveals how his work provides an alternative perspective, within Cuba's 1930s radical Left, to the PCC's class-over-race discourse. Pedroso's work challenges the dominant "non-racialized class identity" that emerged from 1930s Cuban communism and that continues to predominate in Cuba today.[70]

PEDROSO'S RELATIONAL POETICS IN LADLA-CUBA'S *MASAS*

"Zafra-1934" (Sugarcane Harvest–1934) (figures 4.1 and 4.2), published for the first time in the June 1934 issue of *Masas*, is one of Pedroso's lesser-known poems. It appeared almost one year after Machado's ouster and addresses how the business of the sugar economy continues in the post-Machado era. This poem directly incorporates many of LADLA's core political positions.

The first stanza opens with a reference to the political unrest immediately following Machado's ouster: "September has passed. / And in Wall Street it is said: / There must be a harvest in Cuba!"[71] By including the date "1934" in the title and opening with a reference to "September," which "has passed," the poetic voice situates the poem in a specific historical moment. It directly alludes to the Sergeants' Revolt of September 1933, a coup led by Fulgencio Batista that overthrew the provisional government of Carlos Manuel de Céspedes y Quesada and replaced it with a five-man coalition, the Pentarchy of 1933. That coalition named Batista as head of the armed forces and formed a new government, declaring one of the Pentarchy's members, Ramón Grau San Martín, as president. Grau San Martín held the presidency until January 1934, when Batista forced him to resign and Carlos Mendieta replaced him. The first stanza suggests that after all that has occurred, Wall Street wants to proceed with business as usual in Cuba, just under a new government: "Enough of revolutionary agitation. / There must be a sugar harvest in Cuba!"

ZAFRA · 1934

■

HA pasado Septiembre.
Y en Wall Street se dice:
  "Hay que hacer zafra en Cuba!...
¿$2.000,000 de toneladas? 2.200,000?...
¿Qué cuota le impondremos a la india antillana?...
Basta ya de agitación revolucionaria.
¡Hay que hacer zafra en Cuba!"

Poco después transmite el cable:
"Embarcará hacia Cuba Mr. Caffery"
Días más tarde informan los periódicos:
"El enviado personal de Roosevelt ha llegado a la Habana".

Visitas. Comidas. Teje y desteje de entrevistas.
Declaraciones públicas:
"Cuba es Libre". "Ayudaremos a Cuba",
"La zafra es la riqueza de Cuba",
Comentan los salones aristocráticos:
"Mr. Caffery es un perfecto gentleman".
Y las masas oprimidas también comentan:
"Mr. Caffery pasea con Batista."
"Mr. Caffery almorzó con Batista."

Boca mordaz, sardónica, de sonrisa felina;
manos audaces de gangster diplomático;
cabellera de humo y de sol de invierno;
nariz corva y violenta de halcón,
ojos duros de acero;
fotografía en las revistas.
(Una intención que la gente no capta, pero apresan las masas:
HAY QUE HACER ZAFRA EN CUBA!)
¡La zafra! ¡La zafra!

Columbia dijo un día: ¡Machado!
Columbia clamó ayer: ¡Céspedes!
Columbia lanzó luego: ¡La Junta!
También gritó Columbia: ¡Grau San Martín!
Y Batista ordena ahora: ¡Mendieta! ¡Mendieta!

¡Hay que hacer zafra en Cuba!
¡La zafra! ¡La zafra!

La burguesía pide: orden, orden.
El A.B.C. pretende fascistamente: el poder.

Los caudillos políticos gritan: la patria, la patria.
Y las masas obreras: ¡Hambre! ¡Hambre! ¡Hambre!

¡La zafra! ¡La zafra!

¡Hay que hacer zafra en Cuba!
Ciudades populosas al sol del trópico;
Cielo de pórfido, mar de esmeralda;
Harlems criollo de los solares;
bars, burdeles, casinos;
llamas carnales
mujeres embriagantes como cocteles;
negros, canciones, mercados, bongoses, maracas...
Y en nuestras calles y hasta lo rojo de nuestra entraña:
The Royal Bank,
National City Bank,
Standard Oil Company;
First National Bank,
Electric Bond y Share Company;
Chase National Bank,
Cuban Telephone Company...
(¡Hay que hacer zafra en Cuba!)

Noche del trópico. Cielo azul, estrellado.
Aire suave, gorgear de pájaros, rumor de selvas;
tierra de llama pródiga reventando semillas;
sumergibles anfibios
surcan los ríos los caimanes;
las ceibas abren al cielo sus brazos amorosos.
Y en los bateyes y plantaciones:
—Compañeros, oprimidos, explotados...!
—Tac-tac... gime un haitiano.
—Tac-tac... tiembla un criollo.
Noche de ron, de rumbas y canciones guajiras.
Noche que el arte apresa rica de ritmo y de color.
Brisa olorosa a pulpa de mango y de piña.

—Tac-tac... tac-tac...
Sólo dolor de carne sobre el mundo,
nacido de la noche y del color de la noche,
sin patria, sin nombre, sin raza,
ahora ha caído un hombre!
—Tac-tac... tac-tac...

4.1–4.2 Regino Pedroso, "Zafra-1934," *Masas* (June 1934). Courtesy of Biblioteca Nacional de Cuba José Martí.

Noche azul de palmares y cocoteros;
noche del trópico fragante y cálida!
Selvas sin tigres, sin elefantes ni hipopótamos.
Pero se caza bajo la luna...
Agua fuerte del sur de Africa.

¡La zafra! ¡La zafra!
¡Hay que hacer zafra en Cuba!

Mediodía de sol.
En atlánticos de cañaverales un naufragio de gritos...
Reverberar de tierras y músculos.
Torsos curvados sobre las cepas;
brazos desnudos surcan el aire;
cantan las mochas cortando el fruto:
cham... cham... cham...
Con fatiga y esfuerzo las pilas crecen, crecen...
100... 300 arrobas... 500...
Cham... cham... cham...
Cantos cansados,
cantos que evocan tribus esclavas.
Se incendia el cielo, se incendia el viento y la sangre.
Llueve sudor sobre los surcos.
Y ante los hombres, caña; sobre los hombres, caña; sobre la vida,
(caña.

¡La zafra! ¡La zafra!

Tardes vencidas.
Verde cansancio de platanales.
Caravanas de hambrientos por los caminos;
mujeres harapientas sin pan, sin leche;
niños terrosos de paludismo...
Y el horizonte, caña; sobre la tierra, caña; bajo los cielos, caña.

¡La zafra! ¡La zafra!

—¡Más salario! ¡Nos morimos de Hambre!
(Decreto Ley No. 3.)
¡Hay que hacer zafra en Cuba!
—¡Abajo la reacción! ¡Abajo el fascismo!
(Ley de Defensa de la República.)
¡La zafra! ¡La zafra!

—Compañeros: Contra los Trusts!
¡Contra el Terror y el Hambre!
¡Contra la explotación! ¡Campesinos y Obreros...!
Luchas de masas campesinas. Huelgas, huelgas...
(Preston. Santa Lucía. Daiquirí. Báguanos. Tacajó. .)
Cuban Cane Company,
Chaparra Sugar Company,
United Fruit Company,
Antilla Sugar Company...
—¡Mueran los Latifundios! ¡Abajo el Imperialismo!
¡Pan y Libertad! ¡La Tierra! ¡La Tierra!...
Comunistas, comunistas...
Barcos de guerra Yankis, trenes de tropa...
Masacres, masacres, masacres...
Molienda de carne obrera con springfields.

¡La zafra! ¡La zafra!
¡Hay que hacer zafra en Cuba!

Colombia bananera; México petrolero.
Haití. Santo Domingo. Nicaragua. Panamá. Salvador.
—¡América oprimida y proletaria!—
¿Cómo son vuestras zafras?...
En nuestros campos:
continentes de cañaverales bajo oleadas de sol;
guardarrayas inmensas donde el rifle florece
rosas de plomo que cantan en las noches;
bocas de cementerio los surcos se abren largos, largos...
Carretas, bueyes cansados, campesinos, barracones y cárceles.
Grandes ingenios. Turbinas. Hornos gigantes. Tándems enormes.
Chimeneas que elevan sus protestas de llamas al cielo...
Masas férreas que muelen, muelen, muelen pueblos de caña
y vidas de hombres;
la miel dorada y dulce corre a torrentes por los canales;
cantan los músculos, ruedan millones, y corre la sangre;
el sudor proletario cristaliza en los tachos en granos de oro;
y en nuestros puertos,
en monstruos racacielos de los mares,
para los amos imperialistas,
embarques, embarques, embarques...

¡La zafra! ¡La zafra!
Caña, caña... ¡Hambre!
Caña, caña... ¡Sangre!

La Habana, 1934.

REGINO PEDROSO

The stanza that follows alludes to the 1934 arrival of the new US ambassador, Jefferson Thomas Caffery, his meetings with Batista, and his friendliness toward the new regime. Through descriptions of his appearance, the poem characterizes Caffery as a conniving criminal, with his "feline smile," "steely eyes," and "bold hands of a diplomatic gangster." "The masses catch" Caffery's true intentions: "THERE MUST BE A SUGAR HARVEST IN CUBA!" If the US government "said one day: Machado!," it supported "yesterday" the provisional government of Carlos Manuel de Céspedes y Quesada, then the "junta" or Sergeants' Revolt, then Grau San Martín, and now Mendieta.[72] The poem then repeats the refrain, "There must be a sugar harvest in Cuba!," suggesting that the US government remains unconcerned about what kind of government leads Cuba as long as the sugar harvest proceeds.

The refrain "There must be a sugar harvest in Cuba" resonates closely with LADLA-Cuba's political discourse during the Machado years. Consider its November 1925 call to action: "Wall Street needs for there to be a sugar harvest in Cuba. The life of Cuba depends exclusively on the sugar harvest. Cuban farmers cannot survive if there is not a sugar harvest. President Machado has promised Wall Street that there will be a sugar harvest in Cuba."[73] This call to action explains that the *colonos* (small landowners and sugar farmers) do not want to grind their sugarcane, because the current price of sugar does not cover production costs. Machado, however, is attempting to violently force the *colonos* and their workers to proceed with the "suicide sugar harvest" so that Wall Street can make a profit.[74] The document ends with an invitation to the reader to join LADLA-Cuba's efforts to fight both Machado and Wall Street. With the refrain "there must be a sugar harvest in Cuba," Pedroso's "Zafra-1934" relies on similar rhetoric from the earlier Machado era to point to Batista's continued cooperation with the interests of US capital. In both Pedroso's poem and LADLA-Cuba's call to action, the insistent repetition of references to the "sugar harvest" underlines a political system that revolves around a sugar monoculture economy that ultimately serves the industry's foreign investors rather than the Cuban majority.

The poem proceeds by naming the various winners in this monoculture economy: "The Royal Bank / National City Bank / Standard Oil Company / First National Bank / Electric Bond and Share Company / Chase National Bank / Cuban Telephone Company." They all cry in unison, "There must be a sugar harvest in Cuba!" The poem juxtaposes these companies, situated in urban centers, and their obsession with the sugar harvest with a counterimage of tropical biodiversity: "buzzing of jungles; / land of lavish flame bursting seeds; / submarine amphibians / alligators sail through the rivers; / ceibas open their loving arms to the sky." Through a proliferation of signifiers, the poem describes with ecstasy a landscape characterized by multiplicity that serves as a counterpoint to monocrop plantation economies that reduce biodiverse regions to a singular capitalist commodity. This tropical extractive economy, the poem suggests, occurs not just in Cuba but in tropical zones in Africa as well.

The poem then draws a connection between the landscape and the people working in the "sugar refineries and plantations," who are described not as workers but with the more affective and politically strident terms "comrades, oppressed, exploited." The workers become metonymically merged with the cane such that the act of cutting cane simultaneously refers to a cutting, or violence, enacted on the workers' bodies. The poem repeats the onomatopoeic sound of cutting sugarcane, "tac . . . tac," but suggests that this sound refers to a Haitian worker's groans and the trembling of a "criollo" (native-born) worker. The poem then expands its focus on these individuals' suffering, using the "tac . . . tac" sound of cutting cane to signal the "pain of flesh over the world / born of the night and of the color of night/ without nation, without a name, without race."[75] "Tac . . . tac" communicates the painful groans not only of cane workers in Cuba but also of a global mass of workers whom the poem describes as dark-skinned ("the color of night") and existing outside clearly defined national or racial categories. In the stanza that immediately follows, the poem repeats its previous description of tropical biodiversity, thus creating a parallel between biodiversity and an ethno-racially diverse mass of workers that would represent a more humane and ecologically sound society compared to monoculture and extractive capital.

The poem builds on the opposition between extractive companies and workers to draw out the dissonance between the repeated compulsory call to harvest and the oppressiveness of a sugarcane society. The repetition of the word *sugarcane* in the verses "and before the men, sugarcane; / over the men, sugarcane; / over life, / sugarcane" creates a monotony in which the fullness and diversity of life are reduced to the cycles of the sugar industry that exist "over" humanity and all of life itself. This verse is immediately followed by the repeating refrain "The sugar harvest! The sugar harvest!," an abbreviated version of Wall Street's call "There must be a sugar harvest in Cuba!" from the first stanza.

These two oppositional perspectives, the oppressiveness of the monoculture economy and the frenzy of the harvest, become a call-and-response between the leaders of the sugar industry and protesting workers. The workers call out, "Higher salary! We are dying of hunger!" and the response they receive is simply, "There must be a sugar harvest in Cuba!" They call for "struggles of peasant masses. Strikes, strikes . . . ," and the response to these struggles is imperialist violence: "Yankee warships, military trains . . . / Massacres, massacres, massacres."

Whereas the poetic voice alludes to a geography beyond Cuba at other points in the poem, even referencing sugarcane workers around the world, in the second-to-last stanza the poem explicitly diverges from its focus on the sugar industry to reflect on extractive industries in other Latin American countries: "Banana-producing Colombia; oil-producing Mexico / Haiti. Santo Domingo. Nicaragua. Panama. Salvador /—Oppressed and proletarian America!—How are your harvests?" It then describes "continents of sugar plantations," "large mills," "gigantic kilns," and "enormous tandem mills." Just as sugarcane came to represent the entirety of life in earlier verses, here the continent, through synecdoche, is represented as a massive sugar mill that grinds "peoples of sugarcane / and lives of men." It turns their blood to caramel, and their "proletarian sweat crystalizes" into "grains of gold" and "monstrous skyscrapers in the seas,/ for the imperialist masters."[76]

The illustration (figures 4.1 and 4.2) by José Manuel Acosta that accompanies Pedroso's poem depicts this image of exploitation. At the bottom of the second page, a gigantic mill grinds the bodies of Black and white laborers (in sleeveless shirts), who are being driven into the mill at gunpoint by machine guns on tripods, manned by abstract figures. At the top of the first page, a tripartite image depicts smoke rising from the plantation mill, which spawns a columned plantation home (which could also be a reference to the US White House) that appears on the same visual plane with large urban buildings. Beneath the plantation home, men in suits line up to clean the boots of a large, seated man, as if prostate before a god.

The image communicates succinctly the anti-extractive argument of Pedroso's "Zafra-1934," and the poem aligns explicitly with LADLA's hemispheric approach to monoculture and extractive industries. Whereas the poem stands mostly as a condemnation of this system, it also suggests the potential for a new political community in its continental, and at times global, vision of "comrades, oppressed, exploited" calling for a future beyond the sugar economy.[77] Such a vision based in the networks of exploited peoples across a transnational extractive zone appears more explicitly in Pedroso's book-length work *Nosotros*, published the year before. In this book, Pedroso similarly engages LADLA's vision for political community forged out of extractive economies; however, he does so largely through incorporating Junco's relational solidarities with Black immigrant and Chinese labor.

However, before discussing *Nosotros*, I turn to another of Pedroso's poems, "Hermano negro" ("Negro Brother"), which also first appeared in *Masas*.[78] This poem, one of Pedroso's most famous and which has been translated into several languages, has been read within the context of Black communism and as a "call for an Afro-Diasporic movement against imperialism."[79] My analysis builds on these readings by considering "Hermano negro" within the immediate political dialogues in which Pedroso and LADLA-Cuba were engaged at the time of its publication. "Hermano negro" appeared in the last issue of *Masas* (January 10, 1935), the issue that led to the editorial team's imprisonment, alongside a poem by Ramón Guirao called "Imperialismo yanqui" (Yankee imperialism). "Hermano negro" uses the connection between subjects as its central focal point. Through apostrophe, the poem's first stanza begins by establishing mutuality between the poetic voice and the "negro brother" to whom the poem is addressed. Through claiming that "you are in me . . . I am in you . . . Your voice is in my voice . . . Also I am of your race," the two subjects become nearly indistinguishable.[80] From the outset, the poem frames the critique that it will deliver not as an admonishment to a distanced other but as a self-critique articulated from within brotherhood. As I will argue, the poem builds on this initial relationship established between the poetic voice and the interpellated subject in order to stimulate antiracist solidarity throughout the hemisphere and eventually the globe.

Similar to "Zafra-1934," the poem presents uncultivated nature as a space of freedom ("You were free around the land, / like the beasts, like the trees") that contrasts with the system of plantation slavery ("Yet when you became a slave; / feeling the whip").[81] It draws parallels between the history of slavery and a present-day plantation system in which "they trade with your sweat / they trade with your pain."[82] In an indictment of Enlightenment-era notions of civilization and humanism—created in interdependent contrast to the social construction of the enslaved—Pedroso describes how all aspects of Black life have been predetermined as barbaric: "Do you love sometimes? / Ah, if you love, your flesh is barbarous! / Do you shout sometimes? / Ah, if you shout, your voice is barbarous! / Do you live sometimes? / Ah, if you live, your race is barbarous!"[83] Here, Pedroso anticipates later interventions by Black political theorists like Frantz Fanon on the ways that the white gaze fixes Black subjects into social constructions of blackness, what Fanon calls the "myth of the Negro," which is imbued with white imaginaries of savagery and barbarity.[84]

The poem then asks a rhetorical question similar to Martín Castellanos's question in *Masas* in which he asked, "Does the oppression of the Negro respond to the color of his skin or the curl of his hair?" and answered, "Clearly anyone can see that it does not."[85] Pedroso's poem asks a similar question about the predetermined stigmatization of Black life: "And it is only for your skin? / It is all for your color?"[86] Whereas Martín Castellanos claimed that this oppression was not based on race, the response of Pedroso's poem to this question is more nuanced and reflective of the positions expressed by Junco. The poem responds with, "It is not only for color; more because you are, / beneath the bigotry of race, an exploited man."[87] Here, the poem acknowledges what Junco described as Black people's "doubly exploited condition, as a race and as a class."[88]

The poem characterizes blackness through a shared experience of exploitation: "Negro more for hunger than for race!"[89] It pleads with the "negro brother," which is also a message to the poetic voice himself, to refrain from participating in ways that "the rich make of you a game," referring to how white elites enjoy Black cultural forms while denying Black people their basic rights ("There are men that pay your laughter with hunger").[90] This moment of the poem has been interpreted as a direct critique of the *afrocubanismo* movement's "superficial approach to racial solidarity."[91] Instead of participating in surface-level celebrations of Black culture, the poetic voice commands the interpellated subject to "silence a little your maracas" and "soften a little your drum" in order to "learn here / and look there / and listen over there in Scottsboro, in Scottsboro, in Scottsboro."[92]

With the repetition of the word *Scottsboro*, Pedroso refers to the series of 1930s legal cases after nine Black teenagers were falsely accused of raping two white women aboard a train in Scottsboro, Alabama. The process was marred by injustice, such as all-white juries and rushed trials. International Labor Defense, the US Communist Party's legal wing, took up their defense. The so-called Scottsboro Boys case provoked international outcry and was covered extensively in left-wing publications around the world. Pedroso alludes to these cases as exemplars of the severe injustices faced by Black people. As Frank Andre Guridy writes, Pedroso's poem communicates that "what bound black communities together were not the Lindy Hop, the *son*, and the rumba, but rather the struggle against global racism."[93] Importantly, like Junco's position, the poem does not reference the Scottsboro case as a way of externalizing racial injustice to the United

States. Rather, Pedroso uses the case as an opening to describe discrimination faced by Black peoples throughout the hemisphere, including in Cuba, writing, "Negro in Haiti, Negro in Jamaica, Negro in New York, / Negro in Havana."[94] Through the repetition of "in Scottsboro, in Scottsboro, in Scottsboro," the poem claims that the injustice of Scottsboro is not a unique case but occurs repeatedly "here . . . there . . . and over there."[95]

By addressing the transnational nature of this oppression, the poem builds on the connection between the poetic voice and the poem's interpellated subject established in the first stanza and then expands that relationship outward, drawing links between Black peoples throughout the hemisphere. Notably, the poem specifically addresses conditions faced by Black Haitians and Jamaicans, who made up the majority of Cuba's immigrant worker population. With the phrase "more brother in longing than in race," the poem claims that a longing for justice represents the true brotherhood that supersedes biologically deterministic notions of race.[96] In line with the hemispheric globalism core to LADLA's vision, the poem then expands from this hemispheric brotherhood to the globe, commanding the subject to draw upon this shared suffering to call for revolution: "Give to the world, with your rebellious anguish / your human voice."[97]

Through Pedroso's "Hermano negro," Junco's interventions on the Negro Question continued to reverberate in *Masas*, despite Junco's marginalization from LADLA-Cuba at that point. In addition to aligning with LADLA's hemispheric globalism, the poem reflects Junco's analysis of Black people's doubly exploited condition as well as his discussion of Black immigrant labor. In his comments in 1929, Junco also called on his colleagues to devote more attention to the Chinese immigrant population. In *Nosotros*, Pedroso takes this call seriously, engaging more deeply with Junco's vision for relational solidarity politics with Black immigrant and Chinese labor.

RELATIONAL POETICS IN *NOSOTROS*

In the months leading up to Machado's 1933 ouster, a group of activists pooled the money to illegally publish Pedroso's first collection of poetry, *Nosotros* (Us), written from 1927 to 1933.[98] The original book's cover featured a drawing by Afro-Cuban artist José Cecilio Hernández Cárdenas, who trained in Mexico with Diego Rivera, of a red muscular torso turning an industrial blue wheel. The cover image apparently caused such consternation at the printing press that Pedroso was asked to remove the three hundred copies from the print shop before the ink had dried. To avoid police repression, the book jacket did not include the print shop's name and provided the address of an abandoned building for the publishing house.[99] In an interview, Pedroso said that during the 1933 general strike, *Nosotros* was considered "subversive and dangerous" and one could be put in jail for owning a copy.[100] Even so, the book was immediately celebrated in workers' and activists' circles. A review published in the February 1933 issue of *Cultura Proletaria* (Proletarian culture), a magazine put out by the Cuban commercial sector's workers' union, announced the coming of "our long-awaited proletarian poet" and euphorically described the reviewer's experience of reading the book on the bus on his way to work in a factory and later in the street, since these spaces represented "our reading salon."[101]

Pedroso dedicated *Nosotros* to "my exploited brothers," identifying thus the collective of the book's title.[102] The book begins with a unique "Auto-bio-prólogo" (Auto-bio-prologue) in which Pedroso proclaims, "I believe I have, more than any other, the right to introduce my book." Although Pedroso himself had never left the island, in his "Auto-bio-prólogo" the poetic voice presents himself to his audience through the metaphor of an international traveler, and specifically an immigrant worker, arriving at a border customs office, the "border of the public."[103] As Catherine Addington has suggested, Pedroso places the reader in the position of border officer, who searches his bag (the book, or "this luggage of pages") and who will decide whether or not the poet will be allowed to cross.[104] By placing the reading public in the role of border officer, Pedroso acknowledges from the outset that the reader will likely view him, an Afro-Chinese-Cuban working-class writer, with suspicion. However, by choosing to introduce himself, writing, "I come from the PROLETARIAT, and here I am with the future of this luggage of pages," he does not attempt to achieve acceptance as a poet through soliciting a prologue written by a more respected upper-class poet who would introduce him to established literary circles.[105] Instead, Pedroso addresses his reader's suspicion head-on, proclaiming "Here I am" unapologetically and acknowledging his marginalized status within the literary community.

The "Auto-bio-prólogo" is structured like a customs form in which the poetic voice both completes the form and calls into question the limitations of its categories. It lists name, age, place of birth, and profession, as well as more subjective categories like "ideology," "objective," and "self-critique."[106] By questioning and analyzing each category, Pedroso inverts the power dynamic between immigrant and border agent, who stand in for the poet of color and the reading public, pushing his readers to examine their own prejudices and expectations of who can write poetry. By turning the page, and thus allowing the poet to cross the border, the reader is invited into a stance of openness toward both the poetry and immigrant subject that the "Auto-bio-prólogo" invokes.

The "Auto-bio-prólogo" lists the poet's profession as "exploited" and describes his education not through degrees at elite universities but through "the workshops, the fields, the factories, and the sugar plantations." The poet as immigrant worker presents himself as representative of workers across a largely extractive economy. For place of birth, the poet defines himself as a globalist beyond national borders and writes that "within a narrow political geographic concept," he was born in Unión de Reyes, Matanzas, Cuba, "but I can say, more dialectically, that I have been born in the world."[107] For age, he states that although his political consciousness is a mere five years old, he was born "only by biological fate" in 1898, placing his birth in the year of the Spanish-American War and the beginning of the US imperial presence in Cuba (but two years after Pedroso's actual birth, in 1896).[108]

He describes his "race" as "human," calling attention to race as a social construct, with a "pigmentation" of "black-yellow (with no other mixture)."[109] In describing his "pigmentation" as "black-yellow (with no other mixture)," he diverges explicitly from the dominant discourse of *cubanía*, which envisions Cuban culture to be based in *mulataje*, or a mixture of European and African ancestry and culture. Through this statement, the poet also makes explicit that he is not among the Chinese in Cuba who have historically sought to identify with white Cubans.[110] Instead, as Debbie Lee writes, Pedroso "rejects any claim to European ancestry . . . His self-alienation from the body that originally alienated him frees him from the restraints, thus placing the power of self-definition in his own hands."[111]

The "Auto-bio-prólogo" characterizes his ideology first through national and regional geography as a "son of America; born in a country economically and politically enslaved to Yankee imperialism," then through his experience of racialization, "classified by traditional concepts of religion, philosophy, and bourgeois sciences, as an individual of inferior race—Ethiopian-Asian"; and finally through socioeconomic class, "belonging—proletarian—to the most oppressed and exploited class." Only then does he respond to the question of ideology, presenting his communist and anti-imperialist politics as an inevitable result of his identity and circumstances: "What could be my ideology with these three historical-geographic, ethnic and socioeconomic destinies? . . . That which comes from Marx, is synthe-sized in Lenin and today rises up to the world with the International of Justice."[112] Drawing from this ideology, he presents his book of poems as a new political poetics, "the new expression" that will provoke "fire in souls and a call in consciences." If such an expression is considered politics, he writes, "then we will have to admit . . . that a politics so conducted is also humanly aesthetic."[113]

Thus far, Pedroso's "Auto-bio-prólogo" has been interpreted within the framework of Cuban identity discourses. Yet, considering Pedroso's involvement in LADLA-Cuba, I think it equally productive to consider how his work engages LADLA's hemispheric globalism and anti-imperialist politics. Pedroso's choice to position the reader as a border agent and the poet as an immigrant worker should be understood not only as an attempt to address potential prejudices against an Afro-Chinese-Cuban working-class poet within literary circles but also, more specifically, as an attempt to address anti-immigrant prejudice among the radical Left most likely to read Nosotros.

By putting the communist-leaning reader of Nosotros into the position of a border agent who chooses to allow entry to the poet-immigrant worker, Pedroso speaks directly to his colleagues who hold nativist views. By pick-ing apart each category on the customs form, he opposes these views with a radically globalist, pro-immigrant, and antiracist position such that we might read his "Auto-bio-prólogo" as a poetic manifesto of LADLA's pol-itics. Additionally, through positioning the poet as an immigrant worker of partial African descent and describing his ideology as emerging simul-taneously from both his race and class position, the "Auto-bio-prólogo" resonates with Junco's 1929 interventions. It clearly aligns with Junco's emphasis on Black immigrant labor, integrated analysis of racial and class exploitation, and critique of anti-Black and anti-immigrant racism among working classes.

In 1929, Junco also drew attention to Chinese labor in Latin America and criticized his colleagues for not taking this population into account. Pedroso channels this critique as well, presenting the poet as an immigrant worker of Afro-Chinese ancestry. In a clear example of "self-orientalism," in which the poet employs an essentialist discourse to disrupt dominant notions of Cuban identity, the poetic voice critiques anti-Chinese racism among working classes through a tongue-in-cheek reference both to the Marxist position on religion and to anti-Chinese stereotypes, claiming that he does not carry "opium nor opportunism as contraband" in his baggage.[114]

In a way similar to Junco's positions, the "Auto-bio-prólogo" criticizes anti-immigrant, anti-Black, and anti-Chinese racism and calls for a radically open vision of political community, to which the title *Nosotros* alludes.

The engagement of Pedroso's "Auto-bio prólogo" with LADLA's political platform remains constant throughout much of *Nosotros*. For example, we find a parallel analysis of overlapping forms of colonialism in the poem "Los conquistadores" (The conquistadors), which links three waves of conquest in Latin America, from the Spanish to the British to US finance capital. LADLA's hemispheric globalism appears in this poem as well, connecting British expansion in Latin America to China, where the British ventured with their "dreadnought" battleships "as far as the ancient land of Li Tai Pei."[115]

The poem "Elegía de hierro" (Iron eulogy) parallels the anti-extractive discourse of "Zafra-1934." This poem, which depicts a worker who has been hired to replace someone who died from a work-related accident, contains an opening dedication to "one of the many that I have seen disappear ground up by the deaf gears of capitalist mechanization," an image similar to the sugar mill that grinds the bodies of workers in "Zafra-1934."[116] In one of his most famous poems, "Salutación fraterna a un taller mecánico" ("Fraternal Greetings to the Factory")—which Pedroso wrote while working on an electric motor in a train factory and which was translated into English by Langston Hughes and published in *New Masses*—the noisiness of a factory is described as a "temple of love . . . of faith, of burning idealism, and of communion of the races."[117] In this space, the workers speak of "Marx, of Kuo Ming Tang, of Lenin," and the poem uses the practice of metallurgy as a metaphor for the formation of a "collective soul . . . forged in the hatred of social injustices."[118]

Pedroso further develops this political vision in "Salutación a un camarada culí" (Salutation to a coolie comrade), which directly situates Chinese immigrant workers as foundational to this envisioned political collectivity. Similar to Pedroso's other works, this poem focuses on the connection between subjects. Through apostrophe and the framework of a *salutación* (salutation), the poetic voice interpellates a Chinese laborer. In its "salutation" to a "coolie," the poem references the approximately 125,000 Chinese laborers, known as *culíes* from the British term *coolies*, who arrived in Cuba to work in the sugar industry between 1847 and 1874. They came on eight-year contracts intended to substitute for the reduction in enslaved African labor.[119] Cuba, the last of the Spanish-American colonies to abolish slavery, had become the world's leading sugar producer by the mid-nineteenth century. As the African slave trade wound down in the Spanish colonies, ending with the last ships in 1865 and 1866, the importation of Chinese workers rose correspondingly. Of the Chinese immigrant workers who entered the Spanish colonies between 1865 and 1874, over half went to Cuba. The importation of coolies allowed for the continuation of Cuba's plantation-based economic structure.[120]

Those who were recruited, or "more accurately deceived or kidnapped," came from the southeastern agricultural provinces of Fujian and Guangdong.[121] Approximately one-fifth died during the 120-day journey before reaching their destination, and due to extremely harsh working conditions, many died prior to completing their contracts.[122] The trade ended in Cuba in 1874 due to an investigation into its inhumane conditions by Chinese imperial commissioner Ch'ên Lan-pin.[123] Those who survived and were not forced to sign new contracts often moved to cities to become artisans, cooks, butchers, gardeners, tailors, street vendors, and merchants, and Havana's Chinatown became among the most populous in the hemisphere.[124] These communities expanded through an estimated five thousand Chinese who arrived in Cuba from California and Mexico between 1860 and 1875.[125] In Cuba's wars of independence, as Junco mentioned in his comments in 1929, Chinese soldiers, or *chinos mambises*, actively participated in the independence struggle. Later, after World War I, Chinese labor immigration was reinitiated because of expansion in the sugar industry.

Despite the long-standing presence of Chinese Cubans, Cuban national identity in the 1930s was framed through *mulataje*, the mixture of African and European ancestry and culture, eliding its Chinese population and the influence of its culture. Several scholars have noted that "Salutación a un camarada culí," and the poems in *Nosotros* more generally, reframe this identity discourse to recognize Chinese Cubans and open a path for alternative articulations of Cubanness.[126] While I agree with this reading, I would also point out that the poem does not specifically name a Cuban geography and evokes a more continental Latin American experience, drawing attention to Chinese workers within Cuba but also beyond.

Extant criticism has also pointed out that "Salutación a un camarada culí" is one of several poems in *Nosotros* that contains overtly orientalist tropes. It makes multiple stereotypical references to opium consumption, Genghis Khan, and the worker's "ancestral instinct," and it describes Chinese workers' language as "exotic."[127] In her insightful analysis of this exoticism, Huei Lan Yen states that at the time of the book's publication, Pedroso had never been to China, had little memory of his father, and had obtained much of his knowledge of Chinese culture through reading.[128] Pedroso would have had some exposure to Cuba's Chinese community, and many scholars have challenged the notion that cultural ties are held only by second-generation immigrants with direct contact to native-born family members.[129] Despite this, several of Pedroso's poems, including "Conceptos del nuevo estudiante" (Concepts of the new student) and "El heredero" (The heir), associate "the Chinese past" with "a negative set of oppressive and passive traditions" to be overcome, which Ignacio López-Calvo reads as evidence of the poet's tendency toward internalized racism and self-hatred.[130] López-Calvo points to the rejection of Chinese philosophy as passive in "Salutación a un camarada culí," where the "present becomes the threshold to a bright future of freedom and hope offered, from the poet's perspective, by Cuba."[131] Alternatively, Yen maintains that even as the poem relies on these exoticizing tropes and Western representations of the Orient, it ultimately aims to disrupt dominant frameworks of Cuban identity.

Any close reader of Pedroso's work will find moments when the poet reifies racist stereotypes as well as moments when he subverts them. However, a nuanced analysis of Pedroso's work must consider his political context, specifically regarding anti-Chinese sentiment within the 1930s labor movement as well as the influence of Chinese nationalist and communist struggles within LADLA. Considering Pedroso's close involvement in LADLA-Cuba, I read "Salutación a un camarada culí" as a poem that— similar to Modotti's photography—draws connections between subjects, focusing on forging solidarities across transnational extractive economies.

The poem begins with an "exaltation" to the coolie comrade, who rises up "from the depths of the centuries" and "from long years of humiliation." Such exaltation of a Chinese immigrant worker in itself constitutes a political statement in 1930s Cuba. The poetic voice draws connections between himself and his comrade, mostly through a shared Chinese ancestry: "I am from your same race yellow man." He imagines a shared past for them, which he characterizes in stereotypical but explicitly class-based terms: "Perhaps / we had the same Mandarin grandfathers / venal and sickly . . . or maybe, happier, they were farmers rice planters."[132] Beyond this imagined shared ancestry, the link between them is also ideological: "We are doubly bound together by the ties / of lineage and the new ideological unrest."[133] This shared "ideological unrest" has been read as a celebration of coolies' participation in the Cuban national struggle.[134] However, we may also read it as an allusion to Chinese communism and anti-imperialism (indicated in the use of "comrade" in the title) and thus as a challenge to anti-Chinese sentiment within workers' movements.

After the Chinese Nationalist Party consolidated power in 1927 and began purging communists, leftist Chinese in the Americas formed separate Marxist political groups, and in Cuba former left-wing Chinese Nationalist Party members found refuge in the PCC.[135] Reading "ideological unrest" as a shared commitment to political ideas more clearly explains the stanza that follows, in which the poetic voice claims that the coolie has "awakened . . . what is in me of Asia," previously repressed, because "I was numbed by pan-Americanism and Hispano-Americanism."[136] López-Calvo interprets this reference to pan-Americanism and Hispano-Americanism as follows: "According to the poetic voice, meeting the coolie comrade has awakened in him an awareness of his Asian heritage, which had been dormant because of his yearning to bring together all Hispanic peoples in the Americas."[137] Yet, considering LADLA's overt critique of the regionalist positions of pan-Americanism and Hispano-Americanism, discussed in chapter 2, this context provides a more informed reading of this line of the poem as a rejection of ideological regionalism in favor of LADLA's connections to the hemisphere and to colonial contexts in Asia and Africa. Indeed, the verses that immediately follow draw links to Asia and Africa, calling them "two great humiliated, defeated continents."

Even as the poem compares disparate contexts, it also acknowledges differences: "My destiny is sadder than yours" because "from the Rio Grande to the Tierra del Fuego—continental homeland—is also destroyed by imperialism."[138] The poetic voice claims belonging to a "continental homeland" whose experiences both differ from and draw near to African and Asian contexts. The Chinese example of political struggle, the poem suggests, serves as inspiration, and despite European and Japanese threats of colonial occupation, Chinese communists will continue to fight for liberation. They will help stimulate revolutionaries on the American continent: "I will hear in your ideology . . . the frenetic motor of our era / Until arrives . . . the ship of the new American Revolution." Whereas the poem contains a simplistic rejection of the "traditional moorings" of China's past, I argue that the celebrated present that "becomes the threshold to a bright future of freedom and hope" is not necessarily provided by the Cuban example.[139] Rather, the poem presents Cuba and the entire American continent as looking to China as the motor of future liberation.[140] Reading this poem in the context of Pedroso's close involvement in LADLA-Cuba yields a more complex interpretation. Even as we recognize the poem's tendency toward orientalism, we should also recognize that the poem attempts to undermine anti-Chinese racism among Latin American workers and presents Chinese communists as a model for Latin American revolutionaries to follow.

With these readings, I do not intend to overdetermine Pedroso's poetry, and I recognize that writers are shaped by multiple influences. However, I also find it productive to understand Pedroso's poetics within the context of his immediate political commitments. Reading his work alongside LADLA-Cuba's political platform not only results in more nuanced analyses of his poetry but also reveals how Junco's 1929 interventions continued to influence some Cuban radicals in the years after his expulsion from the PCC. Pedroso draws on Junco's understanding of the doubly exploited condition of Black workers through race and class and engages his vision for relational solidarity politics that is attentive to the unique conditions of Black and Chinese immigrant labor.

PEDROSO'S LEGACY AND CUBAN RACIAL POLITICS

Communist organizing in 1930s Cuba has had long-term implications both on the island and around the globe. As De la Fuente has argued, the fact that workers were "able to organize cross-racial and multinational unions in Cuba is nothing short of remarkable. No other country in Latin America had received so many immigrants of different ethnic and geographical origin at the same time." Employers in Cuba divided "the labor market along ethnic lines" and "blamed immigrants for the destitution of Cuban workers." In response, communists worked to create a unified labor movement of native and foreign workers that led to the forging of a "nonracialized class identity" during this period that would form the basis for the primacy of class in Cuba today.[141]

Although I agree with De la Fuente's analysis of the PCC's formation of a class-based struggle, the examples of Pedroso and Junco suggest a broader diversity of thought among 1930s Cuban Marxists. Pedroso and Junco offer alternative perspectives that recognize differentiated experiences of race and class exploitation, particularly for Black and Chinese immigrant communities. Pedroso's poetics draw connections while recognizing a diversity of experiences. The fact that this vision emerged from intellectuals within LADLA is not a coincidence since LADLA's more flexible ideological framework created the space for alternative thinking on Black struggles, immigrant rights, and racial oppression.

In today's Cuba, scholars and activists alike have commented on the problems posed by the race-blind discourse of Cuba's postrevolutionary state. Mark Sawyer described this discourse as one of "inclusionary discrimination"—a mix of Latin American exceptionalism, in which the prerevolutionary framing of Cuba as a raceless nation is used to support a myth of racial democracy, and Marxist exceptionalism, in which class-based socialist reforms are purported to have eliminated racial inequalities.[142] In essence, the "nonracialized class identity" of the 1930s PCC has continued to characterize postrevolutionary Cuba's racial politics. By looking back to 1930s Cuba to highlight and understand alternative visions that emerged out of the radical Left and that challenged the PCC's discourse, this chapter represents an effort to challenge this dominant narrative of Cuban intellectual history. The Cuban Marxist Left has never been a monolith, and people like Junco, who have been largely erased from that history, or those like Pedroso, who are viewed as cultural icons but not as political theorists, provide important footholds for a more dynamic view on Cuban racial politics today.

II   KNOTS IN THE NET

LADLA'S LIMITS AND ENTANGLEMENTS

FIVE

ETHNIC IMPERSONATION AND MASCULINE EROTICS

JAMES SAGER / JAIME NEVARES AND LADLA–PUERTO RICO

I am also necessitated for the present time to use, in connection with League activity, instead of my last name, my middle name. It is Nevarez. —**JAMES SAGER TO FEDERICO ACOSTA VELARDE,** president of Puerto Rican Nationalist Party, December 10, 1925

About your travelings, now I see what a good time you have spent while I have been all the time at home, here in Mayagüez. —**AMPARO TO JAMES SAGER,** October 19, 1926

In August 1925, James Nathanson Sager, a twenty-three-year-old Jewish man from Boston, arrived in Puerto Rico to visit a friend.[1] Within a few months, Sager had reinvented himself as "Jaime Nevares," sometimes written as "Jaime Nevárez," "Jaime Nevarez," or "Jaime Nevares Sager," a political organizer who would become known in nationalist and anti-imperialist circles on the island as the founder of both LADLA–Puerto Rico and the island's first communist organization, Liga Comunista de Puerto Rico (Puerto Rican Communist League). Although Sager lived in Puerto Rico for less than two years, he would leave behind a messy but enduring legacy.

As Sager built his political networks in Puerto Rico through reaching out to local organizers, he shared with them the truth that he was an "American worker" from the mainland, but the name he most often used in these communications was fabricated.[2] Although his use of the first name Jaime may have simply followed the common tendency in Spanish-speaking contexts to hispanicize visitors' English names, Nevares was a name of Sager's invention. Sager claimed Nevares as his middle name, explaining that he used it as a surname for security purposes in connection with political activities.[3] This invention of a Spanish middle name suggests that his name change represented not only an attempt to protect his identity but also a form of ethnic impersonation intended to help draw into his orbit Puerto Rican nationalists suspicious of US cultural encroachment. After Sager left Puerto Rico to work in other parts of Latin America and on the US-Mexico border, he continued using the name Nevares Sager for a few years and maintained the nickname Jaime for the remainder of his life.

The true identity of Jaime Nevares was first uncovered by historian Sandra Pujals, who found Sager's personal archive among the Bertram David Wolfe Papers at the New York Public Library and who also tracked Sager's movements after he left the island. Pujals examined Sager's transformation into Jaime Nevares to illuminate "the psychological feature of identity reinvention" within communist history and "the historical inaccuracy of official documentation in view of agents' own imaginary self-construction, impersonation, and falsification of personal data or facts."[4] This chapter revisits Sager's personal archive to reveal further insights regarding not only Sager's work in Puerto Rico but also the internal workings of LADLA's Continental Committee in relation to the US section, Latin American participation in the 1927 Brussels Congress, and LADLA's complex relationship to nationalists. In particular, it moves in new directions by using Sager's case to reflect on the limitations of LADLA's political vision and, by extension, of transnational solidarity movements more broadly.

The story of Sager's ethnic impersonation and the founding of LADLA–Puerto Rico is not necessarily representative of the broader hemispheric networks at the heart of this book. For example, in the history of LADLA-Cuba, studied in chapter 4, one does not find examples of US citizens operating in leadership roles or engaging in ethnic impersonation. Although many LADLA activists used aliases to avoid political persecution, and although these activists held a "transnational and globalized outlook that surpassed traditional parameters of national identity," they did not tend to take on new ethnicities.[5] And yet, Sager was not the only ethnic impersonator within LADLA's leadership. The man who encouraged Sager to establish LADLA–Puerto Rico was himself a Jewish US citizen named Charles Francis Phillips claiming to be a Mexican expatriate named Manuel Gomez. Phillips, a former Columbia University student and the son of a wealthy businessman, moved to Mexico City to avoid conscription in World War I. There, he was involved in the early formation of the Mexican Communist Party. When he was deported to Guatemala for political activities, he obtained a Guatemalan birth certificate from a waiter named Manuel Gómez and used this birth certificate to apply for a Guatemalan passport to slip back into Mexico. From there, he got a tourist visa to the United States, where he claimed to be a Mexican coal miner.[6] In Chicago, Gomez directed the Anti-Imperialist Department of the Workers Party (WP) and in April 1925 became the secretary of LADLA-US. Over the course of almost two years, the two men corresponded frequently, with Gomez in a supervisory role over Sager. Because they corresponded using the surnames "Sager" and "Gomez," I also employ these names in the following pages.

This chapter provides a counterpoint to the book's analysis thus far of LADLA's momentous contributions to theorizing relational solidarity politics. It studies the limitations of a political project built on bridging differences and considers how solidarity discourses can obscure disparities and frame experiences of oppression as interchangeable. Both Sager's and Gomez's acts of ethnic impersonation are closely related to the disproportionate mobility of these two US citizens in comparison to many of their Latin American counterparts and suggests that they likely made false equivalences between the conditions faced by Jewish minorities in the continental United States and those faced by their Latin American and US Latinx colleagues. These cases exemplify the potential for LADLA's politics of relation across difference to become entangled in overidentification and enmeshment.

Sager, a reportedly handsome man, had an appearance consistent with LADLA's leadership, which was dominated by young, attractive, and able-bodied individuals. While this movement consisted of a nationally and ethnically diverse group of people and focused on Indigenous, Black, and immigrant organizing, several key leaders' ease of travel through international borders was facilitated by white, mestizo, and/or light skin privilege. Moreover, as LADLA members circulated at political conferences and worked in close proximity, they often formed romantic and sexual relationships that were asymmetrical in terms of these individuals' level of access to funding, mobility, and international networks. The youthfulness of

LADLA's membership and the unevenness of many of these relationships is intimately tied, as I will explain, to LADLA's role in the construction and dissemination of the trope of the eroticized male Latin American revolutionary subject.

In addition to exploring the problem of overidentification in solidarity movements, this chapter sheds light on the history of the masculine erotics of the radical Left in the American hemisphere. It considers the potential limitations of political movements built on solidarities that cross ethnic, national, and linguistic boundaries and studies how such politics can veil rather than clarify differences in experience. Ultimately, it interrogates how solidarity movements like LADLA have often been constructed through the mobility and access afforded to a few key players.

JAMES SAGER IN PUERTO RICO, AUGUST 1925–APRIL 1927

Before his arrival in Puerto Rico, Sager worked as a dental technician in Boston, where he held WP membership.[7] Sager described his move to Puerto Rico as both a search for employment and a visit to his friend Antonio Colorado, the son of well-known Puerto Rican filmmaker and activist Rafael Colorado.[8] Sager may have also been looking to distance himself from his family, as he wrote to his mother, "I will not return to Boston for a long-time yet, maybe not for a few years or perhaps never."[9] Although his friend Antonio lived in San Juan, Sager initially settled in Mayagüez, where Antonio's father employed him in his photography shop.[10] He seems to have arrived in Puerto Rico with little money. He also sought work from the South Porto Rico Sugar Company and, according to his letters, had a job "on a plantation six days a week."[11]

Sager spoke some Spanish before arriving but not with enough fluency to write his letters and pamphlets in Spanish, which he had translated. Within a few weeks of his arrival, Sager wrote to WP headquarters in Chicago about his move to Puerto Rico. He wrote that he was not aware of any "organized, activist, Communist group on the island," and that he was in touch—likely through his well-connected friend—with trade union members, "a few of whom claim to be Communist sympathizers."[12] The WP connected Sager with Manuel Gomez, who directed the new US section of LADLA from Chicago. Sager then wrote to Gomez about the possibility of organizing LADLA–Puerto Rico and requested copies of LADLA's program and *El Libertador*.[13] Gomez encouraged Sager to organize LADLA–Puerto Rico, with Sager serving as provisional secretary, and explained that although LADLA "has the endorsement of the Communist International," it is "not a Communist organization" and "tries to draw in all forces willing to join in the struggle against American imperialism," such as "students' organizations, peasants' organizations, trade unions and other workers' organizations, groups of intellectuals, etc."[14]

In Gomez's next communication three days later, the not yet established Puerto Rican section was listed on the English version of LADLA's letterhead. Gomez wrote a handwritten note, drawing attention to the new letterhead: "Please notice that *you* are now a section!!!"[15] Shortly afterward, Sager told Antonio Colorado that because he needed to do his political work "underground," he would likely "assume a different name."[16] By December 7, 1925, little more than three months since his arrival, Sager distributed a flyer calling on Puerto Rican workers to join the organization and signed by LADLA–Puerto Rico secretary "Jaime Nevárez S."[17]

LADLA–Puerto Rico was officially established in Mayagüez on December 14, 1925 and included members of the Puerto Rican Nationalist Party (Partido Nacionalista de Puerto Rico, PNPR), the cigar makers' union, and the Socialist Party.[18] LADLA–Puerto Rico proclaimed a platform of independence for Puerto Rico and from "domination by the imperialist forces of Wall Street," which would require unity with similar movements in "the other countries from both continents and the far East."[19] It "appealed to the exploited working masses" and stated that national independence represented the "first and most essential step toward the emancipation of the working class."[20] Later, LADLA–Puerto Rico expanded its political platform, calling for the removal of Puerto Rican soldiers from Panama and critiquing antilabor corruption within Puerto Rico's trade union organization, the Free Federation of Workers (Federación Libre de Trabajadores).[21] Sager informed both Gomez in Chicago and Xavier Guerrero (administrator of *El Libertador*) in Mexico City of the group's formation and requested additional material for distribution.[22] He enclosed LADLA–Puerto Rico's founding statement, explaining that although the group was composed of only Mayagüez residents, "it can serve as a basic unit around which an all Porto-Rico section can in time be built."[23] Sager would make a concerted effort to deliver on this promise.

In March 1926, Sager reported optimistically that beyond the section in Mayagüez, LADLA sections were forming in San Juan, Ponce, and Cayey.[24] The Ponce section was already in formation, under the leadership of Félix

Lugo, whom Sager described as "a true proletarian, a tobacco worker, who because of his activities in behalf of his class, was blacklisted by the powerful Porto Rican American Tobacco Co."[25] He described Lugo as a communist, "a writer, a soap box artist" who "has popularity among the workers around Ponce."[26] Although the Ponce section became quite active under Lugo's leadership, the Cayey section, which Sager urged anarchist Emiliano Ramos to organize, never got off the ground because of Ramos's discomfort with LADLA's relationship with communists. The San Juan branch did not become active until Sager moved from Mayagüez to San Juan in April 1926.[27]

Sager's personal papers reveal a steady pace of political activity, particularly in the production of political literature. The newspapers La Tribuna and El Mundo published on LADLA–Puerto Rico's activities, and occasionally the PNPR's journal, El Nacionalista de Ponce, published its press releases.[28] LADLA–Puerto Rico distributed a protest resolution condemning the Machado regime's imprisonment of Mella, which it sent to the Daily Worker in Chicago and to LADLA-Cuba.[29] It circulated statements in support of the PNPR and of striking tobacco workers, other statements criticizing the US military occupation of Nicaragua and the Philippines, and solidarity statements with workers of the world on May Day. When Marines from the US Caribbean Fleet arrived in Puerto Rico, LADLA–Puerto Rico distributed a leaflet addressed to them that critiqued the occupation of Nicaragua and referred to Marines as "workers" exploited by the banking industry's imperialist interests.[30] It also sent reports on US imperialism in Puerto Rico to LADLA headquarters in Mexico City for publication in El Libertador and to the Chicago office for publication in the Daily Worker.[31] It distributed El Libertador and El Machete, and publications from other radical Puerto Rican organizations affiliated with LADLA–Puerto Rico.[32]

As the organization's secretary, Sager established contact with activist Rothschild Francis, editor of The Emancipator in the Virgin Islands, leading to the establishment of a LADLA section there.[33] Around the same time, he wrote a letter to the editor of the Daily Worker about the plight of Puerto Rican workers in cotton fields in Arizona, suggesting ties between their circumstances and those of workers from the Virgin Islands employed in Puerto Rican sugar mills.[34] Sager also reported that he picketed with tobacco strikers and spoke at mass meetings of the Tobacco Workers Strike Committee, particularly aiding efforts to recruit women employed by cigarette distributors.[35]

Although Sager had more success in establishing LADLA–Puerto Rico, he also worked to found a "Communist League of Porto Rico with the view of ultimately developing as the Communist Party of Porto Rico."[36] Gomez urged Sager to avoid too much overlap in the two organizations' leadership since it would threaten the "true character of the League as a united front organization."[37] Sager began organizing various communist cells in August 1926 in San Juan, Ponce, and Mayagüez. These were small groups, with the largest, in Ponce, having only nine members.[38] In March 1927, organizers from these cells met to establish the overarching Puerto Rican Communist League (Liga Comunista de Puerto Rico), which immediately affiliated with LADLA.[39] Although significant overlap existed between LADLA–Puerto Rico and the Puerto Rican Communist League, Sager attempted to attract a distinct membership to each and reported that Communist League members were all "workers, the largest proportion of them tobacco workers," as well as "workers in the repair shops of the American Railroad Co."[40] Sager's description of the communist organization appears accurate. An organizer from the Ponce cell, Clemente Sárraga, explained that signatures on their founding document may have contained spelling errors since all members "are workers, who have been denied by the damned ruling system the opportunity to educate themselves a little better."[41] In addition to these workers, the San Juan cell apparently included three Puerto Rican dissident soldiers of the Sixty-Fifth US Infantry, who distributed propaganda materials among the military.[42] Despite these efforts to establish a communist organization, when Sager left Puerto Rico in April 1927, LADLA–Puerto Rico was far more established than the fledgling Communist League.

LADLA–PUERTO RICO AND THE PUERTO RICAN NATIONALIST PARTY

From their earliest communications, Gomez urged Sager to convince PNPR leadership to affiliate with LADLA.[43] The PNPR had been established only three years prior to Sager's arrival.[44] Sager encouraged Antonio Colorado to join the PNPR to serve as a liaison in this effort.[45] In December 1925, Sager wrote in English to PNPR President Federico Acosta Velarde, a twenty-nine-year-old lawyer and son of a judge. Sager introduced himself and LADLA to Acosta Velarde, explaining that LADLA aligned with the PNPR in calling for "complete national independence for all colonies and semi-colonies."[46] He informed Acosta Velarde of LADLA's activities in Mexico, Cuba, and the United States and requested help in establishing contact with those interested in affiliating. Acosta Velarde responded enthusiastically to Sager's initial letter, explaining that he already subscribed to *El Libertador* and was in communication with its director, Úrsulo Galván. He promised his affiliation to LADLA–Puerto Rico and encouraged Sager to reach out to PNPR Vice President Pedro Albizu Campos. While Sager signed his initial letter to Acosta Velarde with "James N. Sager," his second communication acknowledging receipt of Acosta Velarde's reply explained that "in connection with League activity" he would need to use his middle name, "Nevarez."[47]

When Sager wrote to Albizu Campos, the latter did not respond directly to Sager but instead wrote a colleague who had joined LADLA–Puerto Rico, "expressing fear that the organization is Communist."[48] Over time, Sager came to understand Vice President Albizu Campos, rather than President Acosta Velarde, as "the leading mind and tone giver of the nationalist movement and especially the party" and "the author of most of the militant manifestoes."[49] Albizu Campos, with whom the Puerto Rican nationalist cause would become most associated, was a thirty-four-year-old lawyer and Harvard Law School graduate. Although he joined the PNPR in 1924, Albizu Campos would not assume its presidency until 1930, when his leadership transitioned its platform to the more militant ideological position for which the PNPR became known.[50] Albizu Campos's concerns about LADLA–Puerto Rico appear to have influenced Acosta Velarde, since shortly after his initial letter, Acosta Velarde wrote a more tepid follow-up. In this second letter—which, notably, was addressed to James N. Sager and not to James Nevarez—he explained that he had read Sager's letter of introduction at the most recent PNPR meeting and that all members enthusiastically supported LADLA–Puerto Rico. However, the PNPR could not officially affiliate without General Assembly approval. In response to Sager's request to use the middle name Nevarez, Acosta Velarde said he would circulate Sager's letter among friends but could not publish a letter in the PNPR's newspaper that was not backed by "a responsible signature."[51] In a subsequent communication, Acosta Velarde denied Sager's request to publish his initial letter in which Acosta Velarde had affiliated with LADLA–Puerto Rico, stating that he had not been aware that the "Anti-Imperialist League has communist tendencies" and reiterating that although "we sympathize with the League for its anti-imperialism . . . we cannot nor should we affiliate with it for its communism."[52]

Several times, Sager arranged individual meetings with Albizu Campos and Acosta Velarde to try to convince them that LADLA was not communist but a united-front organization. He also suggested affiliation could benefit the PNPR financially.[53] Albizu Campos apparently expressed sympathy with communism and openness to receiving potential aid from the Soviet Union.[54] However, he felt that affiliation with LADLA–Puerto Rico would threaten the PNPR's unity, alienating those like Acosta Velarde with a "right tendency."[55] Additionally, Albizu Campos believed that LADLA–Puerto Rico's growth would detract from the PNPR's ability to "concentrate the struggle for independence" under its leadership.[56] LADLA–Puerto Rico would be "aiding imperialism to split the movement."[57] Albizu Campos proposed LADLA–Puerto Rico's dissolution and suggested that "the only other organization that would be appreciated is one that would confine its activities to the trade unions," helping to align trade unions with the PNPR.[58] For his part, Acosta Velarde apparently recognized "that the League is a non communist organization" but felt affiliation would leave the PNPR "open to attack as being Bolshevik, which would lead to disastrous consequences."[59] The reticence of the PNPR's leadership to affiliate with LADLA–Puerto Rico caused some nationalist members from the Mayagüez section to resign from LADLA.[60]

Gomez expressed surprise to Sager that the nationalists associated LADLA with communism since "this is not the impression in Latin-America generally."[61] Indeed, before meeting Sager, Acosta Velarde thought highly of LADLA and subscribed to El Libertador. Similarly, when planning a lecture tour throughout Latin America, Albizu Campos said he was interested in meeting "the leaders of the League in Mexico." However, when Gomez invited Albizu Campos to add a US visit to his tour at the invitation of LADLA-US, Albizu Campos apparently declined because, "being an avowed enemy of the U.S., it would not be consistent for and ethical for him to set foot in the U.S."[62] Additionally, when Gomez asked if he could accompany Albizu Campos on his tour, Albizu Campos declined, suggesting Gomez send financial support instead.[63]

The differences in the PNPR's positive perception of LADLA's leadership in Mexico City versus Sager's Puerto Rican section suggests that a major deterrent to attracting the PNPR was Sager himself, a Jewish US citizen and non-native Spanish-speaker who had only recently arrived on the island. The fact that Sager's primary contact was not with LADLA's Continental Committee but with Gomez in the US section also posed a problem. The PNPR framed its independence movement within a firmly hispanophile political platform of "Ibero-American union" and "continental hegemony of Latin American nations" that "spoke Spanish, were Catholic, and shared a common past" of Spanish colonialism.[64] Because of this, they likely would have felt more comfortable with LADLA's Latin American leadership in Mexico City than with Sager or Gomez. Moreover, the connection between LADLA-US and the WP, and thus the Comintern, was perhaps more obvious than the connection between LADLA's Mexico City headquarters and the PCM.

Equally significant, Gomez and Sager reproduced the very colonial power relationship between the mainland and the island that the PNPR was fighting to overcome. In a letter to Salvador de la Plaza, administrator of *El Libertador*, Sager explained why Gomez's US section, rather than LADLA's Continental Committee, oversaw the Puerto Rican section: "P.R., being a colony dominated politically by the US, comrades in the United States have the obligation to develop and help the cause and its struggles on the island; but since Puerto [Rico] is a Spanish-speaking country, the cooperation of comrades in Mexico and in Cuba is of vital importance."[65] Sager justified LADLA's structure of oversight between the mainland and the island through the logic of colonial rule. Similarly, the Puerto Rican Communist League was conceived as a district organization of the WP since, as Executive Secretary Charles Emil Ruthenberg wrote, "Porto Rico is under American control."[66] We can only assume that Sager understood his own leadership in both LADLA–Puerto Rico and the Puerto Rican Communist League through a similar colonial lens. The reliance on US oversight proved to be a logistical problem, however: Although Sager distributed *El Machete* and *El Libertador* when he had copies, he frequently struggled to obtain political literature in Spanish.[67] LADLA's Continental Committee also criticized the arrangement as exemplary of Gomez's refusal to recognize that central leadership of LADLA remained with the Continental Committee in Mexico.[68] They said that Gomez's tendency to send out circulars in English to sections throughout Latin America caused confusion and suspicion since "all sections . . . except Mexico and the United States recognize . . . the headquarters of the league" as being in Mexico.[69] It apparently did not occur to either Sager or Gomez that putting the PNPR into direct contact with activists from other Latin American contexts, like Julio Antonio Mella or Salvador de la Plaza, would lead to more favorable results.

Sager held serious doubts over whether the PNPR would be able to build the mass movement that Albizu Campos envisioned. The PNPR, he wrote, is "the party of the native petty bourgeoisie, small land owners, trades

people, professionals, and their intellectual retainers."[70] For "class conscious workers," he explained to Gomez, "the struggle for independence is
but an issue in their class struggle against capitalism," and while the PNPR
had "nationalist bourgeois aspirations," it had no class consciousness.[71]
Sager believed that the island needed "a workers' party with a program for
independence based on the class struggle that can gain influence and leadership among the masses" and thought any movement for independence
should have a "pro labor political and economic program."[72] He laid out
these concerns in a meeting with Acosta Velarde, explaining that LADLA–
Puerto Rico could be used as a mass organization in support of the PNPR
and "will stand ready to unite with the N.P. [nationalist party; the PNPR]
in the struggle for independence."[73] However, Acosta Velarde did not respond favorably to this idea. Ultimately, Sager ignored the PNPR's objec-
tions, moving ahead with the work of LADLA–Puerto Rico.[74]

Sager's frustrations with the PNPR continued throughout his time in
Puerto Rico. Although all PNPR leaders were quite young, Sager characterized the organization as suffering from a generational difference, where the
"young nationalists," like PNPR members Samuel Quiñones and Vicente
Géigel Polanco, supported LADLA–Puerto Rico, in contrast to the older
nationalists.[75] In one letter to Gomez, he called the PNPR "a sect, a group
of a few lawyers and law students," and claimed they were uninterested not
only in workers' issues but also in other nations' independence from colonial rule.[76] To LADLA's Continental Committee, he reported that the PNPR
"just rallies to the slogan of 'Independence for Porto Rico' and is rather
'Anti North American and pro la raza' than 'anti imperialist.'"[77] In communications with Salvador de la Plaza in Mexico City and with LADLA-Cuba
secretary Jorge Vivó, Sager expressed similar assessments, writing, "The
Nationalist Party is very weak and does not and never will appeal to the
workers and peasants with its purely nationalist ideology. The workers and
peasants of PR are class conscious and will welcome the more class approach of the anti-imperialist struggle."[78] Nevertheless, he explained, "our
relations are cordial and . . . many nationalist party members are active in
the League section."[79] Salvador de la Plaza wrote back to this message, reminding Sager that LADLA–Puerto Rico was intended as a united front
that would support nationalists and attract petty bourgeois elements while
leaving the communist party to combat imperialism from within the class
struggle.[80]

Despite his lack of experience on the island, Sager's judgments were not
completely unfounded. Scholarship on the PNPR has similarly described

its leadership during this period as a "semi-private cultural club" made up of primarily Catholic, urban, "educated, well-off men of European descent."[81] Its political positions in this period have been described as "extremely moderate, respectful and 'good-mannered'" and focused on preserving cultural heritage.[82] The organization has been described as maintaining an "elite leadership" and exhibiting a classist and paternalistic cultural nationalism that clashed with working class issues and glorified a Spanish past through its uncritical perspective toward Spanish colonialism.[83]

Sager also noted that within the PNPR, there were "ugly bourgeois petty prejudices," revealed by the fact that although "all leading up elements recognize in Albizu as being the most devoted and the most capable party worker as well as a fanatical nationalist yet he is never chosen for the presidency of the party."[84] The reasoning for this, Sager explained, was racial prejudice: "A few white skinned nationalists have confided to me that Albizu, being a Negro plus Indian, cannot be given the highest place since such action may injure the prestige of the nationalist movement among 'certain elements' outside of PR, especially in the US. . . . [T]he white majority fear least their nationalist movement may be pointed to as a 'mere Negro movement.'"[85] Despite this apparent racism within the PNPR, Sager claimed that Albizu Campos "on all occasions, with much conviction, preaches the 'absence' of race problems in PR and among latin peoples in general, in contrast to U.S." Sager described Albizu Campos's racial politics as "extremely unfortunate" since "because of his background" he should identify with working people and "not with these foul bourgeois cynical white skinned lawyers, who deserve no more than his hatred."[86]

Sager's evaluation of the racially prejudiced views of some PNPR leaders toward Albizu Campos, the mixed-race son of a father of Basque descent and a mother of African descent, is also supported by anecdotal and scholarly evidence. When José Vasconcelos visited Puerto Rico in 1926 for a lecture series with the University of Puerto Rico, he met with Nationalist Party leadership and recorded in his journal a racist comment made at this meeting about Albizu Campos.[87] Partially due to his race, several PNPR leaders strongly opposed Albizu Campos's presidential candidacy in 1930 and resigned when he was elected.[88] Even so, Albizu Campos—as Dolores Austin has written—"chose to overlook racial prejudice in his own society and to highlight U.S. racism because this fit with his very Hispanophilic world-view. He portrayed Latin society as one in which all races lived harmoniously."[89] His idealized portrayal of Puerto Rican race relations may have derived from his experience of the rigid Black/white color line on the

US mainland during his time at Harvard and during his military service. The racism of his Puerto Rican colleagues may have felt less strident in comparison. Alternatively, he may have found it politically advantageous to his own advancement within the PNPR to stress that Puerto Rico lacked the racism of the continental United States.

Although Sager made some correct assessments, his self-assured judgments of the PNPR suggest that, at twenty-three years old, Sager was likely quite arrogant. He was not Puerto Rican, not fluent in Spanish, and had not even been on the island for six months, and yet in the PNPR's view he was already inhibiting the nationalist movement's growth. At the same time, considering that the scholarly record largely supports Sager's evaluations, we can assume that Puerto Rican activists—like tobacco worker Félix Lugo, with whom Sager was collaborating in LADLA—heavily influenced his opinions. It is also possible that Sager, who was working on sugar plantations, may have gained a better understanding of certain aspects of working-class issues even during his short time on the island in comparison to PNPR leaders.

Despite tensions between the PNPR and LADLA–Puerto Rico, Gomez reported to WP leadership that "the official organ of the party, 'El Nacionalista de Ponce,' reprints our news releases and has printed several friendly editorials."[90] Similarly, LADLA–Puerto Rico distributed statements in support of the nationalists' activities, and in summer 1926, Sager was invited to speak at the PNPR's mass meeting.[91] Privately, however, Sager noted, "I feel that some n.p.'s do not look on very pleasingly at increasing the sight of the League coming into the limelight, and it is perhaps best to sail a bit slowly until we get some definite orientation with the n.p. 'El nacionalista' did not publish our resolution as well as other things submitted to it. It would be unfortunate openly to antagonize the n.p."[92]

Gomez urged Sager not to give up on the PNPR, insisting that "in Porto Rico, we must remember, the next point on the order of business is national revolution. . . . You should make every effort to link up your Nationalist Party with your Porto Rican section."[93] He instructed Sager to "go out of your way to heap special favors" on PNPR leadership and to be careful not to "steal the limelight from NP but on the contrary give them as much publicity as possible."[94] When Gomez alerted Sager to the upcoming "Conference of Colonial and Semi-Colonial Peoples," to be held in Brussels and to which Puerto Rico's "nationalist, radical, and progressive organizations" should send representatives, Sager found a new opportunity to connect with PNPR leadership.[95]

PUERTO RICO AND THE 1927
BRUSSELS CONGRESS

Sager wrote to Albizu Campos about the upcoming congress in Brussels and encouraged the PNPR to send a delegate. He mentioned, as Gomez had informed him, that the conference organizers would pay travel expenses for delegates from organizations with limited budgets. The PNPR promised to send as its representative Pedro Jota Rosa, editor of *Voz Latina*, who was living in Paris. However, since the organizers postponed the Brussels Congress several times, first from March to November 1926 and then to February 1927, Rosa had already returned to Puerto Rico by its convening.[96] Moreover, the congress's provisional committee alerted delegations that subsidies would be provided only under exceptional circumstances and organizations should fund their own travel.[97] Gomez believed that "PORTO RICO MUST BE REPRESENTED" in Brussels.[98] He promised that LADLA-US could fund one delegate but urged Sager to "use every effort to get the N.P. to send a delegate and finance him."[99] The PNPR would only agree to send a delegate if LADLA would pay his expenses. The San Juan section of LADLA–Puerto Rico chose as its delegate Samuel Quiñones, "a law graduate, leader of nationalist youth movement, and of students federation," because he believed he could also secure the PNPR's endorsement since he was a member.[100] However, the PNPR ultimately declined to endorse Quiñones and instead named Mexican intellectual José Vasconcelos, who had visited Puerto Rico earlier that year, as well as Argentine socialist Manuel Ugarte, both of whom already planned to attend.[101] In the end, only Vasconcelos was able to attend.[102]

Although Gomez promised that LADLA-US would pay Quiñones's expenses, the money ($380) had not arrived by late January. At that point Quiñones renounced his representation of Puerto Rico at the congress, publishing a letter of resignation in leading Puerto Rican newspapers.[103] Quiñones did not blame LADLA for lack of funding but rather the PNPR president for an unwillingness to endorse him and help finance the trip.[104] Sager explained to Gomez that "when we about gave up hope in money coming, he felt it would be the proper move to resign using the opportunity to denounce the attitude of Velarde toward the league." He assessed that "had the np sincerely desired Porto Rican representation, they could have raised more than sufficient money six months ago."[105] Quiñones's public denouncement of PNPR President Acosta Velarde caused "quarreling" among them, leading Sager to conclude that "the present np is completely impotent and is not destined for anything important."[106] Ironically, although the Brussels Congress intended to unite movements in a common struggle, in the case of Puerto Rico, it became the impetus for division both within the PNPR and against LADLA–Puerto Rico.

The money finally arrived from LADLA-US nine days before the congress, but Quiñones did not yet have a passport. Although Quiñones blamed the PNPR "for not accepting cooperation with the League in raising funds for the sending of a delegate representing both bodies," Sager admitted that the lack of Puerto Rican representation in Brussels was "just as much the fault of Quiñones . . . for being asleep to the last moment."[107] Ultimately, Puerto Rico was represented in Brussels by Vasconcelos, Peruvian journalist César Falcón, and a French citizen of Cuban descent, Louis Casabona.[108] None of them was Puerto Rican, and Vasconcelos's speech did not mention Puerto Rico.[109] Despite this, the PNPR approved the Brussels resolution on Puerto Rico and planned to affiliate with the LAI. This affiliation posed a problem for Sager's work with LADLA–Puerto Rico. As Sager wrote to LADLA's Continental Committee, "If Nationalist Party affiliates to Brussels organization, would it not be preferable for Porto Rican Section of League to retire in favor of Nationalist Party as basis for broad united front?"[110] In essence, the creation of the LAI in Brussels, and the newly forged relations between the LAI and local organizations, threatened to overshadow LADLA's work in certain locations like Puerto Rico.

Perhaps partially due to this problem, on April 6, 1927, only six weeks after the Brussels Congress, Sager left Puerto Rico. He left Vicente Géigel Polanco, former leader of the University of Puerto Rico Students' Federation and leader of Juventud Nacionalista (nationalist youth), in charge as LADLA–Puerto Rico secretary, and he put Géigel Polanco directly in touch with LADLA's Continental Committee.[111] Ultimately, Sager had little success in ever attracting the PNPR's core leadership to LADLA, despite his claims to the contrary.[112] Rather than building a united front, Sager sparked a rift within Puerto Rico's fledgling nationalist movement.

SAGER AND LADLA'S MONEY TROUBLES

Beyond his lack of familiarity with the island, Sager faced other obstacles. He attributed his decision to leave Puerto Rico to financial difficulties and increased police surveillance. Whatever money he may have brought with him in August 1925, it soon ran out. During his first several months in Mayagüez, Sager complained he was unable to devote the necessary time to organizing LADLA–Puerto Rico because he lacked financing and worked on a plantation six days a week.[113] When he moved to San Juan in April 1926, he took with him a letter of introduction from his previous employer.[114] However, once he arrived in San Juan, Sager was unemployed for a few months and never found any stable employment from that point forward. On May 6, 1926, he mentioned to Gomez that although Albizu Campos had invited him to his home in Ponce, he was unable to pay the bus fare, "unless the Chicago office is in a position to assist."[115] By May 13, he said that due to lack of employment, he would likely need to leave Puerto Rico, "but I cannot think of deserting the many Party tasks to be accomplished here."[116]

Over the course of his communications with Gomez, Sager's initial hints at financial troubles became increasingly overt, and he hoped that in founding LADLA–Puerto Rico, he would be placed on the WP payroll. Gomez mostly ignored his financial concerns, offering half-hearted words of support.[117] Gomez sometimes held unrealistic expectations of what Sager could accomplish with no funding, suggesting, for example, that he arrange a banquet for Vasconcelos's visit to Puerto Rico.[118] Gomez himself was having difficulty convincing the WP to fulfill its financial obligations to LADLA. In February 1926, Gomez reported to WP leadership that LADLA was suffering from "a shortage (I might better say, a complete absence) of finances."[119] Although the WP had committed to finance LADLA and to send $200 a month to Mexico City, it was not fulfilling its obligations. Gomez recommended that a "party employee be dropped from the payroll and that his wages be appropriated to make up the bulk of the $200 to be sent to Mexico each month."[120]

Having no luck with Gomez, Sager looked for other sources of support. He reached out to Bertram Wolfe at the Workers School in New York City. While not able to support a paid organizer, the Workers School sent some money to LADLA–Puerto Rico.[121] Additionally, Sager wrote to WP Executive Secretary Charles Emil Ruthenberg about founding a communist party, and Ruthenberg occasionally sent funds to Sager to help maintain his work.[122] Sager's creative efforts to find solutions to these financial problems suggest that his interest in founding a Puerto Rican communist party may have derived partially from his hope for better funding under Ruthenberg's direction. By September 1926, Sager claimed his poverty was resulting in hair loss, teeth disintegration, a skin parasite, malaria, and depression. "I feel that a breakdown is ahead," he wrote.[123] In November, he reported that he had been fired from his job, had been identified by the San Juan police, and expected to be arrested soon.[124] By January, he remained jobless and felt that his political reputation would prevent him from obtaining future employment. He wrote to Gomez that "I am compelled to ask money of the luc[k]ier members of the League," and he explicitly asked Gomez for money.[125] In early February 1927, Sager was making plans to leave for New York to attend the Workers School under Wolfe's direction, but he did not yet have money for a coat or boat ticket.[126]

Considering Sager's financial condition, it comes as no surprise that after the money earmarked for Quiñones's trip to Brussels went unused, Sager did not return the money to Gomez. Instead, LADLA–Puerto Rico paid to send a cable to the Brussels Congress, purchased its first stationery, and printed propaganda leaflets.[127] Although Sager recommended that the rest of the money "be turned over to the PR Section" and to "Secretary Polanco and the treasurer José Taboas Fernández for League purposes," Gomez instructed him to return the money at once.[128] Instead, Sager purchased his transportation to New York City.[129] Once in New York, he offered to pay the money back in installments and sent the first installment of $40. Whether he ever paid back the debt in full is unclear but doubtful, considering that he did not stay in the United States for long.[130]

In the end, Sager assessed that "the PR Section is a real thing now and will grow and succeed in its mission."[131] His efforts to organize a communist organization, however, were less successful. He wrote, "Regards the Communist League, nothing is being done. I believe that if I could remain longer in Porto Rico, and give to it the same attention I did to the Anti-Imperialist League, we could accomplish just as much."[132] He acknowledged that "my work in Porto Rico was left uncompleted, as a matter of fact we were just beginning to get real, concrete results."[133] Despite financial difficulties, youth, and lack of experience, over a mere twenty months Sager established two organizations that connected organizers both within and beyond Puerto Rico. Several key factors appeared to contribute to his modest successes, including his ethnic impersonation, his perceived connection to power and money, and his physical appearance as a light-skinned, able-bodied young man whom others considered attractive. All these factors, analyzed in more depth in the remainder of this chapter, derive directly from the mobility, access, and privilege that Sager, as a Jewish US citizen from the mainland, enjoyed in comparison to his Puerto Rican counterparts. These elements of Sager's story are significant not only in complicating our understanding of LADLA but also in considering problems that can arise within solidarity movements more broadly.

ETHNIC IMPERSONATION AND
MASCULINE EROTICS

Although Sager's ethnic impersonation as Jaime Nevares had little impact in attracting PNPR leadership, he seemed to believe that signing pamphlets addressed to "Puerto Rican Workers and Peasants" with "J. Nevares" aided in bringing others to LADLA.[134] In a profoundly hypocritical move for an organizer committed to Puerto Rican independence and self-determination, Sager often spoke on behalf of Puerto Ricans as if he were Puerto Rican. He explained to an organizer of the Brussels Congress that "this conference is timely for us Porto Ricans. If you Europeans desire to have an idea what Wall Street domination holds in store for you, turn your eyes to our little island country in the Caribbean."[135] While Sager falsely presented himself as Puerto Rican, his work was being overseen by yet another ethnic impersonator, Charles Francis Phillips, a US citizen posing as a Mexican American named Manuel Gomez. Although Sager signed his real name in his letters to Gomez, their letters do not discuss the Nevares name that appeared in Sager's pamphlets, and it is doubtful that Sager knew Gomez's true identity. In both cases, ethnic impersonation, facilitated by these men's light skin privilege, enabled their movements across borders and allowed them to navigate circles of varying class backgrounds.

It is also notable that both Sager and Gomez were Jewish, an identity category that "disrupts the very categories of identity because it is not national, not genealogical, not religious, but all of these in dialectical tension with one another."[136] In the 1920s United States, Jewish people faced intense anti-Semitism, including university quotas, exclusion from certain professions, heavy policing, and anti-immigrant laws that restricted Jewish immigration from Eastern Europe.[137] In the US South during this time, signs at segregated establishments "might read 'no blacks or Jews.'"[138] This anti-Semitism greatly expanded after the 1929 economic collapse, for which fascist movements would blame Jewish people, whom they conflated with the evils of finance capitalism.[139] Similar to Puerto Ricans living on the mainland, Jews were often viewed by white Anglo-Saxon Protestant culture as foreign, and they were under pressure to assimilate, which often took the form of "changing ethnically marked names . . . to attain or sustain a middle-class status."[140] Jews were also racialized in ways similar to white and mestizo Latinx in the continental United States by being cast as what Matthew Frye Jacobson describes as "provisional whites" or "white Others."[141] As Charles B. Hersch explains, although "all ethnicities are hybrid . . . diasporic Jewish identities are particularly so, and the hybridity of Jewishness has at times made Jews racial shape-shifters."[142] In other words, ethnic identity may have always felt like an unstable category for both Sager and Gomez. In attempting to recruit PNPR members, Sager was addressing himself to a group of Catholics of Hispanic descent.[143] Although he used the Jewish last name Sager in some of his communications with PNPR members, we should consider that his chosen name, Nevares, signaled not only a Hispanic identity but also a Catholic one. Part of Sager's motivation for appropriating a Hispanic name may have been related to experiences or fears of anti-Semitism.

Sager's letters and writings reveal that he cared deeply about anti-imperialism, workers' rights, and Puerto Rican independence. Although he never wrote about his Jewish background, he likely could identify with some aspects of Puerto Rican experiences of oppression and racialization. Sager's disgust with the white supremacist rejection of Albizu Campos by some PNPR members suggests that he personally held antiracist views. In his concern for Black immigrant workers from the Virgin Islands employed in Puerto Rico, he may have drawn links between the tendency in Latin America to negatively associate US companies with Black immigrant workers and the fascist conflation of Jews with finance capital. Sager's positions allied with antiracist views among US Jewish communities more broadly. The 1920s Yiddish press and English-language Jewish press in the United States harshly criticized US racism, supported Black civil rights, and frequently drew "connections between black and Jewish suffering."[144] These political affinities became expressed musically through the Black-Jewish exchanges of 1920s jazz even as some 1920s Jewish jazz musicians used blackface to demean Black artists and emphasize Jews' differences from African Americans.[145] Thus, Black-Jewish exchanges in this period should not be understood through a simplistic framework of shared oppression.

As leaders in LADLA, which focused on connecting movements across national, linguistic, and ethnic differences, Sager and Gomez held deep investments in the liberation of people different from themselves. They believed that solidarity, the sharing of mutual responsibility and action in a common cause, requires a form of crossing over in which one takes upon oneself the concerns of others as if they are one's own. However, Sager and Gomez also exemplify how such crossings can become twisted into overidentification, enmeshment, and even impersonation.

Although not writing about ethnic impersonation per se, Janet Jakobsen has warned against the dangers of using analogies to forge solidarities in social movements, arguing that the use of analogy to "show that one form of political oppression and or struggle is like another . . . may actually undercut, rather than enable, alliances among movements."[146] Through an analysis of analogies used in twentieth- and twenty-first-century LGBTQ civil rights movements to compare discrimination based on sexual orientation and gender identity to race discrimination, Jakobsen argues that a central problem of analogy is the way that it can simplistically frame "the relation between oppression to one of similarity."[147] Because "the meaning of the first term in an analogy (e.g., sexism) depends on the second term to which it is analogized (racism), the analogy tends to make the first term the center of analysis while marginalizing (if including at all) any analysis of the second term."[148] This can simplify relationships between oppressions, framing social categories "as distinct entities rather than complexly interrelated social possibilities."[149] Analogy politics can fail to recognize historical differences and exploit those whose experiences are "invoked as the stable ground of analogy" but who are not well-represented in the movement.[150] Jakobsen calls instead for "a form of comparison that can recognize the complexity of relation named by it . . . in which *both* likeness *and* difference could be the basis for connection and collaboration."[151] She calls for a politics of "relation" over analogy, in which social movements are based on "linkage as a projection of complicity."[152]

This political vision of relation and linkage, instead of analogy, echoes what I have described as LADLA's politics of relational solidarity, a vision of solidarity based on the relations (but not conflations) of differing forms of capitalist exploitation. Sager's case, however, provides a lens onto the potential limitations of political movements built on such relations, even when those movements intend to facilitate collaboration between distinct yet interconnected struggles. Sager's case shows how solidarity politics can be misconstrued to veil rather than clarify differences, and his overidentification offers an example of how nets of relation can become entangled in a knotted and ineffectual mess.

Although his ethnic impersonation may have made him feel closer to the Puerto Rican cause, in truth it shielded him from examining his own privileges and complicity with the very colonial structures of domination he was trying to abolish. Sager consistently believed he understood Puerto Rican issues better than his Puerto Rican colleagues, and it was not until he left the island that he ceded leadership of the two organizations he founded to Puerto Rican organizers. As Laura Browder writes of ethnic impersonators who "adopt the voice of another group in order to gain political effectiveness," the success of that political project "rests on their ability to manipulate stereotypes, thus further miring their audience in essentialist racial and ethnic categories."[153] Sager's characterization, in his letter to Brussels, of the "untold misery of our island" where "our people are slowly starving" played into such European stereotypes of Puerto Rico.[154]

Even though Sager's ethnic impersonation did not ease the concerns of PNPR leadership, his perceived connections to powerful people and funding sources did help him gain proximity to both Albizu Campos and Acosta Velarde. Sager mentioned on several occasions that Albizu Campos was "very poor" and that "the nationalist party is dead broke."[155] It appears that it was Sager's promise of potential funding from LADLA-US that caused PNPR leaders to even tolerate Sager at all. Albizu Campos suggested in several instances that the PNPR would welcome funding but otherwise was uninterested in collaborating. While Sager did not put PNPR leadership directly into contact with LADLA's Continental Committee, he did attempt to attract the PNPR by connecting them to prominent Latin American radicals abroad. For example, Gomez informed Sager of LADLA affiliations by well-known Latin American intellectuals, like Argentine socialists Manuel Ugarte and Alfredo Palacios, and suggested that Sager mention these names to PNPR leadership.[156] In anticipation of Vasconcelos's visit to Puerto Rico, Gomez instructed Sager to get in touch with him upon his arrival and invite Albizu Campos and Acosta Velarde to a LADLA–Puerto Rico meeting with Vasconcelos as keynote speaker. "His name commands respect from Cuba to Argentina," Gomez wrote of Vasconcelos, and "it will give you access to an entire new element in PR."[157] Sager's perceived access to funding and to these prominent figures afforded him invitations to Albizu Campos's home on several occasions and to speak to the PNPR mass assembly. Despite Sager's greater affinity for Albizu Campos, he had more success with PNPR members, whom he described as "foul bourgeois cynical white skinned lawyers" and whom he claimed held racist views. This fact suggests that Sager's own proximity to whiteness (and its indexing of power and wealth) may have played a role in his appeal to those members. Ultimately, Sager's actual access to money and influence was as much a farce as his contrived identity, but it was the perception of the contrary that mattered.

In addition to his false identity and perceived connections, Sager was apparently physically attractive. Upon seeing Sager's photograph, Gomez noted that "all my fears regarding your possible starvation in Puerto Rico have vanished. One look at your picture (or at least the photo you sent!) convinces us that you can always get a job in the movies."[158] Sager tried to challenge this perception, writing that "although I appear to be in good health in the photo I sent," malnutrition caused such rapid hair loss that "I'll be able to act for a part in a movie as Lenin."[159] Later Gomez said, "Every woman who comes into this office goes into e[cs]ta[s]ies over your photograph which is displayed on our wall!"[160] Another letter to Sager from a Puerto Rican woman named Luz, whom he met in Mayagüez, called Sager the "Romeo of Mayagüez," echoing Gomez's perception of the young man's erotic appeal.[161]

Sager used his good looks to his advantage. In Mayagüez, he developed a relationship with a Puerto Rican woman whose correspondence used only the name "Amparo." Amparo wrote to Sager in English, the likely language of her education due to US colonial policies dictating English as the official language of public schools.[162] In her letters, she addressed him both as "Jaime" and "Jimmie," meaning that she likely knew Sager's true name. In Amparo's words, while Sager lived in Mayagüez, he showered her with poems and "sweet words," but once he moved to San Juan, he did not write for six months. Sager decided to renew contact with her around the same time as his most severe financial need. Amparo's ecstatic reply to his letter provides a window into their seemingly imbalanced level of emotional investment in the relationship: "It seemed to me a dream when I received your sweet letter, which caused me a great excitement and at the same time happiness when I saw that you have not forgotten me during such a long time of six months." Beyond differing emotional investment, Amparo's letters reveal that Sager enjoyed a level of mobility not afforded to her, an inequity tied to their differently gendered experiences. She wrote, "About your travelings, now I see what a good time you have spent while I have been all the time at home, here in Mayagüez."[163] In her view, "Jimmie" was someone who moved through the world while she remained stationary.

While Sager did not ask for financial help in his first letter to Amparo, he did so shortly afterward. Perhaps as an added incentive, he also sent a photograph of himself. Amparo responded, "I would like to help you but it is impossible because you know that I am a very poor girl." She chided him for his communist activities, saying that he was to blame for his own suffering, and although she claimed she "read very carefully" the political materials he sent, including copies of *El Machete*, these materials did not seem to hold her interest since she turned them "page by page . . . to see if I could find your picture in it but I didn't find any." Although Amparo's bilingualism was clearly superior to Sager's language skills, her way of "reading" these political materials by looking for pictures of her long-lost lover in their pages also suggests a potential asymmetry in education levels, or at least in political education. Amparo signed her last letter with "two thousand kisses," but after she did not send Sager any money, there does not appear to have been any further contact between them.[164] Whether or not Sager maintained contact or any emotional attachment to Amparo, it is abundantly clear that his relationship with her was uneven in many ways. That imbalance in power and access paralleled the colonial dynamic of the mainland United States to Puerto Rico.

Considering this, the case of James Sager raises important questions about both LADLA's political project and about solidarity movements more broadly. Through his ethnic impersonation, Sager seemed to take the movement's attempt to draw parallels between experiences of oppression (like that of Puerto Ricans with oppressed groups in the US mainland) to mean that these experiences were interchangeable and that he was authorized to speak for Puerto Ricans. In addition, his false ethnicity allowed him to avoid confronting his own imperialist and extractive behaviors toward his Puerto Rican friends, colleagues, and lovers. Although Sager's case is not necessarily representative of LADLA's larger movement, his many privileges—including ties between his lighter skin and a mid-1920s sexual economy in which whiteness was highly valued—were not unique. Several LADLA leaders' ease of travel through international borders was likely also facilitated by white, mestizo, and/or light skin privilege. Moreover, the overwhelming majority of activists in this movement, including Black and Indigenous activists, were young and able-bodied.

While LADLA exhibited a relational politics and aesthetics, one of its most lasting images is the now famous portrait of Julio Antonio Mella, taken by Modotti and circulated around the world after his death. In this image, Mella, a man of European descent, embodies youth, strength, and virility.[165] The portrait captures a revolutionary, masculine erotics that would become solidified in the aesthetics of the Latin American Left decades later through the figure of Che Guevara.[166] Such individualist and masculinist images appear periodically in LADLA's propaganda materials, especially in relation to Mella and Nicaraguan revolutionary Augusto

César Sandino, standing in contradistinction to a more nuanced aesthetic political vision based in interconnectivity.

These aesthetics, where Mella's erotic body emblematizes the youth and able-bodiedness of LADLA, connect to these activists' sexual politics. As LADLA members circulated at political conferences and worked together, they often formed romantic and sexual connections. Like Sager's relationship with Amparo, many of these exchanges were uneven. For example, although Nahua artist Xavier Guerrero was already an accomplished artist when he met Tina Modotti, he was also a dark-skinned Indigenous man from a working-class background with experiences different from those of Modotti, with her Italian American immigrant background. In September 1928, while Guerrero was in the Soviet Union, Modotti wrote him an emotional letter breaking off the relationship. She had fallen in love with Mella, who was recently separated from his wife, Oliva Zaldívar, who was in Cuba raising Mella's child.

When Mella was imprisoned and left for Mexico in 1925, Zaldívar, a law student, was pregnant. Zaldívar eventually followed Mella to Mexico City, where she suffered a miscarriage. She became pregnant again in late fall 1926, only for Mella to be traveling from January to June 1927 to the Brussels Congress and Moscow. A few months after her daughter Natasha's birth in August 1927, Zaldívar decided to formally separate from Mella, returning to Cuba and to her studies. Mella and Modotti fell in love in the summer of 1928.[167]

In Modotti's letter to Guerrero, she importantly took responsibility for her own political convictions, rejecting a male chauvinist view that would frame her convictions as dependent on her relationship to a man: "I've thought even more of the effect this step will have on revolutionary action. This has been my greatest worry, greater even than my worry about you. Well, I've come to the conclusion that however it turns out, whether I'm with you or with someone else . . . whatever usefulness I can bring to the cause, to our cause, will not suffer. The work I do for the cause is not a reflection or a result of loving a revolutionary man, but a deep-seated conviction in me."[168] Even with this declaration of her radical commitments, Modotti was in fact leaving Guerrero for a younger, college-educated man of European descent. While she does not address these aspects of her decision, her comments exhibit a self-consciousness around whether her attraction to Mella in this case contradicts her political commitments. She seems to be asking herself what bearing, if any, such sexual and romantic affinities have on "revolutionary action" centered around antiracism and anti-imperialism.

Such questions are not easily answered, and when we examine LADLA's erotics, we find other suggestive cases. Mexican artist David Siqueiros met Uruguayan poet Blanca Luz Brum at the founding conference of the Confederation of Latin American Labor Unions in Montevideo in May 1929, where Sandalio Junco delivered his comments.[169] During the conference, Siqueiros and Brum began their long and tumultuous love affair, and Brum returned with Siqueiros to Mexico City. Graciela Amador, Siqueiros's wife and a PCM leader, was reportedly devastated by the affair and by Brum's presence in their circles in Mexico City. The PCM also expressed serious suspicion about Brum's political commitments and access to sensitive information. Siqueiros was removed from the PCM Central Committee shortly after his return to Mexico from Uruguay and eventually expelled from the party due to his relationship with Brum.[170] The PCM's concerns may have had some basis since although Brum was then a close confidante of Peruvian Marxist José Carlos Mariátegui, years later she became an ardent supporter of the right-wing dictatorship of Augusto Pinochet in Chile. According to Brum, despite her blond hair and European features and the fact that Siqueiros chose her over his Mexican wife, Siqueiros wanted her to dress and wear her hair like a Mexican woman. Brum compared this aspect of their relationship to the dynamic between Diego Rivera and his wife, Mexican artist Frida Kahlo, writing, "Diego tried to erase in her any vestige of her German race. Making her dress like an Indian. With shawls, necklaces, dashes of gold and emeralds, braids wrapped around that head of long hair. Siqueiros, for his part, darkened my hair, braided it, and both established through our personas a true competition of Mexicanized women. Frida and I laughed at these costumes that we wore happily."[171] Significant evidence exists to show that Siqueiros abused Brum both physically and emotionally, and Brum refers here to an extreme level of control that he exercised over her body. At the same time, Brum demonstrates profound disrespect toward Indigenous cultures, viewing the clothing of Indigenous peoples as a "costume" that she could don to satisfy her lover. Considering her cultural insensitivity, the reader should call into question the parallels she draws between herself and Kahlo, who was of partial Indigenous descent and whose relationship to Indigenous clothing and culture would have been different. If Brum and Kahlo laughed about Brum's "costume," Kahlo may have been laughing at Brum, not with her.

Although Brum is not a reliable narrator, I cite the above passage to point to the cognitive dissonance of the sexual preferences of some of LADLA's key activists. In doing so, I do not intend to reduce the mysteries of love and attraction to a rigid race and class analysis; rather, I seek to identify a pattern of self-consciousness among LADLA activists for the ways their sexual preferences could mirror the very colonial and racist hierarchies they were trying to overthrow. Modotti's tortured and self-reflective letter and Siqueiros's apparent request for Brum to appear as Mexican as the wife he no longer desired provide insight into the internal tensions that these contradictions may have provoked.

In the case of Sandalio Junco, long after his return to Cuba, he traveled to Mexico City for the Confederation of Latin American Workers conference in September 1938.[172] During his time there, it appears that he fathered a son with a Mexican woman, since Mexican citizen Jesús Junco Roldán, born in 1939, listed his father as Sandalio Junco Junco, the same name as on Junco's travel visa.[173] Junco had a wife and three sons back in Cuba, but I have not been able to ascertain whether Junco maintained long-distance contact with this son in Mexico or even knew of his existence. Either way, Junco was assassinated in 1942, when the child was only three years old. As a Black Cuban man, Junco's movements between borders would have been subject to more scrutiny than those of his white and mestizo counterparts. Even so, Junco traveled frequently, including to the Soviet Union, Mexico, the Southern Cone, and Miami, Florida. Junco's travels across various international borders while a woman raised his child elsewhere parallels how Mella's political activities led to his absence from his child's life prior to his assassination or how Sager left his Puerto Rican girlfriend for political pursuits while she had been "all the time at home . . . in Mayagüez."[174]

In essence, it would be a mistake to celebrate LADLA's integrated analysis of differentiated experiences of oppression without acknowledging that LADLA was made up of mostly young, able-bodied people with high levels of mobility. Many of these individuals were forced into exile due to political persecution, and for some, their political commitments eventually cost them their lives. It does not minimize their suffering or courage to also remember the people they left behind, who had little choice but to gather the pieces and move forward.

JAMES SAGER AFTER PUERTO RICO

When Sager left Puerto Rico in April 1927, he left in his wake a divided Puerto Rican nationalist movement. Although he succeeded in attracting a slightly younger generation of Puerto Rican nationalists who were becoming increasingly radicalized, most of these activists had little funding or experience. Unsurprisingly, neither LADLA–Puerto Rico nor the Puerto Rican Communist League would last long after Sager's departure.[175] The PNPR, on the other hand, would expand greatly in importance from 1930 onward. In fact, around the same time as Sager's departure, Albizu Campos also left the island for a nearly three-year Latin American tour. When he returned in 1930, he took the reins of the PNPR, moving it toward the more militant position for which it is known.[176]

Sager traveled from San Juan to New York City, where he began taking classes with Bertram Wolfe at the Workers School. There, he made contact with Puerto Ricans and got a job at a factory, where he hoped to organize with African American workers.[177] Within two weeks of his arrival, he met Venezuelan LADLA leader Gustavo Machado, who was traveling through New York on his way back to Mexico City from the Brussels Congress.[178] Perhaps because of his meeting with Machado, Sager did not stay in New York long, traveling to Colombia shortly afterward "to serve the movement of foreign comrades."[179] In Colombia, he continued using the name Nevares Sager and moved in with a militant Colombian woman named Eufrosina Forero.[180] There, Sager appears to have helped organize the infamous December 1928 United Fruit *bananeras* (banana workers) strike, which ended in a massacre of the strikers by the Colombian army.[181] According to Pujals, who has tracked Sager's movements after he left Puerto Rico, Sager's career as an organizer seems to have paused after this point. She suggests this may have been due to a combination of the 1928 shift in Comintern strategy away from the united-front approach, the subsequent weakening of LADLA, and criticisms of the poor management of the *bananeras* strike.[182]

However, within a few years, Sager had become a political organizer in Texas. In 1933, he "arrived in San Antonio as a representative for the American Federation of Labor to coordinate a strike in the Finck Cigar Company."[183] At this point, he appears to have dropped the middle name Nevares but maintained the nickname Jaime. He joined the labor group Alianza Obrera (Worker Alliance) in Laredo, Texas, where he met the now renowned Mexican American activist Manuela Solís, whom he married in 1936 (figure 5.1). Solís and Sager (figure 5.2) played a key role in establishing the South Texas Agricultural Workers' Union, which coordinated union organizing among Mexican field and packing workers.[184] In 1938, Sager and Solís moved to San Antonio, where they joined forces with Chicana activist Emma Tenayuca in organizing a strike of thousands of pecan shellers, most of whom were women of Mexican descent.[185] While Sager

5.1 Manuela Solís Sager and James "Jaime" Sager, undated. Courtesy Esperanza Peace and Justice Center, San Antonio, Texas.

5.2 Manuela Solís Sager and James "Jaime" Sager (front row, left), 1971. Courtesy Esperanza Peace and Justice Center, San Antonio Texas.

initially played a leadership role in the strike, his communist affiliations threatened to compromise its potential success, and he eventually stepped down, ceding leadership to his wife.[186] Considering that Manuela Solís Sager became the far more recognizable name in the history of Chicano activism, it would appear that Sager eventually learned to take a back seat and decenter himself, supporting local organizers instead.

While in Texas, Sager used slightly different names (such as "Jacob Sager Master"), potentially to avoid military conscription.[187] However, he does not appear to have engaged in further ethnic impersonation. Whereas Sager devoted the rest of his life to labor organizing in Texas, often at his own peril, his former mentor Manuel Gomez was accused in 1928 by the Continental Committee of embezzling money intended for Sandino's army in Nicaragua and was removed from his position as LADLA-US secretary and replaced by communist activist Paul Crouch (who later became a government informant).[188] Gomez eventually became politically disillusioned and reinvented himself as an economic consultant and businessman named Charles Shipman.[189]

The case of James Sager and LADLA–Puerto Rico leaves many unresolved questions. Did Sager eventually learn to collaborate in the struggles of others without falling into the trap of over-identification? Alternatively, did he falsely take on his wife's ethnicity, as he had with his Puerto Rican collaborators? And to what extent can we extrapolate from this individual to characterize LADLA as a whole? As I have argued, the story of James Sager and LADLA–Puerto Rico is unique. Yet it sheds light on broader problems within LADLA and solidarity movements in general. It illuminates how a politics of relation must be understood as a complex art of collaboration. It shows that although solidarity demands more than empathy or allyship, it is also a political position that can easily compress sharp differences. When we consider James Sager, we observe the life arc of an individual committed to social justice, who may or may not have been capable of learning from his mistakes over time. Sager serves as a warning to those engaged in solidarity activism to tread lightly, step aside and listen to locals, recognize and allow for differences in experience, and, perhaps most importantly, think critically and openly about one's privileges and complicity with power.

SIX

HANDS OFF NICARAGUA AND THE SANDINO FANTASY

NAVIGATING NATIONALISM, INTERNATIONALISM, AND ANTI-FASCISM

LADLA steadily grew across the American continent from 1925 to 1927, but its growth exploded after January 1928 when it created its Manos Fuera de Nicaragua (Hands Off Nicaragua, MAFUENIC) campaign to support the insurgency of Augusto César Sandino. This chapter studies how LADLA used this financial and propaganda campaign to tie together a range of different struggles under the banner of Sandino and to establish new LADLA sections throughout the continent. The MAFUENIC campaign helped LADLA solidify links between anti-imperialism, the fight against authoritarian dictatorships, and antifascism. It had particular success in drawing together a Greater Caribbean movement (which included the Caribbean islands, Central America, Mexico, Colombia, and Venezuela) around the Sandinista cause. In this Greater Caribbean, LADLA used the Nicaraguan struggle to underline connections between the United Fruit Company's transnational holdings, the US government's actions in the Panama Canal zone, and the racial policing of labor by local authoritarian and fascist governments.

These connections were pivotal to LADLA's continued commitment to a broad coalition, even after the Comintern shifted to its more sectarian platform. Maintaining this unity represented a complicated effort that required merging its internationalist commitments with nationalist movements. This chapter thus builds on existing historical scholarship on MAFUENIC but moves in new directions by analyzing the campaign's narrative and aesthetic aspects. Through this analysis, it outlines how LADLA understood the relationship between anti-imperialist internationalism and nationalist struggles against authoritarian and fascist dictatorships as well as the complications it faced in balancing those commitments.[1] The MAFUENIC campaign, I argue, projected an image of Sandino that perfectly harmonized all of LADLA's diverse commitments. Such fantasy and projection around Sandino represented both the reason for the campaign's widespread expansion and its most severe shortcoming. MAFUENIC ultimately relied too heavily on the individual figure of Sandino, whose nationalist commitments did not align neatly with LADLA's opposition to nativism and authoritarianism. The campaign contained a contradiction between a networked, transnational movement and a nationalist project centered around an individual male hero. As LADLA's relationship to Sandino became increasingly complicated, it turned the campaign's focus away from Sandino and toward the martyred Julio Antonio Mella, a shift that would ultimately threaten to undermine LADLA's core values. In this sense, the MAFUENIC campaign represents both the height of LADLA's movement and the turning point toward its eventual dissolution.

THE SANDINO BANNER

In February 1928, a new banner (figure 6.1) hung from the office of LADLA's Continental Committee in Mexico City's historic center.[2] The banner featured a painting of Nicaraguan revolutionary Augusto César Sandino (whose name appeared below his face) created by Mexican artist Xavier Guerrero, who signed the banner with his moniker "indio" (Indian). Above Sandino, the banner included the words "¡Manos fuera de Nicaragua!" (Hands Off Nicaragua!), referring to LADLA's new grassroots solidarity campaign to support the Nicaraguan insurgency.

Some activities of this solidarity campaign, established in January 1928, were captured by photographer Tina Modotti. In spring 1928, Modotti's camera photographed the MAFUENIC Central Committee inside LADLA's office as committee members counted donations from their fundraising campaign in the presence of a notary (figure 6.2).[3] The committee featured in this photo included an international and multilingual group of people, like the Peruvian Jacobo Hurwitz, who served as MAFUENIC's secretary; Venezuelan exile Salvador de la Plaza; and Mexicans Jorge Fernández Anaya and Rafael Ramos Pedrueza. Modotti is seated between the Venezuelan Gustavo Machado and the notary, meaning that someone else pressed the camera's shutter. On the other side of the notary sits Joseph Jolibois fils of the Haitian Patriotic Union. Behind the group, the same Sandino banner hangs on the wall alongside other drawings by Xavier Guerrero.

A few months after this photo was taken, Modotti captured another important moment inside LADLA headquarters. In this October 1928 photo (figure 6.3), a group posed around a giant American flag reportedly captured by Sandino's soldiers from US Marines.[4] After MAFUENIC representative Gustavo Machado traveled to Nicaragua to deliver $1,000 to Sandino's personal secretary and then stayed two months with Sandino's guerrilla army on Nicaragua's northern border, Sandino gifted the flag to MAFUENIC in appreciation of its fundraising.[5] Machado returned to Mexico with the flag and with Sandino's endorsement of him as the official representative in Mexico of the Ejército Defensor de la Soberanía Nacional de Nicaragua (Army in Defense of the National Sovereignty of Nicaragua, EDSN). Sandino's half brother, Sócrates Sandino, also traveled with Machado to Mexico.[6] Later, PCM Secretary General Hernán Laborde was expelled from his seat in the Mexican legislature after he waved this flag in the chamber of deputies and made a speech against US imperialism.[7] Then Jacobo Hurwitz took the gifted flag to Frankfurt, Germany, where he presented it before the LAI's Second Congress in July 1929.[8] Although the Sandino banner is not visible in the photo of the reception of the flag, it would have been hanging just outside the frame.

The image of Sandino on the banner hanging both outside and inside LADLA headquarters bore little resemblance to Augusto César Sandino himself. Machado commented on this fact in annotations he made on a magazine spread about the campaign.[9] Next to a reproduction of the banner's portrait, Machado wrote, "General Sandino should forgive us. This is the product of the imagination of a Mexican Indian painter who drew a self-portrait—Sócrates protests against this drawing: He only likes where he is handsome, 'fifí' [posh] as they say here."[10] Machado's annotation is notable for several reasons. First, Machado suggested that the Nahua artist Guerrero drew Sandino, the mestizo son of a white landowner and

Das Lokal der **Antiimperialistischen Liga** in Mexiko-City,
die den Kampf der „Hände weg von Nicaragua" leitet

6.1 Office of LADLA's Continental Committee, Mexico City, 1928.
From Bach, "Bei."

6.2 Tina Modotti, *Manos Fuera de Nicaragua* (1928).

6.3 Photograph of MAFUENIC members in LADLA headquarters. Records of the United States Marine Corps, US National Archives, RG 127, entry 37, photo USNA1–2.9. From Schroeder, *The Sandino Rebellion*.

an Indigenous domestic worker, as himself. Second, Machado believed that this self-portrait deserved an apology, reporting that it also bothered Sandino's half brother, Sócrates, not only for its lack of resemblance but also because the portrait was not "handsome." Both Sandino's light-skinned half brother, Sócrates, and Machado believed that the portrait's resemblance to an "Indian" was not an attractive portrayal. In describing Sócrates (and by implication Augusto César Sandino himself) as "fifí," or pretentiously invested in physical appearance, Machado communicated his own critical distance from Sócrates's disapproval of the portrait.[11] Even so, Machado unquestioningly reproduced Sócrates's association between Indigenous features and the portrait's apparent unattractiveness.

Machado's belief that the painting was a self-portrait would suggest that Guerrero saw himself reflected in Sandino and in his army. While that may be true, the drawing also bears little resemblance to Guerrero, a highly skilled artist capable of reproducing his own likeness had he intended to produce a self-portrait. Others have commented on the portrait's lack of resemblance to Sandino, including historian Michael J. Schroeder. Referring to the same spread, which was published in the October 1928 issue of the German magazine *Arbeiter-Illustrierte-Zeitung* (Workers Pictorial Newspaper), edited by LAI founder Willi Münzenberg, Schroeder writes,

"The portrayal of Sandino's struggle here is pretty fantastical—perhaps symbolized most vividly by the image of Sandino himself, which bears virtually no physical resemblance to the guerrilla chieftain. The Sandino portrayed here has much darker skin, much rounder eyes, and exhibits an almost African phenotype."[12] Schroeder's suggestion of the potential Afro-descendancy of the man in the portrait (what he falteringly calls "an almost African phenotype") would also call into question whether Guerrero intended the image as a self-portrait.

Rather than a self-portrait of Guerrero, I find it more productive to understand this image as Machado initially described it: a product of Guerrero's imagination. It represented a projection of the artist's desire for who Sandino could be rather than an accurate depiction of who he was. Guerrero had surely seen a photograph of Sandino. The hat, collar, and direction of the man's gaze suggest that the drawing was likely based on the now famous, but blurry, full-body shot of Sandino standing with hands on hips, taken in January 1928.[13] The Sandino of Guerrero's imagination, or perhaps the Sandino of the blurry and darkened photo on which the portrait was based, was a dark-skinned man.[14] This version of Sandino was perhaps Indigenous, or Afro-descendant, or both; he was simultaneously serious, with his mouth turned down, and starry-eyed, looking up to the sky. And this Sandino was a younger-looking man than the still young but weathered thirty-three-year-old guerrilla leader.

The Sandino on the MAFUENIC banner represented a projection of not only Guerrero's desires but, as I will argue, those of LADLA as well. Here, Sandino embodied LADLA's ideal political subject, initially envisioned as an Indigenous worker in Latin America's extractive economies and over time broadened to Black communities (native-born and immigrant) and to Chinese immigrants. Although Machado's comments about what he considered "handsome" reveal that he held anti-Indigenous prejudices, LADLA as an organization consistently expressed its commitment to fighting both racial inequities within capitalism and the prejudices of white leftists like Machado. The dark skin and ethnic ambiguity of the man in the portrait provided a mirror through which Latin America's particularly agrarian working classes could see themselves reflected. It appeared to matter less to LADLA who Sandino was in reality and more what he represented to those who saw the banner hanging from LADLA's balcony or printed in *El Libertador*.

The desired political vision projected onto the Sandino banner provides insight into the MAFUENIC campaign more broadly. LADLA used the

Nicaraguan cause to tie together a range of different struggles under the banner of *sandinismo* and establish new LADLA sections throughout the continent. The MAFUENIC campaign helped LADLA solidify links between anti-imperialism, the fight against authoritarian dictatorships, and antifascism. These links were key to LADLA's continued commitment to a broad coalition, even after the Comintern shifted to its more sectarian platform. This was a complex balancing act that required merging LADLA's internationalist commitments with local, nationalist movements. Although LADLA presented an image of Sandino that perfectly harmonized these positions, the real Sandino was of course more complicated.

The story of the Comintern's relationship to Sandino has often been narrated as one of overwhelming support that then dissolved into traitorous abandonment.[15] Within that story, LADLA's MAFUENIC campaign is usually mentioned as an arm of Comintern policy in the region. But this familiar narrative fails to account for fissures between the Comintern's positions and those of LADLA and the broader LAI. The MAFUENIC campaign exemplified LADLA's continued commitment to the united-front approach that brought together anti-imperialists across social classes. Looking more closely at LADLA challenges the traditional way that the history of Comintern-affiliated organizations in Latin America (and outside Europe) are narrated, wherein ideological positions are often assumed to have been dictated from the center to the periphery. In truth, MAFUENIC was a grassroots campaign—its money came from individual donations, not the Comintern—and LADLA's Continental Committee did not abandon Sandino even when the Comintern did.[16] MAFUENIC's collapse was instead caused by the Mexican government's intense repression of LADLA organizers in the early 1930s, which resulted in the deportation of much of its leadership. This occurred at the same time that the Comintern tightened its grip on the LAI, attempting to bring the relatively independent organization into lockstep with the new sectarian line. The confluence of these two external factors was disastrous for LADLA.

Despite these external factors, MAFUENIC was also weakened by its overreliance on the individual figure of Sandino, who was never who LADLA imagined him to be and whose nationalist commitments did not always align with LADLA's fierce opposition to nativism and authoritarianism. Regardless of state repression or increased Comintern oversight, the campaign contained fundamental contradictions—emblematic of LADLA as a whole—between a relational, internationalist movement and a nationalist project centered around a charismatic hero. The conflictual ideologies found in MAFUENIC and analyzed in this chapter continue to play a role in Latin American politics, making MAFUENIC a case study deserving of closer examination.

BUILDING MAFUENIC

Activists from around the world gathered at the February 1927 Brussels Congress only one month after US Marines occupied Nicaragua. In this occupation, the US military intervened in the Nicaraguan Civil War between the Conservative government and Liberal "Constitutionalist" army, which formed in response to a Conservative coup that removed Nicaragua's democratically elected government. The Nicaraguan occupation became "the chief rallying ground of Latin American anti-imperialists" at the Brussels Congress.[17] The conference's manifesto discussed international support for the Nicaraguan resistance, and its Latin American resolution described Nicaragua as one of "the places where imperialist pressure is manifested with greatest violence."[18] Both LADLA and the LAI condemned the 1914 Bryan-Chamorro Treaty, through which the United States obtained sovereignty over large portions of Nicaraguan territory and acquired the rights in perpetuity to any canal built within the country.

After Sandino refused to sign the May 1927 peace accord, vowing instead to continue fighting until US Marines left the country, the Nicaraguan occupation again became the focus of discussion at the LAI's General Council meeting in Brussels in December 1927. From there, the LAI began to make plans for a widespread solidarity campaign in support of Sandino's army.[19] The campaign began one month later, in January 1928, during the US-supervised elections in Nicaragua, which LADLA—in support of Sandino's stance—characterized as a farce intended to compromise Nicaraguan sovereignty.[20]

After LADLA reported that it had received a request from Sandino for medical supplies, it formed the MAFUENIC Central Committee, made up of representatives from several organizations.[21] The Swiss Communist Fritz Sulzbachner (aka Federico Bach), who was serving as LAI representative in Mexico, played a key role in founding the campaign.[22] The Central Committee named as its general secretary the Peruvian Jacobo Hurwitz (who had worked with Mella and LADLA-Cuba in Havana prior to moving to Mexico) and designated *El Libertador* as MAFUENIC's official organ.[23] The committee sent invitations to a broad list of organizations, specifying that providing medical supplies represented the campaign's only political position.[24] It immediately began raising funds to send to Sandino, naming February 11–12, 1928, as Hands Off Nicaragua Days in both Mexico and the United States.[25]

From its inception, the campaign had a transnational reach. LADLA's Continental Committee instructed all sections throughout the continent to establish MAFUENIC committees in order to increase the scale of fundraising efforts. MAFUENIC committees were also created in several cities within Mexico.[26] In January 1928, the LAI held a rally in Paris in support of Sandino and the EDSN, and LADLA-US organized a rally of approximately thirty thousand people in New York.[27] At these and subsequent rallies, LADLA activists sold Hands Off Nicaragua stamps and lapel pins and distributed pamphlets.[28] Volunteers hung posters in Mexico's major cities and made collections at union meetings, in the streets, and at public events. [29]

Providing a glimpse into the participation of women in the campaign as well as their relegation to supporting roles, El Libertador described how "women of consciousness" planned to collect money for upcoming MAFUENIC days.[30] Later, "señoras y señoritas" (married and unmarried women) were invited to LADLA headquarters to sign up for the May 1928 fundraising effort, which would commemorate the one-year anniversary of the Sandino resistance.[31] Women who sympathized with the Nicaraguan cause collected the vast majority of the money for MAFUENIC.[32] Funds were collected at rallies held throughout the country.[33] News of the campaign's rallies and donations were reported in El Libertador and in the MAFUENIC bulletin, written by Hurwitz and distributed by leftist newspapers in Mexico and abroad. One MAFUENIC report claimed these bulletins had been reproduced in five hundred Spanish-language newspapers, as well as in other languages.[34]

In early February 1928, MAFUENIC's first representative, Carlos Aponte, traveled from Mexico City to Nicaragua to deliver the campaign's initial donation. Aponte, a member of the Venezuelan Revolutionary Party (Partido Revolucionario Venezolano, PRV) who left Venezuela for Cuba after participating in an armed insurrection against the dictator Juan Vicente Gómez, became involved in LADLA-Cuba before moving to Mexico City.[35] Aponte stayed in Nicaragua for one year, where he was promoted to lieutenant colonel and to second adjutant within the EDSN.[36]

Shortly after Aponte's arrival, in April 1928, Gustavo Machado joined him in Nicaragua, where he met with Sandino and delivered a $1,000 MAFUENIC donation to Sandino's private secretary, Honduran writer Froylán

Turcios.[37] Prior to serving as MAFUENIC's delegate, Machado had a long career as a political activist. Born into an upper-class family in Caracas, he became a leader in the National Assembly of Students and was imprisoned at sixteen for organizing protests against Gómez. Later, while enrolled in law school, he participated in a failed coup against Gómez and then sought exile first in New York and then in Paris. Upon completing his legal studies at the Sorbonne, he made his way to Cuba as the Cuban American Sugar Corporation's legal representative. However, instead of representing the interests of this American-owned corporation, he participated in anti-imperialist activities and befriended Mella.[38] Machado became involved with LADLA-Cuba and its associated magazine, *Venezuela Libre*. When Mella, along with the Venezuelan Salvador de la Plaza, left Cuba for Mexico in January 1926, Machado became LADLA-Cuba's "secretary of the exterior."[39] Shortly afterward, Machado was deported to Mexico, where he joined Mella and De la Plaza on LADLA's Continental Committee and where he eventually became the administrator of *El Libertador*.[40] After more than two months with Sandino's army, Machado returned to Mexico as Sandino's official representative, bringing Sócrates with him.[41] LADLA greeted them with a large outdoor assembly in Mexico City, where they exhibited the captured American flag that Sandino had gifted to MAFUENIC.[42] Many rallies followed over the coming months.[43]

Around the time of Machado's return to Mexico, MAFUENIC sent another representative to Nicaragua, the Salvadoran Agustín Farabundo Martí, who was secretary of LADLA–El Salvador. In early 1928, Martí traveled to New York at the invitation of LADLA-US, where he was detained after a raid on the New York office. He then left the United States for Mexico City, arriving in May 1928. Shortly afterward, he traveled to Nicaragua, where he quickly gained Sandino's trust. Martí would become MAFUENIC's primary point of contact with the EDSN moving forward.[44]

The campaign functioned not only to support Sandino's struggle but also to expand LADLA. Within Mexico, this expansion was facilitated through the organizational structure of the National Peasant League, and by July 1928, *El Machete* reported that a MAFUENIC committee had been established in every state capital city in Mexico, and that "thanks to this campaign, in almost every place in the country, there is formed a section of the Anti-Imperialist League of the Americas."[45] This pattern within Mexico was reproduced throughout the continent. LADLA sections were formed or reorganized in Uruguay, Brazil, Ecuador, Guatemala, Costa Rica, and Panama, and LADLA–El Salvador expanded its local sections significantly.[46] On his way to Nicaragua, Machado interviewed LADLA-Guatemala members, who shared about their successful campaign, which included selling Sandino-branded cigarettes and organizing large rallies.[47] LADLA-US, which had been active in Chicago and New York for several years, also expanded during the campaign, creating sections in Salt Lake City, Seattle, and San Francisco and specifically Spanish-speaking sections in "Los Angeles, Kansas, Colorado and Pittsburgh."[48]

The expansion afforded by the campaign came at an opportune time for LADLA's Central Committee, which was struggling financially to keep the organization afloat. *El Libertador* reported financial difficulties due to unpaid subscriptions and noted that it did not rely on subventions or advertisements.[49] It requested that each LADLA section name two individuals responsible for selling subscriptions, and it printed notes of gratitude to exemplary colleagues, like Tina Modotti, who donated to *El Libertador*.[50] MAFUENIC thus provided an opportunity to increase LADLA's financial support.[51]

LADLA's rapid expansion did not go unnoticed by authorities. In Machado's interview with LADLA-Guatemala, he learned that police had violently broken up a pro-Sandino rally; "the wounds of some had not yet scarred, others were recently released from prison."[52] LADLA-Guatemala was forced to operate underground and reported that distributing *El Libertador* had become criminalized.[53] Similarly in Cuba, because of police persecution, MAFUENIC activities occurred clandestinely.[54] In the United States, when the campaign sent donation requests using their own Hands Off Nicaragua stamps, the US Postal Service refused to deliver the envelopes, threatening LADLA members with imprisonment and fines.[55] Activists were arrested at MAFUENIC protests in Washington, D.C., Los Angeles, and New York, and the Federal Bureau of Investigation (FBI) began investigating Manuel Gomez during this period.[56]

The US State Department and FBI kept a file of documents distributed by LADLA-US in support of the EDSN.[57] The FBI's investigation of LADLA-US for treason reported that at a February 1928 meeting in New York, Manuel Gomez stated that although the money would be sent to Sandino "under the term (guise) of medical supplies, bandages and clothing; no one can stop us from sending money and other things under such terms (methods) and no one will suspect that the money is really going for all kinds of war purposes."[58] This statement would suggest MAFUENIC donations were used for weapons in addition to other supplies.[59] LADLA's Continental Committee eventually accused Gomez of embezzling money intended for the Nicaraguan struggle, leading to Gomez's ouster as secretary of LADLA-US.[60]

MAFUENIC'S PAN-CARIBBEAN MOVEMENT AGAINST "TROPICAL FASCISM"

LADLA's rapid expansion during this period can be attributed to how it used MAFUENIC to deftly join multiple struggles under one roof. LADLA often referred to the campaign as the "Frente Único MAFUENIC" (MAFUENIC United Front), and LADLA introduced its new logo—a hammer, sickle, and pen, which symbolized the merging of class positions—during this moment, hanging it from the office balcony beneath the Sandino banner (figure 6.1). Although MAFUENIC began a few months before the Comintern's 1928 Sixth Congress, in which it officially shifted away from its united-front approach to its class-against-class policy, this shift did not change the campaign's tone moving forward. Instead, the campaign maintained an open-arms approach, which Hurwitz described as follows: "The communal, spontaneous, and extremely sincere effort by poor farmers, poor workers, soldiers, all those who feel that the cause of Nicaragua is the cause of the destitute, those dispossessed by a common enemy, Yankee imperialism . . . we know the unending list of organizations of all factions, of all tendencies, of all colors, joined in one cry of protest against the disgrace and one voice of support to our campaign."[61]

As the campaign united a wide range of interests, it allowed LADLA to draw stronger connections between the fight against imperialism and struggles against local authoritarian governments. A June 1928 article by Salvador de la Plaza, entitled "The Continental Situation," detailed these connections, arguing that imperialist states create "a new kind of country," a semicolony, which "has lost its economic freedom in order to depend on another stronger and richer country, seemingly conserving its political freedom and sovereignty and its international statute."[62] In a colonized country, "economic penetration is almost always from the colonizing country, while in semi-colonies, this penetration is from various imperialist countries."[63] Following independence from Spain, Latin America became subject to British capital, which dominated mines and transportation and "permitted the development of a small, parasitic bourgeoisie and the stabilization of tyrannical governments."[64] The first quarter of the twentieth century, he explained, had been characterized by a struggle between the

United States and England, in which the United States eventually gained control of Latin American markets. Similarly, in his speech before the LAI General Council a few months earlier, De la Plaza explained that US expansion into Latin America was motivated by the "search for primary materials and cheap manual labor from Indigenous people."[65] He argued that within semicolonial countries, the ruling classes were so committed to conserving their internal political power that, if forced to choose, they preferred to lose their economic power by cooperating with imperialist industries. This led to a tendency toward authoritarian dictatorships propped up by imperialist interests. For this reason, he argued, any nationalist struggle against authoritarianism must have a social and economic basis and must be connected to an international workers' rights struggle.

LADLA theorized a continental struggle that had a simultaneously nationalist and internationalist character. As De la Plaza explained, "Almost all the governments of Latin America are agents of Washington, which allows for the characterization of the anti-imperialist struggle as a movement of national liberation."[66] This interdependent relationship between an internationalist movement and nationalist struggles allowed activists throughout the continent to identify with the Nicaraguan cause. For example, Haitian Patriotic Union president and MAFUENIC Central Committee member Joseph Jolibois fils drew parallels between the US military occupations of Haiti and Nicaragua, writing that "the two causes should be one."[67] El Libertador similarly compared Nicaragua's attenuated sovereignty to Venezuela's subjection to the whims of Standard Oil and Royal Dutch Shell, advising Venezuelan revolutionaries to look to Nicaragua for inspiration.[68] Machado claimed that "the struggle of Nicaragua is the struggle of Latin America" and "Nicaragua defends continental sovereignty."[69]

MAFUENIC had particular success in drawing together a Greater Caribbean movement. El Libertador announced that LADLA and MAFUENIC would host a Caribbean Anti-Imperialist Conference, which it also referred to as the "Pro-Nicaragua Conference," in Mexico City. This conference would be organized by the MAFUENIC Central Committee and would use the Nicaraguan struggle as the basis for a broader discussion about imperialist practices in the Greater Caribbean.[70] Both Sandino and Froylán Turcios would be invited as guests of honor, and Machado would preside. The planned program would begin with a discussion of the Nicaraguan case, followed by presentations on imperialism in the Caribbean and then an analysis of "imperialist penetration in the rest of the countries of Latin America."[71] MAFUENIC Central Committee member Marco Antonio Montero traveled throughout Central America, meeting with leaders of LADLA sections in Panama, Costa Rica, Honduras, Guatemala, and El Salvador, inviting them to send delegates to the conference.[72]

LADLA used the Nicaraguan context to frame a Greater Caribbean region characterized by similar experiences of economic domination. The cover of the January 1928 issue of *El Libertador* (figure 6.4) clearly illustrates this vision. Over a map of the Caribbean Sea and Gulf of Mexico, the cover image marks places not by their cartographic name but by their extractive industry. Oil rigs flying American flags mark northern Mexico, the *henequén* (sisal hemp) industry marks the Yucatán peninsula, and Central America is depicted as United Fruit territory. Dead bodies riddle the landscape from the Antilles to northern Mexico to the base of Central America. A caricature of Cuban President Gerardo Machado kneels on the island of Cuba and raises his hands in surrender to the urban and militarized North above him. Above the image appear the words "Hail Augusto C. Sandino!" and "Down with the Pan American Congress!," the latter a reference to the upcoming 1928 Pan-American Conference to be held in Havana. LADLA heavily criticized the discourse of "pan-Americanism" as a hypocritical posture of goodwill that ultimately led to US intervention in Latin America.[73] This cover image draws parallels between the violence of extractive industries in various Caribbean contexts and creates a counterpoint between Sandino's anti-imperialist struggle and Latin American governments' cooperation with the US agenda of pan-Americanism.

Within the Caribbean, LADLA theorized what Mella termed "tropical fascism," or "an adaptation of fascism to colonial conditions . . . to the relations with imperialism."[74] Mella had been calling Cuban President Gerardo Machado a "tropical Mussolini" for years, and in November 1928, Mella used this term to describe how Machado demonstrated characteristics of fascist regimes, such as "attempt at stabilization through dictatorial methods of incipient capitalism," consolidation of power into one party, police persecution, violence, and censorship of leftist groups.[75] In contrast to the independent national economies of European fascist states, Mella argued, tropical fascism "is exercised in favor of the bosses of imperialist industry."[76] While these tropical fascist regimes adopt a protectionist, pro-labor rhetoric, they also cooperate with American sugar companies to import immigrant workers, relying on the nativist demonization of these workers to uphold their power domestically. LADLA used its conceptualization of a Caribbean and tropical extractive zone to theorize intersections between imperialism, authoritarian governance, and racial violence. In October 1928, Mella

6.4 LADLA, *El Libertador* 2, no. 14 (January 4, 1928), cover.

spoke about this notion of "tropical fascism" in a meeting of the International Anti-Fascist League, in which Modotti opened with a discussion of fascism in Italy. Others present made comparisons to the regime of Juan Vicente Gómez in Venezuela and that of Adolfo Díaz in Nicaragua. The meeting ended with cries of "Hail to Sandino and the Anti-Fascist International League, and death to Mussolini."[77] Through creating a dialogue between MAFUENIC and antifascist movements, LADLA attempted to unite anti-authoritarian nationalist struggles, internationalist anti-imperialism, and the growing movement against the rise of fascism worldwide.

The banana industry, and especially US-owned United Fruit, became a focal point of LADLA's efforts to draw links between authoritarian governance and racial violence in the Caribbean. LADLA blamed the US occupation of Nicaragua on the interest of US companies United Fruit and Cuyamel Fruit in the potential construction of a Nicaraguan canal. Nicaragua, LADLA argued, was particularly susceptible to US intervention because of the control that these companies exercised on nearby governments of Guatemala and Honduras. LADLA-Guatemala concentrated its efforts on protesting United Fruit.[78] LADLA's new Costa Rican section published a manifesto on "the banana question," organized agitation against the concession of Costa Rican land for the Nicaraguan canal, and pressured the national legislature to revoke United Fruit land contracts.[79] In the case of Colombia, the massacre of United Fruit banana strikers in the Caribbean town of Ciénaga in December 1928, in which the Colombian army killed hundreds of strikers, became a rallying cry for LADLA's Greater Caribbean movement.

After Marco A. Montero traveled throughout Central America advertising the Caribbean Anti-Imperialist Conference among LADLA sections, he wrote an in-depth comparative analysis of United Fruit and Cuyamel Fruit holdings in Central America. Montero argued that these companies controlled the entire Atlantic coast of many Central American countries and were expanding to the Pacific coast. On Panama's border with Colombia, United Fruit violently squelched strikes by native-born workers and imported Antillean workers to replace them. This led to resentment by local workers, "fomenting a racial problem that extends through all of Central America where UNITED operates as a mistress of exploitation."[80] In Costa Rica, he argued, these companies used anti-Black racial prejudice among white and mestizo Costa Ricans to facilitate anti-labor violence by local police and military. Throughout the region, United Fruit "establishes around its banana industry, a multitude of industries in order to ensure its absolute autonomy and maintain control over commerce . . . robbing in its commissaries—company stores—the meagre salary that it has given its workers."[81] This issue was most acute in Costa Rica and Guatemala, where United Fruit owned every stage of production and distribution and where it monopolized commerce within its land concession. The US government, Montero added, paid for the creation of local national guards to violently suppress labor struggles. For this reason, "all union struggles in those countries have an anti-imperialist base."[82] Sandino's struggle, in turn, "is the only serious obstacle" to the economic domination of these US industries.[83] Montero and LADLA used United Fruit to draw connections between the Nicaraguan context, the United Fruit Company's activities in Central America and the Greater Caribbean, and the racial policing of labor by local authoritarian governments.

Although the Caribbean Anti-Imperialist Conference was scheduled for March 1929, it appears to have been cancelled, likely because of the repression campaign against the PCM and LADLA that began under the Portes Gil government.[84] However, Montero reported that through his travels and efforts to ensure participation, the Sandinista cause had served as an effective rallying cry for connecting struggles transnationally. He wrote, "Central America is a field of intense imperialist penetration, but it is also an ample field of anti-imperialist possibilities."[85] He recommended that LADLA sections in these countries focus on organizing banana workers and on "destroying racial prejudice and attracting to us Black workers looking for fraternization in the anti-imperialist struggle."[86] Despite the conference's cancellation, this anti-imperialist vision for the Greater Caribbean would have a significant impact on the region that would outlast the MAFUENIC campaign, LADLA, or Sandino's struggle, and which is discussed further in this book's final chapter.

THE SANDINO FANTASY

As LADLA used MAFUENIC to connect anti-imperialist internationalism, antiracism, and nationalist struggles against authoritarian and fascist dictatorships, it projected an image of Sandino that embodied all these commitments. In a letter to the MAFUENIC Central Committee, published in *El Libertador*, French communist and LAI member Henri Barbusse described Sandino as "the banner of national and social emancipations, of the liberation of the races and the masses exploited by capitalism and by universal

imperialism."[87] Through similar descriptions, LADLA constructed Sandino as its ideal revolutionary and the personification of its united front.
It framed Sandino as a continental figure and a model to be replicated
throughout the region. "Sandino does not have borders," El Libertador
claimed, describing him as "the good and decent consciousness of Latin
America" who "demands solidarity from all the oppressed."[88] El Machete
made similar claims, arguing that Sandino would foment "the struggle of
new Sandinos that will arise in all of America" and that "each one of its
nations has hundreds of Sandinos that will know how to fight and defeat
imperialism."[89]

The idea that Sandino's struggle would foment more revolutions
throughout the continent was not mere rhetoric. For example, in June 1929,
MAFUENIC Central Committee members who trained with Sandino's
EDSN helped lead a raid on a military fort in Curaçao to obtain weapons
to overthrow Venezuelan dictator Juan Vicente Gómez. MAFUENIC representative Carlos Aponte left Sandino's camp in Nicaragua to participate
in this insurrection along with MAFUENIC representative Gustavo Machado.[90] After the group plundered weapons from the fort and stole an American ship, which they used to sail from Curaçao to the Venezuelan coast,
the Venezuelan military suppressed the revolt, and Aponte and Machado
escaped into Colombia.

In viewing Sandino as a continental leader, whose example would lead
to more revolutions, LADLA positioned Sandino as linked to Mexico's fate
in particular. El Libertador claimed, "When sooner or later the Yankee marines disembark again in a Mexican port, a Mexican Sandino will arise. The
workers of Nicaragua, joined with the workers of the rest of the countries,
will help Mexico then. It is more of a question of mutual aid, of solidary
action, of a common struggle."[91] LADLA characterized helping Sandino
as helping Mexico, participating in a mutual struggle, and it framed supporting Sandino as interchangeable with supporting whichever struggle
its members identified as their own. Whether they were invested in a national, continental, or workers' movement or in antiracist, anticapitalist, or
antifascist organizing, supporting Sandino aligned with their cause.

Sandino's image appeared not only from the balcony of LADLA's headquarters and in El Libertador but also on posters, cigarette packs, and graffiti. Activists wrote songs about him, which were performed at MAFUENIC
rallies.[92] "Who is Sandino?," El Libertador asked rhetorically, answering
with "A miner. A son of the people."[93] As in Guerrero's mixed-race portrait
of Sandino, LADLA presented Sandino as an everyman, in whom anyone

could see themselves reflected, especially if they were working class and non-white. *El Libertador* frequently emphasized that most MAFUENIC donations came from workers of limited economic means. Financially supporting Sandino gave these workers cultural capital (Sandino-branded cigarettes, for example), but it also allowed them to participate, even if they had little time and money, in a movement that LADLA framed as belonging to them.

LADLA's construction of Sandino adheres to what some scholars have called "character work" in social movements that rely on traditional character tropes within narrative structures to advance the "emotional work of mobilization."[94] In this character work, a movement leader is forged into a cultural symbol, "the international image of the movement, necessary for attracting crowds, media attention, contributions."[95] If Sandino appeared as MAFUENIC's narrative hero, envisioned as a perfect conglomeration of all LADLA's political projects, then the narrative villain of this movement found expression in the slogan "Hands Off Nicaragua." The slogan "Hands Off," commonly employed by early twentieth-century communists in support of self-determination movements and still used in the present day, contains an implication of violence against someone who is defenseless, requiring a third party to step in as protector.[96]

LADLA framed the presence of the US Marines in Nicaragua in precisely these terms, focusing especially on violence committed against women and children. At a MAFUENIC rally, US journalist Carleton Beals claimed that "the Marines, recruited from the most degenerate and depraved sectors of the United States, do not know what respect toward human life is."[97] On a similar note, Machado wrote from Nicaragua that Marines tortured women and children to interrogate them about the whereabouts of their adult male family members. He also described how local women fled from him, thinking he was a US Marine, and thus implied that Marines committed acts of sexual violence against Nicaraguan women.[98] Carlos Aponte reported similar abuses from Nicaragua, describing a three-hour bombing of an Indigenous community that left around fifty dead, most of whom were women and children.[99] The cover image for *El Libertador*'s June 1928 issue (figure 6.5), drawn by Diego Rivera, presented Nicaragua as an Indigenous woman being stabbed by a bayonet on a gun labeled "U.S.A."[100] Through its focus on violence toward Indigenous women, MAFUENIC represented the Marine occupation in particularly gendered and raced terms.

By analyzing MAFUENIC's narrative devices, I do not intend to question the veracity of the human rights abuses committed by Marines in Nicaragua. Rather, I seek to explain how MAFUENIC undermined the US media

6.5 Diego Rivera, *El Libertador* 2, no. 18 (June 1928), cover.

strategy that consistently described Sandino as a "bandit" by presenting him instead as a paternal protector of Indigenous people, and especially of women and children. By focusing on the violence toward noncombatants, MAFUENIC emphasized these occupied communities as *indefensos* (defenseless), in need of Sandino as their defender.[101] The US media employed "the legend of banditry," Machado wrote, to criminalize "liberators" and describe as "racial hatred" the times "when oppressed people are incited and protest."[102] LADLA inverted this rhetoric, consistently depicting the Marines as bandits instead. As Joseph Jolibois fils claimed in comparing Haiti and Nicaragua, "It is not the 'bandit' Sandino who is the author of the acts of banditry in Haiti, to which the same Yankee marines that operate in Nicaragua can respond."[103]

LADLA's increasing focus on Sandino through MAFUENIC follows the pattern that Erica Edwards describes as the "spectacle of charismatic leadership."[104] Writing on the history of US Black liberation movements, Edwards characterizes this spectacle as "a storytelling regime . . . a set of performative prescriptions" and "a dynamic interplay between performance, power, and aesthetic idealization" that adheres to "normative masculinity" and a "gendered economy of political authority."[105] LADLA's characterization of Sandino faithfully followed this prescribed set of narrative tropes. In more contemporary social movements, scholars have noted a historical shift wherein recent movements intentionally avoid charismatic leaders in favor of horizontal, "leaderless" (or "leader-full") organizational structures. Contemporary organizers have learned the historical lesson that the imprisonment and assassination of key leaders can easily squelch a movement. Beyond this learned experience, these movements also critique remnants of authoritarianism within the structure of the political community.[106] Such a shift away from the narrative of charismatic leadership has ushered in a transformation in political aesthetics, abandoning the traditional focus on the singular, male hero to emphasize relational political community. Although LADLA did not transcend patriarchal gender roles, the organization's initial vision had much in common with these contemporary horizontal and anti-authoritarian social movements. As LADLA became more focused on Sandino, it moved further from this initial vision, and the paternalism and hypermasculine hero worship of the campaign threatened to undermine the movement's core values. MAFUENIC provides insight into a core tension within LADLA: This movement innovated a networked political and aesthetic vision—what I have called a politics and aesthetics of *redes*—at the same time that it increasingly upheld the charismatic leader of Sandino through the campaign.

Two articles published in *El Libertador* in 1929 addressed "the question of leadership" in relation to LADLA's anti-authoritarian stance.[107] These articles were written by Italian communist Vittorio Vidali, a member of LADLA's Continental Committee and secretary of the Mexican Anti-Fascist League. The articles sought to differentiate between caudillos and "the leader in the revolutionary struggle."[108] A caudillo, Vidali explained, "is one who by acts of bravery, and by taking advantage of a particular situation of general discontent, becomes the leader of an insurrectionary movement."[109] This man (the article uses masculine pronouns) may be from a working-class background and purport to hold anti-imperialist sentiments, but he has a "petty bourgeois mentality and ideology" in that he "does not want to destroy the economic system based on the private ownership of the means of production, nor fight for the complete emancipation of the exploited class."[110] This type of leader is anathema to "the base of the *anti-caudillista* character of our continental organization."[111] The type of leader that LADLA supported, in contrast, does not seek "to control the masses, convinced that those that follow him are an army of idiots that should be controlled."[112] Rather, "our leader is controlled by the masses, and in the very moment in which he escapes this control or deviates from the path that defends the interests of the working class that he represents, he ceases to be a leader."[113] LADLA allowed for leaders, but only if "they have been built on the base of the organization of the exploited masses."[114] Vidali upheld the example of the Venezuelan struggle as a nationalist movement with key leaders but built on a mass base. The publication of these two articles on the "question of leadership" in *El Libertador* evinces a self-conscious awareness that the ongoing idealization of Sandino and his nationalist cause threatened to muddle the "*anticaudillista* character" of the organization. LADLA's conditioned and tenuous commitment to upholding leaders would be central to the complications that arose in its relationship with Sandino.

LADLA's increasing shift from a vision of relational solidarity and networked political community to the individual focus on Sandino was likely an issue of practicality. Although LADLA grew steadily throughout the mid-1920s, it struggled financially prior to MAFUENIC and had difficulty attracting the very Indigenous and Black communities it claimed to represent. As the campaign grew, so did LADLA's ability to reach these communities. Arguably, it is more practical in the short term to organize around an individual with whom people can identify than with a cause promoted by a broad network. The charismatic leader, as Edwards writes, functions as a familiar "discursive sign, a narrative fixity."[115] Predictably, however, Sandino was a human being whose positions changed over time and who, despite LADLA's projections, did not manage to balance all LADLA's interests at once. The Sandino fantasy was bound to disappoint.

SANDINO THE PERSON

In many ways, Sandino upheld LADLA's vision, and he frequently employed the language of *frente único* (united front) to describe his movement.[116] His army included fighters from a wide range of Latin American countries and social classes, as well as representatives from the Comintern, LADLA, and LADLA's rival APRA. For this reason, *El Libertador* claimed, "the struggle in Nicaragua . . . has been carried out not as a national struggle but as one of continental and international transcendence, since fighters of all countries against imperialism have participated."[117] Sandino also courted the support of a wide range of leftist groups and individuals, including leading intellectuals in Latin America like José Vasconcelos and Gabriela Mistral. He intentionally presented his movement through an ideological flexibility that would translate for diverse parties.

But such flexibility and inclusivity also meant that Sandino was ideologically moveable and difficult to pin down. The son of a wealthy landowner and an Indigenous domestic servant, Sandino fled Nicaragua during his youth after a brawl with the son of a prominent Conservative leader. He went to Honduras, where he worked in gold mines and sugar and banana plantations, then to Guatemala, eventually arriving in Tampico, Mexico, in 1923, where he worked for American-owned oil companies.[118] Although Tampico was a hotbed of labor movement activity in the early 1920s, there is no evidence that Sandino participated in labor struggles there.[119] However, he was immersed in anti-imperialist circles in Mexico through Freemasonry and with "spiritualist friends."[120] Sandino returned to Nicaragua in May 1926 to take part in the uprising of the Liberal Party, with which his father had long identified, against the Conservative regime of Emiliano Chamorro. There, he worked in the American-owned San Albino gold mine, where he used his position as paymaster assistant to organize workers for the uprising. By October 1926, he had gathered a group of twenty-nine men and approached the Liberal General José María Moncada about obtaining arms and ammunition. Based on his experience working in US-owned extractive industries, Sandino shared LADLA's pro-worker and anti-imperialist stance focused on extractive economies. At the same time, Sandino was fundamentally committed to regime change in Nicaragua. While he began his struggle on behalf of the Liberal Party, he quickly became disillusioned with its leadership and eventually broke with General Moncada over his negotiations with the US government in the 1927 supervised elections.[121]

Due to Sandino's travels throughout Central America and Mexico, he also held a Latin American regionalist ideology based in *indohispanismo* (Indo-Hispanism). As Rodolfo Cerdas Cruz writes, "It is notable that this internationalism by Sandino was not an internationalism of the proletariat but rather an 'indo-hispanic' internationalism, although in some documents he speaks of the liberation of the global proletariat."[122] In Sandino's first manifesto of July 1927, he defined his movement as existing on a "great horizon of internationalism" on behalf of "the entire continent of our language."[123] He described himself as a "patriot" who had "arisen from the bosom of the oppressed, who is the soul and nerve of the race," which he defined as the "Indo-Hispanic race."[124] This regionalist and Indo-Hispanist vision would overwhelmingly characterize Sandino's ideology throughout his career, and it had much in common with the ideas of an intellectual like Vasconcelos who—as discussed in chapter 2—portrayed Latin American anti-imperialists as Spanish-speaking mestizos.[125] This position differed quite markedly from LADLA's hemispheric globalism and solidarity with Black and Chinese workers.

Sandino's Latin American regionalism and Indo-Hispanism meant that he was willing to negotiate with Latin American politicians who differed from him ideologically. LADLA found this aspect of Sandino's politics troubling, an issue that especially came to a head after the November 1928 election of President Moncada. After the election, when many of Sandino's soldiers returned to civilian life since the impetus of the initial Liberal uprising had been resolved, Sandino found himself in a weak strategic position.[126] Sandino wrote to Froylán Turcios to report that he had created a revolutionary junta of dissident groups that planned to organize a coup against Moncada and to name Dr. Pedro José Zepeda to the presidency instead. This plan, Sandino wrote, would only move forward if US Marines remained in the country. In the case of US withdrawal, he planned instead to travel to Mexico, where he would depend on MAFUENIC support to gather the necessary arms to invade Nicaragua and oust Moncada from power without the collaboration of other dissident groups.[127] Turcios wrote back a strongly worded letter to say that as someone who had spent years disseminating "the glory of the LIBERATOR SANDINO," he could not support Sandino in "heading up a civil war to put this one or that one in the presidential seat of Nicaragua."[128] He added that he could not support the trip to Mexico nor Sandino's transformation into a "caudillo in a civil war, in a miserable fratricidal battle," and for this reason, he resigned from his position as Sandino's personal secretary.[129]

After the resignation of Turcios, who had served as a major link between Sandino and the international community, Sandino decided to travel abroad to rally support. In January 1929, he wrote to Mexican President Emilio Portes Gil with a request to enter Mexico, in the hope that he could secure financial and military support from the Mexican government.[130] A few months later, Sandino wrote Argentine President Hipólito Yrigoyen, proposing that Argentina host a hemispheric conference of government representatives, including the United States, to discuss the future of the Nicaraguan canal. Importantly, he proposed that this conference include the governments of Gerardo Machado in Cuba, Juan Vicente Gómez in Venezuela, and Augusto Leguía in Peru, leaders he had previously called "bloodthirsty despots."[131] He believed this conference would "guarantee Indo-Hispanic sovereignty and independence and the friendship of the America of our race with the United States on a basis of equality."[132]

In descriptions of Sandino's ideology, he is often quoted as saying that his movement was "not far left nor far right but a united front ... we ensure the cooperation of all social classes, without classifications of 'ists.'"[133] This quote uses the language of LADLA's united front but distances the movement from communist associations. Sandino, however, wrote these words in September 1929 after Moncada's election, when his weak position led him to try to cooperate more fully with Latin American government leaders, including ones that were staunchly anticommunist. In other words, while Sandino always held fluid ideological positions, the November 1928 election led to a shift in his rhetoric that confounded not only his personal secretary but also MAFUENIC's leaders.

In the lead-up to Sandino's arrival in Mexico, MAFUENIC Secretary Hurwitz used *El Libertador* to express confusion around the changes happening in Sandino's movement. Hurwitz wrote that he did not understand the full context of Turcios's resignation nor why Sandino was leaving Nicaragua.[134] Although Hurwitz urged readers to continue supporting Sandino until they could learn more, he wrote that MAFUENIC would request further clarification on Sandino's commitment to the anti-imperialist struggle, an explanation of his plan to install Dr. Zepeda into the presidency, and an official statement regarding Turcios's resignation. The article that followed Hurwitz's statement, "The Anti-Imperialist League and General Sandino," expressed concern over Sandino's invitation to "all of the governments of America, agents of imperialism, to a conference in Buenos Aires to discuss if the capital that should be invested in the opening of the canal should be all or partially from U.S. bankers."[135] In essence, Sandino's interest not only in a coup in Nicaragua but also in cooperating with some of LADLA's leading enemies—like Machado, Leguía, and Gómez—caused LADLA to question his alignment with its project. LADLA stated that if EDSN fighters found that "the war against the invader" was no longer sustainable in Nicaragua, then they should "transfer their action to other fields of struggle against imperialism, without accepting any compromise that the invaders propose to them directly or indirectly."[136] LADLA began to recognize that whereas Sandino drew upon internationalist support for his struggle, he was ultimately focused on national regime change and willing to consider various options for accomplishing that goal. LADLA was forced to come to terms with how Sandino's nationalist goals did not exactly align with its own, resulting in LADLA's statement that "we cannot conceive of the struggle against imperialism as circumscribed to only one piece of territory in America; it is continental and international. If one trench is lost, one has to build another, and an exit by Sandino and the rest of the members of the Army with the aim of swelling the anti-imperialist ranks in any other place in the continent would not be a desertion."[137]

In a brief recognition of how LADLA's projection of Sandino differed from the man himself, *El Libertador* stated that Sandino's potential cooperation with "agents of imperialism" represented "a betrayal of the revolutionary masses of America and of the entire world that have seen in him a representative of the struggle that sooner or later all peoples would have to carry out in defense of their own sovereignty."[138] The true betrayal was less Sandino's abandonment of his own ideals and more his betrayal of what others "have seen in him," or the fantasy that MAFUENIC had so carefully constructed.

Despite these misgivings, when Sandino arrived in Mexico in July 1929, MAFUENIC organized a welcoming rally of more than five thousand workers.[139] Sandino in turn sent out a "fraternal greeting, by way of the Anti-Imperialist League of the Americas and the Hands Off Nicaragua Committee, to the peoples of America."[140] After his arrival, *El Libertador* shared with its readers many of the answers to the questions that Hurwitz had previously raised. It argued that Turcios, who had now accepted a diplomatic position under the pro-American government in Honduras, had betrayed Sandino. LADLA explained that Sandino was attempting to "reestablish relations between the Army and the anti-imperialist organizations in the Continent and the world" and that even if Sandino could not continue his struggle in Nicaragua, he would not abandon the anti-imperialist cause.[141] Sandino had complained that MAFUENIC's representative Gustavo Machado—who had left Mexico to participate in the revolt—had recently been unsupportive and noncommunicative.[142] *El Libertador* countered that MAFUENIC's reception of Sandino in Mexico would prove that "Machado, the Hands Off Nicaragua Committee, and the Anti-Imperialist League of the Americas have not been idle while he and the Liberating Army defended with weapons the sovereignty of the continent."[143] Yet even as LADLA expressed support for Sandino, it described his vision for a continental conference on the Nicaraguan canal as an "illusion," which "General Sandino will lose as soon as he confirms that the silence in response to his letter to President Yrigoyen and to the other presidents of Latin America, servile agents of imperialism, has a political and economic basis and is not a 'diplomatic' discourtesy."[144] In fact, none of those presidents ever replied to his invitation.[145]

THE 1929 SECOND LAI CONGRESS AND
THE DECLINE OF THE SANDINO FANTASY

As Sandino arrived in Mexico, LADLA representatives were already en route to the LAI's Second Anti-Imperialist World Congress in Frankfurt. In the lead-up to the congress, LADLA published a pamphlet with the conference agenda and goals. It said that the congress would hold "a grand and significant homage to our Nicaraguan heroes" since they are "the symbol of all peoples of colonial and semi-colonial countries."[146] The agenda that LADLA published was a provisional one distributed by LAI organizer Willi Münzenberg. This agenda, which circulated widely in Latin America and featured many of the same speakers from the 1927 Brussels Congress, became a point of controversy.[147]

The controversy was caused by the fact that despite the Comintern's shift to the class against class line, which "endorsed the categorisation of political opponents as 'social fascists,'" the LAI did not change its united front rhetoric.[148] As Fredrik Petersson writes, "The shift from the united front strategy to the principle of 'class against class' was a contradiction in terms of the LAI's activities."[149] LADLA, in turn, also did not change its united front stance to align with the Comintern's new position, as the MAFUENIC campaign clearly demonstrated. Instead, LADLA dedicated itself even more fully to the united front, using Nicaragua as its rallying cry.

After Münzenberg distributed the 1929 Frankfurt Congress's provisional agenda, which displayed the LAI's continued faith in the united front through the speakers' ideological diversity, the Comintern responded by creating an LAI political commission to bring the organization into line. Although the LAI had operated relatively independently from the Comintern up to this point, this arms-length relationship would shift in the lead-up to the Frankfurt Congress. The Comintern's Executive Committee formed a secret delegation to ensure communist control of the congress. As Petersson writes, "In comparison to the 1927 Brussels Congress, an event where the communists had remained in the background in order to evaluate the reactions and behaviour of the congress crowd, the Frankfurt Congress displayed a diametrically opposed attitude."[150] Such influence can be seen clearly in the manifesto produced from the Frankfurt Congress, which focuses on the threat of war against the Soviet Union and includes an extensive section on the danger of "reformists" within nationalist movements, citing specifically the example of China's Kuomintang.[151]

The shift in the Comintern's relationship to the LAI would have an impact on LADLA's increasingly complicated relationship with Sandino, although not necessarily to the degree that has been assumed in extant scholarship. In the lead-up to the congress, LADLA's Continental Committee sent a cable to LADLA-US with a statement from Sandino to be read at a banquet for US delegates traveling to Frankfurt. In it, Sandino stated, "My next step is to get together with the world anti-imperialist fighters to make our liberation an international movement. . . . I will keep my promise to Henri Barbusse, that I will continue to fight till I have helped liberate not only Nicaragua, but all the Latin-American peoples."[152] Despite the unity with the "world anti-imperialist fighters" expressed in this cable, in the greeting Sandino wrote to the Frankfurt Congress he used his more staunchly regionalist and Indo-Hispanist discourse, emphasizing the unity of his army with "the peoples of Latin America as a racial unity."[153] LADLA published this greeting in El Libertador alongside an article about the congress, which explained that LADLA delegates were en route, delineated their planned contributions, and celebrated the congress as evidence of the true formation of a united front. Without specifically calling out Sandino's rhetoric in his greeting, the article subtly reminded its readers that "existing among many thinkers of Latin America . . . [is] an overly nationalist concept. . . . [T]he members of LADLA are perhaps the only ones who understand that it is not necessary to limit the struggle to Latin America; rather, the imperious necessity exists to unite not only with the anti-imperialist forces of our Continent, but also with those of the whole world."[154] The article also asserted that any nationalist movement lacking the support of the international anti-imperialist community was bound to fail, and it emphasized the continued significance of MAFUENIC's role in backing the Nicaraguan struggle.

Despite these allusions to LADLA's differences with Sandino, the seventeen Latin American representatives who attended the Frankfurt Congress displayed strong support for the EDSN. Hurwitz used the congress to ceremoniously deliver to the LAI the flag that Sandino gifted to MAFUENIC and "was greeted with tremendous applause."[155] Although the Frankfurt Congress became the staging ground for the communist split from noncommunist delegates, "thereby initiating a process to definitively subordinate the LAI and its International Secretariat to the Comintern," this did not result in a split from Sandino.[156] LADLA representatives at the Frankfurt Congress used the divisive climate to oust APRA from the LAI once and for all, and even after Sandino's chosen representative refused to support this effort, there was still no break with Sandino.[157] On the contrary, the congress named Sandino to the new LAI Executive Committee.

Meanwhile, in Mexico the Portes Gil interim government was radically shifting the state's tolerant political climate toward communists, engaging instead in a repression campaign.[158] In January 1929, when Mella was assassinated in Mexico City, Portes Gil ignored LADLA's calls for Mexico to break ties with the Machado regime. In the coming months, the assassination of several Mexican communist leaders followed.[159] In mid-1929, PCM headquarters were raided, and the PCM and publication of its newspaper, *El Machete*, were outlawed.[160] After the PCM continued to print *El Machete* illegally, its printing press was confiscated and its members arrested.[161] *El Libertador* was also outlawed during this time, never to resume publication. LADLA-US released several resolutions condemning "the anti-labor activities of the government of President Portes Gil" and organized a large protest in front of the Mexican consulate that ended in police brutality and arrests.[162] All the while, Sandino was receiving a monthly stipend from the Portes Gil government, from which he hoped to receive weapons and additional financial support.[163]

Although LADLA continued to publicly support Sandino at this moment, it began to focus its energies elsewhere. It used many of the tools that had been successful in constructing the figure of Sandino during the MAFUENIC campaign to rally instead around the martyred Mella. After his assassination, Mella was similarly forged into a larger-than-life figure who exemplified all LADLA's projected desires for the liberation of the continent. Just as Sandino's image had been reproduced in *El Libertador* and on posters, cigarette packs, and graffiti, LADLA turned Mella's image into a recruiting tool and symbol of its broader movement. LADLA and the Mexican section of the International Red Aid (IRA) reproduced Modotti's profiled portrait of Mella on placards and pinback buttons, and collected Mella's books into a library that could be used by workers.[164] At several commemorations held in his honor, a massive painting of Mella—based on the same Modotti photograph and even larger than the Sandino banner at LADLA's headquarters—hung in the background. There, "during the entire ceremony, hundreds of portraits and buttons of comrade Mella were sold."[165] LADLA and the IRA also sold masks of Mella's face and ended meetings by singing *el corrido de Mella* (the Mella ballad).[166] Perhaps most important for Mella's celebrity, leftist publications both within Latin America and outside the region announced his assassination and reproduced his portrait.[167]

Much in the same way that Sandino was used to tie together many causes, Mella became the emblem of these connections. For example, at one of his commemorations, Modotti said:

> In Mella they killed not only the enemy of Cuba's dictatorship, but the enemy of all dictatorships. . . . Machado, or the caricature of Benito Mussolini, has committed yet another crime: but there are corpses that cause trembling and whose death represents for the assassins a threat equal or greater than their life as fighters. . . . Julio Antonio Mella, assassinated by the president of Cuba, is now a symbol of revolutionary struggle against imperialism and against its agents, and his name is a banner. He is in the struggle of workers and peasants throughout the continent; he is in the consciousness and in the mass movements of workers; he is among the soldiers that fight together with Sandino; he is among the strikers in Colombia, machine-gunned by imperialist capital. On this night marking one month since the cowardly assassination, we

honor his memory, and we promise to continue his path until achieving the victory of all the exploited of the world, and in this way, we honor his memory in the form that he would have most liked: not crying, but fighting![168]

Modotti's words frame Mella as an enemy of dictatorship, fascism, and imperialism alike. His spirit permeates the struggles of the continent, including Sandino's movement in Nicaragua.

In this and other events, Mella was frequently compared to Sandino. For example, *El Machete* printed the lyrics to the "Song of Julio Mella," which included the lines "It is not the body that matters, murderer! It is the powerful, immortal action that is named IDEAL with Sandino, that with Mella is named IDEAL."[169] The lyrics forge Sandino and Mella together into the spirit of the idealized revolutionary.

The comparisons between Mella and Sandino, and Mella's replacement of Sandino in LADLA's rhetoric, is perhaps not surprising since social movements historically have had difficulty sustaining the elevation of living individual leaders. Martyrs—victims of violence who are "refigured as strong" to "represent the moral power of the movement"—are easier symbols to control.[170] Dead heroes avoid the complications of living ones since, as sociologists of social movements have noted, "they are symbols, not decision makers."[171]

LADLA's turn to Mella had consequences for the movement. Although Sandino's projected image was one of the charismatic leader, an image steeped in heteronormative masculinity, he was also envisioned as embodying the Black and Indigenous worker, even if this depiction was more fantasy than reality. In contrast, Mella was a university-educated man of European descent who wore a white-collared shirt in his famous portrait. As LADLA's liberatory political vision of *redes* gave way first to the elevation of a charismatic man of color and next to the projection of white masculinity that would later be reproduced at midcentury in the figure of Che Guevara, LADLA seemed to lose sight of a core element of its vision. Although LADLA grew substantially through the MAFUENIC and Mella campaigns, and although it may have been more practical to rally around heroic individuals, some of the movement's most significant contributions seemed to dissipate in that process. Whether LADLA's Continental Committee could have eventually recovered its initial vision is unknown, since shortly after this point its leadership faced ruinous circumstances outside their control.

In January 1930, the Portes Gil government formally severed Mexico's relationship with the Soviet Union, citing communist protests as the work of foreign agitators.[172] A few weeks before this diplomatic break with the Soviet Union, and only a few days before Sandino was supposed to have his long-awaited meeting with Portes Gil, an article appeared in the Comintern's *La Correspondance internationale* that claimed Sandino had made a deal with the United States for $60,000 and would be taking up permanent residence in Mexico.[173] The LAI came to Sandino's defense. Willi Münzenberg and V. Chattophadyaya of the LAI International Secretary published a rejoinder in *La Correspondance internationale*, arguing that this accusation was a rumor started by the imperialists and affirming their support for Sandino as an LAI Executive Committee member. They claimed LADLA had carefully investigated the matter and found the accusations to be false, and they asserted that Sandino was continuing to fight not only US imperialism but also those Latin American governments that were imperialist agents, including the Mexican government. They called for increased solidarity with Sandino and LADLA.[174]

As the Portes Gil government severed ties with the Soviet Union, repressions and deportations increased. By the end of 1929, the PCM reported to the Comintern that "it had become 'almost completely impossible' for LADLA to operate: it could no longer print and circulate materials, and many of its core organizers 'have left the country or are preparing to leave, in order to avoid certain deportation by the government.'"[175] In January 1930, Sandalio Junco, who had replaced the deceased Mella as LADLA's secretary, was arrested and set to be extradited to Cuba. However, LADLA and several other organizations—American Negro Labor Congress and International Labor Defense—organized protests in Junco's defense. The protests succeeded in pressuring the Mexican government to instead send Junco to Germany, using money raised by participating organizations.[176] From Germany, Junco went to the Soviet Union.[177] The next month, when Pascual Ortiz Rubio took office as president of Mexico and suffered an assassination attempt by a Catholic extremist, Tina Modotti, along with several other communists, was arrested on false charges of plotting the assassination. After a two-week imprisonment, Modotti was deported to Europe, landing in Berlin, where she met up with LAI leadership.[178] Several of Sandino's close associates in Mexico were arrested, including Agustín Farabundo Martí and Esteban Pavletich.[179] The LAI produced a manifesto, "Against Terror, Reaction and Betrayal in Mexico," condemning the Mexican government's actions.[180] Although LADLA called for rallies and protests across the continent against these arrests and deportations, this repression would eventually lead to the dissolution of LADLA's Continental Committee.[181]

In this context of intense repression, in January 1930, the PCM sent Sandino a list of conditions for its continuing support. The PCM requested that Sandino either return to Nicaragua immediately or agree to an international tour on behalf of the LAI and that he openly condemn the Mexican government. PCM leadership, along with LADLA and MAFUENIC representatives, then met with Sandino on February 3, 1930.[182] Several LADLA and MAFUENIC members in attendance did not sign these demands because they did not believe that the PCM should attempt to control MAFUENIC.[183] Sandino agreed to the LAI international tour and to condemn the Mexican government but requested a formal written invitation, financing for his trip, and emergency funding to replace what he would lose from the government.[184] Sandino then sent communications to LAI leaders Willi Münzenberg and Henri Barbusse expressing his willingness to do the tour.[185]

However, weeks passed, and no formal invitation or LAI funding ever came.[186] Neither LADLA nor MAFUENIC could be of much help since Machado and Salvador de la Plaza had left Mexico, other core leaders had been deported, and others, like Diego Rivera and Federico Bach, had been expelled from the PCM due to the Comintern's new sectarian line.[187] Shortly thereafter, Sandino met with former President Portes Gil, who offered him safe passage to Nicaragua, two machine guns, ammunition, and 2,000 pesos. In April 1930, Sandino left for Nicaragua without ever making the promised condemnation of the Mexican government. He simultaneously broke with his personal secretary, Agustín Farabundo Martí, who had served as PCM representative within the EDSN.

The outraged PCM released statements in April and May 1930 calling Sandino a traitor.[188] However, at the same time, LADLA released a statement condemning the Mexican government's lack of tangible support for Sandino. In a statement written "to all the revolutionary anti-imperialist organizations," LADLA's Continental Committee asserted that "the government knows that Sandino, far from abandoning the struggle makes great efforts to reorganize his troops and resume the offensive in Nicaragua."[189] In this sense, contrary to how some scholars have represented this history, LADLA's Continental Committee and its MAFUENIC campaign did not abandon Sandino, and Sandino's inability to find alternative funding and support in Mexico was likely not as much a product of MAFUENIC's betrayal as the result of the state's repression of leftists, who were forced to either flee the country or go underground.[190]

Once Sandino's former personal secretary Agustín Farabundo Martí was released from prison, he did not return to Nicaragua but traveled instead to El Salvador. Martí would later write that he believed Sandino had betrayed the world anti-imperialist movement to "become a liberal, petty bourgeois caudillo with aspirations of governing Nicaragua within semi-feudal and semicolonial bourgeois molds."[191] Later, when facing a firing squad after the January 1932 failed uprising in El Salvador, Martí used his final words to say that he did not continue fighting with Sandino because "his banner was only a banner of independence, a banner of emancipation, but he was not pursuing aims of social rebellion."[192] Arguably, despite Martí's implication that Sandino had changed, Sandino was always deeply nationalist with more liberal tendencies. His adherence to LADLA's ideology was never more than tenuous and vacillating, and his movement certainly did not represent the PCM's more orthodox communist line. Martí expressed disillusionment with the Sandino fantasy, which MAFUENIC had disseminated across the continent, rather than with the reality of the man himself.

In this sense, the MAFUENIC campaign stands as a powerful case study of the vulnerability of solidarity movements built around particular charismatic leaders and represents both the height of LADLA's movement and its eventual dissolution. Although LADLA sections would continue to operate in several countries throughout the continent, the Continental Committee in Mexico City would never be reconstituted. In the final chapter, I consider how LADLA's project became subsumed by the subsequent formation of the Comintern's Caribbean Bureau and simultaneously memorialized in 1930s–40s Latin American literature, including in literary works by writers active in the MAFUENIC campaign.

SEVEN

REMEMBERING LADLA

THE CARIBBEAN BUREAU AND THE RISE OF LATIN AMERICAN EXTRACTIVE FICTIONS

I put bananas first before men, because on banana
plantations, fruit occupies first place, or really the only
place. —CARMEN LYRA, *Bananos y hombres*, 1931

With these opening words, Costa Rican communist writer (and former MAFUENIC campaign director) Carmen Lyra explained the title to her 1931 collection of short stories, *Bananos y hombres* (Bananas and men), a text that would usher in a proliferation of social realist, fictional depictions of the banana industry in Central America and the Caribbean over subsequent decades.[1] In the collection's opening story, a young Black Costa Rican single mother named Estefanía spends her life wandering between banana plantations on the country's Caribbean coast looking for work and taking up with different partners (Chinese storeowner, Honduran field worker) to secure housing and food for her daughter. On the banana plantations, Estefanía experiences poverty, sexual assault, and other forms of violence. She eventually finds work as a cook for the son of one of the plantation owners. There, she also manages the company commissary, where she does "not allow one cent to be lost at the commissary, nor allow a single egg to vanish."[2] With the profits, the plantation owner and his son pay for their social club membership in the city, and the daughter buys clothes and vacations to the United States and Europe. Yet when their loyal employee Estefanía falls ill with malaria, no one in the family comes to her aid. After she eventually dies, her grave is marked with a "rough, wooden cross," which the story's narrator later finds washed up on a beach. The name on the grave marker has almost completely faded, leaving only "Estefanía R. Perhaps Rojas, perhaps Ramírez or Ramos."[3] "Estefanía R.," the narrator explains, is "one of so many women who have passed through the banana plantations."[4] Her life and death evince the story's final line: "On the banana plantations more consideration is reserved for the death of a banana than for that of a laborer."[5]

This tragic, hard-hitting story, which opens Lyra's collection, is in many ways typical of a broader genre of proletarian, social realist fiction published in Latin America in the 1930s–40s. I refer to this genre as *Latin American extractive fictions*, referencing novels and short stories that take place in Latin American and Caribbean extractive economies, such as banana, sugar, tobacco, and rubber plantations and oil fields.[6] Most of these works were published in the interwar period in the Caribbean and Central America, although Colombian José Eustasio Rivera's depiction of the Amazonian rubber boom in his famed *La vorágine* (The vortex) was published earlier in 1924. Latin American extractive fictions range from Costa Rican banana novels, like the well-known *Mamita Yunai* (1941) by Carlos Luis Fallas Sibaja and tobacco novels like the Puerto Rican Enrique Laguerre's *La llamarada* (The blaze) (1935) to oil novels about Venezuela's Caribbean coast such as Ramón Díaz Sánchez's *Mene* (1936) and the so-called *novela de la caña* (sugarcane novel) published in the Dominican Republic, Puerto Rico, and Cuba.[7]

Although the works in this genre are each unique, Latin American extractive fictions share many elements, primarily focusing on the experiences of exploitation and interactions of a multinational and multiracial group of laborers on corporate plantations within a primarily US-owned extractive economy. They are also overwhelmingly male-centric (written by male authors and featuring male protagonists and narrators). In this sense, despite the masculine framing of the title of Lyra's *Bananas y hombres*, Lyra's work is atypical in that it is written by a woman and opens with the depiction of a woman's experience in the banana industry. Cuban writer Luis Felipe Rodríguez alludes to the shared thematic of these works in his book of short stories about the sugarcane industry, *Marcos Antilla: Relatos de cañaveral* (Marcos Antilla: Tales from the canefield) (1932). In the title story, "Marcos Antilla," the narrator explains, "I have been a rubber plantation worker in Colombia and Brazil, like the hero of *La vorágine*; a miner in Peru, a galley worker in the salt mines of Chile; a banana dockworker in the Antilles and in Central America and also a canecutter in Santo Domingo and in my homeland and everywhere I saw the sweat of the American slave dripping onto the sold native product."[8] The laborer's experience in the sugar industry, depicted in *Marcos Antilla*, parallels similar experiences throughout the region. In the allusion to Rivera's *La vorágine*, Rodríguez overtly situates his book within a broader set of Latin American extractive fictions that depict corporate plantations in other contexts.

Unsurprisingly, Latin American extractive fictions were mostly written by writers with leftist politics, some with direct connections to LADLA and to the organization that succeeded it, the Caribbean Bureau (Buró del Caribe, BC, 1931–36). For example, Carmen Lyra headed up LADLA's Hands Off Nicaragua (MAFUENIC) campaign in Costa Rica.[9] She published *Bananos y hombres* in 1931, the same year that she and other members of LADLA–Costa Rica founded the Costa Rican Communist Party (Partido Comunista de Costa Rica, PCCR), which fell under the BC's direction.[10] PCCR archives reveal that Lyra served as the primary point of contact with the BC's leadership in New York.[11] The PCCR's membership also included Lyra's literary descendant Carlos Luis Fallas Sibaja, who authored *Mamita Yunai*, the most famous banana novel. *Mamita Yunai*—which was reprinted in three continents and translated into more languages than any other Costa Rican title to date—began as a series of articles authored by Fallas in the PCCR's newspaper, *Trabajo*.[12] The examples of these Costa Rican writers' direct ties to LADLA and the BC are not unique. Luis Felipe Rodríguez, author of *Marcos Antilla*, for instance, was a LADLA-Cuba member and served on the editorial board of its magazine *Masas*, studied in chapter 4.

Within literary criticism, Latin American extractive fictions are generally situated within the broader *novela de la tierra* (novel of the land), a genre dedicated to presenting an autochthonous Latin American identity and experience and reflecting interwar regionalist ideologies.[13] However, despite the regionalist framework through which these works have been read, many of them directly engage the global questions central to both LADLA and the later BC. This chapter thus proposes a critical rereading of these extractive fictions, contending that they participate in a transnational political exchange and cosmopolitics in which they attempt to render the global by using regional contexts to examine global capitalist relations. While these texts are not all exactly alike and do not fall neatly into a set rubric, I argue that, as a genre, these works can and should be read within the context of LADLA's history. Specifically, they should be read alongside the discourse of the organization that succeeded LADLA, the Comintern's BC, which attempted to organize workers on US-owned corporate plantations in the 1930s.

The BC, created in 1931, emerged directly out of LADLA's networks and continued its ideological project in many ways. It especially did so by uniting movements across the Greater Caribbean region and attempting to address the specific forms of violence and exploitation faced by racialized labor, including Black immigrant labor, within the region's extractive economies. While this final chapter examines the BC's activities, it primarily considers how the political project conceived by LADLA (and the later BC) would become interpreted and represented within Latin American extractive fictions. This chapter sheds light on how the region's writers would come to understand, remember, and narrate LADLA's vision.

Using several case studies, I consider how many Latin American extractive fictions meditate on LADLA's project and on the difficulties of forging transnational and transracial political collectivities. These fictions largely align with the ideologies of LADLA and the BC by depicting the shared oppression of a racially diverse set of workers in extractive economies, critiquing the violence inflicted upon racialized workers through policing and exploitative labor conditions, and meditating on the potential for more equitable relations than that of racial capitalism. However, these texts fall far short of representing LADLA's furthest-reaching antiracist positions. Instead, they tend to reproduce a tension found within interwar Latin American anti-imperialisms more broadly by vacillating between antiracist critiques of US-owned companies and expressing anti-imperialist positions based in the rejection of Black immigrant workers employed by these companies. Such ambiguity toward Black immigrant labor takes different forms depending on the text. Some narratives critique the racist exploitation of Black immigrant workers but do not incorporate these workers into a transnational vision of collective organizing, which the text reserves only for mestizo subjects. Others displace onto Black immigrant workers the author's anti-imperialist critique, engaging in overtly nativist and anti-Black depictions of West Indian and Haitian employees. In other cases, an exoticized representation of Black immigrants is coupled with a self-critical reflection on the difficulties of forging multiracial political communities. In this sense, the authors of Latin American extractive fictions draw on key elements of LADLA's worldview but obviate its furthest reaching antiracist perspectives. The ambiguous racial politics of these fictions arguably parallel the gap between the stated ideals of LADLA and the BC and their difficulties in implementing such ideals on the ground.

Although most Latin American extractive fictions are not widely read outside their immediate national and regional contexts, their impact on the literary production of some of Latin America's most well-known writers has been profound. Works like Pablo Neruda's "La United Fruit Co." (1950), the novels in Miguel Ángel Asturias's Banana Trilogy (1950–60), or the representation of the 1928 United Fruit massacre of Colombian banana workers in Gabriel García Márquez's *One Hundred Years of Solitude* (1967) reveal these works' influence on subsequent literary generations. At the core of these fictions are questions that remain relevant to political organizing across linguistic, racial, and national borders in the region. They are worth revisiting, as they shed light on how LADLA has been represented for broader consumption, what elements of this history these fictions memorialize, and which of LADLA's key contributions have been forgotten along the way.

FROM LADLA TO THE CARIBBEAN BUREAU

When Mexico's government cracked down against radical elements in 1929–30, much of LADLA's core leadership was deported or jailed. Tina Modotti was deported in February 1930. She traveled to Germany at the invitation of LAI leadership, and after eight months in Berlin she left for the Soviet Union.[14] Upon his deportation, Sandalio Junco followed the same route from Berlin to the Soviet Union, eventually returning to Cuba in January 1932.[15] Gustavo Machado fled to Colombia after the failed June 1929 raid on a military fort in Curaçao. The dispersal of many of LADLA's key leaders resulted in the dissolution of its Continental Committee in Mexico City. Several of the local sections, like in the United States and Cuba, remained active throughout the early 1930s. Despite the collapse of its Continental Committee, some of LADLA's key leadership would reconvene in the BC in New York City.[16]

Because of the Comintern's shift to its class-against-class line, which abandoned the broad alliances on which LADLA was based, the communist-controlled BC would come to eclipse LADLA in importance in the early 1930s. In the months prior to his death, Mella was having conflicts with the PCM over its move away from united-front organizing, particularly in relation to trade unions, which led to his removal from the PCM's Central Committee.[17] From 1929 through the early 1930s, several of LADLA's core leaders, like Diego Rivera or Sandalio Junco, were ousted from their local communist parties for their non-orthodox positions.[18] Even so, the BC emerged directly out of LADLA's networks and attempted to continue much of its ideological project. It especially did so by uniting movements across a Greater Caribbean region, whose connections were defined through extractive economies. In uniting these movements, the BC relied directly on the networks forged in Central America and the Caribbean through LADLA's MAFUENIC campaign.

Since its 1926 founding, the Comintern's Latin American secretariat was based in Buenos Aires, but because of the distance between Buenos Aires and the Caribbean and Central America, Latin American communists advocated for the creation of an additional secretariat headquartered in Mexico.[19] In December 1930, a Caribbean subcommittee of the Confederation of Latin American Labor Unions (Confederación Sindical Latino Americana, CSLA) was established in New York City.[20] The following month, US communist Alexander Bittelman sent a proposal to the Comintern's Executive Committee for the founding of a Central American secretariat, based in New York.[21] This led to the creation of the BC out of the CSLA Caribbean subcommittee.[22] Since it was LADLA (and not the Comintern's Latin American secretariat in Buenos Aires) that had established networks throughout Central America and the Caribbean in the late 1920s, the new BC would largely continue the work of LADLA's now defunct Continental Committee.[23]

LADLA's MAFUENIC campaign, discussed at length in the previous chapter, was especially successful in drawing together a Greater Caribbean movement. A crucial focal point of LADLA's Greater Caribbean discourse was the role of the banana industry, and especially US-owned United Fruit, in authoritarian governance and racial violence throughout the region. LADLA used United Fruit to underline connections between the Nicaraguan context, the United Fruit Company's activities, and the racial policing of labor by local authoritarian governments.

The BC would build on the networks established by MAFUENIC, using the campaign's Greater Caribbean framework as its organizing rubric. The direct link between LADLA and the BC comes into view when examining the BC's core activists, which included Gustavo Machado from LADLA's Continental Committee; Agustín Farabundo Martí of LADLA–El Salvador, who was sent to Nicaragua by MAFUENIC; Rubén Martínez Villena, Leonardo Fernández Sánchez, and Jorge Vivó from LADLA-Cuba; and Alberto

Moreau from LADLA-US.[24] The BC's periodical *Mundo Obrero* (Workers' world) (1931–33), included articles and artwork from LADLA activists, including Tina Modotti and Xavier Guerrero.[25]

The trajectory of Cuban activist Leonardo Fernández Sánchez is exemplary of how LADLA's networks shaped the later BC. Having begun his political work as a teenage student organizer in Havana, Fernández Sánchez helped found LADLA-Cuba and organized protests demanding the release of his friend Julio Antonio Mella. He attended the 1927 Brussels Congress as a LADLA-Cuba representative. He then lived in Mexico City with Mella at the beginning of 1928 and in October of that year traveled back to Cuba, from where he went to the United States. While living in New York City, Fernández Sánchez became active in various organizations and eventually formed part of the BC, writing articles about the economic crisis faced by sugar workers in Cuba for *Mundo Obrero*.[26]

Although the BC's leadership demonstrates clear continuities from LADLA, much had changed in the lives of these activists. The US stock market crashed just a few months after LADLA triumphantly presented Sandino's captured American flag to the 1929 LAI Congress in Frankfurt. The Great Depression would have significant implications for Latin America's extractive economies, including the sugar industry. To stabilize highly fluctuating sugar prices, US banks and sugar refineries created an agreement with several Caribbean nations to establish export quotas. The agreement, Plan Chadbourne (1931), resulted in reduced harvest seasons, massive unemployment, strikes, and heightened anti-immigrant sentiment. The volatility in the sugar industry would eventually contribute to the overthrow of Gerardo Machado's dictatorship in Cuba and to the military coup that put Rafael Leónidas Trujillo Molina in power in the Dominican Republic.[27]

The banana industry was equally transformed. In the case of Costa Rica, where the United Fruit Company was founded, the country had been the largest banana exporter in the world in 1913 and produced a stable amount of product between 1917 and 1929. However, between 1929 and 1943, banana production "declined to almost nothing."[28] Increased unemployment and reduced wages led to the 1934 banana strike in Limón and to United Fruit's eventual decision to move its entire operations from the Atlantic coast, where workers were more organized, to the Pacific.[29]

Like the MAFUENIC campaign, the BC conceived of the Greater Caribbean as united by the experience of early twentieth-century extractive economies. It defined this region as unified by a monoculture system in which plantations were predominantly owned by foreign corporations that practiced vertical integration and wage and immigrant labor. *Mundo Obrero* described United Fruit as operating "an absolute monopoly in the production of bananas throughout all countries of the Caribbean. It has large landholdings in Guatemala, Honduras, Costa Rica, Colombia, etc. It has a tremendous influence in the national political life of these countries through a long chain of political maneuvers, the purchasing of native and political mercenaries, and the use of the Department of State of the United States, the Marines, and the Army, in order to firmly establish the dominance of the dollar."[30] In the case of Costa Rica, *Mundo Obrero* argued that United Fruit not only held a monopoly on banana exports but also dominated property ownership, electricity, and commerce "in its entire fiefdom of Limón" and owned the country's railroads and the majority of its mines.[31] The BC claimed that independent farmers' dependency on selling their product to United Fruit resulted in exploitation and expropriation of their lands and that United Fruit workers were subjected to unfair payment in the form of credit at overpriced company stores and subpar medical treatment at company hospitals.[32]

Through the BC's focus on United Fruit and other US companies like Standard Oil, it theorized the space of the Caribbean through the shared plantation culture of the company town that proliferated across a loosely defined geography. Such a conceptualization of the region is illustrated by the cover of the July 1932 issue of *Mundo Obrero* (figure 7.1). The cover image presents the governments of Machado in Cuba, Plutarco Elías Calles in Mexico, and Juan Vicente Gómez in Venezuela as allied with the US government (the snarling man in a top hat in the lower left corner). All these figures, the image suggests, collaborate in the economic domination of the US industries of sugar and oil, whose depictions appear in the upper right corner. The caption states, "Only the strong arm of the solidarity of workers and farmers under the direction of the working class will be able to defeat the power of imperialism and its lackeys."[33] The strong arm with the hammer and sickle that chokes the three "lackeys" of imperialism stands in for a resistant political collectivity that will crush this unholy alliance and that coalesces within the very US-owned extractive economy that ties sugar to oil. The exploitative practices that link the three Latin American governments are also those that connect the "masses of exploited workers and farmers of the Caribbean" for whom the BC claimed to speak.

In addition to building on LADLA's geographic imaginary, the BC would also continue LADLA's efforts to bridge racial and linguistic differences, particularly in relation to Indigenous and Haitian and West Indian workers.

7.1 BC, *Mundo Obrero* (July 1932), cover.

As Sandalio Junco argued in 1929, because US-owned companies were responsible for the recruitment of Black immigrant workers, many native-born workers expressed their anti-imperialist stance through antiblackness. This intersection of anti-immigrant sentiment with antiblackness, Junco argued, was profoundly damaging to Black native-born citizens, to Black immigrants, and to the unity of the anti-imperialist movement as a whole. Although Junco was eventually ousted from the Cuban Communist Party, his argument in 1929 for outreach to West Indian and Haitian immigrant workers would become a central platform of the BC.

In line with the Comintern's agenda on the Negro Question, the BC would specifically focus on the radicalization and unification of the region's racial minorities.[34] The BC's correspondence, meeting minutes, and letters of instruction to local communist parties reveal a preoccupation with the need to organize with Black workers in US-owned extractive industries as well as frustration with particular local communist parties for their failure to do so.[35] Regarding this priority, Sandra Pujals writes of the BC: "The anti-imperialist armies in Sandino's Nicaragua for example now struggled in tandem with forces against the Juan Vicente Gómez dictatorship in Venezuela and the Gerardo Machado regime in Cuba. Even when so far apart, and despite their national particularities, these anti-imperialist legions and the movements to end dictatorships in Venezuela and Cuba also joined those who opposed the lynching of Blacks in the Southern states of the U.S. . . . and simultaneously marched along those who opposed racial discrimination of Black workers in Jamaica and Trinidad or indigenous plantation workers in El Salvador."[36] In a way similar to LADLA, the BC's rhetoric joined all these struggles in a broad fight against what it simply defined as "Yankee imperialism."[37] In the article "Day of Anti-Imperialist Struggle" from *Mundo Obrero* (August 1931), the BC demonstrated this expansive vision by suggesting that Yankee imperialism oppressed Mexican immigrant labor in the United States alongside African Americans and "the oppressed masses of Latin America."[38] The connections that *Mundo Obrero* drew between immigrant labor, African Americans, and "the oppressed masses of Latin America" was not mere rhetoric. In the case of the sugar industry, the early twentieth-century military occupations that facilitated the US takeover of the industry exported a post-Reconstruction model of sociopolitical organization based on strict racial hierarchies to sugar-producing areas in the Caribbean.[39] In the Caribbean sugar zone, a direct correlation existed between the inequities of local labor conditions, the rise of immigrant labor, and a US brand of white supremacist ideology that impacted Latin American and US Black workers alike.

The BC used the term "white terror" to describe the transnational police forces charged with disciplining this racialized labor.[40] As the article "The Dictatorship of the United Fruit Company" argued, the problem was not just that the company "possesses and controls the lackey governments of many of the countries of the Caribbean; but rather that the COMPANY ITSELF directly exercises governmental functions, especially in the cases of suppressing the struggles of workers and peasants who are employed by said company."[41] United Fruit banana plantations "are practically armed camps," and in the case of workers' strikes, "armed company gangs set out to crush these struggles with the greatest violence and crimes and always with the support of the armed forces of the lackey governments of these countries."[42] If company police and local armed forces were unsuccessful in suppressing the movement, the article explained, then "the United Fruit Company knows that they always have at hand the American warships and Marines 'to protect' their lives and properties, whenever necessary."[43] Referring in shorthand to the violence carried out by this transnational policing as "white terror," the BC framed land dispossession, racism, and policing as inherent to the logic of extractive capital, in which police and military enforce dispossession of resource-rich lands and where racism and violence are used to extract additional value from racialized labor.

According to Alberto Sánchez, the Puerto Rican editor of *Mundo Obrero*, agricultural workers' confrontation with white terror in the forms of policing and lynching linked the experiences of Mexican workers in California and Colorado with those of Black workers in Camp Hill, Alabama, and agricultural workers throughout the Caribbean.[44] As *Mundo Obrero* attempted to reveal connections between varying local contexts, it used the corporate plantation as the primary lens not just for theorizing a larger plantation and extractive region but for considering global capitalist relations more broadly. The title of the BC's publication is indeed a reference to the world, and in the pages of *Mundo Obrero*, the corporate plantation represented a global space where workers of the world came into contact and a site for the potential creation of a resistant political collectivity among diverse peoples. *Mundo Obrero* sought to facilitate a community of solidarity that transcended nationality, language, and race.

However, even as the BC continued LADLA's efforts to connect racialized populations throughout the region, focusing on Indigenous and especially Black immigrant communities, its discourse followed the more sectarian, class-based line of the Third Period, meaning it defined its collectivity strictly through the category of labor. In a September 1931 article about the Scottsboro Boys case called "Let's Save the Black Workers of Alabama," published in *Mundo Obrero* by the head of the CPUSA's Central Committee for Negro Work, Robert Minor, national and linguistic differences are overcome through emphasizing the teenagers' proximity to labor.[45] Although they were unemployed, Minor emphasizes they are "sons of workers and farmers, sons of our class."[46] Moreover, although *Mundo Obrero* purported to support Indigenous, Black, and immigrant workers, it exhibited an overall lack of attention to the specific circumstances they faced. Despite the BC's insistence to local communist parties that "special manifestos for Indigenous and Black peoples in their own languages are of great importance," the BC's own *Mundo Obrero* targeted a Spanish-reading public.[47] While it discussed immigrant labor—like Haitian and West Indian workers throughout the Caribbean, Chinese workers in Curaçao, and Mexican workers in the United States—it directed little attention to the importance of leadership by these communities in shaping its project. In a December 1931 article by US communist William Simons entitled "Let's Organize Sugar Workers in Cuba," *Mundo Obrero* encouraged communists to infiltrate sugar mills in order to reach out to "the Black masses" as well as to the "semi-proletariat," by which it meant *colonos* (small landowners and sugar farmers) who had been hit hard by production quotas.[48] Here, the implied reader appears to be a citizen who does not belong to those "Black masses" whom the reader is encouraged to influence. Moreover, while *Mundo Obrero* concentrated on reaching out to racial minorities, it did not directly address the issue of anti-Black racism prevalent among white and mestizo workers, which often undermined these coalitions.[49]

Many of the representations of Black workers in *Mundo Obrero* related primarily to the US context, and in these depictions, the BC frequently demonstrated a paternalistic attitude toward Black American workers. Consider the April 1932 article "Let's Save from Death the Nine Black Youth of Scottsboro."[50] The anonymously authored article stated that "the same murderous imperialism that oppresses the Latin American masses attempts to carry out the lynching of the seven young black men of Scottsboro" (seven of the defendants were initially sentenced to death) and called for international solidarity.[51] While the article proposed a mutual identification between its Latin American interlocutors and the Scottsboro boys, the title itself contained a salvific narrative that reflects a general tendency in *Mundo Obrero* to deemphasize the consistent efforts of Black organizations in the United States to fight for the rights of these young men.[52] Additionally, *Mundo Obrero* tended to focus on images of Black victimization, especially lynchings, rather than Black empowerment. Some of these images took the form of illustrations, which—even as they condemned anti-Black violence—presented Black subjects with exaggerated features in caricatures that call into question the artists' ability to view Black colleagues as true equals.

In practice, the BC's success in recruiting Black workers (whether citizens or immigrants) was uneven and depended on the individual context and local communist party. Whereas significant and effective efforts were made on sugar plantations in Cuba, communist parties elsewhere showed less competence and enthusiasm. In the case of the Costa Rican Communist Party (PCCR), for example, the BC consistently urged the party to recruit West Indian workers employed in the banana industry in Limón.[53] In its letters to the BC, the PCCR reported that during the 1934 banana strike, it had successfully incorporated "enormous masses of workers of color into the struggle" and asked the BC to invite African American communist James Ford or "any other Black worker" to write a message of support to this constituency.[54] However, historical studies have shown that West Indian workers did not, in fact, support the strike and that West Indian newspapers in Limón characterized the PCCR as a white Costa Rican organization disconnected from their concerns.[55]

Despite these problems, the BC would both influence and be influenced by Black political thought from the region. Pujals, one of the few scholars to have studied the BC, has argued that its attempt to unify the workers of a broad region of such diversity helped shape the conceptualization of a shared Caribbean historical experience that appears in some Caribbean literature from the same moment, such as works by C. L. R. James and Nicolás Guillén.[56] Arguably, the BC simply created a political program out of a preexisting pan-Caribbean political imaginary, rooted in shared histories of colonization and slavery, that is expressed in these interwar Caribbean writings. Similarly, I would argue that the BC's ideology and Latin American extractive fictions, which emerged at the same moment, occupy a common plane of signification. While I do not mean to imply that these fictions meticulously follow the BC's formal platform or are necessarily always a product of authors' direct engagement with this organization, I do contend that reading these works alongside this political project provides a more robust understanding of the works' commentary on the social and political contexts they depict. This parallel reading reveals how Latin American extractive fictions use the lens of the corporate plantation to theorize global racial capitalism and to examine the potential and challenges to forging a transnational, translinguistic, and transracial political community.

LATIN AMERICAN EXTRACTIVE FICTIONS

Using several case studies, the following pages consider how interwar Latin American extractive fictions meditate on LADLA's project and that of the later BC. The works examined include *Bananos y hombres* (1931) by Carmen Lyra (director of Costa Rica's MAFUENIC Committee and a founding PCCR member), *Mamita Yunai* (1941) by Carlos Luis Fallas Sibaja (another prominent Costa Rican communist), *Marcos Antilla: Relatos de cañaveral* (1932) by LADLA-Cuba member Luis Felipe Rodríguez, and especially the sugarcane novel *Over* (1939) by Dominican writer Ramón Marrero Aristy. Marrero Aristy's *Over* is particularly striking in that the novel was published nine years into the fascist dictatorship of Rafael Leónidas Trujillo Molina. Despite the novel's communist content and although Marrero Aristy was eventually assassinated by the Trujillo regime for his dissenting views, he had a long-standing career in service to Trujillo. In what follows,

I focus primarily on Marrero Aristy's *Over* as an exemplar of a wider theory of interwar Latin American extractive fictions and as a way of considering the broad reach of the BC's discourse outside its immediate bureaucratic structure.[57] Comparing *Over* to similar works, I show how this text considers both the unique conditions of Black immigrant labor and the difficulties of building political collectivities across racial, linguistic, and national difference.

Born in 1913 outside the sugar-producing zone of La Romana, Marrero Aristy lived a life shaped by the sugar industry.[58] As a teenager, he worked for two years in a *bodega* (company store) for the Central Romana Sugar Corporation, established in 1911 when the New Jersey–owned South Porto Rico Sugar Company purchased twenty thousand acres in the region.[59] During his employment at the *bodega*, Marrero Aristy sent a few short stories to the Dominican periodical *La Opinión*, and after seeing their popularity, he moved to Santo Domingo to become a journalist.[60] Marrero Aristy's sustained exposure to the sugar industry would form the plot of *Over* as well as the basis for much of his ideology, in which he was an adamant opponent of the labor practices of US-owned sugar companies. Like Marrero Aristy, many other authors of Latin American extractive fictions had experience in the extractive industries depicted in their works. Carlos Luis Fallas Sibaja, for example, worked on United Fruit plantations before authoring *Mamita Yunai*, with "Yunai" referring to the popular pronunciation of the name United Fruit and "Mamita" as an ironic reference to the company as an evil stepmother.[61]

Because of the novel's left-leaning perspective, Marrero Aristy's *Over* was reportedly banned and removed from bookstores only a few days after its appearance and would not have its second printing until two years after Trujillo's death. Despite this, historian Michiel Baud has argued that Marrero Aristy grew close to the Trujillo government primarily due to the novel's publication.[62] During Trujillo's rise to power, leftist sentiments were not uncommon among his supporters, and Marrero Aristy was one of several writers who espoused socialist positions prior to becoming part of the intelligentsia that created the ideology and mythology that helped Trujillo maintain power.[63] Some have argued that at the moment of its first printing, the novel's harsh critique of US sugar companies aided Trujillo in placing pressure, especially through taxes, on foreign-owned sugar mills he intended to eventually appropriate.[64]

Trujillo's attention to Marrero Aristy raised the writer to the level of a national literary figure, and the author began focusing his journalism on the regime's achievements, apparently in exchange for handsome compensation.[65] While between 1933 and 1939 Marrero Aristy published two books of short stories as well as his novel, he ceased publishing fiction after he began working for Trujillo, focusing solely on journalism and history.[66] In the early 1940s, for the first time since Trujillo seized power, successful strikes took place on sugar plantations in the eastern side of the country, forcing sugar mills to raise wages. In response, Trujillo announced a social services plan for Dominican workers, and in 1945 he created a Ministry of Labor that began building a social security system.[67] In 1945, Marrero Aristy wrote a number of articles on "the position of the laborer" that reflected favorably on the regime, and he was subsequently named undersecretary and later secretary of the Ministry of Labor.[68] In this capacity, Marrero Aristy worked as a negotiator between striking sugar workers and the Trujillo government.

Due to his political dexterity, the author was sent to Cuba several times between 1943 and 1946 to negotiate with the international labor movement and with Dominican communists exiled there. In Havana, he met with major Cuban communist figures, like Blas Roca and Juan Marinello, as well as with prominent members of the Dominican exile community like Juan Bosch.[69] The negotiations led to what Bernardo Vega has referred to as a brief "interlude of tolerance": in exchange for the promise that Cuban communists would cease publishing attacks on Trujillo, Dominican exiles could return to operate the first opposition party in the country in sixteen years, the Dominican Popular Socialist Party (Partido Socialista Popular, PSP), and Dominican workers could organize without fear of retaliation.[70] In mid-1946, however, Trujillo ordered the assassinations of various PSP members, more than forty were imprisoned, and many more went into exile. By May 1947, the PSP had disbanded and its newspaper no longer circulated.[71]

Whether Marrero Aristy's earlier communist leanings carried through in these negotiations and into his later years remains unclear. The journalist Germán Emilio Ornes described Marrero Aristy as a true Marxist. Similarly, the Dominican communist Pericles Franco Ornés commented that in their negotiations, "I had the impression that Marrero was neither representing nor serving Trujillo's interests."[72] In November 1957, Marrero Aristy wrote a lengthy apology to Trujillo in which he begged forgiveness for an incident when, while serving as secretary of labor, he sent a private letter to Trujillo about the actions of the Café Dominicano Company, established by Trujillo two years prior. Marrero Aristy expressed concern that the company was consolidating production and distribution and receiving preferred tax treatment.[73] This monopoly, he wrote, created unfair competition and negatively impacted smaller coffee farmers and workers.[74] Under unknown circumstances, Marrero Aristy's confidential memorandum was leaked to the Dominican newspaper *La Nación*, and shortly after its publication, coffee farmers around the country organized protests against Trujillo's Café Dominicano Company. The incident drove a wedge between Marrero Aristy and his powerful benefactor from which he would never recover. In what was widely viewed as a political assassination, in July 1959 Marrero Aristy and his driver were found dead in a car at the bottom of a ravine near the mountain town of Constanza.[75]

The official posts held by Marrero Aristy are indicative of his liminal position between the Trujillo government and his apparently leftist ideology, an ambiguity that certainly appears in *Over* and that would likely have some relation to his assassination. Even following the experiment with the communist exiles, he grew increasingly close to Trujillo, occupying several official government positions, representing the country at press and labor conferences abroad, publishing his groveling *Trujillo: Síntesis de su vida y su obra* (Trujillo: Synthesis of his life and his work) (1949), and eventually becoming secretary of labor in 1957. Throughout his career, Marrero Aristy wrote articles on the sugar industry that critiqued the negative impact that the US commercial monopoly had on local Dominican businesses, sugar mills, and workers.[76] At the same time that he willingly offered up his journalism as a propaganda tool of the regime, he maintained a focus on the social and economic conditions of the working poor.

Regardless of what Marrero Aristy's views may have been at the end of his life, his 1939 novel *Over* is as much a reflection on communist organizing in sugar-producing regions as it is a criticism of the Dominican middle class to which Marrero Aristy belonged. While I do not suggest that he necessarily had direct contact with the BC or owned copies of *Mundo Obrero*, I do contend that his novel engages with communist internationalist discourse on Caribbean sugar plantations, a discourse that was directed by the BC in the years leading up to the novel's publication.

RACE AND THE "WORLD OF THE PLANTATION"

From its earliest scenes, *Over* alludes to a relationship between its content and communist organizing on sugar plantations. In his initial interview with the US-owned sugar company, the protagonist/first-person narrator, Daniel, is surprised to be asked if "you have ever on the street come across a communist," a subtle suggestion of the possibility of the presence of communism within the novel's setting.[77] Taking this cue, I use *Over* to suggest parallels between interwar Latin American extractive fictions and the BC's discourse. Specifically, these fictions tend to parallel the BC in the following ways: One, they express a pan-Caribbean consciousness by considering the problems in Caribbean extractive industries beyond a national frame; two, they critique those industries through a focus on racial inequality; three, they imagine the possibility for the formation of a new political community; and four, they place the responsibility for building this community on an educated middle class, or what *Mundo Obrero* calls the "semi-proletariat."[78] While some of these works end in triumphant workers' revolts, *Over* differs in that the collective it envisions is never realized, largely because of the failings of the very semi-proletariat in which it places its hope. I read *Over* as engaging communist debates around organizing on sugar plantations and as a self-conscious critique of the nationalism and racism that would prevent some from supporting Black immigrant workers, curtailing thus a broader project of revolutionary internationalism and relational solidarity.

Interwar Latin American extractive fictions like *Over* often center the experiences of middle-class, mixed-race men working in midlevel positions in US-dominated industries.[79] The protagonists of these works—such as in Fallas's *Mamita Yunai* or Laguerre's *La llamarada*—frequently belong to the petty bourgeoisie that the monoculture monopoly has reduced to wage labor or unemployment.[80] From this vantage point, the protagonist/narrator examines what Marrero Aristy calls "the world of the plantation," a multinational and multilingual space that can be read as a microcosm of a Caribbean extractive region and beyond.[81] At the beginning of many of these works, the narrator feels a profound class and racial distance from those on the lowest end of the company's hierarchy, such as canecutters, who are usually represented as Haitians and West Indians. However, over the course of the narrative and through a shared experience of exploitation, the narrator often grows to identify more fully with these coworkers, a coming-to-consciousness that serves to enlighten the reader. The pro-worker and antiracist consciousness reached by the narrator is highly uneven across the genre.

In *Over*, after being disowned by his wealthy father, Daniel finds employment as a *bodeguero* (commissary clerk) at an unnamed US-owned sugar mill. Despite his distaste for the company's policies, Daniel becomes increasingly trapped in its logic of exploitation. Although references to Haitian migration over land make clear that the novel takes place in the Dominican Republic, Marrero Aristy never names the company or the precise location of the novel's setting. Additionally, the novel does not provide a year or even a decade when the action takes place and includes no references to the national political context. This decision by the author could be viewed as a political strategy; by never naming Trujillo or the Dominican context, he places all blame on foreign companies.[82] Yet we might also consider that the vague time and place of the action reflect the literary strategy that Magalí Armillas-Tiseyra calls "dislocation," in which the absence of reference to place serves to dissociate the narrative action from a specific geography to better engage a transnational space, in this case a sugar-producing region.[83] In this sense, the narrative aligns with the BC's rhetoric in that it uses the Caribbean sugar plantation as the lens for formulating a more transregional analysis.

Similar to the BC's *Mundo Obrero*, the novel directs one of its more strident critiques toward the US sugar industry's racial hierarchy. From his first interactions with the company, Daniel notices a stark power differential between the American and European management and the employees. The management are all large white American men who "speak loudly and walk like soldiers." Meanwhile, the company's Dominican office employees move "like shadows . . . speaking softly," tied to their desks "like a typewriter or other service instrument."[84] The American who hires Daniel, Mr. Robinson, is said to only acknowledge the presence of other white people, to the point that he has never greeted employees who have worked for him for ten years. In his interview with Mr. Robinson, Daniel perceives an expression of contempt in Mr. Robinson's eyes, as if the manager fears dirtying his blue eyes by looking at people different from himself.[85] Similarly, the German assistant manager does not speak to Daniel, driving him to the *bodega* in his loud American car "the way you take a thing."[86]

If the American managers occupy the pinnacle of the company hierarchy, Dominicans and some West Indians are hired for midlevel positions, with Haitian and West Indian canecutters in the most subjugated positions. This power structure is communicated in the text through Daniel's own perceptions and the amount of textual space attributed to speakers from each group. When Daniel interacts with his white bosses, Daniel speaks only to answer their questions. Most of the dialogue occurs between Daniel and those who occupy similar intermediate positions. As soon as Daniel arrives at the *bodega*, he befriends Cleto, the bawdy and drunk Dominican policeman who, despite his jovial demeanor with Daniel, strikes fear in the canecutters. Beyond Cleto, Daniel also befriends several other *bodegueros*, as well as Dionisio, a Black Dominican who works as the company foreman. While there are some exceptions, Haitian and West Indian canecutters have no voice in the novel. If the novel treats Americans as caricatures of tyrannical power, the canecutters remain consistently marginal to the narrative and are presented as an unthinking mass.

The racial hierarchy in the text indexes a system of exploitation based on a profit-motive in which the company store plays a central role. The company prohibits the canecutters from growing their own crops on company land and, in essence, from making purchases at local stores, since most of their earnings are given as company store credit. Within Daniel's first weeks in his job at the *bodega*, the foreman Dionisio informs him that if he wants to stay employed, he must steal from the workers by giving them slightly fewer goods than what they purchase. He explains that the *bodega* actually receives fewer goods from the company than what is reported, and the company expects the clerk to pass this shortage on to the workers. This is the system of "over," the English word that is the title of the novel and that becomes shorthand for the exploitative practices at all levels of the industry. When Daniel learns of the extremely poor conditions of the company hospital, he thinks that this is simply "another over! Is everything here *over*?" "Over," he says, is "a fever, an insanity," and an "obsession with more" that infiltrates every level of the company.[87] The *bodega* operates as a synecdoche for the problems within the sugarproducing region of the Dominican Republic that can be extrapolated out to the broader industry.

According to the *bodeguero* Eduardo, although the company describes the *bodegas* as merely "'stores attending to the necessities of the workers in the sugarcane fields,'" in reality they are "the death of the region. They have joined together with the *latifundio* the most vast commercial monopoly in the country, abusing their employees and workers who, afraid to lose bread, do not even dare unionize to obtain protection because it would be considered a crime. . . . This, which has the position of a simple industry, has invaded every corner of the regional economy and has killed the native small merchant."[88] Eduardo argues that the US sugar industry has combined the legacy of colonial plantation practices (*latifundio* system) with a twentieth-century regime of control under the monopoly capital of US corporations. This monoculture monopoly has had a devastating effect on local merchants and the entire economy. The *bodega* emblematizes this system, where the company does not simply harvest and process sugarcane but sells all other commercial goods.

The system of "over" implicates all employees, except the canecutters, who ultimately suffer its worst consequences. This means that employees like Daniel are both victims and victimizers within the system. They are simultaneously "meat for the grinder" but also that which "lubricates the machine."[89] Daniel views himself as occupying an intermediate position in which he resents both those he exploits as well as his "absolute masters."[90] This intermediate position is perhaps most clearly expressed in the novel through the speech varieties with which the various characters speak.

In line with the interest of the wider *novela de la tierra* genre in preserving regional culture and autochthony, Marrero Aristy attempts to represent the multiple speech varieties on the plantation.[91] The speech of characters like Cleto and Dionisio displays the lenition and *s*-deletion common to Caribbean Spanish varieties, whose exaggerated representations communicate the characters' working-class background. The representations of the Spanish spoken by Americans and Haitian workers are especially parodic and suggest the narrator's contempt for these two groups. The American bosses speak in an exaggerated anglicized Spanish.[92] Similarly, the author emphasizes the Haitian workers' tendency toward lambdacism, such as in an exchange in which a Haitian canecutter says that Dominicans are "palejele," which a Dominican corrects with "¡Parejero no, degraciao!" (Not arrogant, you bastard!), repeating the same word with the *r* sound.[93] While these speech caricatures appear throughout the text, the only characters who speak in standard Spanish are the store clerks, including the West Indian *bodeguero* George Brown, who speaks fluent Spanish. The *bodegueros* represent an educated middle class that, in mediating between the caricatured American bosses and the rural Dominicans and immigrant canecutters, are integral to the corporate plantation's operation.

As the protagonists of Latin American extractive fictions like *Over* experience racial discrimination from stereotypical white American bosses and as their consciousness develops over the course of the narrative, they befriend employees in varying positions within the company, including at the lowest levels. In *Over*, Daniel begins to form relationships primarily with other store clerks, establishing a transnational community of Puerto Ricans, Dominicans, and West Indians. They develop a habit of getting together in the evenings, drinking and talking about the injustice around them, forming affective bonds and increasingly trusting one another. It is in these conversations where the novel's communist discourse becomes most explicit. As mentioned previously, Daniel is asked in his initial interview with the company if he has ever met a communist, a reference to the company's fear of communist infiltrators.[94] Similarly, in an early conversation in which Eduardo explains the company's monopolistic activities, Daniel suggests that these exploits should be openly denounced, to which Eduardo replies that the critic would be labeled a communist.[95] This potential accusation shocks Daniel, and he lists the reasons that a socialist revolution is impossible, including that the urban population is too "bourgeois" in its mentality. Dominican society, he claims, has not completed "the necessary social stages for such a transformation," and the immigrant workers could not possibly be communists because they think only of food and of returning home.[96] Yet even as Daniel dismisses the idea that communists walk in their midst, the reader is forced to call his statements into question since Daniel clearly demonstrates an understanding and acceptance of Marxist historical materialism.[97]

As the *bodegueros* become more trusting of one another, they begin to espouse increasingly radical ideas. George Brown, whom Daniel calls "el inglesito" (the little Englishman), was promoted to his current position only because of his unique circumstance as the sole survivor of a shipwreck on the eastern coast of the Dominican Republic where the bodies of fifty canecutters washed ashore. As Daniel's relationship with him grows, Brown becomes the voice of the canecutters in the narrative, and specifically of West Indian migrant workers. In keeping with Daniel's interpretation that communism does not exist among the workers, Brown does not articulate his critique of the industry through a class-based analysis. Rather, his perspective is race-based, claiming that the West Indian workers are twice enslaved, under British colonialism and under their current working conditions. He laments that even though World War I clearly showed that "a gun wielded by a white man and a Black man are equally powerful," exemplifying that "there are no superior races or inferior races," his fellow citizens did not heed this lesson to defeat their colonizers.[98] The Dominican Eduardo responds to Brown's comments by articulating a biting transnational critique of the continuation of colonial power through white supremacy in the Caribbean:

> These countries are promised lands for whites ever since Columbus set foot here. Yesterday they enslaved Indians, they stripped them of their land and their gold . . . Today they come to dispossess us and to use us, "requesting" permission from the governments—backed by their great

nation—to make investments "that will benefit the country," but in the end the results are the same. They no longer bring Black people from Africa, because there is no need to go so far to look for them nor to pay so much for them. The ideas of Father Las Casas can continue to be practiced with rented Haitians and *cocolos*.[99]

Eduardo links the practices of British and Spanish colonizers to the role of finance capital and the importation of immigrant labor (Haitians and *cocolos*, or anglophone Caribbean immigrants) in the modern plantation of the US sugar industry. He compares the dispossession of Dominicans from their land to the history of the enslavement of Indigenous peoples in the Caribbean, the transatlantic slave trade, and the exploitation of Haitian and West Indian labor.

As the content of these conversations becomes increasingly political and antiracist, Daniel's internal reflections mirror these sentiments. Daniel meditates on stories he has heard about experiences of immigrating to the Dominican Republic, and he makes overt comparisons to the transatlantic slave trade: "In the belly of the cargo ship, they generally put a quantity of men two or three times more than that which is prudent. There, Black people spend days and nights, one on top of the other."[100] According to Daniel, those who arrive on land from Haiti are similarly crammed into the trunks of vehicles, many dying along the way. They are then enclosed in barbed wire, surrounded by armed police, chosen by foremen, and loaded onto a train to be taken to various sugar mills. Daniel's conversations and reflections become more politicized over the course of the narrative, and the comparisons to histories of colonization and slavery become more pronounced. He imagines that the white boss, "upon contemplating the recently arrived herds of Black people, experiences the pleasure that once intoxicated the soul of his grandfather as he whipped the back of the African that he bought in a market."[101]

This critical depiction of the strict racial hierarchy within US-owned extractive industries is a common element within interwar Latin American extractive fictions. Like *Over*, these texts display a similar tendency to caricature white American bosses. "Mr. Sweetums," assistant manager of the "United Banana Co.," occupies this position in Carmen Lyra's *Bananos y hombres*.[102] In Luis Felipe Rodríguez's *Marcos Antilla*, it is Mister Norton, the South Carolinian who runs the Cubanacán Sugar Company's mill and who "appears to be the heir . . . of a cunning and calculating slaveholder" with his "regressive vision from the old colony of South Carolina."[103] As the critiques of the white bosses become harsher in *Over*, the descriptions of the canecutters become more dramatic in the misery they depict. Eventually, Daniel and his friends start to fantasize about "the revenge of the masses," and Daniel becomes so disgusted with the company that he finally stands up to his boss, calling him one of those "insolent whites" who "look at us like a master would his slave."[104] Similar culminating acts of rebellion appear in other Latin American extractive fictions as well, taking the form of violence toward company police, stealing from the company, or burning cane fields.

Over's critique of the sugar industry parallels LADLA's and the BC's efforts to join anticapitalist and antiracist struggles in a Greater Caribbean extractive region. However, even as the BC's *Mundo Obrero* championed the cause of Black and immigrant workers, it often described these communities with a tone of condescension that treated them as helpless victims to be saved rather than as leaders and organizers themselves. *Over* (alongside other Latin American extractive fictions) contains a similar tension between overt statements of antiracism and disparaging representations of Black subjects, and in this case, especially of Haitians. While the text condemns the treatment of Haitian workers, it simultaneously presents them as an innocent and helpless mass. Early in the narrative, Daniel becomes angry with a Haitian worker for calling him a thief. He calms his anger when he reflects that "they speak without any sentiment of rancor or meanness. They live so defenseless, they have been so used up that they have no more energy. If they say 'thief,' they do not mean to offend."[105] Here, as in other moments in the novel, Daniel views the Haitian canecutters as unthinking and defenseless. His descriptions often compare Haitians to animals, and he describes their hungry faces standing outside the bodega with disgust: "dirty faces, bristled with greasy beards; their large deformed noses, their mouths generally full of rotten roots, and their bulging eyes."[106] Even in his own critique of the exploitation of canecutters and of his bosses' white supremacy, Daniel clearly sees himself as superior to his Haitian counterparts and looks at them with the same disdain with which he is viewed by his employers.

This too is a common feature of interwar Latin American extractive fictions, wherein Black immigrant workers are presented either as sympathetic but helpless victims or as an exotic and sometimes grotesque mass that is estranged from the narrator. In *Bananos y hombres*, the narrator distantly observes a train car "full of blacks loudly laughing, of black women dressed in festive colors."[107] In *Marcos Antilla: Relatos del cañaveral*, the generalized Haitian worker is described as "a victim of chance and of the hands that play Antillean dice."[108] Although *Marcos Antilla* ends with a Black worker burning the cane fields, this rebellion is presented as resulting from "the murky innocence of one that ignores the profound reason of instinct."[109]

Such distanced and condescending representations are perhaps nowhere more explicit than in Carlos Luis Fallas Sibaja's *Mamita Yunai*, which begins with a depiction of West Indian workers taking a train leaving Costa Rica's Caribbean coast, a region abandoned by United Fruit, to seek employment in Panama. The narrator, Sibaja—a Costa Rican activist named after the author who works for the "Workers and Farmers Block" and who passes out propaganda literature among these workers—describes their flight from Costa Rica as the continuation of a long history of escape by Afro-descendants from enslavers and plantation owners.[110] Yet even as Sibaja is deeply critical of this history of racialized oppression, the exoticism and racism with which he views these workers—describing them as "black demons" in "an extravagant carnival parade, from which rose a deafening buzz of a barbarous and savage party"—undermines any illusion of the possibility for equitable relations between the narrator and the immigrant workers he seeks to influence.[111] This aspect of the novel has not gone without comment. Russell Leigh Sharman writes, "In as much as *Mamita Yunai* is an overt critique of the UFC, it also establishes some of the most insidious racial stereotypes in Costa Rican literature. Throughout Fallas's story there are condescending references to Afro-Caribbeans, Chinese, and the various indigenous groups living along the southern coast."[112] Sharman explains that the racist depictions of Afro-Caribbeans in *Mamita Yunai* must be understood within the context of the 1934 banana strike that the PCCR organized on the Caribbean coast. United Fruit brought tens of thousands of Black immigrant workers from the British Commonwealth islands to Costa Rica's Caribbean coast.[113] Because of their high levels of education and linguistic ability in English, these immigrant workers were often placed in more privileged positions within the company hierarchy than those occupied by white and mestizo Costa Rican and Nicaraguan day laborers.[114] When banana production declined disastrously following the 1929 economic collapse, United Fruit contracted the little remaining banana production to West Indian small landowners, who were dependent on the company to purchase and market their product.[115] As Jacob Zumoff writes, "This deproletarianization created the possibility of upward mobility and engendered political conservatism" among West Indian landholders.[116]

In summer 1933, the BC specifically urged the PCCR to recruit "workers who have shown decisiveness in struggle, principally workers in imperialist firms (banana workers), transport industry, as well as recruiting Negro workers in the Puerto Limón region."[117] A few months later, the BC instructed the PCCR to organize on banana plantations, stressing the importance of "the development of our tasks among the 22,000 Negro workers and English-speakers in the Puerto Limón region, raising the struggle against the discrimination of which they are victims and attracting them to common struggles with other workers."[118] In 1934, the PCCR, led by Fallas himself, organized a massive strike in the banana fields. However, even though the strike was successful and United Fruit agreed to many of the demands, the PCCR's strike failed to garner support from West Indian workers.[119] As Sharman writes, "The fatal error made by communist labor organizers was the naïve and implicitly racist assumption" that all Black people in Limón "were part of the proletariat."[120] Zumoff has argued that the PCCR failed to make a struggle against anti-Black racial oppression central to their cause, pointing out that Limón's West Indian newspaper, the *Atlantic Voice*, described the strike leaders as being out of touch with West Indians' cultural identity and political perspectives.[121]

A profound resentment toward West Indian workers comes through in Fallas's *Mamita Yunai*, published seven years after the strike. Whereas in Marrero Aristy's *Over*, the narrator occupies the midlevel management position of the *bodeguero*, through which he is complicit in the oppression of Black workers, in Fallas's *Mamita Yunai*, West Indians run the commissaries and function as agents of the company's exploitative practices. Even the title of Fallas's novel suggests a portrayal of Black laborers as "naïve dependents to the mother company."[122]

In Marrero Aristy's *Over*, West Indians similarly occupy midlevel positions within the sugar company, but because they are on equal footing with the narrator, Daniel, they are represented more humanely. In the Dominican context of Marrero Aristy's novel, it is Haitian canecutters (particularly Haitian women) who are the subject of the most degrading depictions. While the *bodegueros* and foremen repeatedly make misogynistic statements throughout the novel, and the narrator's own wife accuses him of treating her like an animal, Daniel reserves his most misogynistic and racist statements for Haitian women. Prior to meeting his Dominican wife at a privately owned *bodega*, he explains that "there are no women, actually speaking, on the plantation" because "one can find only ugly and smelly Haitian women that don't inspire me."[123] Later when his wife becomes ill, he hires a Haitian woman but fires her within three days because "the black and smelly woman did not know how to cook, she had no manners nor the slightest idea of what cleaning means."[124]

Marrero Aristy published *Over* only two years after *el corte* (the cutting), the 1937 massacre of anywhere between eighteen thousand and twenty-five thousand Haitians on the Haitian-Dominican border; the name metaphorically links stalks of cane to the bodies of Haitian cane-cutters murdered with machetes. Considering the timing of its publication and the racially discriminatory views expressed therein, some have read *Over* as a propaganda text of Trujillo nationalism. Daniel thinks how much he hates "obeying the orders of people whom we would never want to know and oppressing others whom we would want to forever forget."[125] Those whom he would want to forget are the very Haitian workers who were massacred two years prior to the book's publication and against whom Trujillista ideology constructed Dominican nationalism.[126] In fact, later in life, Marrero Aristy would write several articles that helped bolster Trujillo's anti-Haitian border policies.[127]

Among the critics who read *Over* as nationalist propaganda, Doris Sommer argues that Marrero Aristy puts forth a pro-Trujillo populist and patriarchal argument in which the male citizen has been made impotent through economic dependency and must turn to a national father figure to restore patriarchal pride. *Over*, she writes, "makes an impassioned nationalist demand to expel the North American Usurper of the sugar plantations so that a new class of petty-bourgeois administrators and technicians patronized by Trujillo can develop their own Land." While this is a convincing reading, Sommer admits that in many ways the novel does not fit neatly within her argument, and "the text's insistent foregrounding of the exploitation and racism suffered by sugar workers, whether West Indian, Haitian, or Dominican, complicates the narrowly nationalist and white-collar propaganda" that she would otherwise attribute to the book.[128] The overlap between the novel and Trujillista discourse is, she writes, "imperfect" since the "novel often spills over into a radical critique of exploitation" and the racism of many of the Dominican characters toward Haitians undermines any attempt to treat racism as a US import.[129] These discrepancies, she explains, may be why *Over* was issued only once during the Trujillo regime and why the book was subsequently banned.

Even as *Over* expresses discriminatory views toward Haitians, the novel is so critical of racialized oppression within the industry that others have read it not as a defense of Trujillismo but as a veiled critique of Trujillo himself. The assistant manager, Mr. Lilo, whom Daniel describes as "our dictator," is a sexual predator who convinces the *bodegueros* to hand over their daughters in exchange for political favors.[130] As some have pointed out, Mr. Lilo's behaviors have striking resemblance to Trujillo's own predatory behaviors toward the daughters of government officials.[131]

A DREAM DEFERRED

When we consider *Over* alongside the BC's rhetoric, we understand the ambiguity in this text as parallel to the incongruous positions of communist internationalism in Caribbean extractive economies at this moment. The BC consistently critiqued the exploitation of Black labor but often did so through a paternalistic position that failed to create space for Black leadership. Similarly, despite the racial terms through which *Over* frames the protagonist's moment of rebellion, Daniel as a middle-class Dominican is never fully able to move beyond his own racism toward the Haitian and West Indian canecutters. Daniel's friendship with George Brown never leads him to take action alongside West Indian workers. Sharman has made a similar argument about Fallas's *Mamita Yunai*, writing that Fallas's failure to "adequately incorporate the black laborer in the revolution, both politically and literarily, is linked to the more general paradox of blackness in communist ideology."[132]

Whereas in some interwar Latin American extractive fictions the protagonist's developing political consciousness eventually results in a chosen solidarity with the workers and a decision to fight against these inequities, in the case of *Over* the nightly drinking and political discussions among Daniel and his friends simply lead him to become a drunk. Daniel's alcoholism is clearly tied to a choice to turn away from political solidarity. The *bodeguero* Valerio explains that in order to continue taking advantage of the canecutters, you have to stay constantly drunk: "This, buddy, can only be seen through a tunnel of rum. Here, everything is rum."[133] The previous statement that everything is "over" is replaced with the notion that everything is rum. An escape into alcoholism facilitates the bodegueros' continued participation in this oppressive system. Eventually, alcoholism leaves Daniel destitute and reflecting that the mill has actually ground him up. In the end, he dreams only of escape and plans to leave the country.

Daniel never fully emerges as a rebellious hero. Instead, the novel exhibits a self-conscious critique of Daniel's inability to identify completely with the exploited in order to take action; it is a critique of Daniel's own bourgeois perspective, with all its contradictions, and of the classism, racism, and nationalism that prevent him from organizing with his coworkers.[134] Ultimately, I read this text as containing deep pessimism toward the possibility of organizing internationalist resistance, especially in the Dominican context.[135]

Over forms part of the sugarcane novel genre as well as the broader genre of what I have called Latin American extractive fictions. *Over* was published nine years into the Trujillo dictatorship and two years after the 1937 massacre of Haitians on the Haitian-Dominican border. Despite this sociohistorical context, when we consider *Over* within the broader genre of Latin American extractive fictions and the parallels of that genre with BC propaganda, a reading emerges of this novel as a meditation on the limits of transnational and transracial organizing in extractive economies and specifically of the limits of a pan-Caribbean political collectivity. Whereas Latin American extractive fictions may reflect on LADLA's initial vision (and the continuation of certain elements of its project through the BC), these works fall far short of representing LADLA's furthest-reaching antiracist positions. In some ways, Daniel's inability to have solidarity with Haitian and West Indian canecutters signals the challenges to the BC's project that, despite its intentions, never fully incorporated Black workers into leadership and struggled to address racism within its own ranks. As *Over* reflects on a potentially alternative regional and even global relation, it announces, as its title suggests, something that is finished, closed, something that—at least for the time being—would not be.

TWENTY-FIRST-CENTURY *REDES*

In the early hours of November 6, 2017, residents of Cotuí and surrounding towns in central Dominican Republic chained themselves to chairs outside the Barrick Gold Corporation's Pueblo Viejo mine. The *campamento de los encadenados* (camp of the chained) became a rallying point for social justice and academic organizations, attracting activists, journalists, and politicians until police and military forcibly removed the group in June 2018.[1] The open pit mine at Pueblo Viejo was the first mine exploited by the Spanish on the American continent and remains the second-largest gold mine in Latin America and the eighth-largest in the world.[2] Modern mining at Pueblo Viejo, dating to the 1960s, eventually contaminated the surrounding community's primary water source with sulfide ore.[3] Once the Toronto-based Barrick Gold Corporation purchased the mine in 2006, it invested $4 billion in a new extraction method called pressure oxidation, which uses industrial quantities of cyanide to remove leftover low-grade ore, producing seventy-nine tons of waste per ounce of gold.[4] This process has had profound environmental and health effects, forcing local residents to rely on water provided to them by the company.[5] Ongoing protests against Barrick Gold gained further visibility in 2019 when the company announced an expansion of its operations into Yamasá, Monte Plata, where it planned to construct a large tailings dam (an aboveground dam used to store mining waste).[6] Because twelve rivers originate in Monte Plata and because tailings dams are known to fail, this expansion threatened to put the entire region at risk of contamination.[7]

In April 2021, Barrick Gold's actions in the Dominican Republic became a focus of Strike MoMA, a series of protests against the Museum of Modern Art in New York City.[8] A coalition of twelve groups called the International Imagination of Anti-National Anti-Imperialist Feelings (IIAAF) organized ten weeks of activities to call attention to the business ties of several of MoMA's trustees.[9] Much of this protest centered on MoMA's chairman, Leon Black, for connections with convicted sex offender Jeffrey Epstein, but the protests targeted other trustees as well. These included Patricia Phelps de Cisneros, wife of Gustavo Cisneros, who was on Barrick Gold's board of directors.[10] The Cisneros family funds MoMA's Patricia Phelps de Cisneros Research Institute, which houses part of the family's extensive art collection.[11] Strike MoMA protesters gathered outside the museum in June 2021 for a teach-in by Dominican studies scholar Sandy Plácido, who poured a blue gallon container, like those provided to communities around Pueblo Viejo, of red "blood water" over a pile of plantains at the museum entrance.[12] Protesters shouted, "Cisneros cobarde. El agua vale más que el arte" (Cisneros coward. Water is worth more than art), a play on the slogan "Water is worth more than gold," used by anti-Barrick protesters in the Dominican Republic.

Through its focus on MoMA, the IIAAF joined several causes concerned with "the political economy of the art system."[13] Its "framework and terms for struggle" addressed the establishment of New York City on stolen Indigenous lands and its development by enslaved Africans and subsequent generations of immigrants and refugees. It stated its support for the Indigenous "land back" movement, the "fight for Black liberation," and sanctuary for undocumented immigrants, and it drew connections to the struggle against patriarchy epitomized in the feminist *marea verde* in Latin America. This multiplicity of causes is what the IIAAF calls the "interwoven struggles" of its movement, which is "reinvented through the process of organizing and building relations." The IIAAF represents an attempt to "operationalize solidarity," which it describes as "building relations between movements, communities, families, friends. As we weave our struggles together by taking action and holding each other with care, another political imaginary emerges."[14]

I draw attention to this relatively recent history because of how clearly the IIAAF's framework reflects the weavings that have been at the heart of this book—the interlaced threads of artistic production with anti-imperialist, anti-extractive, antiracist, pro-Indigenous, pro-immigrant, pro-worker, and agrarian struggles. Rooting itself in a long history of radical political movements and thinkers in the Americas, the IIAAF named as inspiration the Third World Liberation Front, Women Students and Artists for Black Art Liberation, and the 1960s–70s Guerrilla Art Action Group. It cited Lucy Parsons and W. E. B. Du Bois's conceptualizations of the "strike" as well as Martinican writer Suzanne Césaire's understanding of the relationship between art and freedom movements. It also named Black Panther Party founder Huey Newton's notion of "intercommunalism" as informing the IIAAF's disidentification from the nation-state.[15] Despite these robust citations to a longer legacy of radical organizing in the Americas, the statement contained no references to the Anti-Imperialist League of the Americas, LADLA's activities in New York City, or LADLA's connections with renowned artists like Modotti, who has thirty-three works in MoMA's catalogue.[16] This elision is not surprising since LADLA has been the subject of just one book (by Daniel Kersffeld) thus far, and extant scholarly work on LADLA has focused less on its artistic and cultural production. We do not yet have a collective discursive and aesthetic memory of LADLA with which current social movements can productively engage.

Through this book, I have attempted to contribute to the construction of such a memory of LADLA. Over the previous chapters, I argued that LADLA made three lasting contributions. First, LADLA provides an early twentieth-century example of transnational political organizing across extractive economies through which it theorized the relationship between different oppressions and the links between anti-imperialism, antiracism, and antifascism. By organizing across extractive economies, LADLA rejected Latin America's interwar regionalisms for hemispheric globalism, wherein LADLA expanded on its initially hemispheric connections with worker and minority struggles in the United States to embrace interdependency and solidarity with movements around the world.

Second, LADLA analyzed the relation between differentiated experiences of capitalist exploitation suffered by Indigenous, Black, and immigrant communities. In doing so, it advanced a multiracial and hemispheric analysis of racial capitalism that addressed the racialization of labor and accounted for the ongoing process of violent dispossession faced by Indigenous peoples. In seeking to understand how capitalism differentially impacted different communities, LADLA modeled a form of relational solidarity based on the relation (but not conflation) of varying forms of capitalist exploitation. LADLA's artist-activists, in turn, reflected this political vision through forging a relational aesthetics and poetics.

And third, LADLA offers a case study for thinking through the complexities of transnational and multiracial solidarity movements. Through examining instances of ethnic impersonation, masculinist erotics, charismatic leadership, and asymmetries in access and mobility, I have considered instances when LADLA's efforts to forge transformative political solidarities served to reinforce the very "uneven power relations and geographies" it sought to dismantle.[17] LADLA shows how solidarity movements can serve to obscure differences and have often been built through connections afforded to a privileged few. As the vision of LADLA (and the later Caribbean Bureau) became memorialized through the genre of interwar Latin American extractive fictions, authors would use these works to reflect on the challenges of organizing within extractive economies and of forging solidarities across national, linguistic, and racial differences. Although these fictions would draw on key elements of LADLA's worldview, they would obviate its furthest-reaching antiracist politics and expansive vision of political community.

Considering that one hundred years have passed since LADLA's founding, its anti-imperialist worldview may seem disconnected from the present. Scholars and activists have debated the relevance of Lenin's theory of imperialism (on which LADLA based its understanding) in the post-neoliberal era. In the early twentieth century, Lenin argued that imperialist powers—through cooperation between state military, banks, and national industry—competed for economic control of territories.[18] Today, however, the traditional imperialist state "must willingly cater to the caprices of globalized finance."[19] Contemporary power exists in the overlapping realms of multiple networked actors that include the global media, the financial sector, national governments and military, multinational corporations, special interest groups, and consumers.[20] This context has not led to the absence of war; rather, "the political and military might of the most powerful capitalist state is proximately used for defending the interests and operations of globalized finance capital."[21] Multinational corporations serve a transnational capitalist class that is largely unbeholden to national allegiances, leading to a breakdown in the spatial divisions of traditional imperialism: The financial elite of poorer countries count among the world's top billionaires, and workers from wealthier countries compete with low-wage workers located elsewhere.[22]

Yet even with the differences between Lenin's moment and our own, many have pointed to the ways that commodities—like iPhones or T-shirts—continue to "generate enormous outflows of money" from poorer countries "to transnational corporations headquartered in the core capitalist nations of the global North."[23] Much like the traditional imperialist model, these core capitalist countries continue to extract significant profits from workers in poorer countries and aggressively seek out sites with lower wages and fewer labor protections. This happens both through less coercive methods, like development assistance and promotion of free markets, and through more coercive methods, like military occupation. Wealthier countries, some have concluded, have simply combined old and new forms of domination, and, rather than leaving behind imperialism, "the specific difference between the imperialism of the 20th century and imperialism today is the globalizing dynamics of capital and its diverse large-scale investment and extractive operations."[24]

Whether or not the imperialist model is the most relevant for describing today's power relations, it would be hard to deny that power has become increasingly transnational and that transnational forms of domination will not be overcome through purely national frameworks. Whereas in the first decade of the twenty-first century the world witnessed an outpouring of protest against global financial institutions and corporations in response to the financial crisis, the scale of internationalism seen in these movements has waned. One hundred years after LADLA, we have much to learn from its example. Without social media or easy access to commercial air travel, LADLA managed to connect activists throughout the American hemisphere and draw them into the LAI's global political movement.

Despite the transnational nature of contemporary power, regionalism and nationalism remain important sources of political mobilization. Although the Dominican struggle against Barrick Gold received international attention, activists framed their struggle in national terms, founding their *campamento de los encadenados* on the anniversary of the nation's constitution to signal how their local concerns impacted the country as a whole.[25] This national framing was successful for the time being, since the Dominican government announced in spring 2022 that Barrick's request to expand into Yamasá would not be approved.[26] However, shortly afterward, Barrick announced plans to build a second tailings dam at Puerto Viejo, requiring the involuntary relocation of six communities and resulting in protests in November–December 2024.[27] Barrick also has many other mining operations around the world. As LADLA argued in the case of the petroleum companies Standard Oil and Royal Dutch Shell, a movement against these corporations, "in order to be effective, must become international."[28]

Activists from the Dominican Republic, Argentina, and Papua New Guinea have met virtually to "share experiences and strategies in light of human rights violations committed by Barrick and their home governments."[29] As these activists understand, combatting a multinational corporation requires networks that cross boundaries of nation and language, as well as political discourses that can effectively weave together anticapitalist, ecological, Indigenous, labor, race-based, and gender-based struggles. These organizing efforts are part of a larger trend of twenty-first-century anti-extractivist activism.

At the turn of the twenty-first century, progressive pink tide governments in Latin America attempted to reverse long-standing relations of economic dependency through a model of progressive neo-extractivism, in which profits from the export of raw materials would fund social services. As discussed in the book's introduction, these ventures fostered a complex relationship with socio-environmental and Indigenous movements, and the expansion of these extractive projects led to a proliferation of socio-environmental and territorial conflicts in the region, especially involving *campesino* and Indigenous groups. These movements, as Henry Veltmeyer and James Petras have argued, "are best understood as the latest development in the historical trajectory of class struggle against capitalist exploitation, which engages the direct producers and peasant farmers, the indigenous (and Afro-descendant communities) and the working class and their combined struggle against both capital and the state."[30] As I have argued, LADLA represents an important historical root of these contemporary social movements.

The cultural production of today's anti-extractivist movements also has clear resonances with the relational aesthetics advanced by LADLA's artists, but contemporary activist-artists take this vision a step further through a posthumanist aesthetics of planetary relation. Carolina Caycedo (with whom I started this book) uses her *cosmotarrayas* to communicate "networks of solidarity and resistance in the fight for . . . social justice" and a vision for an alternative relationship to the planet referenced in the cast net, an Indigenous fishing tool.[31] Caycedo is one among many artist-activists in recent years who use their work to envision alternative socio-ecological frameworks. In the U.S. context, adrienne maree brown's Black feminist vision in *Emergent Strategy* (2017) describes political community as birds in flight, oak trees intertwining their roots, and ocean waves, each unique but connected. Richard Powers's Pulitzer Prize–winning novel *The Overstory* (2018) uses trees' communication and interdependence to structure a radical vision for planetary solidarity. Alternatively, we could return to Colombia, where a feminist group of anti-mining and water rights activists called Colectivo Entretejidos (Interwoven Collective) wrap trees in fabric, using the Indigenous cultural practice of weaving to draw attention to the negative impacts of gold mining on both the local ecology and the Indigenous women who live in it.

Wrapping trees in fabric represents, as Colectivo Entretejidos explains, "a symbolic form of embracing the trees to show that one has to care for them and to lead a defense of the land."[32] This action visualizes what Latin American Indigenous women activists have been calling the defense of the "body-territory," a concept that integrates women's rights struggles with environmental activism.[33] As the Guatemalan Maya-Xinka activist Lorena Cabnal explains, caring for the body-territory means that "the defense of the land is immanent to the defense of the bodies that live in it."[34] Similarly, in a report on Indigenous women land defenders in Latin America—written by Guatemalan Maya-K'iché activist Aura Lolita Chávez Ixcaquic, Mexican activist Marusia López Cruz, and the director of the Mexico City–based Americas program, Laura Carlsen—the body-territory is described as follows: "Territory is understood as a web of life that connects with our bodies and histories, which creates a link between the struggles for the defense of women's bodies and the territories that sustain us."[35]

This thinking on the body-territory represents a radical and welcome expansion of traditional solidarity politics, where a vision of mutuality extends to the planet itself. This expansive understanding of solidarity is inherently tied to the alternative visions to extractive capitalism provided by Indigenous land-rights movements, discussed in the introduction, that call for a social ecology based on "reciprocity, solidarity, concordance, interconnectedness."[36] In addition to these Indigenous traditions of resistance to extractivism, such a relational political imagination, I have argued, is also interwoven with the history of LADLA's hemispheric organizing against extractive capitalism, imperialism, and against these systems' ties to racialized oppression and authoritarian governance. Ultimately, this book contends that future efforts to build global movements against extractive racial capitalism will require deep knowledge of the histories of similar movements, like LADLA, that preceded them and as much attentiveness to those movements' errors as to their successes.

ACKNOWLEDGMENTS

I was working in papers related to Tina Modotti at the Getty Research Institute when COVID-19 hit Los Angeles. The pandemic would impact the researching and writing of this book in significant ways, and it could not have been completed without the help of many collaborators. I will always remember University of Virginia (UVA) librarian Jeremy Wilk, who wheeled out a microfilm machine to my car and allowed me to take it to my house for several months so I could keep working. Other librarians made documents available digitally or put me on the schedule as soon as special collections reopened. These included staff at Getty Research Institute, Hoover Institution Library and Archives, Library of Congress, New York Public Library Manuscripts and Archives division, University of New Mexico Center for Southwest Research, and UVA; Archivo General de la Nación and Biblioteca Manuel Orozco y Berra in Mexico City; Instituto de Historia and Biblioteca Nacional de Cuba José Martí in Havana; and International Institute of Social History in Amsterdam. Lillian Guerra put me in touch with Instituto de Historia director René González Barrios, who was a wonderful resource, and Roberto Armengol, Luciano Castillo, Roberto Zurbano Torres, and Anastasia Valecce provided good company in Havana. In Mexico City, Daniel Kent-Carrasco made sure I was well fed and among friends. Running into Jacob Zumoff in the New York Public Library led to helpful reading suggestions, and in Los Angeles, Kaitlin McNally-Murphy and Melissa Simpson Monaghan brought peace to a distressing moment.

My editor, Courtney Berger, and series editors Bruno Bosteels and George Ciccariello-Maher believed in this project and saw it through to the end. The book was funded by a 2020–21 American Council of Learned Societies fellowship, which allowed me to draft much of it, as well as by University of Virginia AHSS/VPR Research Support and summer stipends, which facilitated travel to special collections in several locations. A UVA Americas Center book workshop offered the exciting opportunity to invite

Michael Hardt and Ignacio Sánchez Prado to campus. Special thanks to them and to Duke's anonymous readers for engaging so deeply with the manuscript and for their suggestions for revision.

I started working on some of this material in response to an invitation from Paolo Capuzzo and Roberto Dainotto to a 2017 workshop on communist internationalism at the University of Bologna as well as through my participation in The Red and the Black Conference, organized by Alan Rice and Christian Høgsbjerg at the Institute for Black Atlantic Research. Subsequent speaking invitations from Magalí Armillas-Tiseyra, Estefanía Bournot, Azucena G. Blanco, Rubén Almendros, Ana María Ramírez Gómez, and Jorge Locane, Smaran Dayal and Robert J. C. Young, Ángel Díaz, Gal Kirn and Paola Barreira López, Marwan M. Kraidy, David Luis-Brown, Joshua K. Lund and Mark Sanders, Jorge Marturano, Justin Mitchell and Nancy Armstrong, Justin Read, and Sarah Quesada, as well as an ACLA panel on "Solidarity Aesthetics" organized by Anthony Alessandrini, Anna Bernard, Alys Moody, and Jessica Stites-Mor, all provided opportunities to receive feedback on various portions of this project. Many scholars shaped this book, and I feel especially indebted to those who laid historiographical foundations, particularly Daniel Kersffeld but also Barry Carr, Alejandro de la Fuente, Michael Goebel, Thomas Lindner, Michele Louro, Caridad Massón Sena, Ricardo Melgar Bao, Sergio Moissen, Fredrik Petersson, Sandra Pujals, Margaret Stevens, Holger Weiss, and Jacob Zumoff.

Friends and colleagues read drafts of chapters and provided feedback. The South-South working group (Magalí, Sophie Esch, Sarah Q., and Lanie Millar) gave consistent intellectual and moral support. Daniel Doncel Martín, Eren Jaye, Lauren Mehfoud, and Caroline Whitcomb were outstanding research assistants, Eli Carter lent his sharp eye, and Éric Morales-Franceschini offered his poetic expertise. Lean Sweeney and Joseph Seeley let me workshop a chapter through their Borderlands Colloquia, and Cole Rizki and Matthew Chin followed up with written feedback. Graduate students from Notre Dame's Department of Romance Languages and Literatures brought energy and insights to workshopping chapter 1. Levin Arnsperger read and translated documents from German, and Rachel Price, Omar Granados, and Erick J. Mota collaborated on an urgent request for a scan. Christine Hatzky gifted me her brilliant biography of Mella. The opportunity to contribute to Mark Atwood Lawrence and R. Joseph Parrott's edited volume allowed me to think more deeply about shared ideological tenets between LADLA and OSPAAAL, and anonymous readers for articles in *American Communist History, Atlantic Studies,*

Cultural Critique, and *Latin American Research Review* provided invaluable suggestions for revision that helped shape my thinking.

Colleagues in UVA's Department of Spanish, Italian, and Portuguese have been a significant source of support, and I've been especially buoyed by the friendship of current and former UVA colleagues Eli, Cole, Mimi Arbeit, Steph Ceraso, Marlene Daut, Laurent Dubois, Tatiana Flores, Laura Goldblatt, Charlotte Rogers, Jalane Schmidt, and Penny Von Eschen. Tally Sanford, Sam Riggs, and Linda Newman gave tireless administrative support. Graduate students in my department have taught me a great deal, and many generously offered their feedback at the book workshop. Thanks especially to Catherine Addington, Dani, Yafrainy Familia, Lauren, Elizabeth Mirabal, Mathilda Shepard, and Carlos Velazco Fernández. Monica Popescu (rest in peace) and Christopher J. Lee were patient, and colleagues outside UVA have given their time to provide guidance, including Nacho, Josh, Ericka Beckman, Valérie Loichot, Alfred J. López, and Jacqueline Loss.

My fiction writing group (Fernanda Hong, Jennifer Hale, Alyssa Kagel, Linda Prather, Liza Losada Schor) provided welcome diversion during this time. Hannah gave her incredible compassion. Joseph Pitts was a constant source of kindness. To my friends and family for their love: Eliza, Emme, Dotty, Karen, Ken, Maisie, Mariam, Mary Lauren, Michael, Naeem, Tanory, Sam, and Sari, and to Celeste, Elana, Emily, Dominick, Nanci, Ricardo, and Shiva. My two dogs made me laugh every day, and the Chesapeake Bay steadied me. My best friend and life partner, Andrew, knows all too well the rhythms of living with a writer, and he consistently reminded me to trust the process. Andrew, no matter where we are, I am in "some kind of heaven" with you.

This book is especially indebted to the activists and artists who inspired me to write about them one hundred years later. May this book testify to their courage and imagination.

NOTES

Portions of this book first appeared in *Cultural Critique* 126 (Winter 2025); *Latin American Research Review* 59, no. 3 (2024); *American Communist History* 17, no. 1 (Spring 2018); and *Atlantic Studies: Global Currents* 19, no. 2 (2019). They are reproduced with permission.

A note on translation: If the source is a newspaper or archival document, I provide the original Spanish in the endnotes. If the source is a published book or online resource, I provide the page number for the original Spanish. All translations mine unless otherwise indicated.

INTRODUCTION

1   Caycedo and De Blois, "The River."
2   Caycedo and De Blois, "The River"; Svampa, *Neo-Extractivism*, 36.
3   Acevedo-Yates, "Carolina."
4   "Humanidad rebelde." LADLA, "El Congreso Antimperialista de Bruselas," 3.
5   "The All-America Anti-Imperialist League: Its Opposition and Aims," CS Papers, box 1, file 2; August 11, 1926, letter, RGASPI, f. 542, o. 1, d. 19. Other documents date its founding to the end of 1924. Mella, "Informe," RGASPI, f. 542, o. 1, d. 19. In December 1926, LADLA reported fourteen national sections, in Argentina, Brazil, Colombia, Cuba, Dominican Republic, Ecuador, El Salvador, Honduras, Mexico, Peru, Puerto Rico, Uruguay, Venezuela, and the continental United States. Julio Antonio Mella to Jaime Nevares Sager, December 18, 1926, BDW Papers, box 1. However, the number of sections and their locations fluctuated over time. Within the US national section, the Chicago and New York branches were the most active, but US section documents from 1929 also mention branches in Chicago, Los Angeles, Salt Lake City, San Francisco, and Seattle, as well as a "Midwestern section." "Summary," RGASPI, f. 542, o. 1, d. 35. An article in *El Libertador* describes Spanish-speaking chapters in "Los Angeles, Kansas, Colorado and Pittsburgh." Ruis, "Actividades," 4.
6   Technically, the LAI Executive Committee named LADLA as its organizing bureau for Latin America. I describe LADLA as the LAI's "Americas" section because LADLA was a hemispheric organization and

maintained chapters in the United States, and the LAI's US chapters were synonymous with LADLA's US chapters. LADLA, "Última," 12.

7   Jeifets and Jeifets, *América Latina*, 66, 257; Petersson, *Willi*, 345–47.

8   LADLA had ongoing problems with funding and mostly relied on membership contributions. In its beginnings, LADLA leadership expressed frustration with the Workers Party in the United States for not upholding its financial commitment to LADLA. After it joined the LAI, LADLA leadership consistently tried to advocate for funding from the LAI, and it appears that LAI contributions were quite minimal. See "Auszug" and F. to Willi Münzenberg, August 15, 1927, both in RGASPI, f. 542, o. 1, d. 19; F. Bach to Willi Münzenberg, January 16, 1928, RGASPI, f. 542, o. 1, d. 28; Rafael Carrillo and Xavier Guerrero to Bertram and Ella Wolfe, August 10, 1925, BW Papers, box 4, folder 11. For a detailed discussion of how LADLA conceived its relationship to communist parties—wherein the communist party had representation in the league but did not control it—see transcript from dialogue on the Leagues Against Imperialism at the First Latin American Communist Conference in Buenos Aires in June 1929. SSA, *El movimiento*, 320–30.

9   The first issue of *El Libertador* described its political community as follows: "It will not close its ranks to any genuinely anti-imperialist tendency nor will it open them to any opposing tendency. It will provide news about the anti-imperialist movement throughout the world, about Russia and China, Persia and Morocco, Egypt and India; about the anti-imperialist movement in the United States; about the anti-imperialist movement in Latin America; about union organizations from both continents and about agrarian organizations; nothing and no one that can serve in the struggle against Yankee imperialism will be external to its ranks" (No cerrará sus columnas a ninguna tendencia genuinamente anti-imperialista ni las abrirá a ninguna tendencia contraria. Dará noticias sobre el movimiento anti-imperialista en todo el mundo, sobre Rusia y China, Persia y Marruecos, Egipto y la India; sobre el movimiento anti-imperialista en los Estados Unidos; sobre el movimiento anti-imperialista de la América Latina; sobre las organizaciones sindicales de los dos continentes y sobre las organizaciones agrarias; nada y nadie que puede servir en la lucha contra el imperialismo yanqui será ajeno a sus columnas). LADLA, "El peligro," 2.

10   Scholarship on Cuban and Mexican communism is extensive. For studies of the Mexican Communist Party, see, for example, Carr, *Marxism*; Herman, *The Comintern*; Márquez Fuentes and Rodríguez Araujo, *El Partido*; Neymet, *Cronología*; Peláez, *Partido*; Spenser, *Stumbling*; Spenser, *The Impossible*. For studies of the early history of the Cuban Communist Party, see García Montes and Ávila, *Historia*; Massón Sena, "Evolución."

11   Kersffeld, *Contra*; Melgar Bao, "El universo"; Melgar Bao, "The Anti-Imperialist." Kersffeld uses documents from the LAI archive and RGASPI but mostly relies on archival sources in Mexico, Cuba, and Argentina.

Wood, "Indoamerica," includes documents from RGASPI. In her study of LADLA–Puerto Rico, Pujals's "Becoming" and "¡Embarcados!" uniquely rely on the BDW papers held at the New York Public Library. Hatzky, *Julio*, includes information on LADLA based on RGASPI documents. Lindner, *A City*, which studies anti-imperialism in Mexico City in the 1920s, including LADLA, does use the Hoover Institution's Wolfe and Shipman Papers.

12   Carr, "Pioneering"; Jeifets and Jeifets, "La Comintern"; Jeifets and Jeifets, "Jaime Nevárez"; Melgar Bao, "The Anti-Imperialist"; Melgar Bao, "El universo"; Pujals, "Becoming"; Pujals, "¡Embarcados!"; Wood, "Indoamerica." Beyond Kersffeld's *Contra*, see also Kersffeld, "El Comité," "La Liga Antiimperialista de Costa Rica," and "La Liga Antiimperialista de las Américas."

13   In particular, I refer to Becker et al., *Transnational*; Heatherton, *Arise!*; Lindner, *A City*; Rivera Mir, *Militantes*; and Stevens, *Red*. See also Bosteels, *El marxismo*; Caballero, *Latin America*; Carr, *Marxism*; Concheiro et al., *El comunismo*; Gronbeck-Tedesco, *Cuba*; Kent-Carrasco, "México"; Melgar Bao, *La prensa*; Power, *Solidarity*; Spenser, *Stumbling*; and Spenser, *The Impossible*; as well as the scholarship of Sandra Pujals.

14   Salvador de la Plaza to Jaime N. Sager, March 10, 1926, BDW Papers, box 1.

15   Melgar Bao also uses this more direct translation in "The Anti-Imperialist."

16   Saldaña-Portillo, "Hemispheric Literature," 209. For hemispheric Américas scholarship that takes the Caribbean and Latin America as its point of departure, see, for example, Castellanos et al., *Comparative*; Cohn, *History*; Feinsod, *The Poetry*; Lomas, *Translating*; Luis-Brown, *Waves*; and Saldaña-Portillo, *Indian*.

17   For an overview of stakes and key texts of Global South studies, see Armillas-Tiseyra and Mahler, "Introduction."

18   There is a growing trend toward better accounting for Latin American engagement with twentieth-century transnational anticolonialisms, such as Lewis and Stolte's *The Lives of Cold War Afro-Asianism*, which in spite of the title discusses how Havana became an important site for the development of Afro-Asianisms, or Manela and Streets-Salter's *The Anticolonial Transnational*, which includes a chapter on LADLA in Mexico City.

19   See Young, *Postcolonialism*, 192; Young, "Postcolonialism," 17.

20   Here I draw from historiography provided in Mahler, *From the Tricontinental*, 73–78.

21   For how LADLA anticipated Tricontinental solidarities, see Mahler, "Global."

22   Louro, in *Comrades*, discusses Mexico's role in LAI, but the treatment is limited since her study centers on Nehru. Petersson, in *Willi*, does not mention LADLA, instead focusing on the US-based All-America Anti-Imperialist League (aka LADLA's US section). Although he discusses the creation of Latin American sections, particularly in Mexico, his otherwise excellent and thorough study does not reflect an understanding that LADLA preceded the LAI by two years or that the LAI's Latin American sections were synonymous with LADLA sections. In an edited volume

about the LAI, Goebel, in "Forging," does provide an in-depth look at Latin American participation in Brussels. See also Brückenhaus, *Policing*.

23 Goebel, *Anti-Imperial*; Goebel, "Forging"; Kersffeld, *Contra*; Lindner, *A City*.

24 Petersson, *Willi*.

25 May 1927 report, RGASPI, f. 542, o. 1, d. 16.

26 Robbins, "Blaming"; Lee, "Modern," 28.

27 Latin Americanist historian Steve J. Stern, for example, points to sixteenth-century labor in silver mines in Bolivia and in sugar mills in Brazil and Hispaniola as case studies for how "the fundamentals of Wallerstein's interpretation are severely flawed when viewed from the American periphery." Stern, "Feudalism," 858. He employs these case studies to point to problems in Wallerstein's division of labor into free-wage labor in the core states of Western Europe, forced labor in the periphery, and intermediate forms such as sharecropping in the semiperiphery. Ultimately, Stern calls for closer engagement with Latin Americanist scholars who have led the way in theorizing colonial modes of production in the Americas. For in-depth discussions of Latin Americanist debates on postcolonial studies, see Acosta, *Thresholds*; Coronil, "Elephants"; Lund, *The Impure*. See also Seed, "Colonial," and responses to this essay in Adorno, "Reconsidering"; Mignolo, "Colonial"; and Vidal, "The Concept." These problems are discussed in more depth in Mahler, *From the Tricontinental*, 25–36.

28 Latin Americanist scholars like Enrique Dussel, Aníbal Quijano, and Walter Mignolo began developing the notions of "modernity/coloniality/decoloniality" in the 1990s. This body of scholarship arose largely in response to Wallerstein's limitations on the history of Latin America and the perceived privileging within postcolonial studies of anglophone and francophone contexts as well in an attempt to consider the relationship between older forms of colonial power and the post-Soviet context. While the founding text for this intellectual movement was Quijano's "Colonialidad y modernidad/racionalidad," the project began to emerge primarily through two panels with Fernando Coronil, Quijano, and Mignolo and then with Wallerstein, Quijano, and Dussel in the late 1990s. Mignolo, "Introduction," 10. For an overview of this body of scholarship organized around a shared conceptual corpus, see Escobar, "Worlds."

29 Chakrabarty, "The Legacies"; Lee, *Making*; Prashad, *The Darker*; Weiss, *Framing*. See also Ahmad, *In Theory*.

30 Baldwin, *Beyond*; Djagalov, *From Internationalism*; Elam, *World*; Feldman, *On the Threshold*; Kalliney, *The Aesthetic*; Glaser and Lee, *Comintern*; Lee, *The Ethnic*; Popescu, *At Penpoint*.

31 Glaser and Lee's *Comintern Aesthetics* does include a chapter on Brazilian modernism. For work on the relationship between anticolonial aesthetics and internationalist political structures that takes Latin American intellectuals into account, see, for instance, Bournot, "Négritude"; Djagalov,

From Internationalism; Lee and Mahler, "Bandung"; Locane, "On the World"; and scholarship that has proliferated since 2018 on OSPAAAL.

32　See the works of Carr, Kersffeld, Lindner, Melgar Bao, and Pujals.

33　"Pueblos oprimidos, coloniales y semi-coloniales." LADLA, "El frente," 9.

34　See, for instance, Delpar, *The Enormous*; Flores, *Mexico's*; Legrás, *Culture*; Rosenberg, *The Avant*; Smith, *The Power*.

35　It is commonly referred to under other monikers like *novela criolla, novela regional*, and novela rural. Alonso, *The Spanish American*.

36　Morse, "The Multiverse," 50; Alonso, *The Spanish American*, 75.

37　Becker, "Mariátegui."

38　The LAI archive reveals consistent complaints by members of LADLA's Continental Committee about Gomez's attempts to control LADLA from the United States. See "Auszug"; Mella, "Informe"; 10 mayo 1926 Informe; "The Question," all in RGASPI, f. 542, o. 1, d. 19.

39　Hatzky, *Julio*, 285.

40　Kersffeld, "La Liga Antiimperialista de Costa Rica," 109.

41　Kersffeld, "La Liga Antiimperialista de Costa Rica," 110–11.

42　"Organizar 'todas las fuerzas' anti-imperialistas de la América Latina, de unificarlas en una unidad continental, de aliarlas con los aliados naturales que existen en Europa, en Asia, en África, Y DENTRO DE LOS ESTADOS UNIDOS MISMOS; de despertar a las masas somnolientas de obreros y campesinos, de indígenas y mestizos y blancos, que gimen bajo el yugo del imperialismo (pues el dueño de nuestras industrias es el mismo capital yanqui, y la huelga en la plantación o en la mina; en la refinería o el ingenio, o en el campo de salitre o de petróleo, es siempre huelga contra el amo extranjero)"; emphasis in original. LADLA, "El peligro," 2.

43　Wolfe (Audifaz), "¿Qué es," 5; Carrillo, "El imperialismo," 9; Gudynas, *Extractivismos*, 10, 188.

44　Gudynas, *Extractivismos*, 17.

45　Svampa, *Neo-Extractivism*, 7.

46　"Las industrias extractivas"; "la explotación de la tierra." Wolfe (Audifaz), "¿Qué es," 5; Carrillo, "El imperialismo," 9.

47　"Que tiene la desgracia de poseer riquezas naturales"; "gobiernos autocráticos." Wolfe (Audifaz), "¿Qué es," 5, 6.

48　Frank, *Dependent*, 2. Although dependency theorists agreed on the source of economic dependency, they were divided on potential solutions, with some arguing for nationalization and protectionism and others for the overthrow of capitalism. Riofrancos, *Resource*; Svampa, *Neo-Extractivism*.

49　Beverley, *Latinamericanism*, 7; Stahler-Sholk et al., "Introduction," 4–5.

50　Riofrancos, *Resource*, 6; Svampa, *Neo-Extractivism*, 6.

51　Svampa, *Neo-Extractivism*, 12.

52　Svampa, *Neo-Extractivism*, 16.

53　OCMAL, *Conflictos*.

54　Linares, "The Deadliest."

55　Riofrancos, *Resource*, 12, 3.

56   Svampa, *Neo-Extractivism*, 41.

57   Acosta, "Living," 101.

58   Acosta, "Living," 106.

59   Riofrancos, *Resource*, 12.

60   Borón, *América Latina*, 122; Losurdo, *La izquierda*. According to this perspective, progressive states' reliance on extractivism is caused by factors outside their control, requiring them "to look for a point of equilibrium, being conscious, at the same time, that no government, and much less a leftist one, can turn a blind eye to the necessity of promoting the development of its economy." Borón, *América Latina*, 147.

61   For instance, former Ecuadorian President Rafael Correa's efforts to cease oil extraction in exchange for subsidies from wealthier nations and Ecuador's Plan Nacional Para el Buen Vivir, which envisions a gradual transition to an economy based in ecotourism and *bioconocimiento*, have suffered from wealthier nations' unwillingness to finance their apparent environmentalism. Borón, *América Latina*, 141.

62   Borón, *América Latina*, 164; García Linera, "Geopolitics."

63   Riofrancos, "Extractivism."

64   Melamed, "Racial Capitalism," 78.

65   Kelley, "Foreword," xiv; Robinson, *Black Marxism*; Magubane, *The Political*. See also Ralph and Singhal, "Racial Capitalism," and the work of Oliver Cox, W. E. B. Du Bois, C. L. R. James, Claudia Jones, Orlando Patterson, Eric Williams, and Aníbal Quijano.

66   For an overview of scholarship on racial capitalism in last ten years, see Ralph and Singhal, "Racial Capitalism," 857–58. See also Burden-Stelly, "Modern"; Boyce Davies, *Left*; Kelley, *Freedom*; Koshy et al., *Colonial*; McDuffie, *Sojourning*; Issar, *"Theorising"*; Melamed, *Represent*.

67   Koshy et al., *Colonial*, 1.

68   They also reject Robinson's argument for the incommensurability of Marxism and the Black radical tradition, disagreeing with his claim that Marx and Engels overlooked the question of racism and accusing Robinson of conflating the analytical method of class analysis with the class reductionism practiced by particular communist parties.

69   Meyerson, "Rethinking," 7.

70   Kohan, *Marx*.

71   Coulthard, "From Wards."

72   Jackson, *Creole*, 4.

73   Lowe, *The Intimacies*, 10.

74   Lowe, *The Intimacies*, 11.

75   Byrd, *The Transit*, xxxiv.

76   "La restauración de las tierras robadas." Wolfe (Audifaz), "Apreciaciones," 3.

77   Gómez-Barris, *The Extractive*; Kröger, *Extractivisms*.

78   Gómez-Barris, *The Extractive*, 9.

79   Cirefice and Sullivan, "Women"; Muñoz and Villareal, "Women's Struggles."

80 Gago, "What Latin."

81 Edwards, *Charisma*; Hardt and Negri, *Assembly*.

82 Escobar, *Territories*, 25–26.

83 Hardt and Negri, *Assembly*, 3–14.

84 "La Liga no es nadie—es de todos; veteranos de la lucha y nuevos lucha-dores; organizaciones e individuos, sindicatos y pueblos." LADLA, "El peligro," 2.

85 "No es el órgano de ningún individuo ni de ningún intelectual, ni de todos los intelectuales juntos. En vez de ser órgano personal, trata de ser órgano de un movimiento. La semilla que todos ellos y que muchos más han sembrado empieza ya a brotar y su fruto es 'organización.'" LADLA, "El peligro," 2.

86 Castells, "A Network"; Escobar, *Territories*, 283; Galloway and Thacker, *The Exploit*; Grewal, *Network*.

87 For the concept of relationality, see Figueroa-Vásquez, *Decolonizing*; Lowe, *The Intimacies*; Weheliye, *Habeas*.

88 Other similar concepts include "multiple jeopardy" (D. K. King), "interlocking oppressions" (Combahee River Collective), and "matrix of domination" (Patricia Hill Collins). These concepts are not equivalent to one another nor to Kimberlé Crenshaw's more recognizable notion of "intersectionality." For an overview of these concepts and their differences, see Carastathis, *Intersectionality*.

89 Carastathis, *Intersectionality*, 35. For instance, Foley writes, "Although intersectionality can usefully describe the effects of multiple oppressions, I propose, it does not offer an adequate explanatory framework for addressing the root causes of social inequality in the capitalist socioeconomic system." Foley, "Intersectionality," 11.

90 Carastathis, *Intersectionality*, 35.

91 Meyerson, "Rethinking," 2.

92 Liu and Shange, "Toward," 190. For "coalitional solidarities," see Murib's analysis of queer Indigenous activists' proposal to replace a commitment to "coalitional unity" with one of "coalitional solidarity" that would address diverse goals and incommensurable experiences. Murib, "Unsettling." In discussing "coalitional solidarity," Murib relies on O'Brien, *The Politics*. Scholarship on the concept of solidarity is extensive. See overviews in Featherstone, *Solidarity*; Sangiovanni and Viehoff, "Solidarity"; Stites Mor, *South-South*.

93 Jakobsen, "Queers," 65–66.

94 Jakobsen, "Queers," 69, 71.

95 Jakobsen, "Queers," 80, 79.

96 Lowe's use of "intimacies" to describe the relations between ethnic groups draws from Édouard Glissant's earlier theorization of the Caribbean as born out of creolization, wherein cultures and communities do not simply come into contact or become forged into a neat synthesis but rather engage in a "limitless" relation. Glissant, *Poetics*, 34.

1. A PHOTOGRAPHY OF RELATION

1 Moreau, "Imperialism's."

2 For discussion of Mella's assassination and the police investigation, see Hatzky, *Julio*.

3 Margaret Hooks writes of this photo: "There seems to be a new reserve, almost a wariness in her gaze, as though unwilling to expose more of herself than the very minimum required for the occasion." Hooks, *Tina Modotti: Photographer*, 192. Perhaps in reaction to her depiction in the press, Modotti's appearance at her exhibit is reserved, forcing those in attendance to focus on the artistic work.

4 Hooks, *Tina Modotti: Photographer*, 194.

5 Folgarait, *Seeing*, 139.

6 Cuba continues to celebrate Julio Antonio Mella as one of the country's foremost heroes. A town in Santiago de Cuba bears Mella's name, a large memorial holding his ashes sits in front of the University of Havana, and his face appears on stamps, on the 1,000-peso bill, and in murals.

7 The portrait's positioning also functions as a rejoinder to the ongoing suspicion toward her and the unjust handling of Mella's murder investigation by the Mexican police.

8 Laura Mulvey and Peter Wollen, who published an essay to accompany a 1982 exhibition devoted to Tina Modotti and Frida Kahlo at the White-chapel Art Gallery in London, were the first to produce academic criticism on Modotti's work. Lowe, *Tina*, 10; see Mulvey and Wollen, *Frida*. Raquel Tibol organized a 1983 exhibition in the Museo Nacional de Arte in Mexico City; Hatzky, *Julio*, 351.

9 Folgarait, *Seeing*; Legrás, *Culture*; Mraz, *Looking*, 8; Mraz, *Photographing*, 1.

10 Armstrong, "This Photography"; Kirby, *Tina*; Lowe, "Immutable." Noble has criticized this "form/content binary" in the analysis of Modotti's photography. Noble, *Tina*, 91.

11 Folgarait, *Seeing*; Hooks, *Tina Modotti: Photographer*; Kirby, *Tina*; Smith, *The Power*. Folgarait and Mraz have also analyzed Modotti's photography through a Marxist framework. Mraz, *Looking*. Elena Poniatowska's novel *Tinísima*, based on the author's ten years of research in archives in Mexico, Italy, and the United States, gives Modotti her due as a political thinker and artist, even as the book is a fictionalized account of her life.

12 Gómez-Barris, *The Extractive*, 2.

13 Gómez-Barris, *The Extractive*, 5.

14 Gómez-Barris, *The Extractive*, 9.

15 Gómez-Barris, *The Extractive*, xix. The "ecological native" trope portrays Indigenous people as protectors of the environment. Ulloa, *The Ecological Native*. As Mathilda Shepard writes, "The 'ecological native' trope has the double effect of reinscribing the racialized and sexualized portrayal of indigeneity as closer to 'nature' than whiteness and making Indigenous

peoples disproportionately responsible for remedying environmental problems." Shepard, "Life," 156.

16 I take the term "relational aesthetics" from Nicolas Bourriaud, who used this concept to refer to a trend in late twentieth-century socially engaged art that intended to construct dynamic social experiences rather than mimetically represent objects. Such works build on the Marxist "concept of a 'social interstice,'" wherein art occupies "the liminal space between aesthetics and politics, where the possibility for new forms of interaction can begin to develop." Miller, "Activism." Whereas Modotti's photography has little in common with the 1990s participatory installations that Bourriaud termed "relational aesthetics," this term is useful for describing Modotti's focus on the relation between subjects as a visualization for a potential alternative political relation.

17 Hooks, *Tina Modotti: Photographer*, 81; Spenser, *Stumbling*, 154.

18 Folgarait, *Seeing*, 850. Other texts that attribute Modotti's radicalization to Guerrero's influence include Hooks, *Tina*, 7; Kirby, *Tina*, 5; Saborit, *Una mujer*, 149; Spenser, *Stumbling*, 160.

19 Hooks, *Tina Modotti: Photographer*, 139.

20 Kirby, *Tina*, 7.

21 Noble, *Tina*, xix.

22 Smith, *The Power*, 82.

23 Kirby, *Tina*, 9.

24 Hooks, *Tina Modotti: Photographer*, 7.

25 Folgarait, *Seeing*, 82, 36. See also the statement by Mexican writer Octavio Paz: "At the risk of disillusioning the feminists, I will add that Frida and Tina are alike in something: neither of the two had their own political belief. By following a cause, they followed their husbands and lovers. They are not interesting as militants, but instead as complex and passionate people. As figures, they belong more to the history of passion than to the history of ideology." Noble, *Tina*, 40.

26 Folgarait, Hooks, Kirby, and Smith all acknowledge this background. Folgarait writes that she was "born into a socialist minded family." Folgarait, *Seeing*, 82.

27 Kirby, *Tina*, 1; Lowe, *Tina*, 13–14.

28 Kirby, *Tina*, 1.

29 Hooks, *Tina Modotti: Photographer*, 117.

30 An alternative origin story could focus, for example, on Úrsulo Galván, first director of LADLA's *El Libertador*, who began his organizing work with agrarian committees in Veracruz in 1920. Galván's perspective on agrarian issues would have significant impact on LADLA's political project. Reynoso Jaime, *El agrarismo*, 80.

31 For an insightful narration of Roy's Mexico years, see Heatherton, *Arise!*, 55–62.

32 The following discussion of Roy's time in Mexico and early influence on the PCM is largely drawn from Mahler and Capuzzo, *The Comintern*.

33 Spenser, *Stumbling*, 43.

34 Kent-Carrasco, "Breath," 1078. For discussions of how the Mexican Revolution inspired early twentieth-century radical internationalisms, see Carr, *Marxism*; Heatherton, *Arise!*; Rivera Mir, *Militantes*.

35 Roy, *M. N. Roy's Memoirs*, 76.

36 Price, *The Object*, 18.

37 Carr, *Marxism*, 18.

38 Roy, *M. N. Roy's Memoirs*, 125.

39 The POS was first founded in 1911 by Santibáñez and Paul Zierold, with its activities ending in 1915. The POS was reestablished in 1918 by Santibáñez and Francisco Cervantes López. Carr, *Marxism*, 15–17, 20. POS members were already familiar with Roy's articles in *El Pueblo* when Roy learned of the party's existence and reached out to Santibáñez. Santibáñez, Roy wrote, "was enthusiastic about my articles, because they depicted India, for the first time, in his knowledge, not as a dreamland, but a country very much like his own." Roy, *M. N. Roy's Memoirs*, 76.

40 Shipman, *It Had*, 76; Spenser, *Stumbling*, 43.

41 Roy, *M. N. Roy's Memoirs*, 109; Shipman, *It Had*, 75.

42 Other aliases include Frank Seaman, Charles Shipman, Jesús Ramírez, Charles Gordon, and Charles Tanner.

43 Spenser, *Stumbling*, 12–13.

44 Spenser, *Stumbling*, 91.

45 Carr, *Marxism*, 23–24.

46 Carr, *Marxism*, 27.

47 Roy, *M. N. Roy's Memoirs*, 219–20.

48 Shipman, *It Had*, 81; Roy, *M. N. Roy*, 29; Spenser, *Stumbling*, 53.

49 Carr, *Marxism*, 27; Spenser, *Stumbling*, 57.

50 Spenser, *Stumbling*, 60. At the Second Comintern Congress, Phillips used the alias Jesús Ramírez.

51 Roy, *M. N. Roy*, 38–47.

52 Roy, *M. N. Roy*, 44.

53 Roy, *M. N. Roy*, 48.

54 Haithcox, "The Roy-Lenin." My discussion of the Roy-Lenin debate is derived from Mahler and Capuzzo, *The Comintern*.

55 Shipman, *It Had*, 118; Jesús Ramírez to Comrade Lenin, September 11, 1920, CS Papers, box 1, folder 1.

56 Petersson, *Willi*, 198, 207. Münzenberg to MN Roy, February 13, 1928, RGASPI, f. 542, o. 1, d. 28.

57 Spenser, *Stumbling*, 60.

58 Shipman, *It Had*, 132.

59 Spenser, *Stumbling*, 125, 133.

60 Shipman, *It Had*, 153.

61 Kersffeld, *Contra*, 48. Later, in 1928, Johnstone was sent to India as LAI representative. Louro, *Comrades*, 129.

62   "The All-America Anti-Imperialist League: Its Opposition and Aims," CS Papers, box 1, file 2. Other documents date its founding to the end of 1924. Mella, "Informe," RGASPI, f. 542, o. 1, d. 19.

63   "The All-America Anti-Imperialist League: Its Opposition and Aims," CS Papers, box 1, file 2.

64   Spenser, *Stumbling*, 159; Shipman, *It Had*, 154–55.

65   In the list of illustrations accompanying the digital version of *El Libertador* and completed by Melgar Bao, this illustration is also described as a "personaje con rasgos indígenas" (character with Indigenous features). However, the artist is incorrectly identified as Diego Rivera.

66   Carr, *Marxism*, 35–36. For more on role of artists within PCM, see Smith, *The Power*.

67   Sánchez Soler, *Xavier*, 116.

68   Reynoso Jaime, *El agrarismo*, 80–91; Wood, "Semicolonials."

69   Carr, *Marxism*, 33; Reynoso Jaime, *El agrarismo*, 95.

70   Wolfe's name did not appear on the masthead until the second issue, but in his memoir, Wolfe claims to have edited the first issue as well. Wolfe, *A Life*, 345.

71   Bertram represented the PCM at the Fifth Comintern Congress and the LCAEV at the Peasant International in Moscow in 1924. Wolfe, *A Life*, 325–31.

72   Wolfe, *A Life*, 345; Spenser, *Stumbling*, 159.

73   BW Papers, box 4, folder 11.

74   BW Papers, box 4, folder 11.

75   Bertram Wolfe to Charles Shipman, January 21, 1966, CS Papers, box 1, folder 4; Carr, *Marxism*, 41; Melgar Bao, "Memoria."

76   Shipman, *It Had*, 154–55. For details on WP's early collaboration in forming LADLA, see United States Congress, *Investigation*, 156.

77   Hooks, *Tina*, 93; Smith, *The Power*; Spenser, *Stumbling*, 160.

78   In Gomez's memoir, he lists Wolfe, Guerrero, and Siqueiros as appearing in the photo. Shipman, *It Had*, 156. In Gomez's personal papers, on the reverse side of this photograph, a few names are listed by row. There, Gomez identifies the same three people, as well as Carrillo, Enrique Magón, and Manuel Díaz Ramírez, but he has a question mark for the woman (Modotti) seated to his left. CS Papers, box 3, folder 7. The Center for Southwest Research also has an original copy of this photo, on which some participants signed their names on the reverse side. There, one can make out several other signatures, including Rosendo Gómez Lorenzo and Miguel Contreras, but Modotti did not sign the back of the photo and is not yet identified in the finding aid description.

79   "La residencia en Estados Unidos de la dirección de Liga, despertaría suspicacias muy malas por nuestro movimiento." Rafael Carrillo and Xavier Guerrero to Bertram and Ella Wolfe, August 10, 1925, BW Papers, box 4, folder 11.

80   "El secretariado americano, cumpla los compromisos contraídos con el Secretariado Mexicano, respecto al sostenimiento del 'Libertador,' órgano

de la Liga. Hasta la fecha solo una vez ha cumplido lo prometido." Rafael Carrillo and Xavier Guerrero to Bertram and Ella Wolfe, August 10, 1925, BW Papers, box 4, folder 11.

81 Frustrations with Gomez would continue. After LADLA joined the LAI in 1927, LADLA's Continental Committee consistently complained to LAI leadership about Gomez's practice of sending out communications in English to sections in Latin America as well as his claims to lead the organization as a whole, rather than just the US section. Gomez, in turn, argued that Mexico City leadership was not prepared to lead LADLA and that the Continental Committee should merely be the face of the movement while control would rest with the US section. Gomez's positions were rejected by LADLA's Continental Committee and eventually by the LAI. See August 11, 1926, letter; "Auszug"; Mella, "Informe"; May 10, 1926, Informe; "Outline"; "The Question," all found in RGASPI, f. 542, o. 1, d. 19.

82 Rafael Carrillo to Bertram and Ella Wolfe, December 31, 1925, BW Papers, box 4, folder 11.

83 Mella, "Informe," RGASPI, f. 542, o. 1, d. 19.

84 Julio Mella to Manuel Gomez, August 4, 1926, CS Papers, box 1, folder 1; Manuel Gomez to Jaime Nevares Sager, May 12, 1926, BDW Papers, box 1. Later, when this problem persisted, Mella complained to the LAI, which affirmed that control and leadership remained with the Continental Committee in Mexico. Mella, "Informe"; "The Question," RGASPI, f. 543, o. 1, d. 19.

85 These are the sections listed on LADLA's letterhead in a December 18, 1926 letter from Mella to the secretary of LADLA-Puerto Rico. Julio Antonio Mella to Jaime Nevares Sager, December 18, 1926, BDW Papers, box 1. However, the number of sections and locations fluctuated over time. According to Melgar Bao, in September 1928, LADLA had eleven chapters: Argentina, Colombia, Cuba, the Dominican Republic, Ecuador, El Salvador, Honduras, Mexico, Peru, Puerto Rico, and Uruguay. Melgar Bao, "The Anti-Imperialist," 18. However, documentation from the 1929 First Communist Conference in Buenos Aires suggests that the Peru section did not extend beyond the Peruvian activists living in Mexico City, and LADLA eventually expanded to other locations, particularly in Central America, such as Costa Rica, Guatemala, and Panama. LADLA, "Secciones," 3. LADLA's international secretariat was formed by a representative of several of its various sections. In 1926, these included Enrique Flores Magón (Mexico), Mella (Cuba), Jaime Nevares Sager (Puerto Rico), Juan de Dios Romero (Colombia), Juan F. Karolys (Ecuador), Gustavo Machado (Venezuela), Eduardo Mattos (Brazil), and Manuel Gomez (United States). Kersffeld, *Contra*, 61.

86 "Hay que buscar también alianzas con los obreros petroleros de Europa y Asia y de la América del Sur, puesto que el capital de la Standard y la Royal Dutch Shell es internacional." LADLA, "Los obreros," 6. Although the author of this article is not listed, it was likely written by the publi-

cation's director, Galván, since much of his labor organizing took place within Tampico's petroleum industry.

87 "Para ser efectiva, tiene que hacerse internacional." LADLA, "Los obreros," 6.

88 There, the newly established LAI named LADLA as its Central Organizing Bureau in Latin America.

89 Rivera, "La unión," 7.

90 "Sindicatos; ligas campesinas e indígenas; partidos políticos obreros y campesinos que luchen contra el capitalismo y el imperialismo; agrupaciones estudiantes, culturales, e intelectuales que hayan participado o manifestado su deseo de participar en nuestra lucha; juntas revolucionarias anti-imperialistas como la de Santo Domingo y la de Venezuela." LADLA, "Un Congreso," 3.

91 "Pueblos oprimidos, coloniales, y semi-coloniales." LADLA, "El frente," 9.

92 Louro, Comrades, 8, 22.

93 Franco, Plotting Women, 106. For an analysis of gender in postrevolutionary Mexico, see Smith, Gender. For the complex position of women in the PCM, see Smith, The Power.

94 For instance, an unsigned letter to the LAI mentioned the well-known Mexican musician and activist Concepción "Concha" Michel as one of the "leading comrades of the league" and a member of the Continental Committee. "Auszug," RGASPI, f. 542, o. 1, d. 19. However, I have not found any other documentation regarding the details of her involvement.

95 For the list of international collaborators, see the back cover of the June 1927 issue. Although the masthead of El Libertador does not include women, in one exception, after Bertram Wolfe's deportation from Mexico in June 1925, Ella Wolfe, who stayed in Mexico City for a few more months, is listed in the third issue of El Libertador (June 1925) as the administrator.

96 Hooks, Tina, 110.

97 A pamphlet published following Modotti's death mentions that she was a PCM member and "took part actively" in LADLA and its Hands Off Nicaragua campaign and "was one of the founders of the Italian Antifascist League in Mexico." Mexican photographer Manuel Álvaro Bravo remembered Modotti as responsible for collecting money at PCM meetings. MC Papers, box 1, series 2. The February 1928 issue of El Libertador listed Modotti as donating funds to support the periodical. LADLA, "¡Manos," 17. Comintern agent Vittorio Vidali described Modotti's apartment as a meeting site for activists and a hub for political activity. Hooks, Tina, 152. Other letters reveal that Modotti served as financial intermediary between the Red International of Labor Unions and local activists and that she lent money to activists. RGASPI, f. 534, o. 7, d. 394–95.

98 Smith, The Power, 75.

99 In May 1928, Modotti spoke at an anti-Mussolini rally. PCM, "¡Contra!," 1. In August 1928, she organized a memorial for Sacco and Vanzetti. Hooks, Tina, 155. In November 1928, she spoke at an event calling for Mexico

to break diplomatic relations with Italy. PCM, "La ruptura," 8. She then largely led the response to Mella's assassination organized by the IRA.

100　During the Hands Off Nicaragua campaign, LADLA specifically called on women to take responsibility for fundraising in support of Sandino's struggle. LADLA, "¡Manos," 1.

101　Hooks, *Tina*, 137.

102　LADLA, "Entrega," 1.

103　Tina Modotti to Edward Weston, August 14, 1930, MC Papers, box 1, series 1, R-68.

104　To name a few examples, the photograph appeared on the cover of the February 1930 issue of *Labor Defender*, published by the International Labor Defense, and on a 1932 cover of the Berlin-based magazine *Arbeiter-Illustrierte-Zeitung* (The Workers Pictorial Newspaper), published by LAI organizer Willi Münzenberg, as well as on postcards distributed at a protest in Madison Square Garden.

105　Modotti, "On Photography," 196.

106　Dramundo, "La exposición."

107　Toor, "Exposición," 194.

108　Armstrong, "This Photography," 28.

109　Armstrong, "This Photography," 48–49.

110　Kent-Carrasco, "Pandurang."

111　Hooks, *Tina*, 120.

112　The blur of the photograph was created after the fact through Modotti's processing method. Dame, "Indigenismo," 75.

113　"El indio como base de la lucha anti-imperialista"; "Hasta que entren en la lucha, el movimiento anti-imperialista está condenado a quedar como una mera tendencia literaria de intelectuales, una lucha estéril de folletos y de libros denunciando el imperialismo yanqui en nombre de la 'raza española' que no constituye la raza que predomina numéricamente en los países más sometidos a dicho imperialismo." Wolfe, "El indio," 3. Here, Wolfe references LADLA's explicit opposition to regionalist anti-imperialisms expressed through cultural *hispanoamericanismo*. LADLA also notably opposed the assimilationist expressions of *indoamericanismo* and *indigenismo* upheld by many contemporaries.

114　My reading differs from that of Melgar Bao, who interprets the hat as the pope's tiara and as a critique of the Vatican's role in imperialism. Melgar Bao, "El universo." Lindner relies on this interpretation in the context of the Cristero War but acknowledges that the figure wearing the hat appears "seemingly submissive" and that the Brussels Congress did not take an anti-Vatican stance. Lindner, *A City*, 178. My reading of this figure as Indigenous is, I believe, more consistent with the facial features in Rivera's other depictions of Indigenous people, with LADLA's view of Indigenous as the base of anti-imperialist struggle, and with other illustrations with similar compositions that Rivera drew for LADLA (see figure 6.5).

115　Lund, *The Mestizo*, 5.

116 Lund, *The Mestizo*, 92.

117 Chilsen, "Synthesis," 4.

118 Braun, *Pre-Columbian*, 241.

119 Dame, "Indigenismo," 98; Debroise, "La tehuana."

120 Guynn, "Mexico"; Mraz, *Looking*, 7.

121 Dame, "Indigenismo," 76; Folgarait, *Seeing*, 39.

122 The *charro*-style sombrero became associated with Zapatismo during the Mexican Revolution, and because Zapata's army was made up mostly of Indigenous peasants, it became a racially distinguishing symbol often used in depictions of Indigenous people in postrevolutionary Mexican cultural production. Noble, *Tina*, 118.

123 Armstrong, "This Photography," 43.

124 Armstrong, "This Photography," 48. Similarly, Noble writes, "In a number of images of the maternal body and infant we find Modotti's gaze transfixed by the relationship between the bodies within the frame." Noble, *Tina*, 134.

125 Figarella, *Edward*, 200; Folgarait, *Seeing*, 130.

126 Lowe, *Tina*, 42.

127 Modotti's aesthetic choices anticipate a contemporary transformation in the aesthetics used within recent social movements, which intentionally abandon a focus on the prototypical, male charismatic leader of the past. Such horizontalist movements critique what Erica Edwards calls the violent "spectacle of charismatic leadership." Edwards, *Charisma*, xvi. A shift away from charismatic leadership has ushered in a change in political aesthetics, which transitions from a traditional focus on the singular male hero to emphasize networked and relational political community. Hardt and Negri, *Assembly*.

128 Hooks, *Tina*, 178.

129 Figarella, *Edward*, 201.

2. AGAINST LATIN AMERICAN REGIONALISMS

1 Louro, *Comrades*, 34. For delegates, see file 2, LAI Archive.

2 Front row, from left: Helen Crawfurd (first), Sen Katayama (second), Willi Münzenberg (third), Edo Fimmen (fifth), Lamine Senghor (sixth), Lu Zhonglin (seventh), Jawaharlal Nehru (eighth), George Lansbury (ninth). Back row, from left: Liau Hansin (first), Roger Baldwin (second), Manuel Gomez (third), José Vasconcelos (fifth), Reginald Bridgeman (seventh), Julio Antonio Mella (eighth), Victorio Codovilla (tenth), Helen Stöcker (twelfth).

Louro and Shipman identify a number of these individuals, and the June 1927 issue of *El Libertador* identifies the Latin American delegates. Otherwise, I compared the photo with General Council members. Although *El Libertador* identifies the man to Roger Baldwin's left as Ismael

Martínez, Shipman's memoir and visual observation confirm him as Manuel Gomez.

3   Technically, the LAI Executive Committee named LADLA as its organizing bureau for Latin America. I describe LADLA as the LAI's "Americas" section because LADLA was a hemispheric organization and maintained chapters in the United States, and the LAI's US chapters were synonymous with LADLA's US chapters. LADLA, "Última," 12.

4   Louro's *Comrades* discusses Mexico's role in the LAI, but the treatment is limited since her study focuses on Nehru. Petersson's *Willi Münzenberg* does not mention LADLA, instead discussing the US-based All-America Anti-Imperialist League (aka LADLA-US). Although he addresses the creation of Latin American sections, particularly in Mexico, his study does not reflect an understanding that LADLA preceded the LAI by two years or that the LAI's Latin American sections were synonymous with LADLA sections. Goebel's "Forging," which appears in an edited volume about the LAI, does provide an in-depth look at Latin American participation in Brussels. Note 17 addresses Goebel's "Forging" and other studies of Latin Americans in Brussels.

5   Dinkel, *The Non-Aligned*; Lee, *Making*; Prashad, *The Darker*; Weiss, *Framing*.

6   For Latin America's marginal position within postcolonial studies, see Coronil, "Elephants."

7   Important exceptions to this tendency include the work of Carr, Kersffeld, Melgar Bao, Pujals, Wood, and Zumoff. However, generally LADLA's history, for example, tends to be addressed within the history of Mexican communism and not necessarily as part of a global anticolonial movement.

8   Carpentier, *Reasons*, 298.

9   Carpentier, *Reasons*, 296.

10   Armillas-Tiseyra, *The Dictator*, 95.

11   Armillas-Tiseyra, *The Dictator*, 97.

12   Carpentier, *Reasons*, 296.

13   Goebel, *Anti-Imperial*, 206.

14   As evidence, Goebel cites from a letter Vasconcelos wrote to Manuel Ugarte "complaining about the overbearing presence at the congress of communists and Asians, who would not listen to the Latin Americans. . . . The crucial dividing line between Latin Americans and the delegates from Asia and Africa was that the anti-imperialism of the former related exclusively to the United States, a country that many Asians and Africans, in spite of Wilson's 'betrayal,' tended to identify as a beacon of anti-colonialism." Goebel, *Anti-Imperial*, 206. However, as I argue in this chapter, Vasconcelos's views differed significantly from those of LADLA members, and his perspectives were not representative of the broader Latin American delegation and especially not of LADLA.

15   Prashad, *The Darker*, 28.

16   Dinkel, *The Non-Aligned*, 22.

17 For Mella's biography, see Hatzky, *Julio*.

18 Goebel's *Anti-Imperial* and "Forging" study Latin American participation in Brussels, focusing on disagreements between Mella and Haya de la Torre. "Forging" uses Vasconcelos's and Haya de la Torre's regionalism to characterize the perspectives of all Latin American delegates. Goebel mentions LADLA but overlooks that LADLA (over one-third of Latin American delegates) rejected regionalist perspectives, and he inaccurately argues that the LAI had little cooperation with LADLA after 1927. Lindner provides an overview of Latin Americans' participation in Brussels, attending much more to LADLA's role. However, he relies on Goebel's characterization of the "Latin American regionalism" of all Latin American delegates in Brussels. Lindner, *A City*, 167. Prashad's *The Darker* uses Vasconcelos's speech to incorrectly argue that Latin Americans had difficulty participating in the congress because of their unique colonial and linguistic history. Kersffeld's *Contra* provides an in-depth look at LADLA's participation in Brussels, focusing on the Mella-Haya controversy. My understanding of LADLA in Brussels relies particularly on Kersffeld but moves in different directions by incorporating insights from LADLA-US activists' personal papers, using cultural studies analysis of LADLA propaganda, tracing LADLA's antagonistic position toward Latin American regionalisms, and analyzing LADLA's growing interest in Black communities.

19 Kersffeld, *Contra*, 94. This committee was organized through Münzenberg's Workers International Relief organization and drew from its earlier Hands Off China campaign. Petersson, *Willi*, 154, 260.

20 Dinkel, *The Non-Aligned*, 19; Kersffeld, *Contra*, 96.

21 File 2, LAI Archive.

22 ECCI to Willi Münzenberg, July 2, 1926, RGASPI, f. 542, o. 1, d.3.

23 Beyond Münzenberg, the organizing committee included Henri Barbusse, Nehru, Baldwin, and William Pickens, among others, and also several Latin American intellectuals and politicians like Vasconcelos, Ramón de Negri, Luis Casabona, César Falcón, and Ugarte. Kersffeld, *Contra*, 98. Not all members of the organizing committee were able to attend.

24 Dinkel, *The Non-Aligned*, 19–20; Kersffeld, *Contra*, 96.

25 File 5, LAI Archive.

26 Dinkel, *The Non-Aligned*, 21–22.

27 File 5, LAI Archive. This included speeches by Mella, Gomez, Vasconcelos, Carlos Quijano (Uruguay), and Ismael Martínez (Mexico). Liga, *Das flammenzeichen*, 282.

28 Louro, *Comrades*, 8, 22.

29 Louro's *Comrades* traces these lasting solidarities in the case of Jawaharlal Nehru.

30 LADLA, "Resolución sobre organización," 12.

31 "Sympathieerklärung," file 40, LAI Archive; Power, *Solidarity*, 76.

32 LADLA, "Las resoluciones," 10–12; LADLA, "Última," 12.

33   Other Latin American organizations in the program included: Mexico—
Confederación Regional Obrera Mexicana, Liga Nacional Campesina,
Confederación Obrera de Tampico, Federación de Estudiantes Mexi-
canos; Cuba—Universidad Popular José Martí, Federación Obrera,
Federación de los Estudiantes; Puerto Rico—Partido Nacionalista de
Puerto Rico, Federación Nacionalista de Juventud; Colombia—Partido
Socialista Revolucionario de Colombia, Federación Obrera de Colom-
bia; Venezuela—Partido Revolucionario Venezolano, Federación Obrera
Venezolana; Peru—Federación de los Estudiantes del Peru, Sindicatos
Textiles y de Artes Gráficas, Partido Unionista; as well as Asociación de
Estudiantes Latinoamericanos de París and Haitian Patriotic Union. Liga,
Das flammenzeichen, 236–38.

34   Puerto Rican Samuel R. Quiñones was supposed to attend on behalf of
LADLA–Puerto Rico but did not due to lack of funding. James Sager to
Manuel Gomez, February 2, 1927, BW Papers. The PNPR delegation in-
cluded Vasconcelos; César Falcón, a Peruvian; and Cuban-French citizen
Louis Casabona. File 2, LAI Archive. Manuel Ugarte was also listed in this
delegation but did not attend. Vasconcelos's failure to mention Puerto
Rico is discussed in Goebel, *Anti-Imperial*, 205.

35   Goebel, *Anti-Imperial*, 205–6.

36   LADLA, "El frente," 9.

37   LADLA, "El 2º. Congreso," 2.

38   "La base de la lucha contra el imperialismo se encuentra en las masas
obreras y campesinas, las cuales, como en China, pueden oponerse a la
presión del poder imperialista por grandes movimientos colectivos, por el
boicot y también por otras armas." LADLA, "Las resoluciones," 11.

39   "Es necesario que todos los elementos progresistas se interesan por esta
lucha: los intelectuales, los estudiantes, y la clase media, también afec-
tados económicamente y políticamente por la penetración del imperialismo." LADLA, "Las resoluciones," 11.

40   Goebel, *Anti-Imperial*; Goebel, "Forging"; Lindner, *A City*; Rojas, "Haya."

41   Goebel, *Anti-Imperial*; Lindner, *A City*.

42   LADLA-Cuba member Rubén Martínez Villena wrote this text. Martínez
Villena, *Cuba*.

43   Liga, *Das flammenzeichen*, 70–76.

44   Liga, *Das flammenzeichen*, 68.

45   "Esa independencia fue ficticia para los trabajadores." LADLA, "Liga," 5.

46   "En busca de materias primas y de la obra de mano barata de los indígenas." LADLA, "Liga," 5.

47   These are the sections listed on LADLA's letterhead in a December 18,
1926, letter from Mella to the LADLA–Puerto Rico secretary. Julio Antonio Mella to Jaime Nevares Sager, December 18, 1926, BDW Papers, box 1.
However, the number of sections and locations fluctuated over time.

48   "Su absoluta dependencia económica de la economía extranjera"; "em-
pleado a los dictadores no son sino servidores del capitalismo imperia-

lista." LADLA, "Liga," 4. Rivera did not attend the February 1927 Brussels Congress but participated in LADLA's report to the General Council in Brussels in December 1927 on behalf of LADLA-Mexico.

49 "Su verdadera independencia nacional"; "no es posible sin una conexión íntima y una acción de conjunto con el proletariado revolucionario de los Estados Unidos." LADLA, "Liga," 4.

50 "Un solo movimiento anti-imperialista continental"; "llegar tal vez a salvar a Europa, Asia, y África también." LADLA, "El peligro," 1.

51 Goebel, Anti-Imperial; Prashad, The Darker.

52 Vasconcelos, "Saludo," 2.

53 All quotes from Vasconcelos's speech come from file 39, LAI Archive.

54 García-Bryce, Haya, 2.

55 Kersffeld, Contra; Rojas, "Haya."

56 Goebel, Anti-Imperial, 207.

57 Rojas, "Haya."

58 Kersffeld makes a similar argument when he writes that LADLA "made possible a first synthesis between Marxism of European origin and the anti-imperialist creed present in Latin America." Kersffeld, "La Liga Anti-imperialista de las Américas," 153.

59 García-Bryce, Haya, 21; Mella, "Víctor."

60 In its May 1925 issue, El Libertador published a letter from Mella, sent from Havana, in which he promised to send an article that the editors requested of him. This letter mentioned that he helped found the Anti-Imperialist Committee at the University of Havana, which organized several protests for which students were jailed and fined. Mella's letter promised they would soon form LADLA-Cuba and that a Cuban Communist Party was also in formation. Mella, "Carta," 8. LADLA-Cuba was founded shortly afterward (July 1925). Kersffeld, Contra, 76. The new section sent an announcement to LADLA headquarters to be published in El Libertador (July 1925). For more on LADLA-Cuba, see chapter 4. Around this same time, Mella also helped organize the PCC along with Carlos Baliño, the much older nationalist intellectual who co-founded (with José Martí) the Cuban Revolutionary Party. A Cuban communist section was first created in 1920 after Mikhail Borodin and Charles Francis Phillips (Manuel Gomez) traveled through Cuba on their way to Moscow and met with anarcho-syndicalists Marcelino Salinas and Antonio Peniche. However, this section did not lead to the foundation of a communist party. Later, in 1923, Baliño formed the Agrupación Comunista de la Habana, which would eventually become the PCC. Hatzky, Julio, 155–56.

61 Guanche, Mella, 224.

62 Kersffeld, Contra, 81.

63 "Hacia la Internacional Americana." Mella, "Hacia," 7.

64 Hatzky, Julio, 188–89.

65 "Juicio," 176.

66 "Juicio," 175.

67   Guanche, *Mella*, 225; Kersffeld, *Contra*, 86; Hatzky, *Julio*, 193.

68   Once the PCC learned that Mella was in Mexico City, they sent a letter
      condemning him to PCM's Central Committee. The PCC claimed that
      Mella left the country because he did not want to conform to his disci-
      plinary sentence. They emphasized that they were not opposed to LADLA-
      Cuba but that Mella represented a sect within it that was disconnected
      from communism, practicing instead a "communist Mella-ism" that was
      "irresponsible, suspicious and malicious, opportunist and yellow." "PCC a
      PCM," 188. Later that summer, in response to a similar letter written to the
      US Workers Party (WP), in which the PCC asked for its opinion on Mel-
      la's case, the WP chided the PCC for alienating members of LADLA-Cuba
      and urged them to repair the relationship. While they acknowledged that
      LADLA-Cuba should have also focused its campaign on the twelve work-
      ers arrested with Mella, they criticized the PCC for not embarking on its
      own campaign to free the prisoners and for condemning LADLA-Cuba's
      success. In addition, the WP argued that the two-year suspension and
      smear campaign against Mella was equivalent to an expulsion and that
      Mella's activities in Mexico since his suspension indicated he had every
      intention of continuing communist organizing. "Ruthenberg a PCC," 193.

69   "Fragmentos," 199–201.

70   Goebel, *Anti-Imperial*, 208.

71   Rojas also suggests that because Mella's commitment to communism was
      in question, he took a more extreme position. In spring 1927, Mella was
      invited to the Soviet Union, and subsequently he authored articles in *El
      Machete* that praised the Soviet Union. Rojas, "Haya," 63; Tibol, *Julio*, 77.
      Shortly afterward, the Comintern began its Third Period, in which it
      abandoned its united-front alliances for its "class against class" policy.
      Mella's visit to the Soviet Union and the simultaneous shift in Comintern
      policy likely influenced his turn toward a more orthodox ideology.

72   Rojas, "Haya," 57.

73   García-Bryce, *Haya*, 30; Goebel, *Anti-Imperial*, 207.

74   Liga, *Das flammenzeichen*, 237–38.

75   According to Mella, Haya did not initially receive an invitation to the
      Brussels Congress, but Mella got him a courtesy invitation. Mella, *¿Qué*, 121.

76   Mella, *¿Qué*, 122.

77   Mella, *¿Qué*, 110. See also García Bryce, *Haya*, 5. For Haya's perspective on
      hispanoamericanismo, see Haya de la Torre, "Hispanoamericanismos."

78   García-Bryce, *Haya*, 2.

79   Goebel, *Anti-Imperial*, 207.

80   Goebel, *Anti-Imperial*, 209.

81   Mella, *¿Qué*, 108.

82   In the pamphlet, Mella quoted Lenin's thesis from the Comintern's Sec-
      ond Congress that argued for bolstering bourgeois nationalist movements
      in colonized countries while maintaining the independence of the prole-
      tarian movement since the proletarian movement would need to continue

to fight against the domestic dominant classes once the foreign power had been overthrown. Mella, *¿Qué*, 112. Mella's reliance on Lenin has, at times, been characterized as mere puppeting of Soviet discourse (in contrast to Haya's commitment to local ideas). However, this reading is an oversimplification since, as discussed in chapter 1, Lenin's position toward nationalist movements was influenced by M. N. Roy's interventions at the Second Congress, which Roy based on his comparative analysis of India and Mexico.

83 Mella, *¿Qué*, 105.

84 Mella, *¿Qué*, 104.

85 Mella, *¿Qué*, 113.

86 "Agrupaciones estudiantes, culturales, e intelectuales que hayan participado o manifestado su deseo de participar en nuestra lucha." LADLA, "Un Congreso," 3.

87 Mella's critiques of APRA and Haya sometimes relied on machismo and homophobia to attack his opponent. He criticized Haya's position on Chinese immigration by writing, "There are also, for example, some young *aprista* men who do not exactly stand out for their virile virtues." Mella, *¿Qué*, 99. Here, he seemed to allude to Haya's apparent effeminacy and to rumors of Haya's homosexuality. García-Bryce, *Haya*, 5. While similar homophobic attacks did not appear in *El Libertador*, LADLA never took any explicit stance on gender or sexuality, a silence that, when combined with its predominantly male membership, suggests that the organization would not have protested such comments.

88 Mella, *¿Qué*, 128.

89 "No es Sectaria / Sí Acepta todos los Credos-Progresistas; No Odia al Pueblo de los EEUU / Sí Lucha Contra el Imperialismo Yanqui; No es un Partido Político Continental; Sí Contribuye a la Unidad de la América; No es una Entidad 'Bolsheviqui'; Sí Defiende a la URSS ante los imperialismos; No Tiene Vínculos con los Gobiernos/ Sí Coopera con Toda Obra Antimperialista." *El Libertador*, August 1927, back cover.

90 "Toute sorte de confusionisme démagogique (Panindianisme, régionalisme, etc.)." File 85, LAI Archive.

91 Makalani, *In the Cause*, 134.

92 Makalani, *In the Cause*, 134–35, 137–38.

93 Makalani, *In the Cause*, 142; Turner and Turner, *Caribbean*, 146.

94 Dalleo, *American*; Makalani, *In the Cause*; Robinson, *Black*.

95 Deambrosis Martins, *Vidas*, 9.

96 Liga, *Das flammenzeichen*, 119–23.

97 Turner and Turner, *Caribbean*, 146, 143.

98 "La penetración imperialista en estos países ha agudizado el problema indígena y el de los negros, por la concentración de la tierra, ya que los negros y los indios constituyen la inmensa mayoría de la población agraria." LADLA, "Las resoluciones," 11.

99 These critiques are discussed in the introduction. See Coulthard, "From Wards"; Jackson, *Creole*.

100 "Las razas oprimidas son también nuestro aliado dentro de los Estados Unidos mismos." LADLA, "Las resoluciones," 11.

101 See also September 1928 photograph of HPU banquet for LADLA-US Secretary Gomez, CS Papers, box 4.

102 Turner and Turner, *Caribbean*, 145–46; File 54, LAI Archive.

103 Weiss argues that Moore played a leading role in preparing this document and that it was based on a longer resolution adopted at the UNIA's Fifth Annual Convention in August 1926. The two resolutions have much in common and some lines are reproduced word for word. Consistent with the UNIA's ideology and with the flexible politics in Brussels, the resolution took a more pan-Africanist stance and was "almost completely lacking references to class struggle and class oppression." Weiss, *Framing*, 85. The original UNIA statement argued that "in Latin America, where our people have secured equal social and political rights with all other peoples, the cordial relationships resulting therefrom prove conclusively that there is no inherent antagonism between the races." Whereas the UNIA statement provided a caveat that in Cuba, "foreign interests . . . spell the establishment of an oppressive system of caste and coloured prejudices," the Brussels resolution made no such exceptions. File 55, LAI Archive.

104 "En la América Latina, excepto Cuba, los negros no sufren el yugo de ninguna opresión especial. (En Panamá la intervención yanqui ha trasplantado las costumbres bárbaras de los Estados Unidos contra los negros, que es el mismo origen de las desigualdades sociales de Cuba). La igualdad social y política, así como las relaciones cordiales entre las diferentes razas que viven en otros países, prueban que no existe ningún antagonismo natural entre ellas." LADLA, "Las resoluciones," 14.

105 Turner and Turner, *Caribbean*, 146.

106 "Desenmascaró el imperialismo francés con valor y veracidad." LADLA, "Lamine," 9. The next issue, #16, is one of the few unavailable issues of *El Libertador*.

3. "POR LA IGUALDAD DE TODOS LOS SERES"

1 "Comité de Defensa Proletaria." Poniatowska likely refers to the International Labor Defense. Poniatowska, *Tinísima*, 107.

2 Poniatowska, *Tinísima*, 15.

3 Moissen, "Cuba."

4 "En México le vilipendiaron y en Cuba lo expulsaron." Junco, "¡¡¡Fuera."

5 "Combatido por los mismos que ahora tratan de deificarlo." Junco, "¡¡¡Fuera."

6 "Los negros y los indios constituyen la inmensa mayoría de la población agraria." LADLA, "Las resoluciones," 11.

7 "El terror blanco." LADLA, "El Congreso Sindical," 5. "La intervención yanqui ha trasplantado las costumbres bárbaras de los Estados Unidos contra los negros." LADLA, "Las resoluciones," 14.

8   "El problema de la raza negra y el movimiento proletario."

9   For instance, Adi, "The Negro"; Gilmore, *Defying*; Høgsbjerg, "Communism"; Kelley, *Hammer*; Kelley, *Freedom*; Robinson, *Black*; Solomon, *The Cry*; Stephens, *Black*.

10   Exceptions include Melgar Bao, "Rearmando"; Carr, "Identity"; De la Fuente, *A Nation*; Massón Sena, "La cuestión"; Sullivan, "The 'Negro'"; Stevens, *Red*; Zumoff, "Black."

11   Adi, "The Negro."

12   Becker, "Mariátegui."

13   Stevens, *Red*, 3.

14   See, for example, Roa, *El fuego*, 279.

15   The following works contain the most extensive discussion of Junco to date: Alexander, *A History*; Alexander, *Trotskyism*; Carr, "Identity"; De la Fuente, *A Nation*; Mahler, "The Red"; Massón Sena, "La cuestión"; Moissen, "Cuba"; Moissen, "Documentos"; Tennant, "The Hidden"; Stevens, *Red*; and Wood, "Semicolonials."

16   The original titles are "El problema de la raza negra y el movimiento proletario" and "Resolución sobre el problema de los trabajadores negros."

17   Alexander, *Trotskyism*, 215. James W. Ford mentions Junco as a "native Negro labor leader" in Ford, "The Rising."

18   Alexander, "Negro," 19.

19   ANLC, "Mass," 3.

20   ANLC, "ANLC Demands," 4; ANLC, "International," 4; ANLC, "Mass," 3.

21   Junco arrived in Miami in May 1936 at forty-two years old. Sandalio Junco Junco, travel visa, May 14, 1926.

22   Alexander, *Trotskyism*, 215; Massón Sena, "La cuestión." A 1930 article from the ANLC's *The Liberator* states that Junco "has been thirty years a leader in the labor movement." ANLC, "Mass," 3. This statement would have been an exaggeration since Junco would have been merely six years old in 1900, but it does suggest that he was politically involved from a young age.

23   Gremio de Panadores, *El productor*, 1.

24   Moissen, "Cuba"; Socialist Workers Party, "Stalinists."

25   Alexander, *Trotskyism*, 215; Massón Sena, "La cuestión."

26   The meeting of Latin American labor unions in Moscow occurred immediately following the Profintern's Fourth World Congress, from March 17 to April 3, 1928. Thus, it is likely that Junco also attended this Profintern conference. For discussion of his detainment, see CSLA, "Cuba," 13.

27   *The Negro Worker* claimed that Junco was deported to Mexico by the Machado government. Alexander, "Negro," 19.

28   He lived with a partner named Olga Maya on Calle Dr. Lucio #72. Sandalio Junco to Solomon Losovski, August 15, 1929, RGASPI, f. 534, o. 4, d. 289.

29   ANLC, "ANLC Demands," 4; ANLC, "Mass," 3; CSLA, *Bajo*, 301.

30   ANLC, "Mass," 3.

31   The ANLC reported the two were tortured (along with Barreiros's wife and daughters) by Mexican government officials. ANLC, "Mass," 3.

32 ANLC, "ANLC Demands," 4.

33 ANLC, "Mass," 3; Stevens, *Red*, 114–15; Junco to Losovski, February 11, 1930, RGASPI, f. 534, o. 4, d. 325.

34 Schelchkov, "El marxismo," 226–47; Stevens, *Red*, 120. While in Moscow, Junco attended the Second Latin American Communist Conference in 1930. Martínez-Villena, sick with tuberculosis, dictated his remarks to Junco to be shared at the conference. However, Junco presented a slightly different text in which he diverged from the Comintern's third-period strategy by arguing for the formation of broad alliances and that a proletarian revolution would occur only after a bourgeois-democratic revolution. This led to a rift between Junco and Martínez-Villena. Massón Sena, "La cuestión"; Moissen, "Cuba"; Wood, "Semicolonials."

35 Wood, "Semicolonials."

36 Reig Romero, *El útil*, 101.

37 Federación Obrera de la Habana. Junco was this group's "principal leader." Alexander, *A History*, 59.

38 Moissen, "Sandalio Junco."

39 Reig Romero, *El útil*, 101. Among the OC founding members was Juan Ramón Breá, who had been in exile with Junco in Mexico City where he joined LADLA's Continental Committee and who was also acquainted with Andrés Nin since the two were imprisoned together in Spain in 1931. Jeifets and Jeifets, *América Latina*, 112.

40 Reig Romero, *El útil*, 101; Alexander, *Trotskyism*, 216. At the 1934 Fourth Congress of the communist-led CNOC, Junco's expulsion was explained as the response to his alliances with "anarcho-syndicalists and all kinds of reformists." Instituto, "Resolución," 579.

41 The OC established sections in Havana, Santiago, Matanzas, Oriente, Guantánamo, Victoria de las Tunas, and Puerto Padre. Moissen, "El trotskismo."

42 Alexander, *A History*, 50–51. For an in-depth analysis of the PBL's political positions and engagement with Trotskyism, see Tennant, "The Hidden"; Soler Martínez, "El Partido." For PBL's political program, see Partido Bolchevique, *Programa*.

43 "Una campaña nacional e internacional de insultos y calumnias." Junco, "¡¡¡Fuera."

44 "Obrero intelectualizado." Junco, "¡¡¡Fuera."

45 "Socialismo en un país"; "los verdaderos trabajadores." Junco, "¡¡¡Fuera." A primary PBL critique of Stalinism was of the theory of socialism in one country, which "undermines the fundamental bases of proletarian internationalism." Partido Bolchevique, *Programa*, 61.

46 Alexander, *International*, 228–29; Alexander, *Trotskyism*, 215–24. After the failed strike, Junco returned for a brief period to Mexico, where he became close to Leon Trotsky. Moissen, "Documentos," 38.

47 Confederación de Trabajadores de América Latina. Alexander, *A History*, 75–81.

48 Moissen, "Cuba."

49 Alexander, *Trotskyism*, 223; Hernández, "El asesinato"; Massón Sena, "La cuestión"; Socialist Workers Party, "Stalinists," 1.

50 The Comintern considered Mella to be a Trotskyist, and while Mella never joined a Trotskyist opposition group, he maintained significant differences with both the PCC and PCM. Moissen, "El trotskismo"; Hatzky, *Julio*, 232.

51 Kelley, *Freedom*, 45.

52 Quoted in Kelley, *Freedom*, 46.

53 Adi, *Pan-Africanism*, 158; Weiss, *Framing*, 57. For earlier intersections between Bolshevism and US Black activists, see Høgsbjerg, "Communism."

54 "Theses on the Negro Question."

55 Huiswoud and McKay, "Speeches," 17.

56 Huiswoud and McKay, "Speeches," 18.

57 Huiswoud and McKay, "Speeches," 22.

58 This thesis became integral to the founding of Black-led organizations like the ANLC in 1925 and the League of Struggle for Negro Rights in 1930. Kelley, *Freedom*, 49.

59 File 54, LAI Archive.

60 Weiss, *Framing*, 13.

61 Carr, "Identity," 99. For in-depth discussion of Comintern debates around Black self-determination, see Klehr and Tompson, "Self-Determination"; De la Fuente, *A Nation*, 192.

62 Carr, "Identity," 98–99; Massón Sena, "La cuestión"; Serviat, *El problema*, 116–17.

63 Partido Bolchevique, *Programa*, 40.

64 CSLA, "Hacia," 6–11.

65 CSLA, "Preparando," 31–32.

66 CSLA, "Informe," 38–39.

67 In a photograph, Siqueiros stands onstage with a group of women who display the flag of the newly founded CSLA. *El Trabajador Latinoamericano* 17–18 (June–July 1929), 25.

68 CSLA, *Bajo*, 262, 301–2.

69 CSLA, *Bajo*, 27.

70 CSLA, *Bajo*, 141.

71 CSLA, *Bajo*, 21.

72 CSLA, *Bajo*, 221; LADLA, "Congreso," 5, 8.

73 CSLA, "Crónica," 54.

74 "El problema indígena." CSLA, "Crónica," 68. Portocarrero's alias for the conference was Suriva. Jeifets and Jeifets, *América Latina*. For a transcript of Mariátegui's essay, see CSLA, *Bajo*, 147–59.

75 Kersffeld, *Contra*, 41; Mariátegui, *Seven*, xvii.

76 Mariátegui, *Seven*, xx–xxi.

77 See, for example, Mariátegui, "Una carta," 23.
78 Mariátegui, *Seven*, xxii.
79 Mariátegui, *Seven*, xxvi.
80 Some non-Peruvian colleagues criticized this decision, like Victorio Codovilla, an Italian Argentine who had attended the 1927 Brussels Congress. ssa, *El movimiento*, 333–45.
81 "Unidad Antimperialista," 16.
82 Mariátegui, *Seven*, xxvi–xxvii.
83 He also published the csla conference invitation as well as csla bylaws in *Amauta*. "1er. Congreso," 96–97; "Proyecto," 98–100; Mariátegui, *Seven*, xxvi–xxvii.
84 csla, *Bajo*, 148.
85 csla, *Bajo*, 150–52.
86 csla, *Bajo*, 155.
87 "Tiene también sus características del problema racial." csla, "Crónica," 69.
88 csla, "Crónica," 69.
89 csla, *Bajo*, 160.
90 csla, *Bajo*, 161.
91 csla, *Bajo*, 162.
92 See Helg, *Our Rightful*.
93 csla, *Bajo*, 165.
94 Carr, "Identity," 106–7; De la Fuente, *A Nation*, 195.
95 Carr, "Identity," 84.
96 Alexander, *A History*, 55; Carr, "Identity," 84–85, 106; De la Fuente, *A Nation*, 190–91; Tennant, "The Hidden."
97 Tennant, "The Hidden." Soler Martínez makes a similar argument in "El Partido," 284–85.
98 Tennant, "The Hidden."
99 Junco, "Abajo," 8–9.
100 csla, *Bajo*, 166.
101 csla, *Bajo*, 168–69.
102 csla, *Bajo*, 169.
103 csla, *Bajo*, 170.
104 csla, *Bajo*, 172.
105 For more on James's argument, see Høgsbjerg, "Communism."
106 West et al., *From Toussaint*, 19.
107 For a discussion of opposition between Garveyism and communism in Cuba and its relation to Black immigrant labor, see Carr, "Identity," 85–86.
108 He claimed that the Unión de Obreros Antillanos in Eastern Cuba represented a good example of an organization that had successfully attracted and organized migrant workers. csla, *Bajo*, 175.
109 csla, *Bajo*, 176.
110 csla, *Bajo*, 173.
111 csla, *Bajo*, 177.
112 csla, *Bajo*, 178.

113 Jeifets and Jeifets, *América Latina*, 579.

114 SSA, *El movimiento*, 324.

115 SSA, *El movimiento*, 322–25.

116 SSA, *El movimiento*, 324, 326.

117 "Hacer todo lo posible por salvar a la Liga . . . para que la Liga sea lo que debe ser: un poderoso organismo anti-imperialista de masa, que sin exclusiones ni restricciones de secta, sin prevenciones contra ninguna ideología, realice en frente único contra el imperialismo." SSA, "Declaración," 8.

118 Specifically, he acknowledged the campaign against Machado in Cuba and against terror in Haiti, Chile, and Peru, as well as the success of its Manos Fuera de Nicaragua (Hands Off Nicaragua) campaign. SSA, *El movimiento*, 327.

119 He also criticized LADLA's tendency to focus on US imperialism, neglecting the ongoing presence of British imperialism in the region, and he argued for a more global perspective that would build solidarity with struggles around the world and focus on Spanish imperialism in Morocco. Members of Brazilian, Venezuelan, and Panamanian sections objected to the claim that LADLA had not been attuned to British imperial interests in the region.

120 "El problema de las razas en América Latina." Becker, "Mariátegui," 456.

121 SSA, *El movimiento*, 265, 288.

122 SSA, *El movimiento*, 265.

123 SSA, *El movimiento*, 288; Becker, "Mariátegui," 466.

124 Becker, *Mariátegui*, 22–36.

125 Becker, "Mariátegui," 471.

126 SSA, *El movimiento*, 266.

127 SSA, *El movimiento*, 270.

128 SSA, *El movimiento*, 284.

129 SSA, *El movimiento*, 288.

130 SSA, *El movimiento*, 292.

131 SSA, *El movimiento*, 293.

132 SSA, *El movimiento*, 291.

133 SSA, *El movimiento*, 294.

134 SSA, *El movimiento*, 298.

135 SSA, *El movimiento*, 299.

136 SSA, *El movimiento*, 314.

137 SSA, *El movimiento*, 309.

138 "Proletariado revolucionario"; "unir a todos los explotados de las diversas razas para la lucha contra el imperialism." SSA, "Problema," 29.

139 Junco, "El proletariado," 23–26.

140 "La humillación, el desprecio y el insulto de que hace objeto al negro toma cada día carácteres de una naturalidad tal que empieza a no producir la indignación y de seguir aceptándose." Junco, "El proletariado," 23.

141 "Un verdadero tráfico negrero." Junco, "El proletariado," 24.

142 "Tiene que demostrar también que sabe comprender todos sus deberes y se incorporará a la lucha de sus hermanos de las colonias africanas y de las Antillas, levantando la bandera de sus reivindicaciones como raza." Junco, "El proletariado," 26.

143 "Cual es su doble condición de explotados, como raza y como clase." Junco, "El proletariado," 23.

144 Melgar Bao, "Rearmando," 161.

145 Junco, "El proletariado."

146 Weiss, "Calling."

147 West et al., *From Toussaint*, 19.

148 For example, one of the three cofounders of Black Lives Matter, Opal Tometi, worked as the executive director of the Black Alliance for Just Immigration (BAJI), which formed as a result of the perceived absence of Black immigrants in immigrants' rights protests in the United States. BAJI joins African Americans, Black immigrants, and immigrant rights groups in a common struggle against structural racism and discrimination. This organization argues for the relationship between neoliberal economics, mass migration, and anti-Black racism, which coalesce in the lived experiences of Black immigrants. Oso et al., "Transformational."

149 Rahier, "Introduction."

150 For example, constitutional reforms initiated by Hugo Chávez in Venezuela and Evo Morales in Bolivia provided strong support for Indigenous rights without mentioning the existence of Afro-descendants. Walsh, "Afro In/Exclusion."

151 Rahier, "Introduction," 5.

4. RELATIONAL POETICS

1 Castellanos, "Algo."

2 "Dentro del proletariado." Castellanos, "Algo," 7.

3 "Su doble condición de explotados, como raza y como clase." Junco, "El proletariado," 23.

4 "¿Responde la opresión del negro al color de su piel o a lo crespo de su pelo?"; "Claramente se ve que no." Castellanos, "Algo," 7.

5 Carr, "Identity," 101. "Faja negra de Oriente"; "son la mayoría." Castellanos, "Algo," 7.

6 "Una lucha de clases que toma una forma nacional." Castellanos, "Algo," 7.

7 "Su actuación personalista y faccionalista." PCC, *Cuidemos*, 3. A PCC report on "the Dr. Martín Castellanos case" noted that in debates in the Political Bureau over whether to form a united front with Grau San Martín's Cuban Revolutionary Party, concerns were raised over whether Grau's group would support the communists' demands for political, social, and economic equality for Black Cubans. PCC leadership decided that as long as Grau accepted the remainder of the communist program

and did not do anything to hinder the PCC's work on the Negro Question, Grau's party could be accepted. In response, Martín Castellanos threatened to leave the PCC, which the report described as evidence of his "political myopia" and "lack of communist conviction." PCC, *Cuidemos*, 7.

8   Perdomo, "Trayectoria," 162.

9   López-Calvo, *Imaging*, 80.

10   Yen, *Toma*, 56, 49.

11   Perdomo, "Trayectoria," 163; Rodríguez Sosa, "Regino."

12   Pedroso, "Vida," 142; Yen, *Toma*, 49.

13   Perdomo, "Trayectoria," 164–65.

14   Yen, *Toma*, 49; Rodríguez Sosa, "Regino."

15   The imprisonment of LADLA-Cuba members occurred within the broader context of the 1935 general strike and police repression against leftist activists. Perdomo, "Trayectoria," 169.

16   Yen, *Toma*, 49.

17   Jackson, *Black Literature*, 26.

18   DeCosta-Willis, *Blacks*; Guarnera, "Our Black América"; Guridy, *Forging*; Luis-Brown, *Waves*.

19   Yen, *Toma*, 50; Guridy, *Forging*, 122.

20   López-Calvo, *Imaging*; Scherer, "Sanfancón"; Yen, *Toma*.

21   Yen, *Toma*, 50.

22   Mella had already been calling for a broad-based anti-imperialist movement, such as in his 1924 pamphlet *Cuba, un pueblo que nunca ha sido libre*. García Montes and Alonso Ávila, *Historia*, 50.

23   This invitation was read at a March 15, 1925, meeting of the Agrupación Comunista de la Habana, which would become the PCC. Kersffeld, *Contra*, 76.

24   Mella, "Carta," 8.

25   Guanche, *Mella*, 224; Kersffeld, *Contra*, 40, 76. A January 7, 1926, report to Cuba's secretary of the interior stated that LADLA-Cuba was founded by Mella, José Acosta, Alejandro Barreiro, Francisco Rey Merodio, Alfonso Bernal del Riesgo, Antonio Penichet, Ángel Arias, R. Madginson, M. Valdés Salvador de la Plaza, Carlos Baliño, Raúl Martínez Villena, L. Alemán, J. Z. Tallet, Alfredo Fons Gí, Leonardo Fernández Sánchez, Aureliano Sánchez Arango, Francisco L. Rodríguez, and Emilio Álvarez Recio. AIHC, Fondo Primer Partido.

26   "Delegación del Partido Nacional Chino, el Kuo-Ming Tang." LADLA, "La Liga Anti-Imperialista en Cuba," 6, 8; Kersffeld, *Contra*, 77. According to a January 7, 1926, report to Cuba's secretary of the interior, a detective interrogated Alfredo Pons Gí, a grocery store owner and the president of the Cuban section of the Kuomintang, who denied that it had designated one of its members as a representative in LADLA-Cuba. AIHC, Fondo Primer Partido.

27   López, "'One,'" 108.

28   Manke, "The Impact," 6.

29 For example, the final line of the manifesto cited Cuban independence leader José Martí. LADLA, "Manifiesto de la Liga," 9.

30 In this manifesto, LADLA framed its discussion of nationalism with the term "racial antagonisms." This relates to the context of 1920s Cuba where the large presence of immigrants in the labor market "tended to obscure racial differences among Cuban workers. Instead, 'race' was construed as a line separating native and foreign workers, rather than native workers of different racial background among themselves." De la Fuente, "Two," 31. Although LADLA-Cuba's manifesto clearly expressed a commitment to internationalism over nationalism, its framing of this commitment in racial terms—and its reference to the Kuomintang delegate as evidence of the organization's supposed inclusivity—could also be read as a self-conscious corrective to the fact that its founding membership was majority white and mestizo. LADLA, "Manifiesto de la Liga," 9.

31 "Secretario Organizador." José Acosta was named vice secretary, Alejandro Barreiros Olivera treasurer, and Francisco Rey Merodio vice treasurer. Others present included Dr. Alfonso Bernal de Riesgo, Antonio Penichet, Ángel Arias, R. Madginson, Carlos Baliño, L. Alemán, José Zacarías Tallet, Lucilo de la Peña, General Rafael de Nogales, Rubén Martínez Villena, Gustavo Aldereguía, José Wong, and the students Leonardo Fernández Sánchez, Aureliano Sánchez Arango, Francisco L. Rodríguez, and Emilio Álvarez Recio. The League had an executive committee, elected annually by its larger constituent assembly. García Montes and Alonso Ávila, *Historia*, 50; Kersffeld, *Contra*, 77; LADLA, "La Liga Anti-Imperialista en Cuba," 6, 8; AIHC, Fondo Primer Partido.

32 "Gran Mitín Internacional Anti-Imperialista." AIHC, Fondo Primer Partido.

33 "Con todos para todos"; "la realidad es muy distinta"; "los que no tienen los mismos derechos que el blanco." AIHC, Fondo Primer Partido.

34 Beyond Afro-Cuban organizations, Mella described reaching out to Spanish exiles, Jewish groups, and the Kuomintang in Cuba. He said that LADLA-Cuba was successful in adopting autonomous subsections for workers, student groups, Chinese groups, and Jewish groups. Mella, "Informe," RGASPI, f. 542, o. 1, d. 19.

35 "Platform of the League." AIHC, Fondo Primer Partido.

36 Hatzky, *Julio*, 172; Kersffeld, *Contra*, 46.

37 *Venezuela Libre*, September–December 1925, 1, 11. The street address was Gral. M. Suárez 216–18 in Havana.

38 Kersffeld, *Contra*, 45.

39 Venezuelan exile Carlos Aponte would also leave Cuba for Mexico City and would work with LADLA on the Hands Off Nicaragua (MAFUENIC) campaign.

40 Reig Romero, *El útil*, 264.

41 Mella, "Hacia," 15.

42 "Esta institución además de sumar millares de adeptos en esta República, es continental. Nuestro alerta pone en pie al proletariado y a la juventud

conscientes de toda América y a nuestra voz de protesta se suman las de 20 Repúblicas guardadoras celosas de su soberanía." AIHC, Fondo Primer Partido.

43 "Secretario del Exterior." Manuel Gomez to Jaime Nevares Sager, January 29, 1926, box 1, BDW Papers; Salvador de la Plaza to Jaime Nevares Sager, March 10, 1926, box 1, BDW Papers.

44 Kersffeld, *Contra*, 86–87. See invitation to LADLA-Cuba to the 1927 Brussels Congress, written by Mella. AIHC, Fondo Primer Partido.

45 Kersffeld, *Contra*, 46; "Gonfalón," 1.

46 "No obstante su nombre, nunca redujo su interés y su acción a las fronteras de un país"; "luchar en la América por la liberación de su pueblo y en contra del imperialismo capitalista"; "continental americano." "Gonfalón," 1.

47 "Llamar a las cosas por su nombre." "Gonfalón," 1.

48 A report to the LAI in the lead-up to the Brussels Congress claimed that *América Libre* was under LADLA-Cuba's control. "Report on Organizations," RGASPI, f. 542, o. 1, d. 16.

49 Several members of LADLA-Cuba, like José Antonio Fernández de Castro and Eduardo Abela, were also members of the avant-garde artist collective Grupo Minorista, and *América Libre* published some Minorista declarations. Kersffeld, *Contra*, 42; "Declaración del Grupo Minorista," 5, 12. Moore describes the Minoristas as a group of elite, white, educated artists in the 1920s whose commitments ranged from the purely culturally oriented to political revolution. They were prominent in advancing the movement of *afrocubanismo*. Moore, *Nationalizing*. As Guridy writes, although "the movement was clearly shaped by white primitivist fantasies about black culture, it nevertheless resulted in greater recognition of the African roots of Cuban culture." Guridy, *Forging*, 94. It should also be noted that the Minorista group became increasingly politically radical over the course of the 1920s. Moore, *Nationalizing*, 196–98.

50 Reig Romero, *El útil*, 270.

51 Villena's letters from Moscow indicate close contact and friendship with both Modotti and Junco. Reig Romero, *El útil*, 276.

52 AIHC, Fondo Primer Partido.

53 "Ha entrado una etapa de máxima actividad"; "Conferencia Frente Único contra el Imperialismo." AIHC, Fondo Primer Partido.

54 "Liga Anti-Imperialista de Cuba," *Masas* 1, no. 1 (May 1934).

55 "Inicio de los trabajos de la Liga-Antiimperialista de Cuba," 15.

56 De la Fuente, "Two," 34.

57 López, "'One,'" 95.

58 De la Fuente, "Two," 31–32.

59 De la Fuente, "Two," 40; López, "'One,'" 117.

60 López, "'One,'" 118.

61 Carr, "Identity," 84.

62 Rosell, *Luchas*, 108.

63 "Sólo con la caída total del régimen económico colonial puede encontrar el negro igualdad y derecho al trabajo." "La cuestión negra," 4.

64 De la Fuente, "Two," 43.

65 De la Fuente, "Two," 32.

66 De la Fuente, "Two," 45.

67 However, the PCC's 1932 platform did mention anti-Chinese discrimination. Rosell, *Luchas*, 206.

68 *Masas* 1, no. 2 (June 1934): 1; Arias de la Canal, *Antología*; Yen, *Toma*, 49.

69 *Masas* included a notable number of poems by Cuban writers like Emilio Ballagas, Felipe Pichardo Moya, Ángel Augier, Ramon Guirao, and Enrique Llarch, as well as one translated poem, "Nuevo cantar" by Langston Hughes. Many of these poems also addressed anti-Black discrimination and exploitation of Antillean workers.

70 De la Fuente, "Two," 45.

71 The original of "Zafra-1934" can be found in figures 4.1 and 4.2.

72 Pedroso, "Zafra-1934," 14.

73 "Wall Street necesita que haya zafra en Cuba. La vida de Cuba depende exclusivamente de la zafra. Los colonos cubanos no pueden subsistir si no hay zafra. El presidente Machado ha ofrecido a Wall Street que en Cuba habrá zafra." AIHC, Fondo Primer Partido.

74 "Zafra suicida." AIHC, Fondo Primer Partido.

75 Pedroso, "Zafra-1934," 14.

76 Pedroso, "Zafra-1934," 15.

77 Pedroso, "Zafra-1934," 14.

78 In this analysis, I rely on the Spanish version of "Hermano negro" first published in *Masas*. Subsequent versions contained various changes. The poem's English translation, including the title, comes from Ruiz del Vizo, *Black*, 48–49.

79 Guarnera, *Our Black*; Guridy, *Forging*, 122.

80 "Tú estás en mí . . . yo estoy en ti . . . Tu voz está en mi voz . . . También yo soy tu raza."

81 "Tú fuiste libre sobre la tierra / como las bestias, como los árboles"; "Y fuiste esclavo; / sentiste el latigo."

82 "Trafican con tu sudor / comercian con tu dolor."

83 "Tú amaste alguna vez? Ah, si tú amas, tu carne es bárbara! / Gritaste alguna vez? / Ah, si tú gritas, tu carne es bárbara! / Viviste alguna vez? Ah, si tú vives, tu raza es bárbara!" Pedroso, "Hermano," 19.

84 Fanon, *Black*, 96.

85 "¿Responde la opresión del negro al color de su piel o a lo crespo de su pelo?"; "Claramente se ve que no." Martín Castellanos, "Algo," 7.

86 "¿Y es sólo por tu piel. ¿es todo por color?"

87 "No es solo por color; mas porque eres, bajo el prejuicio de raza, hombre explotado." Pedroso, "Hermano," 19.

88 "Su doble condición de explotados, como raza y como clase." Junco, "El proletariado," 23.

89   "Negro más por el hambre que por raza."

90   "El rico hace de ti un juguete"; "hay hombres que te pagan con hambre la risa." Pedroso, "Hermano," 19.

91   Guarnera, *Our Black*, 135.

92   "Silencia un poco tus maracas" and "enluta un poco tu bongo" so that he can "aprende aquí / y mira allí / y escucha allá en Scottsboro, en Scottsboro, en Scottsboro." Pedroso, "Hermano negro," 19. Here I diverge from the English translation provided by Ruiz del Vizo's *Black*.

93   Guridy, *Forging*, 123.

94   "Negro en Haití, negro en Jamaica, negro en New York, negro en la Habana."

95   "Aquí . . . allí . . . allá."

96   "Más hermano en el ansia, que en la raza." Here I diverge from the English translation provided by Ruiz del Vizo's *Black*.

97   "Da al mundo con tu agustia rebelde / tu humana voz." Pedroso, "Hermano," 19.

98   In an interview, Pedroso specifically mentioned the involvement of Raúl Roa and LADLA-Cuba members José Antonio Fernández de Castro and José Zacarías Tallet. Rodríguez Sosa, "Regino."

99   Arias de la Canal, *Antología*, 167.

100   Rodríguez Sosa, "Regino."

101   "Nuestro esperado poeta proletario"; "nuestro salón de lectura." Penichet, "Surgió," 3, 4.

102   All translations of "Auto-bio-prólogo" are mine. I rely on the original 1933 version of *Nosotros*, which includes the "Auto-bio-prólogo." As Addington has traced, the 1939 and 1966 editions excluded the "Auto-bio-prólogo" in addition to incorporating other changes. Addington, "'A todos.'"

103   Pedroso, *Nosotros*, 12.

104   Pedroso, *Nosotros*, 12; Addington, "'A todos.'"

105   Pedroso, *Nosotros*, 12.

106   Pedroso, *Nosotros*, 9–10; Addington, "'A todos.'"

107   Pedroso, *Nosotros*, 9.

108   Pedroso, *Nosotros*, 9; Arias de la Canal, *Antología*, 162.

109   Pedroso, *Nosotros*, 9

110   López discusses this historical tendency in "'One,'" 120–21.

111   Quoted in López-Calvo, *Imaging*, 81.

112   Pedroso, *Nosotros*, 9.

113   Pedroso, *Nosotros*, 10.

114   Scherer, "Sanfancón"; Pedroso, *Nosotros*, 12.

115   Pedroso, *Nosotros*, 23–24, translation mine.

116   Pedroso, *Nosotros*, 31, translation mine.

117   Pedroso, *Nosotros*, 18; Arias de la Canal, *Antología*, 166. Translation of this poem comes from Pedroso, "Fraternal," 10.

118   Pedroso, *Nosotros*, 18. I have deviated from Hughes's translation here.

119   López-Calvo, *Imaging*, xi.

120   Hu-DeHart, "Opium," 83.

121   López-Calvo, *Imaging*, 9.

122   Yen, *Toma*, 25.

123   López-Calvo, *Imaging*, 8–9.

124   Yen, *Toma*, 25; López-Calvo, *Imaging*, 2, 11–13.

125   López-Calvo, *Imaging*, 94.

126   Yen, *Toma*, 25; Scherer, "Sanfancón."

127   Pedroso, *Nosotros*, 34–35. All translations of "Salutación a un camarada culí" are mine.

128   Yen, *Toma*, 56.

129   See the work, for example, of Karen Leonard or Matthew Frye Jacobson.

130   López-Calvo, *Imaging*, 81.

131   López-Calvo, *Imaging*, 82.

132   Pedroso, *Nosotros*, 34.

133   Pedroso, *Nosotros*, 35.

134   López-Calvo, *Imaging*, 81.

135   López, "'One,'" 109.

136   Pedroso, *Nosotros*, 35.

137   López-Calvo, *Imaging*, 81.

138   Pedroso, *Nosotros*, 35.

139   Pedroso, *Nosotros*, 36.

140   López-Calvo, *Imaging*, 81. Guarnera reads this moment similarly, writing, "Asia's anti-colonial struggles of the 1920s served as a model for later anti-imperialist movements" and "Pedroso clearly identifies Asian revolutionary fervor as the solution to the desperate situation of Latin America, as he depicts the arrival of revolution in Latin America as the arrival of a ship from the East, her sails blown out by the enthusiasm of the 'nuevos postulados' of socialism." Guarnera, *Our Black*, 125–26.

141   De la Fuente, "Two," 45.

142   Sawyer, *Racial*, 19.

5. ETHNIC IMPERSONATION AND MASCULINE EROTICS

1   INS, Passenger Lists; James Sager, death certificate; Pujals, "Becoming," 404.

2   James Sager to Pedro Albizu Campos, December 1, 1925, BDW Papers, box 1. All further correspondence cited in this chapter comes from BDW Papers unless otherwise indicated.

3   James Sager to Federico Acosta Velarde, December 10, 1925, box 1.

4   Pujals, "Becoming," 394.

5   Pujals, "Becoming," 398.

6   Shipman, *It Had*, 133–51. Phillips used several other names throughout his life, including Jesús Ramírez, Frank Seaman, Charles Shipman, and Lewis Corey.

7   The Workers Party of America was the name of the legal organization used by the Communist Party USA from 1921 to 1929. N. Kutziker to Whomever It May Concern, August 8, 1925, box 2; James Sager to Executive Secretary, Workers Party of America, September 18, 1925, box 1.

8   James Sager to Pedro Albizu Campos, December 1, 1925, box 1.

9   James Sager to Mother, March 9, 1926, box 1.

10 Journeyman Barbers' International Union of America to Chago, April 10, 1926, box 1.

11 V.P. & G.M., South Porto Rico Sugar Company, to James Sager, December 1, 1925, box 1; James Sager to Manuel Gomez, February 2, 1926, box 1.

12 James Sager to Executive Secretary, Workers Party of America, September 18, 1925, box 1.

13 James Sager to Manuel Gomez, November 3, 1925, box 1.

14 Manuel Gomez to James Sager, November 11, 1925, box 1.

15 Manuel Gomez to James Sager, November 14, 1925, box 1, emphasis in original. Pujals uses this instance of Gomez's addition of the "nonexistent Puerto Rican section" to the LADLA letterhead to question the existence of other LADLA sections. Pujals challenges Kersffeld's work on LADLA, saying it has a tendency to "to elevate the scope of the organization." Pujals, "Becoming," 401. However, Kersffeld's work mostly focuses on LADLA's activities in Mexico, Cuba, and Argentina and barely addresses the Puerto Rican section. From my own research, I would argue that each section developed differently in each location and the process of creation of the Puerto Rican section is not representative of LADLA in its entirety.

16 James Sager to Tony, November 24, 1925, box 1.

17 Jaime Nevárez S., "A los Trabajadores de P.R.," December 7, 1925, box 2.

18 Dr. Manuel Guzmán Rodríguez, founder of the newspaper *La Vanguardia*, was elected chairman. Julio Vargas, secretary of the Cigar Makers' Union Local 411 and member of the Socialist Party, was named secretary. Cayelano Drouyn became treasurer. Julio Aponte, Nationalist Party secretary in Mayagüez, signed onto the statement, and Sager mentioned the presence of others, although not by name. James Sager to Manuel Gomez, December 15, 1925, box 1.

19 "La dominación de las fuerzas imperialistas de Wall Street"; "los otros países de ambos continentes y el lejano Oriente." Secretario Internacional, Liga Anti-Imperialista de las Américas, December 14, 1925, box 1.

20 J. Nevares Sager, Secretary of Porto Rican Section, AAAIL, "Move for Independence," March 15, 1926, box 2.

21 James Sager to Salvador de la Plaza, August 14, 1926, box 1.

22 James Sager to Xavier Guerrero, December 15, 1925, box 1; James Sager to Manuel Gomez, December 15, 1925, box 1.

23 James Sager to Manuel Gomez, December 15, 1925, box 1.

24 James Sager to Félix Lugo, March 26, 1926, box 1.

25 James Sager to Manuel Gomez, April 5, 1926, box 1. Lugo originally reached out to Manuel Gomez about starting LADLA–Puerto Rico, and

Gomez referred him to Sager. Félix Lugo to Manuel Gomez, February 19, 1926, box 1. The Ponce section was officially announced in April in the newspaper *La Tribuna*. James Sager to Manuel Gomez, April 5, 1926, box 1. Lugo mentioned the cooperation of the following people in the Ponce section: Clemente Sárraga, Cruz Conde Suárez, Ángel M. Saavedra, Juan Torres, and Juan Cardona. Félix Lugo to James Sager, April 5, 1926, box 1.

26 James Sager to Manuel Gomez, April 5, 1926, box 1.

27 Gomez mentioned that Emilio Delgado served as secretary of the San Juan section. Manuel Gomez to James Sager, July 30, 1926, box 1.

28 Félix Lugo to James Sager, February 19, 1926, box 1; Manuel Gomez, "Report to Politcom," February 8, 1926, box 4.

29 Manuel Gomez to James Sager, January 29, 1926, box 1; "Resolución adoptada por la sección puertorriqueña," undated, box 2.

30 Porto Rican Section, AAAIL, "Appeal to the Sailors," February 18, 1927, box 2.

31 J. Nevares Sager, Secretary of Porto Rican Section, AAAIL, "Move for Independence," March 15, 1926, box 2; J. Nevares, "Día del Primero de Mayo," May 1, 1926, box 2; Salvador de la Plaza to J. N. Sager, July 15, 1926, box 1; Manuel Gomez to James Sager, July 30, 1926, box 1; James Sager to Editor, *Daily Worker*, January 26, 1927, box 1; James Sager to Manuel Gomez, February 15, 1927, box 1; "Manifiesto de la Liga Anti-Imperialista de las Américas, sección de Puerto Rico," undated, box 2. Félix Lugo's Ponce section also sent statements to be published in the US leftist press. James Sager to Manuel Gomez, April 25, 1926, box 1.

32 Julio de Artegas to James Nevares, July 27, 1926, box 1; Juventud Nacionalista de Puerto Rico to Hon. Pres. de la Liga Anti Imperialista de America, July 29, 1926, box 1. The organizations that affiliated included Club Libertad, Asociación de Periodistas, Juventud Nacionalista, Federación de Estudiantes de P.R., and Grupo Modernista. James Sager to Salvador de la Plaza, August 14, 1926, box 1; Manuel Gomez to James Sager, September 3, 1926, box 1.

33 J. Nevares Sager to Rothschild Francis, November 20, 1926, box 1; Rothschild Francis to J. Nevares Sager, November 30, 1926, box 1; Rothschild Francis to J. Nevares Sager, December 5, 1926, box 1.

34 J. Nevares Sager to Editor, *Daily Worker*, October 13, 1926, box 1.

35 James Sager to Manuel Gomez, January 12, 1927, box 1.

36 James N. Sager to C. E. Ruthenberg, February 9, 1926, box 1; C. E. Ruthenberg to M. Sager, July 1, 1926, box 1.

37 Manuel Gomez to James Sager, April 22, 1926, box 1.

38 For a listing of executive committee and members of each section, see Liga Comunista de Puerto Rico Organizational Chart, box 2. For members of Mayagüez Communist League, see Cayelano Droyn to James Sager, September 29, 1926, box 1.

39 Meeting minutes of El Comité Ejecutivo de la Liga Comunista de Puerto Rico, March 6, 1927, box 2.

40 James Sager to C. E. Ruthenberg, August 24, 1926, box 1; James Sager to Manuel Gomez, March 21, 1927, box 1.

41 Clemente Sárraga to J. N. Sager, August 2, 1926, box 1.

42 James Sager to Jay Lovestone, March 15, 1927, box 1.

43 Sager's letters refer to the PNPR as "n.p.," for "nationalist party."

44 Despite its recent formation, PNPR membership had roots among nationalists within the electoral Union Party. Austin, "Albizu Campos," 49.

45 James Sager to Tony, November 24, 1925, box 1.

46 James Sager to Federico Acosta Velarde, December 4, 1925, box 1.

47 JNS to Federico Acosta Velarde, December 10, 1925, box 1.

48 James Sager to Manuel Gomez, December 15, 1925, box 1.

49 James Sager to Manuel Gomez, April 5, 1926, box 1.

50 Ferrao, *Pedro*, 41.

51 "Una firma responsable." Federico Acosta Velarde to James N. Sager, December 22, 1925, box 1.

52 "Liga Anti-Imperialista tiene tendencias comunistas"; "Simpatizamos con la Liga por lo que tiene de anti-imperialista . . . no podemos ni debemos adherirnos a ella por lo que tiene de comunista." Federico Acosta Velarde to James N. Sager, March 8, 1926, box 1.

53 James Sager to Pedro Albizu Campos, April 28, 1926, box 1.

54 James Sager to Manuel Gomez, February 2, 1926, box 1; James Sager to Manuel Gomez, April 5, 1926, box 1.

55 James Sager to Manuel Gomez, April 5, 1926, box 1.

56 James Sager to Manuel Gomez, February 2, 1926, box 1.

57 James Sager to Manuel Gomez, April 5, 1926, box 1.

58 James Sager to Manuel Gomez, April 5, 1926, box 1. Although I am relying on Sager's reporting of his conversations with Albizu Campos, Sager sent this report to Albizu Campos, who concurred that it accurately represented his positions. James Sager to Pedro Albizu Campos, April 28, 1926, box 1; Pedro Albizu Campos to J. Nevares Sager, May 1, 1926, box 1.

59 James Sager to Manuel Gomez, March 10, 1926, box 1.

60 James Sager to Manuel Gomez, April 5, 1926, box 1.

61 Manuel Gomez to James Sager, April 22, 1926, box 1.

62 James Sager to Manuel Gomez, June 22, 1926, box 1.

63 Pedro Albizu Campos to Mr. Nevares, August 12, 1926, box 1.

64 Austin, "Albizu Campos," 53; Power, *Solidarity*, 73.

65 "P.R., siendo una colonia, dominada políticamente por los E.U. de A., los camaradas en los Estados Unidos tienen el deber de desarrollar y ayudar la causa y sus luchas en esta isla; pero como Puerto es un país de habla castellano, la cooperación de los camaradas en México y en Cuba, es de vital importancia." J. N. Sager to Camarada, April 1926, box 1. This letter is undated, but it is a response to an April 26, 1926, letter to Sager from Salvador de la Plaza.

66 James Sager from C. E. Ruthenberg, May 18, 1926, box 1.

67 James Sager to C. E. Ruthenberg, August 24, 1926, box 1; James Sager to Manuel Gomez, January 12, 1927.

68 See "Auszug"; Mella, "Informe"; "The Question"; "10 mayo 1926 Informe," all in RGASPI, f. 543, o. 1, d. 19.

69 "Todas las secciones mencionadas salvo Estados Unidos y Puerto Rico
reconocen . . . la sede de la liga." RGASPI, f. 542, o.1, d. 19.

70 James Sager to Manuel Gomez, February 2, 1927, box 1.

71 James Sager to Manuel Gomez, February 2, 1927, box 1.

72 James Sager to Manuel Gomez, February 2, 1927, box 1; J. Nevares Sager to
Comité Continental de la Liga Anti Imperialista de las Américas, April 15,
1927, box 1.

73 James Sager to Manuel Gomez, March 10, 1926, box 1.

74 James Sager to Manuel Gomez, February 2, 1926, box 1.

75 James Sager to Manuel Gomez, February 2, 1926, box 1; J. Nevares Sager
to Comité Continental de la Liga Anti Imperialista de las Américas,
April 15, 1927, box 1.

76 James Sager to Manuel Gomez, September 15, 1926, box 1.

77 J. Nevares Sager to Comité Continental de la Liga Anti Imperialista de las
Américas, April 15, 1927, box 1.

78 James Sager to Jorge Vivó, June 19, 1926, box 1.

79 James Sager to Jorge Vivó, June 19, 1926, box 1.

80 Salvador de la Plaza to J. N. Sager, July 15, 1926, box 1.

81 Ferrao, *Pedro*, 40; Power, *Solidarity*, 55.

82 Ferrao, *Pedro*, 46.

83 Austin, "Albizu Campos," 95, 99; Ferrao, *Pedro*, 50.

84 James Sager to Manuel Gomez, March 21, 1927, box 1.

85 James Sager to Manuel Gomez, March 21, 1927, box 1. He repeated the same
assessment to LADLA's Continental Committee. J. Nevares Sager to Comité
Continental de la Liga Anti Imperialista de las Américas, April 15, 1927, box 1.

86 James Sager to Manuel Gomez, March 21, 1927, box 1.

87 For more on Albizu Campos's racial and ethnic background and on Vasconcelos's visit, see Power, *Solidarity*, 65–76.

88 Austin, "Albizu Campos," 58–59.

89 Austin, "Albizu Campos," 91.

90 Manuel Gomez, "Report to Politcom," February 8, 1926, box 4.

91 J. Nevares Sager, Secretary of Porto Rican Section, AAAIL, "Move for
Independence," March 15, 1926, box 2; James Sager to Salvador de la Plaza,
August 14, 1926, box 1.

92 James Sager to Manuel Gomez, April 5, 1926, box 1.

93 Manuel Gomez to James Sager, March 6, 1926, box 1.

94 Manuel Gomez to James Sager, May 12, 1926, box 1; Manuel Gomez to
James Sager, April 22, 1926, box 1.

95 Manuel Gomez to James Sager, January 29, 1926, box 1.

96 James Sager to Manuel Gomez, May 13, 1926, box 1.

97 League Against Colonial Suppression Provisional Committee to James
Sager, July 18, 1926, box 1.

98 Emphasis in original.

99   Manuel Gomez to James Sager, September 3, 1926, box 1.

100   Manuel Gomez to James Sager, October 6, 1926, box 1.

101   James Sager to Manuel Gomez, December 14, 1926, box 1.

102   Goebel, *Anti-Imperial*, 205.

103   James Sager to Manuel Gomez, February 2, 1927, box 1.

104   "Samuel R. Quiñones Renuncia," January 28, 1927, box 4.

105   James Sager to Manuel Gomez, February 2, 1927, box 1.

106   James Sager to Manuel Gomez, February 16, 1927, box 1; James Sager to Manuel Gomez, February 2, 1927, box 1.

107   James Sager to Ángel del Río, February 15, 1927, box 1.

108   File 2, LAI Archive.

109   Goebel, *Anti-Imperial*, 205.

110   J. Nevares Sager to Comité Continental de la Liga Anti Imperialista de las Américas, April 15, 1927, box 1.

111   J. Nevares Sager to Comité Continental de la Liga Anti Imperialista de las Américas, April 15, 1927, box 1; James Sager to Vicente Géigel Polanco, April 19, 1927, box 1.

112   James Sager to Manuel Gomez, February 16, 1927, box 1.

113   James Sager to Manuel Gomez, February 2, 1926, box 1.

114   Journeyman Barbers' International Union of America to Chago, April 10, 1926, box 1.

115   James Sager to Manuel Gomez, May 6, 1926, box 1.

116   James Sager to Manuel Gomez, May 13, 1926, box 1.

117   Manuel Gomez to James Sager, August 26, 1926, box 1.

118   Manuel Gomez to James Sager, May 12, 1926, box 1.

119   Manuel Gomez, "Report to Politcom," February 8, 1926, box 4.

120   Manuel Gomez, "Report to Politcom," February 8, 1926, box 4.

121   Max Rock to James Sager, December 10, 1926, box 1.

122   C. E. Ruthenberg to J. N. Sager, May 18, 1926, box 1.

123   James Sager to Manuel Gomez, September 15, 1926, box 1.

124   James Sager to Manuel Gomez, November 10, 1926, box 1.

125   James Sager to Manuel Gomez, January 12, 1927, box 1.

126   James Sager to Manuel Gomez, February 2, 1927, box 1; James Sager to Ángel del Río, February 15, 1927, box 1.

127   James Sager to Manuel Gomez, February 16, 1927, box 1. New letterhead and leaflets dated from this time, included in BDW Papers, substantiate Sager's claim for how money was used.

128   James Sager to Manuel Gomez, February 16, 1927, box 1.

129   James Sager to Manuel Gomez, March 21, 1927, box 1.

130   James Sager to Manuel Gomez, April 25, 1927, box 1.

131   James Sager to Manuel Gomez, February 2, 1927, box 1.

132   James Sager to Ángel del Río, February 15, 1927, box 1.

133   James Sager to Manuel Gomez, April 15, 1927, box 1.

134   "Trabajadores y Campesinos de Puerto Rico"; J. Nevares, "Día del Primero de Mayo," May 1, 1926, both in box 2.

135 J. Nevares Sager to L. Gibarti, May 3, 1926, box 1.

136 Hersch, *Jews*, 3.

137 Hersch, *Jews*, 19; Franklin, "Jew."

138 Jakobsen, "Queers," 79.

139 Jakobsen, "Queers," 75.

140 Fermaglich, "Too Long," 35.

141 Jacobson, *Whiteness*.

142 Hersch, *Jews*, 3.

143 For the importance of Catholicism to the 1920s PNPR, see Power, *Solidarity*.

144 Hersch, *Jews*, 31.

145 Hersch, *Jews*, 8.

146 Jakobsen, "Queers," 65–66.

147 Jakobsen, "Queers," 69.

148 Jakobsen, "Queers," 67.

149 Jakobsen, "Queers," 85.

150 Jakobsen, "Queers," 71.

151 Jakobsen, "Queers," 79.

152 Jakobsen, "Queers," 80.

153 Browder, *Slippery*, 7, 10.

154 J. Nevares Sager to L. Gibarti, May 3, 1926, box 1.

155 James Sager to Manuel Gomez, May 6, 1926, box 1; James Sager to Manuel Gomez, May 13, 1926, box 1.

156 Manuel Gomez to James Sager, May 6, 1926, box 1.

157 Manuel Gomez to James Sager, May 12, 1926, box 1.

158 Manuel Gomez to James Sager, September 3, 1926, box 1.

159 James Sager to Manuel Gomez, September 15, 1926, box 1.

160 Manuel Gomez to James Sager, December 14, 1926, box 1.

161 Pujals, "Becoming," 405.

162 Between 1903 and 1915, English was the official language of instruction in grades 1–12 in Puerto Rico. Between 1917 and 1934, grades 1–4 were officially taught in Spanish while grades 5–12 were taught in English. In practice, the implementation of these policies was inconsistent due to an insufficient number of teachers with high levels of fluency in English. De Jesús Toro, *Historia*, 125.

163 Amparo to James Sager, October 19, 1926, box 1.

164 Amparo to James Sager, undated, box 1.

165 Mella was the son of an Irish-born mother and a father of Spanish descent born in the Dominican Republic. For more on Mella's background, see Hatzky, *Julio*.

166 For discussion of how Che Guevara came to represent the erotics of 1960s revolutionary politics, see Manzano, *The Age*.

167 For more on Mella's marriage, see Hatzky, *Julio*, 212–17.

168 Tina Modotti to Xavier Guerrero, September 15, 1928, MC Papers, box 1, series II.

169 This conference is discussed in depth in chapter 3.
170 For in-depth discussion of this controversy, see Smith, *The Power*, 46–50.
171 Aguchar and Brum, *Falsas*, 65.
172 Alexander, *A History*, 75–81.
173 Jesús Junco Roldán, acta de defunción; Sandalio Junco Junco, travel visa.
174 Amparo to James Sager, October 19, 1926, box 1.
175 Pujals, "Becoming," 407.
176 Ferrao, *Pedro*, 41–46.
177 James Sager to Manuel Gomez, April 25, 1927, box 1.
178 James Sager to Vicente Géigel Polanco, April 19, 1927, box 1.
179 Pujals, "Becoming," 409; James Sager to Manuel Gomez, April 25, 1927, box 1. Before leaving for Colombia, he left his papers with Bertram Wolfe.
180 Pujals, "Becoming," 409.
181 Pujals, "Becoming," 408; Jeifets and Jeifets, *América Latina*, 450.
182 Pujals, "Becoming," 408.
183 Pujals, "Becoming," 410.
184 Pujals, "Becoming," 410; Calderón and Zamora, "Manuela," 32.
185 Calderón and Zamora, "Manuela," 34. In the early 1940s in Texas, Sager worked for the Works Progress Administration Archives Project, perhaps as a cover for his political organizing. James Sager, registration card.
186 Pujals, "Becoming," 411.
187 On his draft card, Sager reported that his name was "Jacob Sager Master" and that he was born in Russia. This name is crossed out on the draft card and replaced with "James Sager (social security)." James Sager, registration card.
188 Hatzky, *Julio*, 285. Crouch's communications as LADLA-US secretary can be found in RGASPI, f. 542, o. 1, d. 35.
189 Shipman, *It Had*.

6. HANDS OFF NICARAGUA AND THE SANDINO FANTASY

1 For existing scholarship on this campaign, cited throughout this chapter, see Carr, "Pioneering"; Cerdas Cruz, *Sandino*; Jeifets and Jeifets, "La Comintern"; Kersffeld, "El Comité"; Kersffeld, *Contra*; Melcher, "La solidaridad"; Staklo, "Harnessing"; and Wood, "Indoamerica."
2 The address was Calle República del Salvador 94.
3 LADLA, "Saludo," 7.
4 LADLA, "Entrega," 1. Sandino's soldiers reported that they captured this flag in the battle of El Zapete in May 1928.
5 LADLA, "Entrega," 1.
6 LADLA, "Saludo," 7.
7 Wood, "Indoamerica," 84.
8 "Information and Press Service No. 4," July 22, 1929, RGASPI, f. 542, op. 1, d. 87.

9   Bach, "Bei."

10   "El general Sandino debe perdonarnos. Esto es el producto de la imagina-
     ción de un pintor indio mexicano que se autoretrató—Socrates protesta
     contra este dibujo; A él solo le gusta donde está buen mozo, fifí como
     dicen por aquí." Bach, "Bei."

11   Although I have translated *fifí* as "posh," the term has a stronger associa-
     tion with vanity.

12   Schroeder, "Bei." Schroeder's work to digitize hundreds of documents
     related to Sandino's struggle greatly facilitated this chapter.

13   "Augusto César Sandino, 1895–1934," Library of Congress, accessed
     June 22, 2021, https://www.loc.gov/pictures/item/2003663600/. Another
     drawing based on this photo appeared in *El Machete*, February 18, 1928.
     PCM, "Los Partes," 1.

14   By portraying Sandino in this way, Guerrero's portrait inverted the
     historic tradition in Latin American portraiture of depicting political
     leaders, such as Simón Bolívar or Antonio Maceo, as lighter-skinned and
     more European than they were in reality.

15   See, for example, Cerdas Cruz, *Sandino*; Melcher, "La solidaridad."

16   F. Bach to Münzenberg, January 10, 1928; F. Bach to Münzenberg, Jan-
     uary 16, 1928, both in RGASPI, f. 542, op. 1, d. 28. Jeifets and Jeifets also
     argue that this was a grassroots campaign with little financial support
     from the Comintern. Jeifets and Jeifets, "La Comintern." Some individual
     LADLA sections, like LADLA–Costa Rica, eventually took a strong stance
     against Sandino. Kersffeld, "La Liga Antiimperialista de Costa Rica," 114–15.

17   Goebel, *Anti-Imperial*, 204.

18   LADLA, "Manifiesto del Congreso," 6. "Los lugares donde la presión im-
     perialista se manifiesta con mayor violencia." LADLA, "Las resoluciones,"
     10–11.

19   LADLA, "Liga," 4; Kersffeld, *Contra*, 138.

20   LADLA condemned the decision of both Haya de la Torre and Vasconce-
     los to participate in the Latin American supervising commission of the
     Nicaraguan elections. LADLA, "Una traición," 6.

21   Kersffeld, *Contra*, 139; The committee was formed on January 18, 1928,
     and inspired by the campaign in support of Sacco and Vanzetti from the
     previous year. The member organizations included LAI; Socorro Obrero
     Internacional; Unión Centro Sud-Americana y Antillana, represented by
     Dr. Carlos León; LADLA (Continental Committee and Nicaraguan and
     Mexican sections); Federación Anticlerical Mexicana, represented by
     Belén de Sárraga; Liga Internacional Pro Luchadores Perseguidos; Hai-
     tian Patriotic Union, represented by J. Jolibois fils; Liga Internacional An-
     tifascista; Internacional de los Trabajadores de la Enseñanza, represented
     by Rafael Ramos Pedrueza; Partido Ferrocarrilero Unitario, represented
     by Hernán Laborde; Liga Nacional Campesina, represented by Úrsulo
     Galván; Federación Minera de Jalisco, represented by David Siqueiros.
     LADLA, "Comité Central," 2–3; PCM, "A la prensa," 1.

22 F. Bach to Münzenberg, January 10, 1928, RGASPI, f. 542, op. 1, d. 28. Wood, "Indoamerica," 80–83. Bach was also the IRA representative in Mexico. Jeifets and Jeifets, *América Latina*, 66; Jeifets and Jeifets, "La Comintern."

23 Hatzky, *Julio*, 181. *El Machete* described Hurwitz as the former secretary of the Peruvian Student Federation, a professor at González Prada Popular University in Peru and José Martí Popular University in Cuba, and a journalist. PCM, "A la prensa," 1.

24 PCM, "A la prensa," 1. This call was circulated in major newspapers, like *El Día* and *El Universal*. Jeifets and Jeifets, "La Comintern."

25 LADLA, "Comité Central," 3.

26 LADLA, "Comité Central," 3; PCM, "Internacionales," 2; Within Mexico, MAFUENIC committees were listed in Guadalajara, Tampico, Ciudad Victoria, Veracruz, Puebla, and Toluca. PCM, "Sábado 11," 1.

27 PCM, "Contra la hipocresía," 1.

28 FBI, "All American Anti Imperialist League," b7c.

29 PCM, "A la prensa," 1. A large chalkboard used to track funds raised hung outside the headquarters of *El Machete*.

30 "Mujeres de conciencia." LADLA, "Comité Central," 2.

31 Hurwitz, "Como derriba," 1.

32 Although MAFUENIC sent an initial 250 pesos to Nicaragua, after the first MAFUENIC days on February 11–12 in Mexico City, the campaign raised another 1,500 pesos. LADLA, "Comité Central," 3; Hurwitz, "Boletín," 1. In subsequent weeks, it raised more money in Veracruz, Guadalajara, and Puebla, and by April the campaign had collected over 4,000 pesos. PCM, "Aumenta," 1; Hurwitz, "Informe de MAFUENIC," 16. In June, it set a new goal to raise 10,000 pesos. LADLA, "Diez mil," 3. These were relatively modest sums, and by mid-1928 Sandino had received less than $20,000 from the campaign. Carr, "Pioneering," 148, 152.

33 In April 1928, for example, five thousand people filled the Virginia Fábregas Theater in Mexico City for a MAFUENIC event where US writer Carleton Beals reported on his recent meeting with Sandino. PCM, "Actividades," 1; LADLA, "Gran mitín," 12. Another rally in Veracruz attracted one thousand attendees. PCM, "Gran mitin del Comité," 1.

34 Hurwitz, "Informe de Mafuenic," 8.

35 Kersffeld, *Contra*, 151; Melcher, "La solidaridad," 22; Cerdas Cruz, *Sandino*, 90–91.

36 Kersffeld, *Contra*, 151.

37 Machado, "La situación," 7; Hurwitz, "Informe de MAFUENIC," 11.

38 Morán Beltrán et al., "Gustavo Machado."

39 "Secretario del exterior." Manuel Gomez to James Sager, January 29, 1926, box 1, BDW Papers; Salvador de la Plaza to Jaime N. Sager, March 10, 1926, box 1, BDW Papers.

40 At this time, Machado was LAI representative in Mexico as well as secretary of the PRV, which he and others founded in Mexico. PCM, "A la prensa," 1.

41 PCM, "La semana," 1. When Machado and Sócrates arrived in Veracruz, the MAFUENIC local chapter organized a welcome reception and rally. LAI representative Federico Bach spoke at the rally, along with Machado, Sócrates, Mella, Hurwitz, and others, including feminist activist Belén de Sárraga. LADLA, "Actividades de Mafuenic," 5; PCM, "Gran mitin de Frente Único," 1. After several days of meetings with workers and student groups in Veracruz and in Xalapa, Machado and Sócrates traveled to Mexico City. LADLA, "Magno mitín," 6; PCM, "El sábado," 1.

42 PCM, "El sábado," 1.

43 LADLA, "Actividades antimperialistas," 8. After the US-supervised election of President Moncada in Nicaragua in November 1928, MAFUENIC led a letter-writing campaign to discourage Mexican President Portes Gil from recognizing Moncada's presidency. PCM, "Sandino es el único," 1.

44 Kersffeld, *Contra*, 152; Cerdas Cruz, *Sandino*, 95–97.

45 Wood, "Indoamerica," 84. "Merced a esta campaña, en casi todos los lugares del país hay formada una sección de la Liga Antimperialista de las Américas." PCM, "Al margen," 2.

46 Kersffeld, *Contra*, 224–25; LADLA, "Nuevas secciones," 2; LADLA, "Secciones," 3.

47 LADLA, "Una muralla," 3.

48 "Summary," RGASPI, f. 542, op. 1, d. 35; Ruis, "Actividades," 4.

49 LADLA, "El Libertador," 16.

50 LADLA, "Crónica," inside cover; LADLA, "Gracias," 17.

51 For example, LADLA-US promised that with the recent creation of four new Spanish-speaking sections, it could increase the paper's subscribers by five thousand. Ruis, "Actividades," 4.

52 PCM, "Sábado," 1. "Las heridas de algunos no se habían todavía cicatrizado, otros estaban recién salidos de la prisión." LADLA, "Una muralla," 3.

53 LADLA, "Una muralla," 3.

54 Hurwitz, "Informe de MAFUENIC," 11.

55 Ruis, "Actividades," 4; LADLA, "Impiden," 1.

56 Kersffeld, *Contra*, 144, 148.

57 FBI, "All American Anti Imperialist League," b7c.

58 FBI, "All American Anti Imperialist League," b7c. Gomez also apparently stated that LADLA-US sent money through either the Mexican Red Cross, Salvadoran Red Cross, LADLA headquarters in Mexico City, or individual couriers.

59 Carr writes, "Significant loads of weapons were also funnelled to Nicaragua from Mexico with the barely concealed support of the Mexican army." Carr, "Pioneering," 145.

60 Hatzky, *Julio*, 285.

61 "El esfuerzo común, espontáneo, enormemente sincero de los campesinos pobres, de los obreros pobres, de los soldados, de todos aquellos que sienten que la causa de Nicaragua es la causa de los desheredados, de los desposeídos por un común enemigo, el Imperialismo yanqui . . .

conocemos la lista interminable de organizaciones de todas las banderías, de todas las tendencias, de todos los colores, agrupadas en un solo grito de protesta por la ignominia y a una sola voz de adhesión a nuestra campaña." Hurwitz, "Informe de Mafuenic," 8.

62   "La situación continental"; "una nueva forma de país"; "ha perdido su libertad económica para depender de otro país más fuerte y rico, conservando aparentemente su libertad política y soberanía y su estatuto internacional." De la Plaza, "La situación," 5.

63   "La penetración económica es casi siempre del país colonizador, mientras que en los semicoloniales, esta penetración es de varios países imperialistas." De la Plaza, "La situación," 5.

64   "Permitieron el desarrollo de una pequeña burguesía parasitaria y la establización de gobiernos tiránicos." De la Plaza, "La situación," 5.

65   "Busca de materias primas y de la obra de mano barata de los indígenas." LADLA, "Comité Continental," 5.

66   "Casi todos los gobiernos de la América Latina son agentes de Washington, lo que permite caracterizar la lucha antimperialista como movimiento de liberación nacional." LADLA, "Comité Continental," 5.

67   "Las dos causas no deben hacer más que una." Jolibois, "La ocupación," 12.

68   LADLA, "Venezuela," 2.

69   "La lucha de Nicaragua es la lucha de América Latina"; "Nicaragua defiende la soberanía continental." Machado, "La situación," 7.

70   LADLA, "La Conferencia," 2.

71   "La penetración imperialista en los demás países de América Latina." LADLA, "La Conferencia," 2.

72   Montero, "La situación," 10.

73   "¡Viva Augusto C. Sandino!"; "¡Abajo el Congreso Panamericano!" For LADLA's critique of pan-Americanism, see, for example, LADLA, "Manifiesto a los pueblos," 8–9.

74   "Fascismo tropical"; "una adaptación del fascismo a las condiciones coloniales . . . y a las relaciones con el imperialismo." Mella, "De Cuba," 6.

75   "Intento de estabilización por medios dictatoriales del capitalismo incipiente." Mella, "De Cuba," 6. Mella first used "Mussolini tropical" in May 1925. Hatzky, *Julio*, 136.

76   "Se ejercita en favor de los señores de la industria imperialista." Mella, "De Cuba," 6.

77   "Vivas a Sandino y a la Liga Internacional Antifascista, y mueras a Mussolini." PCM, "La ruptura," 8.

78   LADLA, "Secciones," 3.

79   "La cuestión bananera." LADLA, "Secciones," 3; LADLA, "Manifiesto del Comité Continental," 9.

80   "Fomentando un problema racial que se extiende por toda Centroamérica donde la UNITED opera como señora de la explotación." Montero, "La situación," 6.

81 "Instaura en redor de su industria bananera, una multitud de industrias para asegurar su autonomía absoluta y mantiene el control sobre el comercio . . . robando en sus comisariatos—tiendas de raya—el escaso salario que ha dado sus trabajadores." Montero, "La situación," 6.

82 "Toda lucha sindical en aquellos países tiene una base antiimperialista." Montero, "La situación," 8.

83 "Es el único escollo serio." Montero, "La situación," 7.

84 AAAIL to All Branches, January 25, 1929, RGASPI, f. 542, op. 1, d. 35.

85 "Centroamérica es un campo de intensa penetración imperialista, pero es también un amplio campo de posibilidades antiimperialistas." Montero, "La situación," 8.

86 "Destruir el prejuicio de razas y atraer hacia nosotros a los trabajadores negros buscando la confraternización en la lucha antiimperialista." Montero, "La situación," 8.

87 "La bandera de las emancipaciones nacionales y sociales, de la liberación de las razas y de las masas explotadas por el capitalismo y por el imperialismo universal." LADLA, "Henri," 3.

88 "Sandino no tiene fronteras"; "la conciencia sana y digna de América Latina"; "reclama la solidaridad de todos los oprimidos." LADLA, "Sandino no," 4; LADLA, "¡Manos," 2; LADLA, "4 de mayo," 3; Correa, "La tragedia," 10.

89 "La lucha de los nuevos Sandinos que surgirán en toda América"; "cada uno de sus pueblos cuenta con centenares de Sandinos que sabrán luchar y vencer contra el imperialismo"; PCM, "Un embajador," 3; PCM, "Hace," 1.

90 Melcher, "La solidaridad," 30; Cerdas Cruz, *Sandino*, 92–93; Jeifets and Jeifets, "La Comintern"; LADLA, "Venezuela comienza," 1.

91 "Cuando tarde o temprano los marinos yanquis desembarquen nuevamente en puerto mexicano, surgirá un Sandino mexicano. Los trabajadores de Nicaragua agrupados con los trabajadores de los demás países ayudarán entonces a México. Se trata, más que de una ayuda mutua, de una acción solidaria, de una lucha común." LADLA, "La semana," 2.

92 LADLA, "Actividades antiimperialistas," 8.

93 "¿Quién es Sandino?"; "Un minero. Un hijo del pueblo." Correa, "La tragedia," 10.

94 Jasper et al., "Character," 117.

95 Jasper et al., "Character," 118.

96 See the Hands Off China campaign of 1925–27, as well as the Hands Off Haiti campaign of 1925–29. Buchanan, *East Wind*, 30–43; Stevens, "'Hands.'" This slogan continues to be used in defense of countries threatened by foreign intervention and has also been used in the #MeToo movement and protests by Muslim women against the French ban on hijabs.

97 "Los marinos, reclutados en los sectores más degenerados y viciosos de los Estados Unidos, no saben lo que es el respeto a la vida humana." LADLA, "Carleton," 9.

98 Machado, "El terror," 6.

99 Aponte, "Desde," 4.

100 In his comparisons of the Nicaraguan context to the occupation of Haiti, Joseph Jolibois fils similarly wrote about human rights abuses by Marines in Haiti, especially focusing on the rape of Haitian women and girls. Jolibois, "La ocupación," 12.

101 LADLA, "La huelga," 11.

102 "La leyenda del bandolerismo"; "libertadores"; "odio de raza"; "cuando el pueblo oprimido se agita y protesta." Machado, "Con Sandino," 1; LADLA, "Barbusse," 18.

103 "No es el 'bandido' Sandino el autor de los actos de bandidaje en Haití de los que pueden responder en cambio los mismos marinos yanquis que operan en Nicaragua." LADLA, "Gran mitín," 12.

104 Edwards, Charisma, xvi.

105 Edwards, Charisma, 16, 19, 21.

106 Hardt and Negri, Assembly, 3–14.

107 "El problema del dirigente." Contreras, "El jefe," 5.

108 "El jefe en la lucha revolucionaria." Vidali was writing under the pseudonym Jorge Contreras. Jeifets and Jeifets, América Latina, 634–36.

109 "Es aquel que por actos de valor y para aprovechar una determinada situación de descontento general, se hace Jefe de un movimiento insurreccional."

110 "Mentalidad e ideología de pequeño burgués"; "No quiere destruir el sistema económico basado en la propiedad privada de los medios de producción, ni luchar por la completa emancipación de la clase de los explotados."

111 "La base del carácter anticaudillista de nuestra organización continental."

112 "Controlar la masa, convencido de que los que lo siguen es un ejército de ignorantes que debe ser controlado."

113 "El dirigente nuestro es controlado por las masas y en el momento mismo en el cual escapa a este control o se desvía del camino en que defiende los intereses de la clase trabajadora que representa, cesa de ser dirigente."

114 "Se han construido sobre la base de la organización de la masa explotada." Contreras, "El jefe," 5.

115 Edwards, Charisma, 20.

116 See, for example, Sandino, "Carta a los gobernantes," 143.

117 "La lucha en Nicaragua . . . se ha llevado a cabo no como una lucha nacional sino de una trascendencia continental e internacional, ya que han participado en ella luchadores de todos los países contra el imperialismo." LADLA, "Sandino en México," 2.

118 Macaulay, The Sandino, 49–52.

119 Macaulay, The Sandino, 53.

120 "Amigos espiritualistas." Sandino, "El regreso," 53; Carr, "Pioneering," 142.

121 Macaulay, The Sandino, 54–60.

122 Cerdas Cruz, Sandino, 57.

123 Sandino, "Manifiesto," 87.

124 Sandino, "Manifiesto," 87–89.

125 As Carr writes, "Sandino almost certainly absorbed elements of Vasconcelos' ideas during his time in Mexico in 1923 to 1926. . . . Vasconcelos' notion of the *Raza Cósmica* is well known but his book *Indología* (1926) has been neglected by scholars in spite of the fact that it was the first substantial essay in which Indoamerica was developed in Latin America. . . . Sandino used the terms 'indohispano' and 'indolatino' extensively from his earliest declarations in 1927." Carr, "Pioneering," 146–47.

126 Macaulay, *The Sandino*, 146.

127 Sandino, "Carta a Froylán Turcios," 148–50; Sandino, "Convenio," 150–52.

128 Turcios, "Carta," 156, emphasis in original.

129 Turcios, "Carta," 156–57.

130 Macaulay, *The Sandino*, 146; Sandino, "Carta al presidente de México," 161.

131 Sandino, "Carta a los gobernantes de América," 143; Sandino, "Carta al Presidente Hipólito," 169–72.

132 Sandino, "Carta al Presidente Hipólito," 170; translation from Macaulay, *The Sandino*, 147.

133 Sandino, "A Gustavo," 180.

134 Hurwitz, "Declaraciones," 2.

135 "Todos los gobiernos de América, agentes del imperialismo, a una conferencia en Buenos Aires para discutir si el capital que debe invertirse en la apertura del canal de Nicaragua debe ser todo o parte de banqueros estadounidenses."

136 "La guerra contra el invasor"; "trasladar su acción a otros campos de lucha contra el imperialismo, sin aceptar ningún compromiso que directa o indirectamente les propongan los invasores."

137 "La lucha contra el imperialismo no podemos concebirla circunscrita a un solo pedazo del territorio de América, ella es continental e internacional. Perdida una trinchera, hay que construir otra y una salida de Sandino y de los demás miembros del Ejército con el fin de engrosar las filas antimperialistas en cualquier otro lugar del continente, no sería una deserción."

138 "Agentes del imperialismo"; "una traición a las masas revolucionarias de la América y del mundo entero que han visto en él un representativo de la lucha que tarde o temprano tendrán todos los pueblos que llevan a cabo en defensa de su propia soberanía." LADLA, "La Liga Antimperialista y el General," 2.

139 LADLA, "La llegada de Sandino," 1.

140 "Fraternal saludo, por intermedio de la Liga Antimperialista de las Américas y del Comité Manos Fuera de Nicaragua, a los pueblos de América." LADLA, "El General," 1.

141 "Reestablecer las relaciones entre el Ejército y las organizaciones antimperialistas del Continente y del mundo." LADLA, "Sandino en México," 2.

142 For more details on Sandino's complaints against Machado, see Jeifets and Jeifets, "La Comintern." Machado failed to tell Sandino about his

departure from Mexico. Sandino had already expressed his positions in letters to Machado, meaning that Hurwitz's many questions serve as indirect evidence of Machado's lack of communication. Staklo, "Harnessing."

143 "Machado, el Comité Manos Fuera de Nicaragua y la 'Liga Antiimperialista de las Américas' no habían estado ociosos mientras él y el Ejército Libertador, defendían con las armas la soberanía del continente." LADLA, "Sandino en México," 2.

144 "Ilusión"; "perderá el General Sandino tan pronto como constate que el silencio a su carta al Presidente Yrigoyen y a los demás Presidentes de la América Latina, agentes serviles del imperialismo, tiene un fundamento político y económico y no es una descortesía 'diplomática." LADLA, "Sandino en México," 2.

145 Campos Ponce, *Los yanquis*, 104.

146 "Un grande y significativo homenaje a nuestros héroes nicaragüenses"; "el símbolo de todos los pueblos de los países coloniales y semicoloniales." LADLA, *Suplemento*, 2.

147 The same agenda circulated, for example, in the Peruvian magazine *Amauta*. "2do. Congreso Mundial Anti-imperialista," 94–97. For more on the controversy, see Petersson, *Willi*, 531–652.

148 Petersson, *Willi*, 607.

149 Petersson, *Willi*, 609–10.

150 Petersson, *Willi*, 617.

151 "Manifiesto," 92–97.

152 CPUSA, "Sandino," 1.

153 "Los pueblos de Latinoamérica como una unidad racial." LADLA, "Mensaje," 8.

154 "Existe en muchos pensadores de la América Latina . . . un concepto demasiado nacionalista . . . son tal vez los miembros de la LADLA los únicos que entienden que no hay que limitar la lucha a América Latina, sino que existe la imperiosa necesidad de unir, no solamente las fuerzas antimperialistas de nuestro Continente, sino a las de todo el mundo." LADLA, "El 2º. Congreso," 2.

155 "Information and Press Service No. 4," July 22, 1929, RGASPI, f. 542, op. 1, d. 87.

156 Petersson, *Willi*, 647.

157 Cerdas Cruz, *Sandino*, 66–67; Staklo, "Harnessing," 96.

158 This turn was largely due to the "assassination of president-elect Álvaro Obregón in July 1928. Though carried out by a Catholic extremist, it brought a surge in government pressure on the left." Wood, "Indoamerica," 85.

159 For example, J. Guadalupe Rodríguez Favela and Hipólito Landero. Peláez Ramos, "El fusilamiento."

160 CPUSA, "Gil," 1; Wood, "Indoamerica," 86.

161 CPUSA, "Suppress," 3; Smith, *The Power*, 42.

162 CPUSA, "Latin," 3; CPUSA, "Workers," 1.

163 Cerdas Cruz, *Sandino*, 102.

164 PCM, "Defensa," 2.

165 "Durante todo el acto se vendieron centenares de retratos y foto-botones del camarada Mella." PCM, "Velada," 1, 4.

166 PCM, "Defensa," 2; PCM, "Mitin," 4.

167 See, for example, the announcement of Mella's death in the Peruvian magazine *Amauta*. "Necrología," 96. See also the covers of the February 1929 *Labor Defender* and 1932 *Arbeiter-Illustrierte-Zeitung*, no. 3.

168 "En Mella mataron no sólo al enemigo de la dictadura de Cuba, sino al enemigo de todas las dictaduras . . . Machado, o sea la caricatura de Benito Mussolini, ha cometido un crimen más: pero hay muertos que hacen temblar y cuya muerte representa para los asesinos una amenaza igual o mayor que su vida de luchadores . . . Julio Antonio Mella asesinado por el Presidente de Cuba es ahora un símbolo de la lucha revolucionaria contra el imperialismo y contra sus agentes, y su nombre es una bandera. Él está en la lucha de los obreros y campesinos en todo el continente; está en la conciencia y en los movimientos de masas de los trabajadores; está entre los soldados que pelean junto a Sandino; está entre los huelguistas de Colombia ametrallados por el capital imperialista. En esta noche al cumplirse un mes del cobarde asesinato, nosotros honramos su memoria y prometemos seguir su camino hasta conseguir la victoria de todos los explotados del mundo, y así honramos su memoria en la forma que más le hubiera gustado: ¡no llorando sino luchando!" PCM, "La velada," 1.

169 "Canción de Julio Mella"; "¡No es el cuerpo el que vale, asesino! Es la acción poderosa, inmortal, que se llama IDEAL con Sandino, que con Mella se llama IDEAL"; emphasis in original. Lyrics for this song were written by Alfonso Sierra Madrigal with music by Luis G. Monzón. PCM, "Canción," 3.

170 Jasper et al., "Character," 124.

171 Jasper et al., "Character," 121.

172 Cerdas Cruz, *Sandino*, 105.

173 Cerdas Cruz, *Sandino*, 103.

174 Cerdas Cruz, *Sandino*, 107–8. See also "Erklärung," April 10, 1930, RGASPI, f. 542, o. 1, d. 39; "Erklärung," RGASPI, f. 542, o. 1, d. 46a. Although the LAI discussed the possibility of expelling Sandino, he remained on the LAI executive committee. "Auszug," January 13, 1930, RGASPI, f. 542, o. 1, d. 37.

175 Wood, "Indoamerica," 81. Wood quotes from "Resolución sobre el Comité Continental" in RGASPI, f. 495, o. 108, d. 102.

176 ANLC, "ANLC," 4; ANLC, "International," 4; ANLC, "Mass," 3; Stevens, *Red*, 114–15.

177 Schelchkov, "El marxismo," 226–47; Stevens, *Red*, 120.

178 Tina Modotti to Edward Weston, April 14, 1930, box 1, series 1, MC Papers.

179 "A todas," 100.

180 "Contra el terror, la reacción, y la traición en México." "Contra el terror," 94–95.

181 "La prisión," 97; "Protokoll," December 19, 1929, RGASPI, f. 542, o. 1, d. 39.

182 PCM members included Hernán Laborde, Enea Sormenti, and Gastón Lafarga. The Cuban Juan Ramón Brea attended as LADLA's delegate, and Carlos León, Federico Bach, and Rafael Ramos Pedrueza on behalf of MAFUENIC. EDSN members José Constantino González, Enrique Rivera Bertrand, Esteban Pavletich, and Agustín Farabundo Martí were also present. Jeifets and Jeifets, "La Comintern."

183 Jeifets and Jeifets, "La Comintern."

184 Jeifets and Jeifets, "La Comintern"; Staklo, "Harnessing," 123–25.

185 Staklo, "Harnessing," 125.

186 Staklo, "Harnessing," 127. The LAI was undergoing a major transition at this moment due to conflicts over the Frankfurt Congress. Petersson, *Willi*, 676.

187 Jeifets and Jeifets, "La Comintern."

188 Staklo, "Harnessing," 129.

189 "A todas las organizaciones revolucionarias antimperialistas"; "El gobierno sabe que Sandino, lejos de abandonar la lucha hace los mayores esfuerzos por reorganizar sus efectivos, y reanudar la ofensiva en Nicaragua." "A todas," 100.

190 For an example of a narrative that faults LADLA for abandoning Sandino, see Cerdas Cruz, *Sandino*.

191 Quoted in Cerdas Cruz, *Sandino*, 111.

192 Quoted in Cerdas Cruz, *Sandino*, 112.

7. REMEMBERING LADLA

1 Lyra, *Los otros*, 107.

2 Lyra, "Estefania," 38.

3 Lyra, "Estefania," 37.

4 Lyra, "Estefania," 39.

5 Lyra, *Los otros*, 110.

6 I follow up on the final chapter of Ericka Beckman's *Capital Fictions* (2013), which studies José Eustasio Rivera's *La vorágine* as exemplary of an interwar literary genre that responds to the previous literary generation's celebration of Latin America's commodity export economy by directly addressing "the exploitative and often murderous practices of extraction" within that economy, or what Beckman calls "the export real." Beckman, *Capital*, 159.

7 The *novela de la caña* is often used to refer to a group of Dominican novels: *Cañas y bueyes* (1936) by Eugenio Moscoso Puello, *Over* (1939) by Ramón Marrero Aristy, and Manuel Antonio Amiamo's *El terrateniente* (1970). De Sarlo, "The Sugar Plantation"; Graciano, *La novela de la caña*; Amiama et al., *La novela de la caña*. However, there are other Dominican sugarcane novels from the same period, such as *Jengibre* (1940) by Pedro Andrés Pérez Cabral and *Los enemigos de la tierra* (1936) by Andrés Francisco Requena, as well as multiple generations of sugarcane novels.

Interwar novels in the rest of Latin America that focus on the sugarcane industry include *A Bagaceira* (1928) by the Brazilian José Américo de Almeida; *La llamarada* (1935) and *Solar Montoya* (1941) by the Puerto Rican Enrique La Guerre; and the five novels in the Brazilian José Lins do Rego's "sugar cane cycle." *Marcos Antilla: Relatos de cañaveral* (1932) by the Cuban Luis Felipe Rodríguez is a collection of short stories but could also be considered within this genre. For a comparative study of sugarcane novels from Brazil and the Caribbean, see Carlotti-Smith, "A Field." See also Carlotti-Smith, "Sugar's"; Smith, "La Novela." For a comparison of *Over* and *La llamarada*, see Reyes-Santos, *Our Caribbean*.

8   Rodríguez, *Marcos*, 38.

9   LADLA–Costa Rica was created in early 1927. Its first actions included issuing a manifesto on the banana industry, urging the Costa Rican legislature to end contracts with United Fruit, and organizing a protest against the concession of the Nicaraguan canal. LADLA, "Secciones," 3. LADLA–Costa Rica joined a range of leftist constituencies and uniquely maintained a close relationship with APRA, through which Lyra entered the organization. Kersffeld, "La Liga Antiimperialista de Costa Rica," 109.

10 Kersffeld, "La Liga Antiimperialista de Costa Rica," 110–11.

11 Ching, "El Partido," 69.

12 Fallas Sibaja, *Mamita*, 6; Sharman, "Red," 141.

13 It is commonly referred to as *novela criolla*, *novela regional*, and *novela rural*. Alonso, *The Spanish*.

14 In a letter to Edward Weston, Modotti mentioned that in Berlin, she went to the home of "Professor G.," referring to Professor Alfons Goldschmidt, who was a "member of the International Antiimperialist League." Tina Modotti to Edward Weston, April 14, 1930, box 1, series 1, R-68, MC Papers. Goldschmidt was a German economics professor who had been the LAI's representative in Mexico City. Jeifets and Jeifets, *América Latina*, 257; Petersson, *Willi*, 345–47.

15 Schelchkov, "El marxismo"; Stevens, *Red*, 120.

16 After Junco's arrest, LAI leadership discussed moving LADLA's Continental Committee to either Montevideo or New York. It appears that a Continental Committee was attempted in Montevideo but that it never got off the ground. "Bericht," September 8, 1930, RGASPI, f. 542, o. 1, d. 37; "Besprechungen," August 21, 1930, RGASPI, f. 542, o. 1, d. 42; and Liga Fraktion to Berlin, April 24, 1930, and "Protokoll," December 19, 1929, both in RGASPI, f. 542, o. 1, d. 39.

17 Hatzky, *Julio*, 260–74.

18 For Rivera's ouster, see Smith, *The Power*, 44.

19 Staklo, "Harnessing," 58–60.

20 Pujals, "De un pájaro," 3.

21 Staklo, "Harnessing," 71.

22 Pujals, "De un pájaro," 3. According to Staklo, the BC's leadership was made up of an ECCI representative (who acted as secretary), a Profintern

representative, an International Communist Youth representative, and representatives from communist parties of Mexico, Cuba and the United States. Staklo, *Harnessing*, 72.

23 Pujals has made this argument as well, explaining that exiled activists in Mexico who were involved with LADLA were forced to move their Caribbean operations to New York due to government repression. Pujals, "De un pájaro," 4.

24 Many of these names are listed on the masthead of the BC's legally distributed periodical, *Mundo Obrero*. The Venezuelan Ricardo Arturo Martínez and the Puerto Rican Alberto E. Sánchez were also leading BC members. Pujals, "De un pájaro," 3–4. Alberto Moreau was a Greek immigrant in the United States named John Bell, who used several aliases. For details on Moreau's and Jorge Vivó's participation, see Jeifets and Jeifets, *América Latina*, 84–85, 641–42. For others involved, see RGASPI, f. 500, op. 1.

25 Buró, "Correspondencia," 19; Buró, *Mundo Obrero* 1, no. 3 (October 1931), back cover. The BC published two periodicals: *Mundo Obrero*, which was legally distributed, and *El Comunista*. RGASPI, f. 500, op. 1, d. 2

26 Ortega, "Este periodista."

27 Ayala, *American*.

28 Zumoff, "Ojos," 217.

29 Zumoff, "Ojos," 223.

30 "Un monopolio absoluto en la producción de bananas a través de todos los países del Caribe. Tiene grandes posesiones de tierra en Guatemala, Honduras, Costa Rica, Colombia, etc. Tiene una influencia tremenda en la vida política nacional de esos países mediante una larga cadena de maniobras políticas, la compra de mercenarios nativos y políticos y la utilización del Departamento de Estado de los Estados Unidos, Marina y Ejército, a fin de establecer firmemente el dominio del dólar." Palacios, "El aniversario," 12.

31 "En todo su feudo de Limón." Gómez, "Las próximas," 14.

32 Palacios, "El aniversario," 12.

33 "Solo el brazo fuerte de la solidaridad obrera y campesina bajo la dirección de la clase obrera, podrá derrocar el poder del imperialismo y sus lacayos."

34 Zumoff, "Black."

35 RGASPI, f. 500, op. 1, d. 4, 5, 9.

36 Pujals, "A 'Soviet,'" 261.

37 Pujals, "A 'Soviet,'" 262–63.

38 "Día de lucha antiimperialista"; "las masas oprimidas de América Latina." Buró, "Día," 5.

39 Gilmore, *Defying*, 22–24.

40 "Terror blanco." Vivaldi, "Se acentúa," 17.

41 "La dictadura de la United Fruit Company"; "no sólo posee y controla los gobiernos lacayos de muchos de los países del Caribe; sino que ejerce ELLA MISMA las funciones gubernamentales directamente, especialmente

en los casos de suprimir las luchas de los obreros y campesinos trabajadores que están empleados por dicha compañía"; emphasis in original.

42 "Son prácticamente campos armados"; "estas bandas armadas de la compañía emprenden el aplastamiento de las luchas con la mayor violencia y crímenes al por mayor, siempre con el apoyo de las fuerzas armadas de los gobiernos lacayos de estos países."

43 "La United Fruit Company sabe que hay siempre a mano barcos de guerra americanos y marinos 'para proteger' sus vidas y propiedades, siempre que sea necesario." Buró, "La dictadura," 5.

44 Sánchez, "Las luchas," 10.

45 "Salvemos a los obreros negros en Alabama."

46 "Hijos de obreros y campesinos, hijos de nuestra clase." Minor, "Salvemos," 21.

47 "Los manifiestos especiales para los indios y negros en sus propios idiomas son de gran importancia." RGASPI, f. 500, op. 1, d. 4.

48 "Organicemos los obreros azucareros en Cuba"; "las masas negras"; "semiproletarios." Simons, "Organicemos," 22, 17.

49 There are similar critiques of *Mundo Obrero* in Zumoff, "Black."

50 "Salvemos de la muerte a los nueve jóvenes negros de Scottsboro." Buró, "Salvemos," 2.

51 "El mismo imperialismo asesino que oprime a las masas latinoamericanas intenta llevar a cabo el linchamiento de los 7 jóvenes negros de Scottsboro." Buró, "Salvemos," 2.

52 Minor, "Salvemos," on the other hand, does mention the work of several US Black organizations.

53 Zumoff, "Ojos," 220. Communications between BC and PCCR are published in Ching, "El Partido."

54 "Enormes masas de trabajadores de color a la lucha"; "cualquier otro trabajador negro." Ching, "El Partido," 64.

55 Ching, "El Partido," 11; Zumoff, "Ojos," 222; Zumoff, "Black."

56 Pujals, "A 'Soviet.'"

57 My analysis of Marrero Aristy's *Over* is drawn from Mahler, "South-South."

58 Graciano, *La novela,* 57. Other sources report that he was born in 1914. Marrero Aristy, *Over,* 7.

59 Ayala, *American,* 106, 270; Graciano, *La novela,* 57.

60 Graciano, *La novela,* 57; Marrero Aristy, *Over,* 7–8.

61 Fallas Sibaja, *Mamita,* 6; Sharman, "Red," 139.

62 Baud, "'Un permanente.'" The second printing in 1963 would include a prologue by Trujillo's chief enemy, Juan Bosch. Graciano, *La novela,* 59.

63 Mateo, *Mito,* 83.

64 Baud, "'Un permanente,'" 183, 193. When Trujillo came to power in 1930, almost all the island's sugar mills were in foreign hands. Under the guise of a nationalist economy, he began seizing small sugar estates, eventually setting his sights on the larger mills under North American control. Within a decade, Trujillo controlled more than 75 percent of all sugar

mills in the country. Trujillo was able to maintain good relations with the US government even as he became its competitor since, due to the decline of sugar prices worldwide, US investors were eager to liquidate their assets. Graciano, *La novela*, 23.

65 Baud, "Un permanente," 184.

66 Graciano, *La novela*, 211.

67 Vega, *Un interludio*, 6–7.

68 Marrero Aristy, "La posición."

69 Vega, *Un interludio*, 31.

70 The reasons behind this shift in Trujillo's positions, which lasted a mere six months (June–November 1946), have been debated. However, generally it has been seen as a way for Trujillo to identify his enemies to later eliminate them and as an attempt to divide the exile community. It has also been described as a way to project an image of tolerance since the United States, in the wake of World War I, was on friendly terms with the Soviet Union and taking a harder, pro-democracy line with its authoritarian allies. Dominican communists reportedly believed that Trujillo's power was nearing its end and that organizing workers within the country would better position them to step into power once he fell. Juan Bosch, who led the social democratic Dominican Revolutionary Party, fiercely opposed these negotiations, writing several articles warning communists to tread lightly with Trujillo. Vega, *Un interludio*, 31.

71 Vega, *Un interludio*, 6–9, 13–17, 25–32, 47.

72 Vega, *Un interludio*, 34.

73 Vega, *Un interludio*, 34.

74 Marrero Aristy, "El Secretario."

75 As with many political assassinations during the Trujillato, the case of Marrero Aristy's death is shrouded in secrecy, and the reasons for his falling out of favor have been subject to multiple interpretations. Some point to this November 1957 incident with the Café Dominicano Company as the turning point; others suggest his assassination was the response to criticisms of the Trujillo government that Marrero Aristy shared with *New York Times* journalist Tad Szulc; yet others claim the writer was conspiring against Trujillo, establishing secret contacts with the exiled opposition in New York. Baud, "'Un permanente'"; Graciano, *La novela*, 58.

76 Baud, "'Un permanente,'" 184–87, 194.

77 Marrero Aristy, *Over*, 25.

78 Simons, "Organicemos," 17.

79 For example, Eugenio Moscoso Puello's *Cañas y bueyes* (1936) depicts the experience of small landowning *colonos* whose lands are appropriated by US companies. In Enrique Laguerre's *La llamarada* (1935), the protagonist, a descendant of small coffee farmers, becomes employed on a US sugar plantation as an agricultural engineer.

80 Sommer, "Populism," 262.

81   Marrero Aristy, *Over*, 62. Similarly, Danielle Smith reads the plantation in sugarcane novels as standing in "synecdochically for the region." Smith, "La Novela," 44.

82   Sommer, "Populism."

83   Armillas-Tiseyra, "Dislocations."

84   Marrero Aristy, *Over*, 27.

85   Marrero Aristy, *Over*, 24.

86   Marrero Aristy, *Over*, 27.

87   Marrero Aristy, *Over*, 167.

88   Marrero Aristy, *Over*, 64.

89   Marrero Aristy, *Over*, 56.

90   Marrero Aristy, *Over*, 50.

91   Alonso, *The Spanish*, 65.

92   For example, "¡Mi no hablando con gentes de tu tamaño!" ("Me not speaking with peoples of your size!"). Marrero Aristy, *Over*, 22.

93   Marrero Aristy, *Over*, 67.

94   Marrero Aristy, *Over*, 25.

95   Marrero Aristy, *Over*, 64.

96   Marrero Aristy, *Over*, 65.

97   Karl Marx describes the stages of production within his theory of history in *Grundrisse*. See Marx, *Marx's Grundrisse*.

98   Marrero Aristy, *Over*, 98.

99   Marrero Aristy, *Over*, 98–99.

100   Marrero Aristy, *Over*, 75.

101   Marrero Aristy, *Over*, 79.

102   Lyra, *Los otros*, 115.

103   Rodríguez, *Marcos*, 97.

104   Marrero Aristy, *Over*, 198, 189.

105   Marrero Aristy, *Over*, 41.

106   Marrero Aristy, *Over*, 49.

107   Lyra, *Los otros*, 109.

108   Rodríguez, *Marcos*, 88.

109   Rodríguez, *Marcos*, 113–44.

110   Fallas Sibaja, *Mamita*, 19–20.

111   Fallas Sibaja, *Mamita*, 14.

112   Sharman, "Red," 141.

113   Sharman, "Red," 137.

114   Zumoff, "Ojos," 215–16.

115   As Zumoff writes, "Banana production in Costa Rica peaked in 1913 when the country was the leading exporter of bananas in the world, it stabilized at lower levels from 1917 to 1929, and from 1929 to 1943 declined to almost nothing. West Indian migration mirrored the export of bananas; it peaked in 1913 and fell off sharply thereafter. From 1914 to 1917, more people left Costa Rica for Jamaica than made the reverse trip." Zumoff, "Ojos," 217.

116   Zumoff, "Ojos," 218.

117   Zumoff, "Ojos," 220.

118   Zumoff, "Ojos," 227.

119   Sharman, "Red," 137.

120   Sharman, "Red," 146.

121   Zumoff, "Ojos," 222–24. See also Zumoff, "Black."

122   Sharman, "Red," 141.

123   Marrero Aristy, *Over*, 107–8.

124   Marrero Aristy, *Over*, 175.

125   Marrero Aristy, *Over*, 89.

126   For more on anti-Haitianism and Dominican national identity, see San Miguel, *The Imagined*.

127   Baud, "'Un permanente,'" 202.

128   Sommer, "Populism," 258.

129   Sommer, "Populism," 263.

130   Marrero Aristy, *Over*, 62.

131   De Sarlo, "The Sugar," 180.

132   Sharman, "Red," 145.

133   Marrero Aristy, *Over*, 199.

134   In this sense, my reading of *Over* aligns with that of critic Berta Graciano, who describes Daniel as distancing himself from immigrant workers and as a victim of the dominant ideology that encourages maintaining the status quo for one's own interests. Graciano, *La novela*, 76, 83. I agree with this interpretation of the contradictions of the protagonist's life but take it further by considering how the novel comments on the broader political context of Comintern organizing in the region.

135   Norberto Pedro James—Dominican poet/scholar of West Indian origin— identifies the presence of "pesimismo dominicano" (Dominican pessimism) in two Dominican sugarcane novels, *Cañas y bueyes* (1936) by Eugenio Moscoso Puello and *Jengibre* (1940) by Pedro Andrés Pérez Cabral. The tradition of Dominican pessimism refers to the moderniza- tion theories of late nineteenth- and early twentieth-century figures like José Ramón López and Américo Lugo who—with some variation—used biological determinism to argue that Dominicans suffered from racial, climactic, and nutritional variables that prevented their moderniza- tion. Ramón López in particular argued that it was malnutrition (and not racial mixture, as others had maintained) that ailed the Dominican nation. Trujillismo would mobilize this intellectual tradition, along with anti-Haitianism, to defend the need for a strongman to lift the nation out of underdevelopment. James points to the ideological elements of Trujillismo—which he argues were hispanophilia, anti-Haitianism, and above all, Dominican pessimism—in the sugarcane novels that he exam- ines. James, "Un estudio," 52–59. One finds a similar tendency toward pes- simism in Marrero Aristy's *Over*. However, I would argue that this novel's pessimism is based not in fatalistic notions of biological determinism but rather in a political critique of nativism, classism, and racism. While

the novel may suggest that the protagonist's inaction derives from the influence of the tradition of Dominican pessimism over his perceptions of himself and his reality, I argue that *Over* does not uncritically reproduce this ideology and does not exactly fit the pattern traced by James.

EPILOGUE

1 Ashly, "The Canadian"; Bosmans, "No todo."

2 Rashotte, "World's."

3 The US company Rosario Mining found gold deposits there in the late 1960s. In 1979, the Dominican government purchased over half of the company, and the Rosario Dominicana state-run mine operated until 1999, when it was shut down due to mismanagement and financial difficulties. Bosmans, "No todo"; Gaine, "Fighting"; Plácido, "Blood," 140.

4 In 2001, the mine was purchased by the Canada-based Placer Dome America Holding Corporation and then sold to Barrick Gold in 2006. Currently, Barrick owns 60 percent of the mine, with 40 percent held by Denver-based Newmont Goldcorp. Bosmans, "No todo"; Gaine, "Fighting."

5 Residents cite a rapidly increasing death rate for both people and livestock, high levels of cyanide in community members' bloodstream, skin lesions caused by contact with cyanide-contaminated water, drastic decline in agricultural production (a primary source of income for these communities), and increase in cancer and respiratory issues. Ashly, "The Canadian"; Gaine, "Fighting"; Plácido, "Blood," 141. See also Open Letter.

6 Ashly, "The Canadian"; Bosmans, "No todo"; Reuters, "Civil"; Schalk, "Barrick."

7 Ashly, "The Canadian"; Open Letter; Plácido, "Blood," 141.

8 Bishara, "'Washing.'"

9 Kenney, "Coalition"; Strike, *Strike MoMA Reader*, 39.

10 Cisneros, "Biography."

11 Strike, "Water."

12 Bishara, "'Washing"; Strike, "Week 9."

13 Strike, *Strike MoMA Reader*, 27.

14 Strike, "Framework."

15 Strike, "Framework."

16 These include "Mella's Typewriter," "Workers' Parade," "Baby Nursing," and the images of Tehuanas analyzed in chapter 1. Although the description of Modotti in MoMA's catalogue briefly discusses her political organizing, only one of the thirty MoMA exhibits in which Modotti's work has been displayed over the last sixty years has had an explicitly political focus. MoMA, "Tina Modotti."

17 Featherstone, *Solidarity*, 6. Featherstone also writes, "Solidarities are use-fully thought of as transformative political relations. There are no guaran-tees about the kinds of transformations wrought by solidarities. They can entrench as well as challenge privilege and can close down as well as open up political possibilities and alliances." Featherstone, *Solidarity*, 16.

18 Lenin, *Imperialism*.

19 Patnaik and Patnaik, *A Theory*, 4.

20 Castells, "A Network."

21 Patnaik and Patnaik, *A Theory*, 4.

22 Hardt and Negri, *Empire*; Veltmeyer and Petras, *The New*, 8.

23 Smith, *Imperialism*.

24 Veltmeyer and Petras, *The New*, 10.

25 Its international renown included an open letter signed by eighty-eight organizations from twenty-one countries that expressed concern over the proposed expansion. Open Letter; Bosmans, "No todo."

26 N Digital, "Diputados."

27 Torres García, "Barrick."

28 "Para ser efectiva, tiene que hacerse internacional." LADLA, "Los obre-ros," 6.

29 NYU, "Negative."

30 Veltmeyer and Petras, *The New*, 18.

31 Acevedo-Yates, "Carolina."

32 Icaza Giraldo, "La protesta."

33 Verónica Gago describes the "body-territory" as "a concept elaborated by different compañeras from Central America to name the anti-extractivist struggles that begin with women's resistance—especially those of Indig-enous, Black, and Afro-descendant women, along with various feminist collectives." Gago, *Feminist*, 6–7. For a visualization of this concept, see "Cuerpo-Territorio" graphic created by Buenos Aires–based art collec-tive Iconoclasistas: https://iconoclasistas.net/portfolio-item/salud-y -extractivismo-2021/.

34 Crespo Rubio, "Mujeres."

35 Carlsen, "The Defense." For the report, see Chávez Ixcaquic et al., "Las mujeres."

36 Acosta, "Living," 101.

BIBLIOGRAPHY

ARCHIVES

AIHC (Archivo del Instituto de Historia de Cuba). Fondo Primer Partido Comunista de Cuba y Julio A. Mella. Havana.

BDW Papers (Bertram David Wolfe Papers). Manuscripts and Archives Division, New York Public Library, New York.

BW Papers (Bertram Wolfe Papers). Hoover Institution Library and Archives, Palo Alto.

CS Papers (Charles Shipman Papers). Hoover Institution Library and Archives, Palo Alto.

Hemeroteca. Biblioteca Nacional de Cuba José Martí, Havana.

LAI Archive (League Against Imperialism Archive). International Institute of Social History, Amsterdam. https://search.iisg.amsterdam/Record /ARCH00804.

MC Papers (Mildred Constantine Research Papers Regarding Tina Modotti). Getty Research Institute, Los Angeles.

RGASPI (Russian State Archive of Socio-Political History), Moscow. Fonds 500 and 542 in https://sovdoc.rusarchives.ru/. Fonds 495, 515, 534, and 542 in Relación de documentos sobre México en el Centro Ruso, Biblioteca Manuel Orozco y Berra, Mexico City.

GOVERNMENT DOCUMENTS

FBI (Federal Bureau of Investigation). "All American Anti Imperialist League." Section 552, b7c. Accessed June 25, 2021. https://vault.fbi.gov/All%20 American%20Anti%20Imperialist%20League%20/All%20American%20 Anti%20Imperialist%20League%20Part%201%20of%201/view.

INS (Immigration and Naturalization Service). Passenger Lists of Vessels Arriving at San Juan, Puerto Rico, 10/07/1901–06/30/1948. RG 85, NAI 2945834, National Archives and Records Administration, Washington, DC.

James Sager, death certificate, July 18, 1979. Texas Department of State Health Services. Texas Death Certificates, 1903–1982. Austin, Texas.

James Sager, registration card. World War II Draft Registration Cards for Texas, 10/16/1940–03/31/1947. Records of the Selective Service System, 147, box 1318. National Archives. St. Louis, Missouri.

Jesús Junco Roldán, acta de defunción. June 1, 1987. Registro Civil. Acta de Defunción, 1861–1987. Mexico City.

Sandalio Junco Junco, travel visa, May 14, 1926. Department of Justice, Immigration and Naturalization Service. "Index to Alien Arrivals by Airplane, 1930–1942." Records of the Immigration and Naturalization Service, RG 85, National Archives and Records Administration, Washington, DC.

United States Congress House Special Committee on Communist Activities in the United States. *Investigation of Communist Propaganda: Hearings Before a Special Committee to Investigate Communist Activities in the United States of the House of Representatives, Seventy-First Congress, Second Session, Pursuant to H. Res. 220, Providing for an Investigation of Communist Propaganda in the United States.* U.S. Government Printing Office, 1930.

RARE NEWSPAPERS AND MAGAZINES

"1er. Congreso Sindical Latinoamericano." *Amauta* 18 (October 1928): 96–97.

"2do. Congreso Mundial Anti-imperialista." *Amauta* 23 (May 1929): 94–97.

Alexander, Charles. "Negro Workers Starving in Cuba." *Negro Worker* 1, nos. 10–11 (October–November 1931): 19.

ANLC (American Negro Labor Congress). "ANLC Demands Mexico Free Sandalio Junco." *The Liberator* 1, no. 34 (December 7, 1929): 4.

ANLC. "International Arena." *The Liberator* 1, no. 35 (December 14, 1929): 4

ANLC. "Mass Protest Saves Lives of Junco and Other Leaders." *The Liberator* 1, no. 39 (January 11, 1930): 3.

Aponte, Carlos. "Desde el campamento de Sandino." *El Libertador* 2, no. 20 (November 1928): 4.

"A todas las organizaciones revolucionarias antiimperialistas." *Amauta* 30 (April–May 1930): 100.

Bach, Federico "Bei dem Rebellengeneral Sandino." *Arbeiter-Illustrierte-Zeitung* (October–November 1928). Records of the United States Marine Corps, RG 127, entry 38, box 30, National Archives and Records Administration. Published in Michael Schroeder, *The Sandino Rebellion Nicaragua 1927–34.* Accessed June 22, 2021. http://www.sandinorebellion.com/Top100pgs /Top100-p20b.html.

Buró del Caribe de la Internacional Comunista. "Correspondencia obrera y campesina." *Mundo Obrero* 1, no. 2 (September 1, 1931): 19.

Buró del Caribe de la Internacional Comunista. "Día de lucha antiimperialista." *Mundo Obrero* 1, no. 1 (August 1931): 5.

Buró del Caribe de la Internacional Comunista. "La dictadura de la United Fruit Company." *Mundo Obrero* 2, no. 9 (April 1932): 5.

Buró del Caribe de la Internacional Comunista. *Mundo Obrero* 1, no. 3 (October 1931): back cover.

Buró del Caribe de la Internacional Comunista. "Propósitos de 'Mundo Obrero.'" *Mundo Obrero* 1, no. 1 (August 1931): 3–4.

Buró del Caribe de la Internacional Comunista. "Salvemos de la muerte
a los nueve jovenes negros de Scottsboro." *Mundo Obrero* 2, no. 9
(April 1932): 2.

Carrillo, Rafael. "El imperialismo y el campesino." *El Libertador* 1, no. 3
(June 1925): 9–10.

Castellanos, Dr. Martín. "Algo sobre la cuestión negra." *Masas* 1, no. 1
(May 1934): 7.

"Contra el terror, la reacción, y la traición en México." *Amauta* 29 (February–
March 1930): 94–95.

Contreras, Jorge. "El jefe en la lucha revolucionaria." *El Libertador* 2, no. 20
(May 1929): 5.

Correa, Rafael. "La tragedia de Nicaragua." *El Libertador* 2, no. 15 (February 1928): 10.

CPUSA (Communist Party of the United States of America). "Gil Starts New
Terror Against Mexico Workers, Raid Communist Party, Suppress Central Organ." *Daily Worker* 6, no. 81 (June 11, 1929): 1.

CPUSA. "Latin Workers Denounce Gil, Hail Venezuelans Who Are Opposed by
U.S." *Daily Worker* 6, no. 98 (July 1, 1929): 3.

CPUSA. "Sandino on Way to World Anti-Imperial Meet, Fighter Against Wall
St. to Attend Paris Congress July 20, Temporarily in Mexico." *Daily
Worker* 6, no. 100 (July 3, 1929): 1.

CPUSA. "Suppress 'El Machete' and Jail Editors." *Daily Worker* 6, no. 151 (August 31, 1929): 3.

CPUSA. "Try to Expel Red Mexican Deputy." *Daily Worker* 6, no. 24 (April 3,
1929): 1.

CPUSA. "Workers Score Mexican Terror in Anti-Imperialist Communist Protest." *Daily Worker* 6, no. 164 (September 16, 1929): 1.

CSLA (Confederación Sindical Latinoamericana). "Crónica sintética del
Congreso Sindical Latino Americano, efectuado en Montevideo del 18 al
26 de May de 1929." *El Trabajador Latinoamericano* 2, nos. 17–18 (June–
July 1929): 51.

CSLA. "Cuba: Atropello contra los delegados de las organizaciones obreras
que asistieron a la Conferencia Sindical Latino Americana realizada en
Moscú." *El Trabajador Latinoamericano* 1, no. 1 (September 15, 1928): 13.

CSLA. "Hacia el Congreso de Montevideo." *El Trabajador Latinoamericano* 1,
no. 1 (September 15, 1928): 6–11.

CSLA. "Informe de la Comisión de Poderes: Composición del congreso, fuerzas
representadas, etc." *El Trabajador Latinoamericano* 2, nos. 17–18 (June–
July 1929): 38–39.

CSLA. "Preparando el Congreso: Carta abierta a todas las organizaciones que
participarán en el Congreso de Montevideo." *El Trabajador Latinoamericano* 2, nos. 10–11 (January 31, 1929–February 15, 1929): 31–32.

"Declaración del Grupo Minorista." *América Libre* 1, no. 3 (June 1927): 5, 12.

De la Plaza, Salvador. "La situación continental." *El Libertador* 2, no. 18
(June 1928): 5.

Dramundo, Baltasar. "La exposición fotográfica de Tina Modotti." *Acción Social*, 1929. Box 2, series 8, Mildred Constantine Papers Regarding Tina Modotti. Getty Research Institute, Los Angeles.

Ford, J. W. "The Rising Revolt in Cuba: Some Tasks for U.S. Workers." *Daily Worker*, April 17, 1930.

Gómez, R. "Las próximas elecciones en Costa Rica." *Mundo Obrero* 1, no. 2 (September 1931): 14.

"Gonfalón." *América Libre* 1, no. 1 (April 1927): 1.

Gremio de Panadores and the Unión de Dulceros y Pasteleros. *El Productor* 1, no. 2 (January 10, 1923): 1.

Haya de la Torre, Víctor Raúl. "Hispanoamericanismos literarios." *El Libertador* 1, no. 4 (July 1925): 16.

Haya de la Torre, Víctor Raúl. "Qué es el APRA?" *Labour Monthly: A Magazine of International Labour* 8 (December 1926): 756–59.

Hurwitz, Jacobo. "Boletín del Comité 'Manos Fuera de Nicaragua.'" *El Machete* 3, no. 102 (February 18, 1928): 1.

Hurwitz, Jacobo. "Como derriba Sandino a los aviones yanquis." *El Machete* 4, no. 112 (May 1, 1928): 1.

Hurwitz, Jacobo. "Declaraciones de Mafuenic." *El Libertador* 2, no. 20 (May 1929): 2.

Hurwitz, Jacobo. "Informe de MAFUENIC." *El Libertador* 2, no. 17 (April 1928): 11, 16.

Hurwitz, Jacobo. "Informe de Mafuenic." *El Libertador* 2, no. 18 (June 1928): 8.

"Inicio de los trabajos de la Liga-Antiimperialista de Cuba—Su manifiesto-programa y sus estatutos." *Masas* 1, no. 5 (September 1934): 15.

Jolibois, Joseph, fils. "La ocupación de Haití." *El Libertador* 2, no. 15 (February 1928): 12.

Junco, Sandalio. "Abajo la demagogía." *El Obrero Panadero* 21 (December 1933): 8–9.

Junco, Sandalio. "El proletariado negro de la América Latina y la Conferencia de Londres." *El Trabajador Latinoamericano* 2, nos. 32–33 (July 1930): 23–26.

"La cuestión negra sobre su tapete." *Masas* 1, no. 5 (September 1934): 4.

LADLA (Liga Antimperialista de las Américas). "4 de Mayo." *El Libertador* 2, no. 17 (April 1928): 3.

LADLA. "Actividades antimperialistas." *El Libertador* 2, no. 20 (November 1928): 8.

LADLA. "Actividades de Mafuenic, gran mitín en Veracruz." *El Libertador* 2, no. 19 (August 1928): 5.

LADLA. "Barbusse en el Congreso de Bruselas." *El Libertador* 2, no. 12 (June 1927): 18.

LADLA. "Carleton Beals con Sandino." *El Libertador* 2, no. 17 (April 1928): 9.

LADLA. "Comité Central ¡Manos Fuera de Nicaragua! Actividades y propósitos." *El Libertador* 2, no. 15 (February 1928): 2–3.

LADLA. "Comité Continental." *El Libertador* 2, no. 15 (February 1928): 5.

LADLA. "Crónica de El Libertador." *El Libertador* 2, no. 15 (February 1928): inside cover.

LADLA. "Desde el campamento de Sandino." *El Libertador* 2, no. 17 (April 1928): 5.

LADLA. "Diez mil pesos para Sandino." *El Libertador* 2, no. 18 (June 1928): 3.

LADLA. "El 2º. Congreso Mundial Antimperialista." *El Libertador* 2, no. 22 (July 1929): 2.

LADLA. "El Congreso Antimperialista de Bruselas." *El Libertador* 2, no. 12 (June 1927): 3–4.

LADLA. "El Congreso Sindical de Montevideo." *El Libertador* 2, no. 22 (July 1929): 5, 8.

LADLA. "El frente único de la lucha por la emancipación de los pueblos oprimidos." *El Libertador* 2, no. 12 (June 1927): 9.

LADLA. "El General Sandino llega a México, dirige un saludo a los pueblos de América." *El Libertador* 2, no. 22 (July 1929): 1.

LADLA. "El Libertador no vive . . ." *El Libertador* 2, no. 15 (February 1928): 16.

LADLA. *El Libertador* suplemento 2, no. 21 (May 1929).

LADLA. "El peligro; las posibilidades; el propósito." *El Libertador* 1, no. 1 (March 1925): 1–2.

LADLA. "Entrega de la bandera norteamericana enviada por el General Sandino al CC 'Manos Fuera de Nicaragua.'" *El Libertador* 2, no. 20 (November 1928): 1.

LADLA. "Gracias a." *El Libertador* 2, no. 15 (February 1928): 17.

LADLA. "Gran mitín en el Teatro Fábregas." *El Libertador* 2, no. 17 (April 1928): 12.

LADLA. "Henri Barbusse al General Sandino." *El Libertador* 2, no. 20 (November 1928): 3.

LADLA. "Impiden la circulación de timbres pro Nicaragua." *El Libertador* 3, no. 101 (February 11, 1928): 1.

LADLA. "La Conferencia Antimperialista de Caribe." *El Libertador* 2, no. 20 (November 1928): 2.

LADLA. "La huelga de Colorado." *El Libertador* 2, no. 15 (February 1928): 11.

LADLA. "La Liga Anti-imperialista en Cuba." *El Libertador* 1, no. 4 (July 1925): 6.

LADLA. "La Liga Antimperialista y el General Sandino." *El Libertador* 2, no. 20 (May 1929): 2.

LADLA. "La llegada de Sandino a Veracruz." *El Libertador* 2, no. 22 (July 1929): 1.

LADLA. "Lamine Senghor." *El Libertador* 2, no. 15 (February 1928): 9.

LADLA. "La Semana Sandino." *El Libertador* 2, no. 19 (August 1928): 2.

LADLA. "Las resoluciones sobre América Latina." *El Libertador* 2, no. 12 (June 1927): 10–11.

LADLA. "Liga Internacional Contra el Imperialismo y Por la Independencia Nacional: Párrafos del informe de la delegación de la Liga Antimperialista de las Américas a la Conferencia del Consejo General Celebrada en Bruselas en los días 9, 10, 11 de Dic. de 1927." *El Libertador* 2, no. 15 (February 1928): 4–5.

LADLA. "Los obreros de Tampico llevan la delantera en la lucha con el capital petrolero." *El Libertador* 1, no. 2 (May 1925): 6.

LADLA. "Magno mitín en México." *El Libertador* 2, no. 19 (August 1928): 6.

LADLA. "Manifiesto a los pueblos de América—La Liga Antimperialista de las Américas y el Próximo Congreso Panamericano de la Habana." *El Libertador* 2, no. 14 (January 1928): 8–9.

LADLA. "Manifiesto de la Liga Anti-Imperialista de Cuba Contra el Imperialismo. Por la justicia social." *El Libertador* 1, no. 5 (August 1925): 9.

LADLA. "Manifiesto del Comité Continental de la LADLA, al pueblo costarricense, a los pueblos de América." *El Libertador* 2, no. 20 (May 1929): 9.

LADLA. "Manifiesto del Congreso Antimperialista de Bruselas." *El Libertador* 2, no. 12 (June 1, 1927): 6.

LADLA. "¡Manos Fuera de Nicaragua!" *El Libertador* 2, no. 15 (February 1928): 2.

LADLA. "Mensaje del General Sandino al 2°. Congreso Mundial." *El Libertador* 2, no. 22 (July 1929): 8.

LADLA. "Nuevas secciones de la Liga Uruguay y Ecuador." *El Libertador* 2, no. 18 (June 1928): 2.

LADLA. "Resolución sobre la raza negra." *El Libertador* 2, no. 12 (June 1927): 13–14.

LADLA. "Resolución sobre organización: Aprobado unánimemente en el Congreso de Bruselas por todas las representaciones." *El Libertador* 2, no. 13 (August 1927): 12.

LADLA. "Saludo y felicitación." *El Libertador* 2, no. 19 (August 1928): 7.

LADLA. "Sandino en México." *El Libertador* 2, no. 22 (July 1929): 2.

LADLA. "Sandino no tiene fronteras." *El Libertador* 2, no. 20 (November 1928): 4.

LADLA. "Secciones de la Liga." *El Libertador* 2, no. 20 (May 1929): 3.

LADLA. "Última resolución del Comité Internacional Ejecutivo sobre la América Latina." *El Libertador* 2, no. 13 (August 1927): 12.

LADLA. "Una muralla gigantesca de traición y vergüenza." *El Libertador* 2, no. 19 (August 1928): 3.

LADLA. "Una traición de Nicaragua." *El Libertador* 2, no. 14 (January 1928): 6.

LADLA. "Un Congreso Anti-Imperialista Continental." *El Libertador* 1, no. 2 (May 1925): 3.

LADLA. "Vasconcelos y nosotros." *El Libertador* 2, no. 15 (February 1928): 8–9.

LADLA. "Venezuela." *El Libertador* 2, no. 20 (November 1928): 2.

LADLA. "Venezuela comienza la lucha antimperialista." *El Libertador* 2, no. 22 (July 1929): 1.

"La prisión de Esteban Pauletich [sic] en México y La Liga Antiimperialista en las Américas." *Amauta*, April–May 1930, 97.

Machado, Gustavo. "Con Sandino en las montañas de Nicaragua." *El Libertador* 2, no. 19 (August 1928): 1.

Machado, Gustavo. "El terror yanqui en Nicaragua." *El Libertador* 2, no. 18 (June 1928): 6.

Machado, Gustavo. "La situación de Honduras." *El Libertador* 2, no. 17 (April 1928): 7.

"Manifiesto del II Congreso Mundial de la Liga Antiimperialista." *Amauta* 27 (November–December 1929): 92–97.

Mariátegui, José Carlos. "Una carta de Mariátegui." *La Correspondencia Suda-mericana* 29 (August 15, 1927): 23.

Marrero Aristy, Ramón. "El Secretario de Trabajo denuncia explotación de los cafetaleros por companía monopolista." *La Nación*, November 17, 1957.

Marrero Aristy, Ramón. "La posición del trabajador." *Boletín del Archivo General de la Nación* 30, no. 113 (September–December 2005): 623–59.

Mella, Julio Antonio. "De Cuba: Machado, el Mussolini tropical, intenta la esta-bilización de su régimen." *El Libertador* 2, no. 20 (November 1928): 6.

Mella, Julio Antonio. "Hacia la Internacional Americana." *Venezuela Libre* 4, nos. 14–18 (September–December 1925): 7, 15.

Mella, Julio Antonio. "Carta de Julio A. Mella." *El Libertador* 1, no. 2 (May 1925): 8.

Minor, Robert. "Salvemos a los obreros negros en Alabama." *Mundo Obrero* 1, no. 2 (September 1931): 20–21.

Modotti, Tina. "La contrarrevolución mexicana." *Amauta* 29 (February–March 1930): 94.

Modotti, Tina. "On Photography." *Mexican Folkways* 5, no. 4 (October–December 1929): 196–98.

Montero, A. "El terror en Santo Domingo contra el naciente movimiento revo-lucionario." *Mundo Obrero* 1, no. 4 (November 1931): 8, 17.

Montero, Marco A. "La situación antimperialista en Centro América." *El Liber-tador* 2, no. 20 (May 1929): 6–8.

Moreau, Albert. "Imperialism's Killers at Work." *Labor Defender* 5, no. 1 (January 1930).

"Necrología." *Amauta* 20 (January 1929): 96.

Palacios, R. "El aniversario de la gran huelga bananera en Colombia." *Mundo Obrero* 1, no. 5 (December 1931): 12.

PCM (Partido Comunista Mexicano). "Actividades del Comité 'Manos Fuera de Nicaragua.'" *El Machete* 4, no. 108 (March 31, 1928): 1.

PCM. "A la prensa y a las organizaciones del continente americano Boletín del Comité 'Manos Fuera de Nicaragua.'" *El Machete* 3, no. 103 (February 25, 1928): 1.

PCM. "Al margen de la V. Conferencia del Partido Comunista de México, los comunistas y la lucha antimperialista." *El Machete* 4, no. 122 (July 7, 1928): 2.

PCM. "Aumenta la colecta nacional pro-Nicaragua." *El Machete* 3, no. 104 (March 3, 1928): 1.

PCM. "Canción de Julio Mella." *El Machete* 4, no. 149 (January 26. 1929): 3.

PCM. "¡Contra el terror fascista!" *El Machete* 4, no. 114 (May 12, 1928): 1.

PCM. "Contra la hipocresía de Coolidge mitin de la Liga contra el imperialismo en París." *El Machete* 3, no. 98 (January 21, 1928): 1.

PCM. "Defensa de las víctimas de la reacción y del imperialismo." *El Machete* 6, no. 149 (January 26, 1929): 2.

PCM. "Defensa de las víctimas de la reacción y del imperialismo." *El Machete* 4, no. 151 (February 9, 1929): 2.

PCM. "El hermano de Sandino y el padre de un marino muerto en Nicaragua se abrazarán públicamente en Nueva York." *El Machete* 3, no. 98 (January 21, 1928): 1.

PCM. "El sábado 7 llegan a la capital Gustavo Machado y Sócrates Sandino." *El Machete* 4, no. 122 (July 7, 1928): 1.

PCM. "Gran mitin del Comité 'Manos Fuera de Nicaragua' en Veracruz." *El Machete* 4, no. 114 (May 12, 1928): 1.

PCM. "Gran mitin de Frente Único en Veracruz, lo organizó el Comité 'Manos Fuera de Nicaragua.'" *El Machete* 4, no. 122 (July 7, 1928): 1.

PCM. "Hace un año que Sandino ofrece a la América Latina el ejemplo de su heroica lucha militar." *El Machete* 4, no. 113 (May 5, 1928): 1.

PCM. "Internacionales." *El Machete* 3, no. 97 (January 4, 1928): 2.

PCM. "La ruptura de relaciones con el gobierno de Mussolini fue pedido en el mitin de la Liga Internacional AntiFascista." *El Machete* 4, no. 138 (November 7, 1928): 8.

PCM. "La semana." *El Machete* 4, no. 122 (July 7, 1928): 1.

PCM. "La velada por el Camarada Mella." *El Machete* 4, no. 152 (February 16, 1929): 1.

PCM. "Los partes de guerra de Augusto C. Sandino." *El Machete* 3, no. 102 (February 18, 1928): 1.

PCM. "Mitin por Mella en Veracruz." *El Machete* 4, no. 150 (February 2, 1929): 4.

PCM. "Sábado 11 y Domingo 12, colecta a favor de los heridos de Nicaragua." *El Machete* 3, no. 101 (February 11, 1928): 1.

PCM. "Sandino es el único representante del pueblo de Nicaragua." *El Machete* 4, no. 149 (January 26, 1929): 1.

PCM. "Un embajador de Sandino." *El Machete* 4, no. 122 (July 7, 1928): 3.

PCM. "Velada en memoria de Mella." *El Machete* 4, no. 150 (February 2, 1929): 1, 4.

Pedroso, Regino. "Fraternal Greetings to the Factory." Translated by Langston Hughes. *New Masses* 6, no. 3 (August 1930): 10.

Pedroso, Regino. "Hermano negro." *Masas* 2, no. 7 (January 10, 1935): 19.

Pedroso, Regino. "Zafra-1934." *Masas* 1, no. 2 (June 1934): 14–15.

Penichet, A. "Surgió nuestro esperado poeta proletario: 'Nosotros' de Regino Pedroso." *Cultura proletaria* 1, no. 2 (February 1933): 3–5.

"Proyecto de estatutos de la Confederación Sindical Latinoamericana." *Amauta* 19 (November–December 1928): 98–100.

Rivera, Diego. "La unión proletaria continental." *América Libre* 1, no. 4 (July 1927): 7.

Ruis, León S. "Actividades antimperialistas—Estados Unidos." *El Libertador* 2, no. 19 (August 1928): 4.

Sánchez, Alberto. "Las luchas de los obreros mexicanos al norte del Rio Grande." *Mundo Obrero* 2, no. 7 (February 1932): 10.

Simons, William. "Organicemos los obreros azucareros en Cuba." *Mundo Obrero* 1, no. 5 (December 1931): 16–17, 22.

Socialist Workers Party. "Stalinists Assassinate Labor Leader in Cuba." *The Militant* (June 20, 1942): 1.

SSA (Secretariado Sudamericano de la Internacional Comunista). "Declaración del Grupo de Izquierda de la Liga Anti-Imperialista." *La Correspondencia Sudamericana* 28 (July 31, 1927): 7–8.

SSA. "Problema de las razas." *La Correspondencia Sudamericana* 15 (August 1929): 25–29.

Toor, Frances. "Exposición de fotografías." *Mexican Folkways* 5, no. 4 (October–December 1929): 192–94.

"Unidad Antimperialista." *Amauta* 13 (1928): 16.

Vasconcelos, José. 1925. "Saludo cordial." *El Libertador* 1, no. 2 (May 1925): 2.

Vivaldi, León. "Se acentúa el terror contra el movimiento revolucionario en el Caribe." *Mundo Obrero* 2, no. 9 (April 1932): 17.

Wolfe, Bertram D. (Audifaz). "Apreciaciones falsas y correctas del problema indígena." *El Libertador* 1, no. 5 (August 1925): 3–4.

Wolfe, Bertram D. (Audifaz). "El indio como base de la lucha anti-imperialista." *El Libertador* 1, no. 4 (July 1925): 3–4.

Wolfe, Bertram D. (Audifaz). "¿Qué es el imperialismo financiero?" *El Libertador* 1, no. 3 (June 1925): 5.

SECONDARY AND OTHER PUBLISHED PRIMARY SOURCES

Acevedo-Yates, Carla. "Carolina Caycedo: From the Bottom of the River." Museum of Contemporary Art Chicago Exhibition Tour, 2021. https://www.youtube.com/watch?v=Cf9A6yD-oxI.

Acosta, Abraham. *Thresholds of Illiteracy: Theory, Latin America, and the Crisis of Resistance.* New York: Fordham University Press, 2014.

Acosta, Alberto. "Extractivism and Neoextractivism: Two Sides of the Same Curse." In *Beyond Development: Alternative Visions from Latin America*, edited by Miriam Lang and Dunia Mokrani, 61–86. Amsterdam: Transnational Institute: Fundación Rosa Luxemburg, 2013.

Acosta, Alberto. "Living Well from an Ecuadorian Perspective: Philosophies Without Philosophers, Actions Without Theories." In *Reframing Latin American Development*, edited by Ronaldo Munck and Raúl Delgado Wise, 99–122. New York: Routledge, 2018.

Addington, Catherine. "'A todos mis compañeros de hoy': Un acercamiento bibliográfico a *Nosotros* (1933) de Regino Pedroso." Unpublished term paper for "The Black Radical Tradition in Latin America," taught by Professor Anne Garland Mahler at the University of Virginia. Fall 2018.

Adi, Hakim. "The Negro Question: The Communist International and Black Liberation in the Interwar Years." In *From Toussaint to Tupac: The Black International Since the Age of Revolution*, edited by Michael O. West, William G. Martin, and Fanon Che Wilkins, 155–75. Chapel Hill: University of North Carolina Press, 2009.

Adi, Hakim. *Pan-Africanism and Communism: The Communist International, Africa and the Diaspora, 1919–1939*. Trenton, NJ: Africa World Press, 2013.

Adorno, Rolena. "Reconsidering Colonial Discourse for Sixteenth- and Seventeenth-Century Spanish America." *Latin American Research Review* 28, no. 3 (1993): 135–45.

Aguchar, Hugo, and Blanca Luz Brum. *Falsas memorias, Blanca Luz Brum*. Montevideo: Trilce, 2001.

Ahmad, Aijaz. *In Theory: Nations, Classes, Literatures*. London: Verso Books, 2008.

Alexander, Robert J. *A History of Organized Labor in Cuba*. Westport, CT: Praeger, 2002.

Alexander, Robert J. *International Trotskyism, 1929–1985: A Documented Analysis of the Movement*. Durham, NC: Duke University Press, 1991.

Alexander, Robert J. *Trotskyism in Latin America*. Stanford, CA: Hoover Institution Publications, 1973.

Alonso, Carlos. *The Spanish American Regional Novel*. Cambridge: Cambridge University Press, 1990.

Amiama, Manuel Antonio, Ramón Marrero Aristy, and F. E. Moscoso Puello. *La novela de la caña*. Santo Domingo: Editora de Santo Domingo, 1981.

Arias de la Canal, Fredo, ed. *Antología de la poesía cósmica de Regino Pedroso*. Mexico City: Frente de Afirmación Hispanista, 2004.

Armillas-Tiseyra, Magalí. *The Dictator Novel: Writers and Politics in the Global South*. Evanston, IL: Northwestern University Press, 2019.

Armillas-Tiseyra, Magalí, ed. "Dislocations." Special issue, *Global South* 7, no. 2 (Fall 2014): 1–10.

Armillas-Tiseyra, Magalí, and Anne Garland Mahler. "Introduction: New Critical Directions in Global South Studies." *Comparative Literature Studies* 58, no. 3 (2021): 465–84.

Armstrong, Carol. "This Photography Which Is Not One: In the Gray Zone with Tina Modotti." *October* 101 (Summer 2002): 19–52.

Ashly, Jaclynn. "The Canadian Mining Company Dominicans Call 'Worse than Columbus.'" *Jacobin*, July 8, 2021. https://jacobin.com/2021/07/canadian-mining-company-barrick-gold-dominican-republic-pollution-health-crisis.

Austin, Dolores. "Albizu Campos and the Development of a Nationalist Ideology, 1922–32." Master's thesis, University of Wisconsin–Madison, 1983.

Ayala, César J. *American Sugar Kingdom: The Plantation Economy of the Spanish Caribbean, 1898–1934*. Chapel Hill: University of North Carolina Press, 1999.

Baldwin, Kate A. *Beyond the Color Line and the Iron Curtain: Reading Encounters Between Black and Red, 1922–1963*. Durham, NC: Duke University Press, 2002.

Barrick Gold. "Operations." *Barrick Gold*. https://www.barrick.com/English/operations/default.aspx#gold-ops.

Baud, Michiel. "'Un permanente guerrillero': El pensamiento social de Ramón Marrero Aristy (1913–1959)." In *Política, identidad y pensamiento social en* la *República Dominicana, siglos XIX y XX*, edited by Raymundo González, 181–212. Madrid: Ediciones Doce Calles, 1999.

Beal, Frances M. "Double Jeopardy: To Be Black and Female." *Meridians* 8, no. 2 (2008): 166–76.

Becker, Marc. *Mariátegui and Latin American Marxist Theory*. Athens: Ohio University Center for International Studies, 1993.

Becker, Marc. "Mariátegui, the Comintern, and the Indigenous Question in Latin America." *Science and Society* 70, no. 4 (October 2006): 450–79.

Becker, Marc, Margaret Power, Tony Wood, and Jacob A. Zumoff, eds. *Transnational Communism Across the Americas*. Champaign: University of Illinois Press, 2023.

Beckman, Ericka. *Capital Fictions: The Literature of Latin America's Export Age*. Minneapolis: University of Minnesota Press, 2013.

Beverley, John. *Latinamericanism After 9/11*. Durham, NC: Duke University Press, 2001.

Bishara, Hakim. "'Washing Their Hands with Our Blood': Activists on MoMA Trustee's Dominican Republic Gold Mine." *Hyperallergic*, June 6, 2021. https://hyperallergic.com/651146/washing-their-hands-with-our-blood -activists-on-moma-trustees-dominican-republic-gold-mine/.

Borón, Atilio. *América Latina en la geopolítica imperial*. Havana: Editorial de Ciencias Sociales, 2014.

Bosmans, Marleen. "No todo lo que brilla es oro: Crece la resistencia popular contra la Barrick Gold en la República Dominicana." *Rebelión*, March 10, 2022. https://rebelion.org/no-todo-lo-que-brilla-es-oro-2/.

Bosteels, Bruno. *El marxismo en América Latina*. La Paz, Bolivia: Vicepresidencia del Estado Plurinacional, Presidencia de la Asamblea Legislativa Plurinacional, 2013.

Bournot, Estefanía. "Négritude et Amérique Latine: From the Black South Atlantic to the Third World." *Comparative Literature Studies* 59, no. 1 (2022): 77–93.

Bourriaud, Nicolas. *Relational Aesthetics*. Dijon: Les Presses du Réel, 2002.

Boyce Davies, Carole. *Left of Karl Marx: The Political Life of Black Communist Claudia Jones*. Durham, NC: Duke University Press, 2008.

Braun, Barbara. *Pre-Columbian Art and the Post-Columbian World: Ancient American Sources of Modern Art*. New York: Harry N. Abrams, 1993.

Browder, Laura. *Slippery Characters: Ethnic Impersonators and American Identities*. Chapel Hill: University of North Carolina Press, 2000.

brown, adrienne maree. *Emergent Strategy: Shaping Change, Changing Worlds*. Chico, CA: AK Press, 2017.

Brückenhaus, Daniel. *Policing Transnational Protest: Liberal Imperialism and the Surveillance of Anticolonialists in Europe, 1905–1945*. Oxford: Oxford University Press, 2017.

Buchanan, Tom. *East Wind: China and the British Left, 1925–1976*. Oxford: Oxford University Press, 2012.

Burden-Stelly, Charisse. "Modern U.S. Racial Capitalism: Some Theoretical Insights." *Monthly Review*, July 1, 2020. https://monthlyreview.org/author/charisseburden-stelly/.

Byrd, Jodi A. *The Transit of Empire: Indigenous Critiques of Colonialism*. Minneapolis: University of Minnesota Press, 2011.

Caballero, Manuel. *Latin America and the Comintern 1919–1943*. Cambridge: Cambridge University Press, 1986.

Calderón, Roberto, and Emilio Zamora. "Manuela Solis Sager and Emma Tenayuca: A Tribute." Paper presented at the National Association for Chicana and Chicano Studies Annual Conference, January 1, 1984, Austin, Texas. https://scholarworks.sjsu.edu/naccs/1984/Proceedings/7/.

Campos Domínguez, Teresa de Jesús. "La revista Mundo Obrero (1930–33) y el Buro del Caribe de la IC." *Pacarina del Sur: Revista de Pensamiento Crítico Latinoamericano* 4, no. 16 (July–September 2013). http://www.pacarinadelsur.com/home/huellas-y-voces/763-la-revista-mundo-obrero-1930–1933-y-el-buro-del-caribe-de-la-ic.

Campos Ponce, Xavier. *Los yanquis y Sandino*. Mexico City: Ediciones X.C.P., 1962.

Carastathis, Anna. *Intersectionality: Origins, Contestations, Horizons*. Lincoln: University of Nebraska Press, 2016.

Carlotti-Smith, Danielle D. "A Field of Islands: The Intertextual Geography of the *Roman de la canne*." PhD diss., University of Virginia, 2012.

Carlotti-Smith, Danielle D. "Sugar's Sequels: Inventing Traditions in the Plantation Saga Novels of Martinique and Brazil." *Canadian Review of Comparative Literature* 38, no. 1 (March 2011): 80–93.

Carlsen, Laura. "The Defense of the Body-Territory." Americas Program, May 5, 2021. https://www.americas.org/the-defense-of-the-body-territory/.

Carpentier, Alejo. *Reasons of State*. Translated by Frances Partridge. London: Victor Gollancz, 1976.

Carr, Barry. "Identity, Class, and Nation: Black Immigrant Workers, Cuban Communism, and the Sugar Insurgency, 1925–1934." *Hispanic American Historical Review* 78, no. 1 (February 1998): 83–116.

Carr, Barry. *Marxism and Communism in Twentieth-Century Mexico*. Lincoln: University of Nebraska Press, 1992.

Carr, Barry. "Pioneering Transnational Solidarity in the Americas: The Movement in Support of Augusto C. Sandino 1927–34." *Journal of Iberian and Latin American Research* 20, no. 2 (2014): 141–52.

Castellanos, M. Bianet, Lourdes Gutiérrez Nájera, and Arturo J. Aldama, eds. *Comparative Indigeneities of the Américas: Toward a Hemispheric Approach*. Tucson: University of Arizona Press, 2012.

Castells, Manuel. "A Network Theory of Power." *International Journal of Communication* 5 (2011): 773–87.

Caycedo, Carolina, and Jeffrey De Blois. "The River as a Common Good: Carolina Caycedo's Cosmotarrayas." Institute of Contemporary Art/Boston,

2020. https://www.icaboston.org/publications/river-common-good
-carolina-caycedos-cosmotarrayas.

Cerdas Cruz, Rodolfo. *Sandino, el APRA y la Internacional Comunista: Antecedentes históricos de la Nicaragua de hoy.* Lima: EDIMSSA, 1983.

Chakrabarty, Dipesh. "The Legacies of Bandung: Decolonization and the Politics of Culture." In *Making a World After Empire: The Bandung Moment and Its Political Afterlives,* edited by Christopher J. Lee, 45–68. Athens: Ohio University Press, 2010.

Chávez Ixcaquic, Aura Lolita, Marusia López Cruz, and Laura Carlsen. "Las mujeres defensoras de derechos humanos lideran la protección colectiva para defender la vida y el territorio." Open Global Rights, February 5, 2021. https://www.openglobalrights.org/women-human-rights-defenders
-lead-in-the-collective-protection-to-defend-life-and-territory/?lang
=Spanish.

Chilsen, Liz. "Synthesis of Art and Life: Tina Modotti's Photography in Mexico and the Building of a Mexican National Identity." *Photo Review* 19, no. 1 (1996): 2–15.

Ching, Erik. "El Partido Comunista de Costa Rica, 1931–35: Los documentos." *Revista de Historia* 37 (January–June 1998): 7–226.

Cirefice, V'cenza, and Lynda Sullivan. "Women on the Frontlines of Resistance to Extractivism." *Policy and Practice: A Development Education Review* 29 (Autumn 2019): 78–99.

Cisneros, Gustavo. "Biography." *Gustavo Cisneros.* https://www.gustavo
cisneros.com/en/biography/.

Cohn, Deborah. *History and Memory in the Two Souths: Recent Southern and Spanish American Fiction.* Nashville, TN: Vanderbilt University Press, 1999.

Collins, Patricia Hill. *Black Feminist Thought: Knowledge, Consciousness, and the Politics of Empowerment.* Boston: Unwin Hyman, 1990.

Combahee River Collective. "A Black Feminist Statement." In *This Bridge Called My Back: Writings by Radical Women of Color,* 2nd ed., edited by Cherríe Moraga and Gloria Anzaldúa, 210–18. New York: Kitchen Table / Women of Color Press, 1983.

Concheiro, Elvira, Massimo Modonesi, and Horacio Crespo. *El comunismo: Otras miradas desde América Latina.* 2nd ed. Mexico City: Universidad Nacional Autónoma de México, Centro de Investigaciones Interdisciplinarias en Ciencias y Humanidades, 2011.

Coronil, Fernando. "Elephants in the Americas? Latin American Postcolonial Studies and Global Decolonization." In *Coloniality at Large: Latin America and the Postcolonial Debate,* edited by Mabel Moraña, Enrique Dussel, and Carlos A. Jáuregui, 396–416. Durham, NC: Duke University Press, 2008.

Coulthard, Glen. "From Wards of the State to Subjects of Recognition? Marx, Indigenous Peoples, and the Politics of Dispossession in Denendeh." In *Theorizing Native Studies,* edited by Audra Simpson and Andrea Smith, 56–98. Durham, NC: Duke University Press, 2014.

Crenshaw, Kimblerlé. *On Intersectionality: Selected Writings.* New York: New Press, 2022.

Crespo Rubio, Alba. "Mujeres en resistencia al extractivismo." SERVINDI, March 25, 2017. https://www.servindi.org/actualidad-noticias/25/03/2017/mujeres-en-resistencia-al-extractivismo.

CSLA (Confederación Sindical Latino Americana). *Bajo la bandera de la C.S.L.A.: Resoluciones y documentos varios del Congreso Constituyente de la Confederación Sindical Latino Americana efectuado en Montevideo en mayo de 1929.* Montevideo: Imprenta la linotopo, 1929.

Dalleo, Raphael. *American Imperialism's Undead: The Occupation of Haiti and the Rise of Caribbean Anticolonialism.* Charlottesville: University of Virginia Press, 2016.

Dame, Shannon. "Indigenismo in the Mexican Photographs of Tina Modotti." Master's thesis, Brigham Young University, 2011.

Deambrosis Martins, Carlos. *Vidas exaltantes: Rolland, Unamuno, Vasconcelos.* Mexico City: Finisterre, 1967.

Debroise, Olivier. "La tehuana desnuda y la tehuana vestida: La fotografía y la construcción de un estereotipo." In *Del istmo y sus mujeres tehuanas en el arte mexicano*, edited by Museo Nacional de Arte, 60–74. Mexico City: Consejo Nacional para la Cultura y las Artes, 1992.

DeCosta-Willis, Miriam, ed. *Blacks in Hispanic Literature.* Baltimore, MD: Black Classic Press, 2011.

DeCosta-Willis, Miriam. "Social Lyricism and the Caribbean Poet/Rebel." In *Blacks in Hispanic Literature*, edited by Miriam DeCosta-Willis, 114–22. Baltimore, MD: Black Classic Press, 2011.

De Jesús Toro, Rafael. *Historia económica de Puerto Rico.* Cincinnati: South-Western, 1982.

De la Fuente, Alejandro. *A Nation for All: Race, Inequality, and Politics in Twentieth-Century Cuba.* Chapel Hill: University of North Carolina Press, 2001.

De la Fuente, Alejandro. "Two Dangers, One Solution: Immigration, Race, and Labor in Cuba, 1900–1930." *International Labor and Working-Class History* 51 (1997): 30–49.

Delpar, Helen. *The Enormous Vogue of Things Mexican: Cultural Relations Between the United States and Mexico, 1920–1935.* Tuscaloosa: University of Alabama Press, 1992.

De Sarlo, Giulia. "The Sugar Plantation as a Place of Caribbean Identity: A Literary Focus." In *Caribbeing: Comparing Caribbean Literatures and Cultures*, edited by Kristian Van Haesendonck and Theo D'haen, 169–82. Amsterdam: Rodolpi, 2014.

Dinkel, Jürgen. *The Non-Aligned Movement: Genesis, Organization and Politics (1927–1992).* Leiden: Brill, 2019.

Djagalov, Rossen. *From Internationalism to Postcolonialism: Literature and Cinema Between the Second and the Third Worlds.* Montreal: McGill-Queen's University Press, 2020.

Edwards, Erica R. *Charisma and the Fictions of Black Leadership*. Minneapolis: University of Minnesota Press, 2012.

Elam, Daniel J. *World Literature for the Wretched of the Earth: Anticolonial Aesthetics, Postcolonial Politics*. New York: Fordham University Press, 2021.

Escobar, Arturo. *Territories of Difference: Place, Movements, Life, Redes*. Durham, NC: Duke University Press, 2008.

Escobar, Arturo. "Worlds and Knowledges Otherwise: The Latin American Modernity/Coloniality Research Program." In *Globalization and the Decolonial Option*, edited by Walter D. Mignolo and Arturo Escobar, 33–64. New York: Routledge, 2010.

Fallas Sibaja, Carlos Luis. *Mamita Yunai*. Santiago de Chile: Quimantu, 1972.

Fanon, Frantz. *Black Skin, White Masks*. Translated by Richard Philcox. New York: Grove, 2008.

Featherstone, David. *Solidarity: Hidden Histories and Geographies of Internationalism*. London: Zed, 2012.

Feinsod, Harris. *The Poetry of the Americas: From Good Neighbors to Countercultures*. Oxford: Oxford University Press, 2017.

Feldman, Leah. *On the Threshold of Eurasia: Revolutionary Poetics in the Caucasus*. Ithaca, NY: Cornell University Press, 2018.

Fermaglich, Kirsten. "'Too Long, Too Foreign . . . Too Jewish': Jews, Name Changing, and Family Mobility in New York City, 1917–1942." *Journal of American Ethnic History* 34, no. 3 (2015): 34–57.

Ferrao, Luis Ángel. *Pedro Albizu Campos y el nacionalismo puertorriqueño*. San Juan: Editorial Cultural, 1990.

Figarella, Mariana. *Edward Weston y Tina Modotti en México: Su inserción dentro de las estrategias estéticas del arte posrevolucionario*. Mexico City: Universidad Nacional Autónoma de México, Instituto de Investigaciones Estéticas, 2002.

Figueroa-Vásquez, Yomaira C. *Decolonizing Diasporas: Radical Mappings of Afro-Atlantic Literature*. Chicago: Northwestern University Press, 2020.

Flores, Tatiana. *Mexico's Revolutionary Avant-Gardes: From Estridentismo to ¡30–30!* New Haven, CT: Yale University Press, 2013.

Foley, Barbara. "Intersectionality." *New Labor Forum* 28, no. 3 (Fall 2019): 10–13.

Folgarait, Leonard. *Seeing Mexico Photographed: The Work of Horne, Casasola, Modotti, and Álvarez Bravo*. New Haven, CT: Yale University Press, 2008.

"Fragmentos de la 'Cuban Resolution' del Secretariado Político de la Internacional Comunista del 28 de enero de 1927." In *Mella: Textos escogidos*, edited by Julio César Guanche, 2:197–201. Havana: Centro Cultural Pablo de la Torriente Brau, 2017.

Franco, Jean. *Plotting Women: Gender and Representation in Mexico*. New York: Columbia University Press, 1989.

Frank, Andre Gunder. *Dependent Accumulation and Underdevelopment*. New York: Monthly Review Press, 1979.

Franklin, Paul B. "Jew Boys, Queer Boys: Rhetorics of Antisemitism and Homophobia in the Trial of Nathan 'Babe' Leopold Jr. and Richard 'Dickie'

Loeb." In *Queer Theory and the Jewish Question*, edited by Daniel Boyarin, Daniel Itzkovitz, and Ann Pellegrini, 121–48. New York: Columbia University Press, 2003.

Gago, Verónica. *Feminist International: How to Change Everything*. Translated by Liz Mason-Deese. London: Verso Books, 2020.

Gago, Verónica. "What Latin American Feminists Can Teach American Women About the Abortion Fight." *Guardian*, May 10, 2022. https://www .theguardian.com/commentisfree/2022/may/10/abortion-roe-v-wade -latin-america.

Gaine, Klaire. "Fighting for Their Water and Their Lives, Communities Take Direct Action Against Barrick Gold in the Dominican Republic." *Upside Down World*, November 30, 2017. https://upsidedownworld.org/archives /caribbean/fighting-for-their-water-and-their-lives-communities-take -direct-action-against-barrick-gold-in-the-dominican-republic/.

Galloway, Alexander R., and Eugene Thacker. *The Exploit: A Theory of Networks*. Minneapolis: University of Minnesota Press, 2007.

García-Bryce, Iñigo. *Haya de la Torre and the Pursuit of Power in Twentieth-Century Peru and Latin America*. Chapel Hill: University of North Carolina Press, 2019.

García Linera, Álvaro. "Geopolitics of the Amazon: Landed-Hereditary Power and Capitalist Accumulation." Translated by Richard Fidler. Climate and Capitalism, 2013. https://climateandcapitalism.com/wp-content/uploads /2013/01/Geopolitics-of-the-Amazon-8x11.pdf.

García Montes, Jorge, and Antonio Alonso Ávila. *Historia del Partido Comunista de Cuba*. Miami: Ediciones Universal, 1970.

Gilmore, Glenda. *Defying Dixie: The Radical Roots of Civil Rights, 1919–1950*. New York: W. W. Norton, 2008.

Gimenez, Martha E. "Intersectionality: Marxist Critical Observations." *Science and Society* 82, no. 2 (April 2018): 261–69.

Glaser, Amelia M., and Steven S. Lee, eds. *Comintern Aesthetics*. Toronto: University of Toronto Press, 2020.

Glissant, Édouard. *Poetics of Relation*. Ann Arbor: University of Michigan Press, 1997.

Goebel, Michael. *Anti-Imperial Metropolis: Interwar Paris and the Seeds of Third World Internationalism*. Cambridge: Cambridge University Press, 2015.

Goebel, Michael. "Forging a Proto–Third World? Latin America and the League Against Imperialism." In *The League Against Imperialism: Lives and Afterlives*, edited by Michele Louro, Carolien Stolte, Heather Streets-Salter, and Sana Tannoury-Karam, 53–78. Leiden: Leiden University Press, 2020.

Gómez-Barris, Macarena. *The Extractive Zone: Social Ecologies and Decolonial Perspectives*. Durham, NC: Duke University Press, 2017.

González Casanova, Pablo. *Imperialismo y liberación en América Latina: Una introducción a la historia contemporánea*. Mexico City: Siglo Veintiuno Editores, 1978.

Graciano, Berta. *La novela de la caña: Estética e ideología.* Santo Domingo: Editora Alfa & Omega, 1990.

Grewal, David Singh. *Network Power: The Social Dynamics of Globalization.* New Haven, CT: Yale University Press, 2008.

Gronbeck-Tedesco, John A. *Cuba, the United States, and Cultures of the Transnational Left, 1930–1975.* New York: Cambridge University Press, 2015.

Guanche, Julio César. *Mella: Textos escogidos.* 2 vols. Havana: Centro Cultural Pablo de la Torriente Brau, 2017.

Guarnera, Anne. "Our Black América: Transnational Racial Identities in Twentieth-Century Cuba and Brazil." PhD diss., University of Virginia, 2017.

Gudynas, Eduardo. *Extractivismos: Ecología, economía y política de un modo de entender el desarrollo y la Naturaleza.* Cochabamba: CEDIB, Centro de Documentación e Información Bolivia, 2015.

Guridy, Frank Andre. *Forging Diaspora: Afro-Cubans and African Americans in a World of Empire and Jim Crow.* Chapel Hill: University of North Carolina Press, 2010.

Guynn, Beth. "Mexico." In *Encyclopedia of Nineteenth Century Photography,* edited by John Hannavy, 922–24. London: Taylor and Francis, 2008.

Haithcox, John P. "The Roy-Lenin Debate on Colonial Policy: A New Interpretation." *Journal of Asian Studies* 23, no. 1 (1963): 93–101.

Hardt, Michael, and Antonio Negri. *Assembly.* Oxford: Oxford University Press, 2017.

Hardt, Michael, and Antonio Negri. *Empire.* Cambridge, MA: Harvard University Press, 2000.

Hatzky, Christine. *Julio Antonio Mella (1903–1929): Una biografía.* Translated by Jorge Luis Acanda. Santiago de Cuba: Editorial Oriente, 2008.

Heatherton, Christina. *Arise! Global Radicalism in the Era of the Mexican Revolution.* Oakland: University of California Press, 2022.

Helg, Aline. *Our Rightful Share: The Afro-Cuban Struggle for Equality, 1886–1912.* Chapel Hill: University of North Carolina Press, 1995.

Herman, Donald L. *The Comintern in Mexico.* Washington, DC: Public Affairs Press, 1974.

Hernández, Félix. "El asesinato de Sandalio Junco, padre del Trotskismo cubano." *Cuba Nuestra: Historia,* March 18, 2011. https://cubabuestra7eu .wordpress.com/2011/03/19/el-asesinato-de-sandalio-junco-padre-del -trotskismo-cubano/.

Hersch, Charles B. *Jews and Jazz: Improvising Ethnicity.* New York: Routledge, 2017.

Høgsbjerg, Christian. "Communism and the Colour-Line: Reflections on Black Bolshevism." In *The Comintern and the Global South,* edited by Anne Garland Mahler and Paolo Capuzzo, 96–120. New York: Routledge, 2023.

Hooks, Margaret. *Tina Modotti.* New York: Aperture, 1999.

Hooks, Margaret. *Tina Modotti: Photographer and Revolutionary.* London: Pandora, 1993.

Hu-DeHart, Evelyn. "Opium and Social Control: Coolies on the Plantations of Peru and Cuba." *Journal of Chinese Overseas* 1, no. 2 (November 2005): 169–83.

Huiswoud, Otto, and Claude McKay. "Speeches to the 4th World Congress of the Comintern on the Negro Question." November 25, 1922. *Bulletin of the IV Congress of the Communist International* 22 (December 2, 1922): 17–23.

Icaza Giraldo, Mateo. "La protesta que embellece el parque central de Jericó." *El Colombiano*, October 15, 2019. https://www.elcolombiano.com/antioquia /la-protesta-que-embellece-el-parque-central-de-jerico-FB11763017.

Instituto de Historia del Movimiento Comunista y de la Revolución Socialista de Cuba, adjunto al Comité Central del Partido Comunista de Cuba. "Resolución sobres cuestiones de organización." In *El movimiento obrero cubano, documentos y artículos* 2, 574–93. Havana: Editorial de Ciencias Sociales, 1981.

Issar, Siddhant. "Theorising 'Racial/Colonial Primitive Accumulation': Settler Colonialism, Slavery and Racial Capitalism." *Race and Class* 63, no. 1 (2021): 23–50.

Jackson, Richard L. *Black Literature and Humanism in Latin America.* Athens: University of Georgia Press, 1988.

Jackson, Shona N. *Creole Indigeneity: Between Myth and Nation in the Caribbean.* Minneapolis: University of Minnesota Press, 2012.

Jacobson, Matthew Frye. *Whiteness of a Different Color: European Immigrants and the Alchemy of Race.* Cambridge, MA: Harvard University Press, 1999.

Jakobsen, Janet R. "Queers Are Like Jews, Aren't They? Analogy and Alliance Politics." In *Queer Theory and the Jewish Question,* edited by Daniel Boyarin, Daniel Itzkovitz, and Ann Pellegrini, 64–89. New York: Columbia University Press, 2003.

James, C. L. R. *World Revolution, 1917–1936: The Rise and Fall of the Communist International.* 1937. Durham, NC: Duke University Press, 2017.

James, Norberto Pedro. "Un estudio sociocultural de dos novelas dominicanas de la era de Trujillo." PhD diss., Boston University, 1992.

Jasper, James M., Michael Young, and Elke Zuern. "Character Work in Social Movements." *Theory and Society* 47, no. 1 (2018): 113–31.

Jeifets, Lazar, and Víctor Jeifets. *América Latina en la Internacional Comunista, 1919–1943, diccionario biográfico.* Santiago: Ariadna Ediciones, 2015.

Jeifets, Lazar, and Víctor Jeifets. "Jaime Nevarez y la fundación del movimiento comunista y antiimperialista en Puerto Rico." *Pacarina del Sur: Revista de Pensamiento Crítico Latinoamericano* 5, no. 21 (October–December 2014). http://pacarinadelsur.com/home/huellas-y-voces/1037-jaime-nevarez-y-la -fundacion-del-movimiento-comunista-y-antiimperialista-en-puerto-rico.

Jeifets, Lazar, and Víctor Jeifets. "La Comintern, el PCM, y el 'caso' Sandino: Historia de una alianza fracasada, 1927–1930." *Anuario Colombiano de Historia Social y de la Cultura* 44, no. 2 (2017): 63–86. https://www.redalyc .org/journal/1271/127151758003/html/.

Jones, Claudia. *An End to the Neglect of the Problems of the Negro Woman!* New York: National Women's Commission, CPUSA, 1949.

"Juicio político del Partido Comunista de Cuba a Julio Antonio Mella por motivo de su huelga de hambre." In *Mella: Textos Escogidos*, edited by Julio César Guanche, 2:160–79. Havana: Centro Cultural Pablo de la Torriente Brau, 2017.

Junco, Sandalio. "¡¡¡Fuera caretas!!! Contra la demagogía, las vilezas, y la incapacidad de los líderes de la CNOC." Havana, January 1934. Archivo Nacional de Cuba. Fondo Especial. Leg. 1. No. 2833. In Sergio Moissen Méndez, "Cuba: ¿Qué pasó con Sandalio Junco?" *Sin permiso: República y socialismo para el siglo XXI*, October 6, 2018. https://www.sinpermiso.info/textos/cuba-que-paso-con-sandalio-junco.

Kalliney, Peter J. *The Aesthetic Cold War: Decolonization and Global Literature*. Princeton, NJ: Princeton University Press, 2022.

Kelley, Robin D. G. "Foreword: Why *Black Marxism*? Why Now?" *Black Marxism: The Making of the Black Radical Tradition*, by Cedric Robinson, xi–xxxiv. Chapel Hill: University of North Carolina Press, 2021.

Kelley, Robin D. G. *Freedom Dreams: The Black Radical Imagination*. Boston: Beacon Press, 2002.

Kelley, Robin D. G. *Hammer and Hoe: Alabama Communists During the Great Depression*. Chapel Hill: University of North Carolina Press, 1990.

Kenney, Nancy. "Coalition of Activist Groups Announces 'Strike' Action Against MoMA." *The Art Newspaper*, March 24, 2021. https://www.theartnewspaper.com/2021/03/24/coalition-of-activist-groups-announces-strike-action-against-moma.

Kent-Carrasco, Daniel. "Breath of Revolution: Ghadar Anticolonial Radicalism in North America and the Mexican Revolution." *South Asia: Journal of South Asian Studies* 43, no. 6 (202): 1077–92.

Kent-Carrasco, Daniel. "México en las memorias de M. N. Roy: Nostalgia, devoción política, e historia." In *Autobiografías y/o textos autorreferenciales*, edited by Alicia Sandoval, 95–118. Puebla: UNAM de Puebla, 2019.

Kent-Carrasco, Daniel. "Pandurang Khankhoje and the Free Schools of Agriculture: *Campesino* Internationalism in Post-Revolutionary Mexico." In *The Comintern and the Global South: Global Designs/Local Encounters*, edited by Anne Garland Mahler and Paolo Capuzzo, 147–71. New York: Routledge, 2023.

Kersffeld, Daniel. *Contra el imperio: Historia de la Liga Antimperialista de las Américas*. Mexico City: Siglo Veintiuno Editores, 2012.

Kersffeld, Daniel. "El Comité Manos Fuera de Nicaragua: Primera experiencia del sandinismo." *Pacarina del Sur: Revista de Pensamiento Crítico Latinoamericano* 15, nos. 50–51 (January–December 2023). http://pacarinadelsur.com/home/oleajes/537-el-comite-manos-fuera-de-nicaragua-primera-experiencia-del-sandinismo.

Kersffeld, Daniel. "La Liga Antiimperialista de Costa Rica: Una escuela de cuadros para el Partido Comunista de Costa Rica." *Revista Estudios, Universidad de Costa Rica* 22 (2009): 105–19.

Kersffeld, Daniel. "La Liga Antiimperialista de las Américas: Una construcción política entre el marxismo y el latinoamericanismo." In *El comunismo: Otras miradas desde América Latina*, edited by Elvira Concheiro Bórquez, Horacio Crespo, and Massimo Modonesi. Mexico City: Universidad Nacional Autónoma de México, 2007.

King, Deborah K. "Multiple Jeopardy, Multiple Consciousness: The Context of a Black Feminist Ideology." *Signs: Journal of Women in Culture and Society* 14, no. 1 (1988): 42–72.

Kirby, Rachel, comp. *Tina Modotti: Revolutionary Photographer, Fotógrafa Revolucionaria*. North Melborne, Victoria, Australia: Ocean Press, 2013.

Klehr, Harvey, and William Tompson. "Self-Determination in the Black Belt: Origins of a Communist Policy." *Labor History* 30 (1989): 354–66.

Knight, Franklin W., and Henry Louis Gates Jr., eds. *Dictionary of Caribbean and Afro-Latin American Bibliography*. Oxford: Oxford University Press, 2016.

Kohan, Nestor. *Marx en su (Tercer) Mundo: Hacia un socialismo no colonizado*. Havana: Centro de Investigación y Desarrollo de la Cultura Cubana Juan Marinello, 2003.

Koshy, Susan, Lisa Marie Cacho, Jodi A. Byrd, and Brian Jordan Jefferson. *Colonial Racial Capitalism*. Durham, NC: Duke University Press, 2022.

Krippner, James, et al. *Paul Strand in Mexico*. Mexico City: Fundación Televisa, 2010.

Kröger, Markus. *Extractivisms, Existencies, and Extinctions: Monoculture Plantations and Amazon Deforestation*. New York: Routledge, 2022.

Lee, Christopher J., ed. *Making a World After Empire: The Bandung Moment and Its Political Afterlives*. Athens: Ohio University Press, 2010.

Lee, Christopher J., and Anne Garland Mahler. "The Bandung Era, Non-Alignment and the Third-Way Literary Imagination." In *The Palgrave Handbook of Cold War Literature*, edited by Andrew Hammond, 183–202. London: Palgrave Macmillan, 2020.

Lee, Richard E. "The Modern World-System: Its Structures, Its Geoculture, Its Crisis and Transformation." In *Immanuel Wallerstein and the Problem of the World: System, Scale, Culture*, edited by David Palumbo-Liu, Nirvana Tanoukhi, and Bruce Robbins, 27–40. Durham, NC: Duke University Press, 2011.

Lee, Steven S. *The Ethnic Avant-Garde: Minority Cultures and World Revolution*. New York: Columbia University Press, 2015.

Legrás, Horacio. *Culture and Revolution: Violence, Memory, and the Making of Modern Mexico*. Austin: University of Texas Press, 2017.

Lenin, Vladimir. *Imperialism: The Highest Stage of Capitalism*. London: Penguin, 2010.

Lewis, Su Lin, and Carolien Stolte, eds. *The Lives of Cold War Afro-Asianism*. Baltimore, MD: Project Muse, 2022.

Liga gegen imperialismus und für nationale unabhängigkeit. *Das flammenzeichen vom Palais Egmont: Offizielles protokoll des Kongresses gegen*

Koloniale unterdrückung und Imperialismus, Brüssel, 10–15, februar. Berlin: Neuer Deutscher Verlag W. Münzenberg, 1927.

Linares, Albinson. "The Deadliest Place for Latin American Activists Is Latin America." NBC *News,* September 20, 2021. https://www.nbcnews.com/news/latino/latin-america-deadliest-region-environmental-activists-rcna2021.

Lindner, Thomas K. *A City Against Empire: Transnational Anti-Imperialism in Mexico City, 1920–1930.* Liverpool: Liverpool University Press, 2023.

Liu, Roseann, and Savannah Shange. "Toward Thick Solidarity: Theorizing Empathy in Social Justice Movements." *Radical History Review* 131 (May 2018): 189–98.

Locane, Jorge J. "On the World Peace Movement and the Early Internationalisation of Latin American Literature." In *Culture as Soft Power: Bridging Cultural Relations, Intellectual Cooperation, and Cultural Diplomacy,* edited by Elisabet Carbó-Catalan and Diana Roig-Sanz, 297–318. Berlin: De Gruyter, 2022.

Lomas, Laura. *Translating Empire: José Martí, Migrant Latino Subjects, and American Modernities.* Durham, NC: Duke University Press, 2008.

López, Kathleen M. "'One Brings Another': The Formation of Early-Twentieth-Century Chinese Migrant Communities in Cuba." In *The Chinese in the Caribbean,* edited by Andrew R. Wilson, 93–127. Princeton, NJ: M. Wiener, 2004.

López-Calvo, Ignacio. *Imaging the Chinese in Cuban Literature and Culture.* Gainesville: University Press of Florida, 2008.

Losurdo, Domenico. *La izquierda ausente: Crisis, sociedad del espectáculo, guerra.* Barcelona: El Viejo Topo, 2015.

Louro, Michele L. *Comrades Against Imperialism: Nehru, India, and Interwar Internationalism.* Cambridge: Cambridge University Press, 2018.

Louro, Michele L., Carolien Stolte, Heather Streets-Salter, and Sana Tannoury-Karam, eds. *The League Against Imperialism: Lives and Afterlives.* Leiden: Leiden University Press, 2020.

Lowe, Lisa. *The Intimacies of Four Continents.* Durham, NC: Duke University Press, 2015.

Lowe, Sarah M. "The Immutable Still Lifes of Tina Modotti: Fixing Form." *History of Photography* 18, no. 3 (September 1994): 205–10.

Lowe, Sarah M. *Tina Modotti: Photographs.* New York: Harry N. Abrams, 1995.

Luis-Brown, David. *Waves of Decolonization: Discourses of Race and Hemispheric Citizenship in Cuba, Mexico, and the United States.* Durham, NC: Duke University Press, 2008.

Lund, Joshua K. *The Impure Imagination: Toward a Critical Hybridity in Latin American Writing.* Minneapolis: University of Minnesota Press, 2006.

Lund, Joshua K. *The Mestizo State: Reading Race in Modern Mexico.* Minneapolis: University of Minnesota Press, 2012.

Lyra, Carmen. "Estefania." In *When New Flowers Bloomed: Short Stories by Women Writers from Costa Rica and Panama*, edited by Enrique Jaramillo Levi. Pittsburgh: Latin American Literary Review Press, 1991.

Lyra, Carmen. *Los otros cuentos de Carmen Lyra*. San José: Editorial Costa Rica, 1985.

Macaulay, Neill. *The Sandino Affair*. Chicago: Quadrangle Books, 1967.

Magubane, Bernard. *The Political Economy of Race and Class in South Africa*. New York: Monthly Review Press, 1979.

Mahler, Anne Garland. *From the Tricontinental to the Global South: Race, Radicalism, and Transnational Solidarity*. Durham, NC: Duke University Press, 2018.

Mahler, Anne Garland. "Global Solidarity Before the Tricontinental Conference: Latin America and the League Against Imperialism." In *The Tricontinental Revolution: Third World Radicalism and the Cold War*, edited by R. Joseph Parrott and Mark Atwood Lawrence, 43–68. Cambridge: Cambridge University Press, 2022.

Mahler, Anne Garland. "The Red and the Black in Latin America: Sandalio Junco and the 'Negro Question' from an Afro-Latin American Perspective." *American Communist History* 17, no. 1 (2018): 16–32.

Mahler, Anne Garland. "South-South Organizing in the Global Plantation Zone: Ramón Marrero Aristy, the *novela de la caña*, and the Caribbean Bureau." *Atlantic Studies: Global Currents* 19, no. 2 (2019): 236–60.

Mahler, Anne Garland, and Paolo Capuzzo, eds. *The Comintern and the Global South: Global Designs/Local Encounters*. New York: Routledge, 2023.

Makalani, Minkah. *In the Cause of Freedom: Radical Black Internationalism from Harlem to London, 1917–1939*. Chapel Hill: University of North Carolina Press, 2011.

Manela, Erez, and Heather Streets-Salter, eds. *The Anticolonial Transnational: Imaginaries, Mobilities, and Networks in the Struggle Against Empire*. Cambridge: Cambridge University Press, 2023.

Manke, Albert. "The Impact of the 1949 Chinese Revolution on a Latin American Chinese Community: Shifting Power Relations in Havana's Chinatown." *Revista Brasileira de Política Internacional* 61, no. 2 (2018).

Manzano, Valeria. *The Age of Youth in Argentina: Culture, Politics, and Sexuality from Perón to Videla*. Chapel Hill: University of North Carolina Press, 2014.

Mariátegui, José Carlos. *Seven Interpretative Essays on Peruvian Reality*. Translated by Marjory Urquidi. Austin: University of Texas Press, 1971.

Márquez Fuentes, Manuel, and Octavio Rodríguez Araujo. *El Partido Comunista Mexicano (en el período de la Internacional Comunista: 1919–1943)*. Mexico City: Ediciones "El Caballito," 1973.

Marrero Aristy, Ramón. *Over*. Santo Domingo: Editora Taller, 1998.

Martínez Villena, Rubén. *Cuba, factoría yanqui*. Havana: Editorial de Ciencias Sociales, 1999.

Marx, Karl. *Marx's Grundrisse*. Edited by David McLellan. London: Macmillan, 1971.

Massón Sena, Caridad. "Evolución de las primeras organizaciones comunistas cubanas." In *El comunismo: Otras miradas desde América Latina*, edited by Elvira Concheiro, Massimo Modonesi, and Horacio Crespo, 279–91. Mexico City: Universidad Nacional Autónoma de México Centro de Investigaciones Interdisciplinarias en Ciencias y Humanidades.

Massón Sena, Caridad. "La cuestión racial en la política del Partido Comunista de Cuba (1925–1940)." *Perfiles de la Cultura Cubana: Revista del Instituto Cubano de Investigación Cultural Juan Marinello*, August–December 2016.

Mateo, Andrés L. *Mito y cultura en la era de Trujillo*. Santo Domingo: Editora Manatí, 2004.

McDuffie, Erik S. *Sojourning for Freedom: Black Women, American Communism, and the Making of Black Left Feminism*. Durham, NC: Duke University Press, 2011.

Melamed, Jodi. "Racial Capitalism." *Critical Ethnic Studies* 1, no. 1 (Spring 2015): 76–85.

Melamed, Jodi. *Represent and Destroy: Rationalizing Violence in the New Racial Capitalism*. Minneapolis: University of Minnesota Press, 2011.

Melcher, Dorothea. "La solidaridad internacional con Sandino 1928–1930." *Iberoamericana (1977–2000)* 13, no. 1 (1989): 20–40.

Melgar Bao, Ricardo. "The Anti-Imperialist League of the Americas Between the East and Latin America." *Latin American Perspectives* 35, no. 2 (March 2008): 9–24.

Melgar Bao, Ricardo. "El universo simbólico de una revista cominternista: Diego Rivera y *El Libertador*." *Convergencia* 21 (January–April 2000): 121–43.

Melgar Bao, Ricardo. *La prensa militante en América Latina y la Internacional Comunista*. Mexico City: Instituto Nacional de Antropología e Historia, 2015.

Melgar Bao, Ricardo. "Memoria cominternista de Nuestra América en los años veinte: Testimonio de Rafael Carrillo Azpéitia." *Pacarina del Sur: Revista de Pensamiento Crítico Latinoamericano* 11, no. 42 (January–March 2020). http://pacarinadelsur.com/home/huellas-y-voces/1842-memoria -cominternista-de-nuestra-america-en-los-anos-veinte-testimonio-de -rafael-carrillo-azpeitia.

Melgar Bao, Ricardo. "Rearmando la memoria: El primer debate socialista acerca de nuestros afroamericanos." *Humanía del Sur* 2, no. 2 (January–June 2007): 145–66.

Mella, Julio Antonio. *¿Qué es el ARPA?* In *Julio Antonio Mella en el "Machete,"* edited by Raquel Tibol. Ciudad de México: Fondo de Cultura Popular, 1968.

Mella, Julio Antonio. "Víctor Raúl Haya de la Torre." In *Mella: Textos escogidos*, edited by Julio César Guanche, 1:97–98. Havana: Centro Cultural Pablo de la Torriente Brau, 2017.

Mella, Julio Antonio, and Ana Cairo Ballester. *Mella: 100 años*. Santiago de Cuba: Editorial Oriente, 2003.

Meyerson, Gregory. "Rethinking Black Marxism: Reflections on Cedric Robinson and Others." *Cultural Logic: A Journal of Marxist Theory and Practice* 6 (2000). https://doi.org/10.14288/clogic.v6i0.192628.

Mignolo, Walter D. "Colonial and Postcolonial Discourse: Cultural Critique or Academic Colonialism?" *Latin American Research Review* 28, no. 3 (1993): 120–34.

Mignolo, Walter D. "Introduction: Coloniality of Power and De-Colonial Thinking." In *Globalization and the Decolonial Option*, edited by Walter D. Mignolo and Arturo Escobar, 1–21. New York: Routledge, 2010.

Miller, Jason. "Activism vs. Antagonism: Socially Engaged Art from Bourriaud to Bishop and Beyond." *Field: A Journal of Socially-Engaged Art Criticism* 3 (Winter 2016): 165–83.

Moissen, Sergio. "Cuba: ¿Qué pasó con Sandalio Junco?" *Sin Permiso: República y Socialismo para el Siglo XXI*, October 6, 2018. https://www.sinpermiso.info/textos/cuba-que-paso-con-sandalio-junco.

Moissen, Sergio. "Documentos para una historia del trotskismo en Cuba." Unpublished document.

Moissen, Sergio. "El trotskismo cubano en la revolución de 1933." *Pacarina del Sur: Revista de Pensamiento Crítico Latinoamericano* 6, no. 23 (April–June 2015). http://www.pacarinadelsur.com/home/abordajes-y-contiendas/1126-el-trotskismo-cubano-.

Moissen, Sergio. "Sandalio Junco: Un perfil del fundador del trotskismo en Cuba asesinado por el estalinismo." *Ideas de Izquierda*, June 18, 2024. https://www.laizquierdadiario.com/Sandalio-Junco-un-perfil-del-fundador-del-trotskismo-en-Cuba-asesinado-por-el-estalinismo.

MoMA. "Tina Modotti." Museum of Modern Art, New York. https://www.moma.org/artists/4039.

Moore, Robin. *Nationalizing Blackness: Afrocubanismo and the Artistic Revolution in Havana, 1920–40*. Pittsburgh: University of Pittsburgh Press, 1997.

Morán Beltrán, Lino, Lorena Velásquez, and Vileana Meleán. "Gustavo Machado y los orígenes del marxismo en Venezuela." *Revista de Filosofía* 23, no. 49 (January 2005). http://www.scielo.org.ve/scielo.php?pid=S0798-11712005000100002&script=sci_arttext.

Morse, Richard M. "The Multiverse of Latin American Identity, c. 1920–c. 1970." In *The Cambridge History of Latin America*, edited by Leslie Bethell, 1–128. Cambridge: Cambridge University Press, 1995.

Mraz, John. *Looking for Mexico: Modern Visual Culture and National Identity*. Durham, NC: Duke University Press, 2009.

Mraz, John. *Photographing the Mexican Revolution: Commitments, Testimonies, Icons*. Austin: University of Texas Press, 2012.

Mulvey, Laura, and Peter Wollen. *Frida Kahlo and Tina Modotti*. Whitechapel Art Gallery, March 26–November 7, 1982.

Muñoz, Enara Echart, and María del Carmen Villareal. "Women's Struggles Against Extractivism in Latin America and the Caribbean." *Contexto Int.* 41, no. 2 (May–August 2019). https://www.scielo.br/j/cint/a/xryLFTDmtg6hpnkz7fy3wKz/?lang=en.

Murib, Zein. "Unsettling the GLBT and Queer Coalitions in US Politics Through the Lens of Queer Indigenous Critique." *New Political Science* 40, no. 1 (2018): 165–76.

N Digital Multimedia. "Diputados favorecen presa de cola de Barrick Gold no se construya en Cuance, Monte Plata." *N Digital*, April 1, 2022. https://n .com.do/2022/04/01/diputados-favorecen-presa-de-cola-de-barrick-gold -no-se-construya-en-cuance-monte-plata.

Neymet, Marcela de. *Cronología del Partido Comunista Mexicano*. Mexico City: Ediciones de Cultura Popular, 1981.

Noble, Andrea. *Tina Modotti: Image, Texture, Photography*. Albuquerque: University of New Mexico Press, 2000.

NYU (New York University Center for Latin American and Caribbean Studies). "Negative Impacts of Barrick Gold's Exploitations on Different Continents: The Cases of Argentina, Papua New Guinea, and Dominican Republic." Online event, October 19, 2022.

O'Brien, Erin E. *The Politics of Identity: Solidarity Building Among America's Working Poor*. Albany: State University of New York Press, 2008.

OCMAL (Observatorio de Conflictos Mineros de América Latina). "Conflictos mineros en América Latina." Accessed August 22, 2023. https://mapa .conflictosmineros.net/ocmal_db-v2/.

Open Letter to Antonio Reynoso, Orlando Mera, Mark Bristow, and Juana Barceló by Earthworks, the Global Justice Clinic from NYU School of Law, MiningWatch Canada, and other organizations. May 4, 2021. https:// miningwatch.ca/sites/default/files/barrick_sign_on_letter_final_2021 _w.signatures_0.pdf.

Ortega, Víctor Joaquín. "Este periodista es el mejor camarada de Mella." *Cuba Periodistas: La Prensa de la Prensa Cubana*, March 25, 2019. https://www .cubaperiodistas.cu/index.php/2019/03/este-periodista-es-el-mejor -camarada-de-mella/.

Oso, Tia, Opal Tometi, and Aly Wane. "Transformational Solidarity Webinar: Why the Migrant Rights Movement Must Show Up for Black Lives." Black Alliance for Just Immigration, March 11, 2015.

Partido Bolchevique Leninista. *Programa del Partido Bolchevique Leninista*. Havana: O'Reilly, 1934.

Patnaik, Utsa, and Prabhat Patnaik. *A Theory of Imperialism*. New York: Columbia University Press, 2016.

PCC (Partido Comunista de Cuba). *Cuidemos la unidad: El caso del Dr. Martín Castellanos*. Havana: Impresora Alfa, 1938.

"PCC a PCM, 31 de mayo 1926." In *Mella: Textos escogidos*, edited by Julio César Guanche, 2:187–89. Havana: Centro Cultural Pablo de la Torriente Brau, 2017.

Pedroso, Regino. *Nosotros*. Havana: Editorial Trópico, 1933.

Pedroso, Regino. "Vida y Sueños." *Antología de la poesía cósmica de Regino Pedroso*, edited by Fredo Arias de la Canal, 129–51. Mexico City: Frente de Afirmación Hispanista, 2004.

Peláez Ramos, Gerardo. "El fusilamiento de J. Guadalupe Rodríguez Favela." *Rebelión* 14 (May 2014). https://rebelion.org/el-fusilamiento-de-j -guadalupe-rodriguez-favela/.

Peláez Ramos, Gerardo. *Partido Comunista Mexicano: 60 años de historia.* Culiacán, Sinaloa, Mexico: Universidad Autónoma de Sinaloa, 1980.

Perdomo, Omar. "Trayectoria vital de Regino Pedroso." In *Antología de la poesía cósmica de Regino Pedroso*, edited by Fredo Arias de la Canal, 162–78. Mexico City: Frente de Afirmación Hispanista, 2004.

Petersson, Fredrik. *Willi Münzenberg, the League Against Imperialism, and the Comintern, 1925–1933.* Lewiston, NY: Edwin Mellen Press, 2014.

Plácido, Sandy. "Blood on Their Hands: Barrick Gold, Gustavo and Patricia Cisneros, and Networks of Imperialist Extraction in the Dominican Republic." In *Strike MoMA Reader*, edited by Strike MoMA Working Group of International Imagination of Anti-National, Anti-Imperialist Feelings (IIAAF). N.p.: Decolonize This Place, 2022.

Poniatowska, Elena. *Tinísima.* Mexico City: Ediciones Era, 1992.

Popescu, Monica. *At Penpoint: African Literatures, Postcolonial Studies, and the Cold War.* Durham, NC: Duke University Press, 2020.

Power, Margaret M. *Solidarity Across the Americas: The Puerto Rican Nationalist Party and Anti-Imperialism.* Chapel Hill: University of North Carolina Press, 2023.

Prashad, Vijay. *The Darker Nations: A People's History of the Third World.* New York: New Press, 2007.

Price, Rachel. *The Object of the Atlantic: Concrete Aesthetics in Cuba, Brazil, and Spain, 1868–1968.* Chicago: Northwestern University Press, 2014.

Pujals, Sandra. "Becoming Jaime Nevares: Imagination and Identity Reinvention in the Communist International's Latin American Network, 1919–43." In *The Global Impacts of Russia's Great War and Revolution, Book 2: The Wider Arc of Revolution Part 1*, edited by Choi Chatterjee, Steven G. Marks, Mary Neuburger, and Steven Sabol, 393–415. Bloomington, IN: Slavica, 2019.

Pujals, Sandra. "De un pájaro las tres alas: El Buró del Caribe de la Comintern, Cuba y el radicalismo comunista de Puerto Rico, 1931–1936." *Op. Cit.: Revista del Centro de Investigaciones Históricas* 21 (2012–2013): 255–83.

Pujals, Sandra. "¡Embarcados! James Sager, la Sección Puertorriqueña de la Liga Anti-Imperialista de las Américas y el Partido Nacionalista de Puerto Rico, 1925–1927." *Op. Cit.: Revista del Centro de Investigaciones Históricas* 22 (2013): 105–39.

Pujals, Sandra. "A 'Soviet Caribbean': The Comintern, New York's Immigrant Community, and the Forging of Caribbean Visions, 1931–1936." *Russian History* 41, no. 2 (2014): 255–68.

Rahier, Jean Muteba. "Introduction: Black Social Movements in Latin America: From Monocultural Mestizaje and 'Invisibility' to Multiculturalism and State Corporatism/Co-optation." In *Black Social Movements in Latin*

America: From Monocultural Mestizaje to Multiculturalism, edited by Jean Muteba Rahier, 1–12. New York: Palgrave Macmillan, 2012.

Ralph, Michael, and Maya Singhal. "Racial Capitalism." *Theory and Society* 48, no. 6 (2019): 851–81.

Ramírez, Sergio, ed. *El pensamiento vivo de Sandino*. San José: Editorial Centroamérica, 1974.

Rashotte, Nicole. "World's 10 Largest Gold Mines by Production." *Investing News*, July 31, 2019. https://investingnews.com/daily/resource-investing /precious-metals-investing/gold-investing/largest-gold-mines/.

Reig Romero, Carlos Eduardo, ed. *El útil anhelo: Correspondencia de Rubén Martínez Villena*. Havana: Centro Cultural Pablo de la Torriente Brau, 2015.

Reuters Staff. "Civil Society Groups Urge Halt to Barrick's Pueblo Viejo Expansion." *Reuters*, May 4, 2021. https://www.reuters.com/article/mining -barrick-dominican-idINL1N2MR1MP.

Reyes-Santos, Alaí. *Our Caribbean Kin: Race and Nation in the Neoliberal Antilles*. New Brunswick, NJ: Rutgers University Press, 2015.

Reynoso Jaime, Irving. *El agrarismo radical en México: Una biografía política de Úrsulo Galván, Primo Tapia, y José Guadalupe Rodríguez*. Morelos, Mexico: Universidad Autónoma del Estado de Morelos, 2020.

Riofrancos, Thea. "Extractivism and *Extractivismo*." *Global South Studies*, November 2020. https://www.globalsouthstudies.org/keyword-essay /extractivism-and-extractivismo/.

Riofrancos, Thea. *Resource Radicals: From Petronationalism to Post-Extractivism in Ecuador*. Durham, NC: Duke University Press, 2020.

Rivera Mir, Sebastián. *Militantes de la izquierda latinoamericana en México, 1920–34: Prácticas políticas, redes y conspiraciones*. Mexico City: El Colegio de México, 2018.

Roa, Raúl. *El fuego de la semilla en el zurco*. Havana: Editorial Letras Cubanas, 1982.

Robbins, Bruce. "Blaming the System." In *Immanuel Wallerstein and the Problem of the World: System, Scale, Culture*, edited by David Palumbo-Liu, Nirvana Tanoukhi, and Bruce Robbins, 41–63. Durham, NC: Duke University Press, 2011.

Robinson, Cedric R. *Black Marxism: The Making of the Black Radical Tradition*. Chapel Hill: University of North Carolina Press, 1983.

Rodríguez, Luis Felipe. *Marcos Antilla: Relatos de cañaveral*. Havana: Ediciones Huracán, 1971.

Rodríguez Sosa, Fernando. "Regino Pedroso: Yunque y verso." Originally published as "Regino Pedroso, yunque y verso." *Bohemia* 68, no. 33 (August 13, 1976): 10–13. Republished in *Habana Radio: La voz del patrimonio cubano*, October 29, 2018. http://www.habanaradio.cu/culturales/regino -pedroso-yunque-y-verso/.

Rojas, Rafael. "Haya, Mella y la división originaria." *Telar* 20 (January–June 2018): 45–67.

Rosell, Mirta. *Luchas obreras contra Machado*. Havana: Instituto Cubano del Libro Editorial de Ciencias Sociales, 1973.

Rosenberg, Fernando J. *The Avant-Garde and Geopolitics in Latin America*. Pittsburgh: University of Pittsburgh Press, 2006.

Roy, Manabendra Nath. *M. N. Roy's Memoirs*. Bombay: Allied Publishers, 1964.

Roy, Samaren. *M. N. Roy: A Political Biography*. New Delhi: Orient Longman, 1997.

Ruiz del Vizo, Hortensio, ed. *Black Poetry of the Americas*. Miami: Ediciones Universal, 1972.

"Ruthenberg a PCC, 15 de julio 1926." In *Mella: Textos escogidos*, edited by Julio César Guanche, 2:191–95. Havana: Centro Cultural Pablo de la Torriente Brau, 2017.

Saborit, Antonio, ed. *Una mujer sin país: Las cartas a Edward Weston y otros papeles personales*. Mexico City: Ediciones Cal y Arena, 2001.

Saldaña-Portillo, María Josefina. "Hemispheric Literature." In *The Cambridge Companion to Transnational Literature*, edited by Yogita Goyal, 203–18. Cambridge: Cambridge University Press, 2017.

Saldaña-Portillo, María Josefina. *Indian Given: Racial Geographies Across Mexico and the United States*. Durham, NC: Duke University Press, 2016.

Sánchez Soler, Juan, Coronel Rivera, and the Museo Casa Estudio Diego Rivera y Frida Kahlo. *Xavier Guerrero (1896–1974): De piedra completa*. Mexico City: Consejo Nacional para la Cultura y las Artes, 2012.

Sandino, Augusto César. "A Gustavo Alemán Bolaños." In *El pensamiento vivo de Sandino*, edited by Sergio Ramírez, 180–81. San José: Editorial Centroamérica, 1974.

Sandino, Augusto César. "Carta a Froylán Turcios." In *El pensamiento vivo de Sandino*, edited by Sergio Ramírez, 148–50. San José: Editorial Centroamérica, 1974.

Sandino, Augusto César. "Carta a los gobernantes de América." In *El pensamiento vivo de Sandino*, edited by Sergio Ramírez, 141–44. San José: Editorial Centroamérica, 1974.

Sandino, Augusto César. "Carta al presidente de México, Emilio Portes Gil." In *El pensamiento vivo de Sandino*, edited by Sergio Ramírez, 161–62. San José: Editorial Centroamérica, 1974.

Sandino, Augusto César. "Carta al Presidente Hipólito Yrigoyen de la Argentina." In *El pensamiento vivo de Sandino*, edited by Sergio Ramírez, 169–72. San José: Editorial Centroamérica, 1974.

Sandino, Augusto César. "Convenio." In *El pensamiento vivo de Sandino*, edited by Sergio Ramírez, 50–52. San José: Editorial Centroamérica, 1974.

Sandino, Augusto César. "El regreso de Nicaragua." In *El pensamiento vivo de Sandino*, edited by Sergio Ramírez, 53–54. San José: Editorial Centroamérica, 1974.

Sandino, Augusto César. "Manifiesto político." In *El pensamiento vivo de Sandino*, edited by Sergio Ramírez, 87. San José: Editorial Centroamérica, 1974.

Sangiovanni, Andrea, and Juri Viehoff. "Solidarity in Social and Political Philosophy." In *Stanford Encyclopedia of Philosophy*, edited by Edward N. Zalta and Uri Nodelman. Summer 2023. https://plato.stanford.edu/archives/sum2023/entries/solidarity/.

San Miguel, Pedro L. *The Imagined Island: History, Identity, and Utopia in Hispaniola*. Chapel Hill: University of North Carolina Press, 2005.

Sawhney, Savitri. "Revolutionary Work: Pandurang Khankhoje and Tina Modotti." *Bouilla Baise Work in Progress*, August 3, 2019. https://bouillabaiseworkinprogress.blogspot.com/2017/08/revolutionary-work-pandurang-khankhoje.html.

Sawyer, Mark Q. *Racial Politics in Post-Revolutionary Cuba*. New York: Cambridge University Press, 2006.

Schalk, Owen. "Barrick, Falconado, and Canadian Imperialism in the Dominican Republic." *Canadian Dimension*, October 24, 2021. https://canadiandimension.com/articles/view/barrick-falcondo-and-canadian-imperialism-in-the-dominican-republic.

Schelchkov, Audrey. "El marxismo militante: La Escuela Internacional Leninista y los cuadros de la Internacional Comunista en América Latina." *Izquierdas* 28 (July 2016): 226–47.

Scherer, Frank F. "Sanfancón: Orientalism, Self-Orientalization, and Chinese Religion in Cuba." In *Nation Dance: Religion, Identity and Cultural Difference in the Caribbean*, edited by Patrick Taylor, 153–70. Bloomington: Indiana University Press, 2001.

Schroeder, Michael. "'Bei dem Rebellengeneral Sandino' by Federico Bach in the *Arbeiter-Illustrierte-Zeitung* (Workers Pictorial Newspaper), Berlin." *The Sandino Rebellion Nicaragua 1927–34*. Accessed June 22, 2021. http://www.sandinorebellion.com/Top100pgs/Top100-p20b.html.

Seed, Patricia. "Colonial and Postcolonial Discourse." *Latin American Research Review* 26, no. 3 (1991): 181–200.

Serviat, Pedro. *El problema negro en Cuba y su solución definitiva*. Havana: Editora Política, 1986.

Sharman, Russell Leigh. "Red, White, and Black: Communist Literature and Black Migrant Labor in Costa Rica." *Afro-Hispanic Review* 24, no. 2 (Fall 2005): 137–49.

Shepard, Mathilda. "Life Politics: Race, Ecology and Dissident Aesthetics in Colombia." PhD diss., University of Virginia, 2022.

Shipman, Charles. *It Had to Be Revolution: Memoirs of an American Radical*. Ithaca, NY: Cornell University Press, 1993.

Smith, Danielle D. "La Novela de la Caña: Insular or International Phenomenon?" *Canadian Review of Comparative Literature* 35, nos. 1–2 (March–June 2008): 40–51.

Smith, John Charles. *Imperialism in the Twenty-First Century: Globalization, Super-Exploitation, and Capitalism's Final Crisis*. New York: Monthly Review Press, 2016.

Smith, Stephanie J. *Gender and the Mexican Revolution: Yucatán Women and the Realities of Patriarchy.* Chapel Hill: University of North Carolina Press, 2009.

Smith, Stephanie J. *The Power and Politics of Art in Postrevolutionary Mexico.* Chapel Hill: University of North Carolina Press, 2018.

Soler Martínez, Rafael. "El Partido Bolchevique Leninista Cubano." EHSEA 15 (July–December 1997): 271–90.

Solomon, Mark. *The Cry Was Unity: Communists and African Americans, 1917–1936.* Jackson: University Press of Mississippi, 1998.

Sommer, Doris. "Populism as Rhetoric: The Case of the Dominican Republic." *boundary 2* 11, no. 2 1–2 (Autumn 1982–Winter 1983): 253–70.

Spenser, Daniela. *The Impossible Triangle: Mexico, Soviet Russia, and the United States in the 1920s.* Durham, NC: Duke University Press, 1999.

Spenser, Daniela. *Stumbling Its Way Through Mexico: The Early Years of the Communist International.* Translated by Peter Gellert. Tuscaloosa: University of Alabama Press, 2011.

SSA (Secretariado Sudamericano de la Internacional Comunista). *El movimiento revolucionario latinoamericano: Versiones de la primera conferencia comunista latinoamericana, junio de 1929.* Buenos Aires: S.S.A. de la I.C., 1929.

Stahler-Sholk, Richard, Harry E. Vanden, and Glen David Kuecker. "Introduction." In *Latin American Social Movements in the Twenty-First Century: Resistance, Power, and Democracy,* edited by R. Stahler-Sholk, H. Vanden, and G. Kuecker, 1–15. Plymouth, MD: Rowman and Littlefield, 2008.

Staklo, Vadim. "Harnessing Revolution: The Communist International in Central America, 1929–1935." PhD diss., University of Pittsburgh, 2001.

Stephens, Michelle. *Black Empire: The Masculine Global Imaginary of Caribbean Intellectuals in the United States, 1914–1962.* Durham, NC: Duke University Press, 2005.

Stern, Steve J. "Feudalism, Capitalism, and the World-System in the Perspective of Latin America and the Caribbean." *American Historical Review* 93, no. 4 (1988): 829–72.

Stevens, Margaret. "'Hands Off Haiti!': Self-Determination, Anti-Imperialism, and the Communist Movement in the United States, 1925–1929." *Black Scholar* 37, no. 4 (2008): 61–70.

Stevens, Margaret. *Red International and Black Caribbean: Communists in New York City, Mexico and the West Indies, 1919–1939.* London: Pluto Press, 2017.

Stites Mor, Jessica. *South-South Solidarity and the Latin American Left.* Madison: University of Wisconsin Press, 2022.

Strike MoMa. "Framework and Terms for Struggle." Strike MoMA. https://www.strikemoma.org/.

Strike MoMa. "Water Is More Precious than Gold." Strike MoMA. https://www.strikemoma.org/week-9.

Strike MoMa. "Week 9." Strike MoMA. https://www.strikemoma.org/week-9.

Strike MoMA Working Group of International Imagination of Anti-National, Anti-Imperialist Feelings, eds. *Strike MoMA Reader*. N.p.: Decolonize This Place, 2022.

Sullivan, Frances Peace. "The 'Negro Question' in Cuba, 1928–1936." In *Transnational Communism Across the Americas*, edited by Marc Becker, Margaret Power, Tony Wood, and Jacob A. Zumoff, 55–78. Champaign: University of Illinois Press, 2023.

Svampa, Maristella. *Neo-Extractivism in Latin America: Socio-Environmental Conflicts, the Territorial Turn, and New Political Narratives*. Cambridge: Cambridge University Press, 2019.

Taylor, Diana. *The Archive and the Repertoire: Performing Cultural Memory in the Americas*. Durham, NC: Duke University Press, 2003.

Tennant, Gary. "The Hidden Pearl of the Caribbean: Trotskyism in Cuba." *Revolutionary History* 7, no. 3 (2000).

"Theses on the Negro Question." *Bulletin of the IV Congress of the Communist International* 17 (December 7, 1922): 8–10.

Tibol, Raquel. *Julio Antonio Mella en "El Machete."* Mexico City: Fondo de Cultura Popular, 1968.

Torres García, María Alejandra. "Barrick Threatens Involuntary Resettlement." *Earthworks*, December 10, 2024. https://earthworks.org/blog/barrick-threatens-involuntary-resettlement/.

Turcios, Froylán. "Carta de Froylán Turcios." In *El pensamiento vivo de Sandino*, edited by Sergio Ramírez, 156–59. San José: Editorial Centroamérica, 1974.

Turner, Joyce Moore, and W. Burghardt Turner. *Caribbean Crusaders and the Harlem Renaissance*. Urbana: University of Illinois Press, 2005.

Ulloa, Astrid. *The Ecological Native: Indigenous Peoples' Movements and Eco-Governmentality in Colombia*. New York: Routledge, 2005.

Vega, Bernardo. *En la década perdida*. Santo Domingo: Fundación Cultural Dominicana, 1990.

Vega, Bernardo. *Un interludio de tolerancia: El acuerdo de Trujillo con los comunistas en 1946*. Santo Domingo: Fundación Cultural Dominicana, 1987.

Veltmeyer, Henry, and James Petras. *The New Extractivism: A Post-Neoliberal Development Model or Imperialism of the Twenty-First Century*. London: Zed Books, 2014.

Vidal, Hernán. "The Concept of Colonial and Postcolonial Discourse: A Perspective from Literary Criticism." *Latin American Research Review* 28, no. 3 (1993): 113–19.

Walsh, Catherine. "Afro In/Exclusion, Resistance, and the 'Progressive' State: (De)Colonial Struggles, Questions, and Reflections." In *Black Social Movements in Latin America: From Monocultural Mestizaje to Multiculturalism*, edited by Jean Muteba Rahier, 15–34. New York: Palgrave Macmillan, 2012.

Weheliye, Alexander G. *Habeas Viscus: Racializing Assemblages, Biopolitics, and Black Feminist Theories of the Human*. Durham, NC: Duke University Press, 2014.

Weiss, Holger. "Calling the Toilers in the African Atlantic." Paper presented at The Red and the Black: The Russian Revolution and the Black Atlantic Conference, Institute for Black Atlantic Research, University of Central Lancashire, Preston, UK, October 14, 2017.

Weiss, Holger. *Framing a Radical African Atlantic: African American Agency, West African Intellectuals and the International Trade Union Committee of Negro Workers*. Leiden: Brill, 2013.

West, Michael O., William G. Martin, and Fanon Che Wilkins, eds. *From Toussaint to Tupac: The Black International Since the Age of Revolution*. Chapel Hill: University of North Carolina Press, 2009.

Wolfe, Bertram D. *A Life in Two Centuries*. Briarcliff Manor, NY: Stein and Day, 1981.

Wood, Tony. "Indoamerica Against Empire: Radical Transnational Politics in Mexico City, 1925–1929." In *The Anticolonial Transnational: Imaginaries, Mobilities, and Networks in the Struggle Against Empire*, edited by Erez Manela and Heather Streets-Salter, 64–88. Cambridge: Cambridge University Press, 2023.

Wood, Tony. "Semicolonials and Soviets: Latin American Communists in the USSR, 1927–1936." In *Transnational Communism Across the Americas*, edited by Marc Becker, Margaret Power, Tony Wood, and Jacob A. Zumoff, 79–100. Champaign: University of Illinois Press, 2023.

Yen, Huei Lan. *Toma y daca: Transculturación y presencia de escritores chino-latinoamericanos*. West Lafayette, IN: Purdue University Press, 2016.

Young, Robert J. C. *Postcolonialism: An Historical Introduction*. Oxford: Blackwell, 2001.

Young, Robert J. C. "Postcolonialism: From Bandung to the Tricontinental." *Historein* 5 (2005): 11–21.

Zumoff, J. A. "Black Caribbean Migrants and the Labor Movement and Communists in the Greater Caribbean in the 1920s and 1930s." In *Transnational Communism Across the Americas*, edited by Marc Becker, Margaret Power, Tony Wood, and Jacob A. Zumoff, 31–54. Champaign: University of Illinois Press, 2023.

Zumoff, J. A. "Ojos que no ven: The Communist Party, Caribbean Migrants and the Communist International in Costa Rica in the 1920s and 1930s." *Journal of Caribbean History* 45, no. 2 (2011): 212–47.

INDEX

Note: Page numbers followed by f refer to figures.

anti-Semitism, 172–73

Aponte, Carlos, 192, 201–2, 288n39

APRA (American Popular Revolutionary Alliance/Alianza Popular Revoluciona-ria Americana), 76, 80, 82–85, 106, 206, 212; LADLA–Costa Rica and, 310n9; Mella's critiques of, 279n87

Arbeiter-Illustrierte-Zeitung, 188, 272n104

archives, 6–8, 53, 266n11; LAI, 7–8; PCCR, 220

Argentina, 75, 119, 175, 208, 251, 260n11; Black people in, 109; LADLA section, 51, 77, 115, 259n5, 270n85, 293n15

Armillas-Tiseyra, Magalí, 69–70, 235, 261n17

Armstrong, Carol, 55, 57, 64

artists, 2, 38, 48, 54, 94, 126; APRA, 80, 84; Black, 173; LADLA, 5, 6, 27, 252; Latin American, 10–11; leftist, 122; Mexican, 40; Minoristas, 289n49; *Mundo Obrero*, 229; PCM, 269n66. *See also* Caycedo, Carolina; Guerrero, Xavier; Modotti, Tina; Rivera, Diego; Siqueiros, David

Asia, 4, 19, 71, 78, 150, 274n14; anticolo-nialists from, 70–71; colonialism in, 10, 14, 68; decolonization in, 10; foreign governments in, 130; Latin American cosmopolitanism and, 11, 69; petroleum workers from, 51

assimilation, 116, 123; of Indigenous peoples, 60; national, 74

Association of New Cuban Revolutionary Émigrés (ANERC), 93, 98

Asturias, Miguel Ángel, 19, 222

Auténtico (Cuban Revolutionary Party), 100–101

authoritarianism, 17, 22, 185, 190, 196, 204

Aymara, 117; language, 22

Bach, Federico (Fritz Sulzbachner), 5, 191, 216, 301n22, 302n41, 309n182

banana industry, 199, 218–19, 223–24, 229, 310n9

bananas, 37, 55, 199, 220, 224–25, 241, 314n115. *See also* plantations: banana; workers: banana

Bandung Conference, 9–10, 68

Barbusse, Henri, 200, 211, 216, 275n23

Barreiro Olivera, Alejandro, 92, 99, 118, 281n31, 287n25, 288n31

Basbaum, Leoncio, 117–18

Batista, Fulgencio, 100–101, 135, 138

Beals, Carleton, 202, 301n33

Becker, Marc, 96, 117, 261n13

Berlin, 6, 72; Du Bois and, 86; Junco and, 36, 222; LAI headquarters in, 116; Mella and, 40; Modotti and, 54, 215, 222, 310n14

biodiversity, 39; tropical, 138–39

Black activists, 4, 7, 14, 95, 103, 113; Bol-shevism and, 283n53

Black Belt, 96, 104, 126

Black communities, 7, 29, 53, 249

Black Cubans, 110, 118, 126, 130, 286n7

Black Latin Americans, 15, 95–96, 109, 118–21

blackness, 142, 244

Black people, 88–89, 108, 110, 112, 114, 119–21, 142–43, 239; in the Americas, 96, 117; in Argentina and Uruguay, 109; colonial economic regime and, 134; double exploitation of, 142; *El Libertador* and, 76; in Limón, 242; manifestos for, 228; in Peru, 118; in the United States, 27, 95, 103

Black populations, 4, 13, 26, 88, 102–4, 106; American, 103, 113–14

Black workers, 15, 86, 102–4, 110–14, 118, 123, 127, 228; in the Americas, 14; BC and, 229, 245; Black political subjectivity and, 126; double exploitation of, 151; exclusion of, 132; fraternization with, 200; Junco and, 99; LADLA-Cuba and, 134; in *Mamita Yunai* (Fallas), 242; *Mundo Obrero* and, 229; organizing, 89, 102, 109, 226; race consciousness among, 122; US, 108–9, 227

Bolívar, Simón, 83, 300n14

Bolivia, 21, 23, 75, 119, 130; Indigenous rights in, 286n150; La Paz, 82; silver mines in, 262n27

Bolshevik-Leninist Party (PBL), 100, 104, 110–11, 125, 282n42, 282n45

Borodin, Mikhail Markovich, 44–45, 277n60

bourgeoisie, 45, 118, 121, 195; Cuban, 110; European, 100; national, 111; native, 114; petty, 164, 234

Brazil, 21, 51, 71, 75, 220; LADLA section, 77, 116–17, 193, 259n5, 285n119; modernism in, 262n31; Palmares, 112; sugarcane nov-els from, 310n7; sugar mills in, 262n27

Colombia (*continued*)
270n85; Machado and, 201, 222; massacre of banana workers in, 19, 181, 199, 222 (*see also* United Fruit Company); Sager and, 181, 299n179

Colorado, Antonio, 158–59, 161

colonialism, 147; British, 129, 238; European, 10, 60, 68, 77; Japanese, 129; settler, 24, 26, 31, 95; Spanish, 164, 166. *See also* anticolonialisms

communism, 45, 72; Black, 97, 104, 141; Chinese, 149; Cuban, 6, 93, 135, 260n10; Garveyism and, 284n107; global, 11; Haya de la Torre and, 80, 83; ideology of, 103; Indigenous cultures and, 84; LADLA and, 162–63; Latin American, 6; Mella and, 83, 278n68, 278n71; Mexican, 6–7, 260n10, 274n7; orthodox, 85; in *Over* (Marrero Aristy), 234, 238; Vasconcelos and, 79

Communist International (Comintern), 40, 44–47, 117, 190, 195, 278n82, 300n16; American Black radicals and, 102; Black self-determination and, 283n61; class against class approach, 17–18, 195, 210–11, 222, 278n71; Executive Committee, 211, 223; Frankfurt Congress, 211–12, 309n186; Junco and, 99, 118; *La Correspondance internationale*, 215; LADLA and, 7, 88, 93–94, 164, 185, 190; LAI and, 47, 72, 211–12; in Latin America, 315n134; Latin American secretariat, 223; Latin Americans' engagement with, 11; Mella and, 82, 283n50; in Mexico, 42; Negro Commission, 102–4; Negro Question and, 226; PCM and, 216; periodicals, 6; popular front, 100; Sandino and, 190, 206; South American Secretariat, 104; Third Period, 278n71, 282n34; united front approach, 5, 73, 181, 195, 211, 222, 278n71; Workers International Relief and, 72. *See also* Caribbean Bureau (Buró del Caribe, BC); Vidali, Vittorio

communist parties, 44, 102, 115–16; BC leadership and, 311n22; Black workers and, 229; class reductionism and, 264n68; LADLA and, 5, 260n8; Latin American, 118, 120; local, 18, 223, 226, 228; orthodox, 6

Confederation of Cuban Workers (CNOC), 98, 110, 282n40

Confederation of Latin American Labor Unions (CSLA), 95, 98, 101, 104–9, 113–16, 223, 283n67, 284n83; *El Trabajador Latinoamericano*, 104–5, 109, 120

Congress Against Colonial Oppression and Imperialism and for National Independence, 4, 52, 67, 72

Contreras, Miguel, 105–6, 269n78

corporations, 251; foreign, 20, 23; multinational, 250; US, 111, 236

corruption, 22, 159

cosmotarrayas, 1–2, 252

Costa Rica, 6, 241; banana production in, 314n115; MAFUENIC campaign in, 220; United Fruit Company and, 199–200, 224–25

Costa Rican Communist Party (PCCR), 18, 220, 229–30, 241–42, 312n53

Coulthard, Glen, 26

Crouch, Paul, 183, 299n188

Cuba, 6, 17, 69, 89, 131, 133, 151–52, 277n60, 284n107, 285n118; anti-Black racism in, 126; Aponte and, 192, 288n39; Black self-determination in, 104; Black workers in, 114, 118; Chinese immigrants in, 120, 145, 147–49; dictatorship in, 54, 224, 227; Fernández Sánchez and, 224; 50 Percent Law, 110–11, 133–34; Haya de la Torre and, 80; José Martí Popular University (UP), 80–81, 129, 131; Junco and, 98–99, 109, 111, 125, 180, 215, 222; Machado and, 193; MAFUENIC and, 194; Martí's, 81; Marrero Aristy and, 232; Mella and, 93, 213, 266n6, 288n34; Morúa Law, 110, 118, 125–26; nationalism in, 288n30; nonracialized class identity in, 135; *novela de la caña* and, 219; Oriente province, 104, 118, 126, 133, 282n41; Pedroso and, 127–28, 135–40, 143, 145, 149–50; Puerto Rico and, 164; sugar plantations in, 229; Tricontinental Conference in, 9; UNIA and, 280n103; Unión de Obreros Antillanos, 284n108; US domination in, 76; US-owned plantations in, 119; Vasconcelos and, 175; Wong and, 129; Zaldívar and, 178. *See also* Batista, Fulgencio; Joven Cuba; LADLA-Cuba; Machado, Gerardo; Organization of

Solidarity with the Peoples of Africa, Asia, and Latin America (OPSAAAL); sugar; sugarcane

Cuban Communist Party (PCC), 35, 80–82, 134–35, 152, 260n10, 287n23; anti-Chinese discrimination and, 290n67; BC and, 311n22; Castellanos and, 125–26, 286n7; Chinese Nationalist Party and, 150; Communist Opposition (OC), 99–100, 282n39, 282n41 (see also Bolshevik-Leninist Party [PBL]); 50 Percent Law and, 133; Junco and, 93, 97–101, 115, 122, 125–27, 134, 151, 226; Mella and, 80–84, 93, 98, 277n60, 278n68, 283n50; Negro Question and, 287n7

cubanía, 128, 145

cultural production, 4, 11; of anti-extractivist movements, 252; interwar Latin American, 12; LADLA's, 249; Mexican, 273n122; radical interwar, 7

cultural studies, 6, 275n18

Curaçao, 201, 222, 228

Cuyamel Fruit, 199

dams, 61; hydroelectric, 1, 20; tailings, 247

Deambrosis Martins, Carlos, 76, 86–88

decoloniality, 10, 262n28

decolonization, 10, 71

de la Plaza, Salvador, 5, 8, 164–65, 186, 193, 196, 216; Brussels Congress and, 77; "The Continental Situation," 195; LADLA-Cuba and, 51, 130–31, 287n25

dependency, 21, 225, 243, 252, 263n48; theorists, 20, 263n48; theory, 20

discrimination, 174, 242, 286n148; anti-Black, 118, 121, 131, 143, 290n69; anti-Chinese, 134, 290n67; of form, 55; immigrant workers and, 108; inclusionary, 152; racial, 103, 110, 116–17, 121, 227, 237

dispossession, 25–26; Indigenous, 12, 26, 30, 88, 94, 249; land, 4, 24, 27, 39, 94, 227–28, 239

Dominican Republic, 6, 130, 219, 224, 235–36, 238–39; activists from, 251; Dominican Popular Socialist Party (PSP), 232; LADLA section, 51, 77, 259n5, 270n85; Limón, 224–25, 229–30, 242; protests against Barrick Gold in, 247–48, 251–52. See also Mella, Julio Antonio

Du Bois, W. E. B., 86, 248, 264n65

economics: Latin American, 21; neoliberal, 286n148

Ecuador, 21, 51, 77, 193, 264n61; LADLA section, 259n5, 270n85

Edwards, Erica, 204, 206, 273n127

Ejército Defensor de la Soberanía Nacional de Nicaragua (EDSN), 186, 92–94, 201, 209, 212, 216, 309n182

El Libertador, 7, 13, 19, 28–29, 51–53, 73, 75–76, 78, 85, 88, 194, 197, 198f, 203, 205, 260n9, 273n2, 280n106; Acosta Velarde and, 163; América Libre and, 132; APRA and, 83; CSLA and, 106; De la Plaza and, 51, 77, 164; Galván Reyes and, 49, 56, 129, 267n30; gender and sexuality and, 279n87; Guerrero and, 48, 51, 159; Haya de la Torre and, 82; illustrations in, 269n65; Jolibois and, 89; LADLA-Cuba and, 130; LADLA–Puerto Rico and, 160; LADLA-US and, 259n5; Machado and, 193; MAFUENIC and, 191, 196, 200, 202, 208–10; Mella and, 277n60; Modotti and, 271n97; PCM and, 212; Rivera and, 52, 59, 60f, 202, 203f; Sager and, 159, 162, 164; Sandino and, 189, 201, 206, 209–11, 213; Senghor and, 90; Wolfe and, 49, 51, 59; women and, 192, 271n95

El Machete, 38, 40, 83, 193, 212, 300n13; Guerrero and, 48; headquarters of, 301n29; Hurwitz and, 301n23; LADLA and, 160; Mella and, 214, 278n71; Modotti and, 41; Sager and, 164, 177; Sandino and, 201

El Salvador, 119; LADLA section, 51, 77, 193, 197, 223, 259n5, 270n85; Sandino and, 217; workers in, 227

enmeshment, 16, 30, 157, 174

enslavement, 95, 112, 119, 239

erotics: LADLA's, 179; masculine, 16, 158, 177, 249; of revolutionary politics, 298n166 (see also Guevara, Che)

Escobar, Arturo, 28, 262n28

ethnic impersonation, 174, 249. See also Gomez, Manuel (Charles Francis Phillips); Sager, James Nathanson (Jaime Nevares)

ethnicity, 17, 116–17, 177, 183

Europe, 19, 70, 78, 190, 219; Eastern, 172; Haya de la Torre and, 82–83; Mariátegui and, 122; Modotti and, 215;

Guevara, Che, 54, 93, 116, 177, 214, 298n166
Guillén, Nicolás, 128–29, 230
Guirao, Ramón, 141, 290n69
Guridy, Frank Andre, 142, 289n49

Haiti, 112, 118, 130, 140, 143, 204, 239; Black
    immigrant workers from, 110; Haitian
    Revolution, 112; terror in, 285n118; US
    imperialism in, 88; US invasion of, 87;
    US occupation of, 89, 196, 305n100
Haitian Patriotic Union (HPU), 86–89, 186,
    196, 276n33, 280n101, 300n21
Havana, 6–7, 143, 261n18, 288n37; Central
    Park, 132; Chinatown, 148; Fernández
    Sánchez and, 224; Hurwitz and, 191;
    Junco and, 14, 36, 98–99, 111; Marrero
    Aristy and, 232; Mella and, 81–82, 92,
    277n60; OC in, 282n41; Pan-American
    Conference in, 197; Pedroso and, 127;
    Tricontinental Conference in, 9; Uni-
    versity of Havana, 80, 82, 93, 129, 266,
    277n60
Hawkins, Isaiah, 6, 108–9
Haya de la Torre, Víctor Raúl, 72, 75–76,
    79, 90; on hispanoamericanismo, 278n77;
    LADLA condemnation of, 300n20;
    Mariátegui and, 106; Mella and, 80–84,
    275n18, 278n75, 279n82, 279n87
hemispheric globalism, 11–12, 14, 71,
    74–76, 85, 91, 249; LADLA's, 76, 78–79,
    128, 135, 143, 146–47, 207
hispanoamericanismo, 11, 69, 74, 83,
    272n113, 278n77
Honduras, 199; LADLA section, 51, 77, 197,
    259n5, 270n85; Puerto Cortes, 111; San-
    dino and, 206; Turcios and, 210; United
    Fruit Company and, 225
Hooks, Margaret, 38, 41, 266n3, 267n18,
    267n26
Huiswoud, Otto, 102–3, 113, 121
Hurwitz, Jacobo, 186, 191–92, 195, 208–10,
    212, 301n23, 302n41, 307n142

identity, 62, 145, 156, 172–75; class, 115,
    134–35, 151–52; cross-national, 134;
    Cuban, 128, 146, 148–49; Dominican
    national, 315n126; essay, 12; false, 16, 176
    (see also Gomez, Manuel [Charles Francis
    Phillips]; Sager, James Nathanson
    [Jaime Nevares]); Latin American, 220;

Mexican national, 60–61; politics, 84;
    racial, 74; West Indian cultural, 242
immigrant communities, 7, 29, 53, 249;
    Black, 134, 151, 228; Chinese, 134, 151
immigrant populations, 4, 26, 120, 122;
    Black, 134; Chinese, 143, 146, 148
immigrants, 15, 105, 123, 133–34, 151, 248,
    288n30; Black, 113, 119–20, 134, 221, 226,
    229, 286n148; Caribbean, 110, 133, 239;
    Chinese, 15, 84, 120, 133, 189; Jewish, 115
immigration, 119–20; Chinese, 120, 148,
    279n87; Jewish, 172
imperialism, 19–20, 23, 44, 52, 73, 85, 132,
    251; agents of, 209–10; aiding, 163; Brit-
    ish, 43, 75, 285n119; in the Caribbean,
    196–97; class struggle and, 165; critique
    of, 93; French, 90; in Latin America, 77,
    150, 229; Lenin's theory of, 250; Mella's
    opposition to, 214; power of, 225; Siquei-
    ros's report on, 106; universal, 200–201;
    Vatican and, 272n114; world, 90. See
    also anti-imperialism; US (Yankee)
    imperialism
India, 42–46, 131, 260n9, 268n39, 279n82;
    Johnstone and, 268n61
indigenismo, 11, 60–61, 69, 74, 272n113
Indigenous communities, 7, 22, 27, 29,
    116–17, 119, 249; APRA and, 84; essen-
    tializing views of, 74; extractive econ-
    omies and, 13, 23, 39, 88, 93; indigenista
    representation of, 64; Indigenous
    workers and, 107; LADLA and, 24, 39,
    58, 60–62, 88, 94
Indigenous cultures, 60, 84, 179
Indigenous groups, 22, 123, 241, 252
Indigenous languages, 47, 107
Indigenous leaders, 59, 61, 107
Indigenous leadership, 4, 47, 66, 107
Indigenous movements, 14, 21, 24, 76, 95,
    123, 252
Indigenous peoples, 59, 61–62, 88, 94, 96,
    112, 116–17, 272n114, 273n122; assimila-
    tion of, 60, 64; clothing of, 179; dispos-
    session of, 26, 249; enslavement of, 95,
    239; environment and, 266n15; erasure
    of, 78; insurrection and, 107; labor and,
    77, 196; land and, 107; oppression of,
    85; primitive accumulation and, 26;
    racialization and, 15; Sandino and, 204;
    self-determination for, 57, 119

Nehru, Jawaharlal, 4, 67, 69–70, 261n22, 273n2, 274n4, 275n23, 275n29

Neruda, Pablo, 19, 222

New York City, 6–7, 44, 143, 192, 194, 310n16; Caribbean Bureau (BC), 18, 122, 220, 222, 311n23; CSLA and, 223; Fernández Sánchez and, 224; LADLA-US branch in, 259n5; Machado in, 181, 193–94; Martí in, 193; Museum of Modern Art (MoMA), 247–49, 316n16; Public Library, 156, 281n11; Sager and, 170–71, 181; Workers School, 170–71, 181

Nicaragua, 54, 130, 140, 160, 191–96, 199, 201–2, 206–11, 213, 216, 226; Jolibois and, 204; Liberal uprising, 206–7; Machado in, 186, 202; Martí in, 217, 223; weapons and, 302n59. See also LADLA-Nicaragua; MAFUENIC (Manos Fuera de Nicaragua/Hands Off Nicaragua) campaign; Sandino, Augusto César

Nin, Andrés, 99, 282n39

novela de la caña, 219, 309n7

novela de la tierra, 12, 220, 237

oil, 140, 225; companies, 206; extraction, 264n61; fields, 18, 20, 219; industry, 20; rigs, 197. See also Standard Oil

Organization of Solidarity with the Peoples of Africa, Asia, and Latin America (OSPAAAL), 9, 11, 263n31

organizing, 16, 73, 194, 223, 234, 245, 248–50, 252; anticapitalist, 25, 201; anticolonial, 130; anti-imperialist, 129; Black, 102, 108, 157; Black internationalist, 86; collective, 221; Comintern, 315n134; communist, 44, 47, 49, 102, 151, 233, 278n68; ethnicity-based, 117; feminist, 27; Galván and, 267n30, 271n86; Indigenous, 14, 16, 24, 59, 107; 157; labor, 98–100, 105, 113, 134, 183, 200, 271n86, 313n70; LADLA's, 13, 23–24, 26, 253, 259n6, 274n3; leftist, 5; political, 2–4, 6, 27–28, 36, 61, 110, 116, 222, 249, 299n185, 316n16; race-based, 109–10, 120, 127; union, 181; united-front, 222

orientalism, 128, 146, 151

Over (Marrero Aristy), 18, 230–31, 233–40, 242–45, 309–10n7, 312n57, 315–16nn134–35

overidentification, 16, 30, 157–58, 174, 183

Padmore, George, 86, 97, 103, 121. See also Negro Worker, The

Panama, 75, 89, 111, 114, 140, 159, 241; border with Colombia, 199; LADLA section, 74, 82, 116, 193, 197, 270n85, 285n119; United Fruit Company and, 105

Panama Canal, 130; zone, 17, 184

pan-Americanism, 8, 44, 47, 150, 197, 303n73

Paris: APRA and, 82; LAI in, 192; Machado in, 193; Modotti in, 40; Rosa in, 168; Second International and, 102

Partido Independiente de Color (PIC), 118, 125

Pavletich, Esteban, 215, 309n182

Pedroso Aldama, Regino, 5, 12, 15, 127–29, 134–35, 150–52, 291n98, 292n140; "Hermano negro," 141–43, 290n78; Nosotros, 12, 134, 140–41, 143–49, 291n102; "Zafra-1934," 135–41, 147, 290n71

Peru, 6, 75, 117, 119, 220, 285n118; Cusco, 59, 107; González Prada Popular University, 106, 301n23; LADLA section in, 51, 77, 82, 259n5, 270n85; Socialist Party of, 106–7. See also Haya de la Torre, Víctor Raúl; Leguía, Augusto; Mariátegui, José Carlos

Pesce, Hugo, 107, 116, 119

Petersson, Fredrik, 211, 261n22, 274n4, 307n147

petroleum: companies, 251; industry, 271n86; Mexican, 72; workers, 51

Philippines, 71, 130, 160

Phillips, Charles Francis. See Gomez, Manuel

Pickens, William, 86, 275n23

pink tide governments, 21, 123, 252

Pittsburgh, 108; LADLA in, 194, 259n5

plantation economies, 4, 139

plantations, 20; banana, 18, 206, 218–19, 227, 242; corporate, 219–21, 224; monoculture, 27; rubber, 18, 219; sugar, 18, 113, 127, 139–40, 145, 167, 206, 219, 229, 232–34, 243; tobacco, 18, 219; United Fruit, 227, 231; US-owned, 119

poetry, 6, 145; Pedroso's, 15, 127–29, 134–35, 143, 151; social, 128–29, 134

police, 27, 194, 199, 239, 247; brutality, 107, 212; company, 227, 240; investigation of

Mella's assassination, 266n2; Machado dictatorship and, 98; Mexican, 266n7; persecution, 197; repression, 144, 287n15; San Juan, 171; surveillance, 169; white terror and, 227

policing, 4, 24, 172, 221, 227–28; of labor, 223; militarized, 123; racial, 4, 12, 17, 26, 184, 200; white terror and, 227

political organizing, 2, 4, 27–28, 36, 110, 116, 222; Modotti's, 316n16; Sager's, 299n185; transnational, 6, 61, 249

politics, 146, 280n103; aesthetics and, 12, 267n16; anticolonial, 9–11; anti-imperialist, 145–46; antiracist, 19, 94, 250; Black internationalist, 15, 96, 122; Cuban, 120, 134, 152; identity, 84; in-ternationalist, 86; Latin American, 191; leftist, 7, 18, 80, 127, 220; Modotti and, 41, 55; Pedroso and, 128–29; racial, 152, 166, 222; of *redes*, 28, 31, 128, 204–5; of relation, 31, 66, 143, 151, 157, 174, 177, 183; revolutionary, 43, 298n166; Sandino's, 207; sexual, 178; solidarity, 13, 16, 27, 31, 66, 126, 143, 151, 157–58, 174, 253; women and, 53

Poniatowska, Elena, 280n1; *Tinísima*, 38, 92–93, 266n11

Portes Gil, Emilio, 35, 99, 200, 208, 212–13, 215–16; MAFUENIC and, 302n43

Portocarrero, Julio, 106–7, 283n74

postcolonial studies, 9, 262nn27–28, 274n6

postcolonial theory, 10

Prashad, Vijay, 70–71, 275n18

primitive accumulation, 24–26

privatization, 21; of land, 24

proletarianization, 24–25; deproletarian-ization, 241

Puerto Rican Communist League (Liga Comunista de Puerto Rico), 155, 161, 164, 181, 294n38

Puerto Rican Nationalist Party (PNPR), 16, 73–74, 159–69, 172–73, 175, 181, 276nn33–34, 295nn43–44; Catholicism and, 298n143; Vasconcelos and, 74, 79, 276n34

Puerto Rico, 74; Black immigrant workers in, 173; Cayey, 159–60; English as official language of instruction in, 298n162; European stereotypes of, 175; independence of, 130, 159; Mayagüez,

158–61, 163, 170, 176, 180, 293n18; *novela de la caña* in, 219; Ponce, 159–61, 167, 170, 294n25, 294n31; Quiñones and, 168; racism in, 167; Rosa and, 168; Sager and, 155–56, 158, 161, 165, 167, 169–71, 176, 180–81, 270n85; United States and, 177; Vasconcelos and, 166, 168–70, 175, 276n34. *See also* LADLA–Puerto Rico

Pujals, Sandra, 7, 156, 181, 226, 230, 274n7, 293n15, 311n23

Quechua, 59, 62, 117; language, 22

Quijano, Aníbal, 262n28, 264n65

Quijano, Carlos, 76, 275n27

Quiñones, Samuel, 165, 168–69, 171, 276n34

racialization, 15, 25, 96, 145, 173; capital accumulation and, 24–25; of labor, 26, 249

racism, 24–27, 30, 103, 174, 227–28, 264n68; anti-Chinese, 146–47, 151; anti-immigrant, 26, 123, 128, 133, 135, 146; anti-Indigenous, 94, 111, 116; antiracism, 53, 88, 124, 178, 200, 240, 249; global, 142; internalized, 149; Jim Crow, 111; of Latin American workers, 108; in *Mamita Yunai*, 241; nativist, 126; *Over* as critique of, 234, 243–45, 315n135; within the PNPR, 166–67; structural, 286n148; US, 166–67, 173. *See also* anti-Black racism

radicalism, 65; Black, 96–97; Latin Ameri-can, 11, 68; twentieth-century, 37

Ramos Pedrueza, Rafael, 186, 300n21, 309n182

raw materials, 20–21, 252

reciprocity, 22–23, 50, 253

redes, 2, 28, 31, 128, 205, 214

Redes (Strand, Zinneman, and Gómez Muriel), 1–2, 3f, 5

Red International of Labor Unions (Profintern), 52–53, 99, 103, 113, 271n97, 281n26, 310–11n22

regionalisms, 251; ideological, 150; inter-war, 11, 71, 90, 249; Latin American, 72, 74–75, 78, 85–86, 128, 207, 249, 275n18

relationality, 29, 39, 265n87; anti-, 24

relational solidarity, 29–30, 205, 234, 249; politics of, 66, 143, 151, 157, 174

Richey, Robo de, 40–41
rights, 191; abortion, 27; African Americans', 89, 229; Black Cubans', 130, 142; Black laborers', 108–9; civil, 173–74; equal, 73, 102, 280n103; human, 202, 251, 305n100; immigrant, 4, 12, 152, 286n148; Indigenous, 22, 59, 61, 77, 95, 107, 286n150; labor, 20, 26; land, 117, 119, 123, 253; reproductive, 28; water, 1, 252; women's, 67, 253; workers', 80, 97, 126, 173, 196
Riofrancos, Thea, 21, 23–24
Rivera, Diego, 13, 40, 52, 59–64, 132, 202, 203f, 269n65, 272n114; Hernández Cárdenas and, 143; Kahlo and, 179; LADLA and, 5, 18, 61, 101, 126, 223, 277n48; LAI and, 77; PCM and, 216, 310n18
Robinson, Cedric, 24–26, 264n68
Rodríguez, Luis Felipe, 5; *Marcos Antilla: Relatos de cañaveral*, 18, 219–20, 230, 239–41, 310n7
Roy, Manabendra Nath, 13, 42–47, 102, 267nn31–32, 279n82; *El Pueblo* and, 43, 268n39. *See also* Lenin, Vladimir
rubber plantations, 18, 219–20
Russia, 44, 260n9, 299n187. *See also* Soviet Union (USSR)
Ruthenberg, Charles Emil, 164, 170

Sacco and Vanzetti, 40, 271n99, 300n21
Sager, James Nathanson (Jaime Nevares), 15–16, 155–77, 180–83, 270n85, 293n18, 294n25, 299n187; Albizu Campos and, 295n58; ethnic impersonation and, 16, 156, 171–72, 174–75, 177, 183; LADLA international secretariat and, 270n85; Works Progress Administration Archives Project and, 299n185
sandinismo, 17, 190
Sandino, Augusto César, 17, 54, 178, 183–217, 226, 300n12; LADLA and, 272n100, 309n190; LAI and, 308n174; Machado and, 188, 204, 210, 306–7n142: Vasconcelos and, 306n125
Sandino, Sócrates, 186, 188, 193, 302n41
San Francisco, 41; LADLA branch in, 194, 259n5
San Juan, 6, 158–61, 168, 170–71, 176, 181
Santibáñez, Adolfo, 44, 268n39

Santo Domingo, 6, 52, 140, 220, 231
Sárraga, Clemente, 161, 294n25
Schroeder, Michael J., 188–89
Scottsboro, 104, 142–43
Scottsboro Boys, 96, 104, 142, 228–29
self-determination, 12, 74; Black, 102, 104–5, 116, 119, 126, 132, 283n61; Cuba's, 81; home-grown, 79; Indigenous, 56–57, 105, 116–17, 119–20; movements, 202; national, 81, 119–20; Puerto Rican, 172; resource extraction and, 23
Senghor, Lamine, 4, 67, 86, 89–90, 103, 273n2
sexism, 30, 174
Sharman, Russell Leigh, 241–42, 244
Simons, William, 115–16, 228
Siqueiros, David, 5, 37, 92, 108f, 120, 179–80, 269n78; CSLA and, 105–6, 283n67; Federación Minera de Jalisco and, 300n21
slavery, 31, 103, 112; abolishment of, 25, 147; African, 95; colonization and, 230, 239; modern-day, 110; plantation, 141; racial, 24, 26
slave trade, 89; African, 148; transatlantic, 109, 239
Smith, Stephanie J., 38, 267n26, 271n93, 299n170, 310n18
socialism, 292n140; in one country, 100, 282n45
social movements, 6, 19, 28–29, 31, 204, 214, 249, 252; aesthetics and, 273n127; analogies and, 174; character work in, 202; horizontalist, 29; Latin American, 18
solidarity movements, 4, 16, 30, 172, 177, 183, 217, 250; multiracial, 7, 249; overidentification in, 158; transnational, 7, 156, 249
solidarity politics, 13, 27, 31, 126, 174, 253; relational, 143, 151, 157 (*see also* relational solidarity)
Solís, Manuela, 181–83
Sommer, Doris, 243
South Africa, 24, 96, 104
Soviet Union (USSR), 85, 105, 123, 211; aid from, 163; Guerrero and, 178; Junco and, 14, 99, 180, 215; Mella and, 278n71; Mexico and, 215; Modotti and, 222; United States and, 313n70; Villena and, 132

violence, 22, 28, 112, 139, 214, 218, 227; anti-Black, 111, 229; anti-immigrant nativism and, 133; anti-labor, 199; toward company police, 240; of extractive industries, 88, 197; imperialist, 73, 140, 191; in Nicaragua, 202, 204; racial, 4, 197, 199, 223; racialized labor and, 221, 228; of US expansion, 77; against women, 202

Virgin Islands, 160, 173

Vivó, Jorge, 131, 165, 223, 311n24

Wallerstein, Immanuel, 10, 262nn27–28

Weston, Edward, 40, 54–57, 63–64, 310n14

whiteness, 175, 177, 266n15

white terror, 24, 95, 227–28

Wolfe, Bertram, 5, 48–51, 170–71, 181, 269n70, 269n78; deportation of, 51, 271n95; "The Indian as the Base of the Anti-Imperialist Struggle," 59, 62, 272n113; Sager and, 299n179

Wolfe, Ella, 5, 48–51, 271n95

women, 27, 30, 53, 105, 283n67; banana plantations and, 219; Black, 97, 240, 317n33; El Libertador and, 271n95; Haitian, 242, 305n100; Indigenous, 61–66, 202, 253 (see also Tehuanas); LADLA-Uruguay and, 115; MAFUENIC and, 192, 202, 272n100; of Mexican descent, 181; Mexicanized, 179; Muslim, 304n96; Nicaragua and, 192, 202; PCM and, 271n93; resistance and, 317n33; rights of, 67, 253; Sandino and, 204; tobacco workers, 160; white, 104, 142; working conditions of, 105

women of color, 29–30

Wong, José, 129–30

Wood, Tony, 7, 26on11

workers, 19–20, 25, 40, 59, 75, 77–80, 90, 106–7, 195, 201, 230, 250; African American, 181; agrarian, 53, 112, 119; agricultural, 13, 39, 133, 228; Antillean, 106, 290n69; banana, 19, 55, 105, 181,

199–200, 222, 242; BC and, 221, 242; campaigns, 116; Chinese, 96, 120, 127–28, 133, 135, 147–48, 150, 207, 228; coffee, 233; Cuban, 99, 110–11, 126, 130, 133, 139, 151, 288n30, 288n34; Dominican, 232, 313n70; Grupo Izquierda and, 115; Haitian, 99, 108, 110–11, 126, 225–26, 237, 240, 243; immigrant, 15, 96, 108, 110–11, 113–14, 122–23, 127–28, 133–35, 148, 173, 197, 221, 226, 228, 234, 238, 240–41, 315n134; Indigenous, 39, 53, 59, 63, 85, 107, 112, 199, 227; industrial, 113; Junco and, 100; LADLA and, 94; Latin American, 52, 105, 108–9, 121, 151, 227; MAFUENIC and, 202, 209, 302n41; in Mamita Yunai (Fallas), 241; Mella and, 92, 213, 278n68; mestizo, 113, 229; Mexican, 52, 84, 181, 228; migrant, 284n108; movements, 52, 126, 134, 150; Nosotros (Pedroso) and, 144–45; organizations, 120, 129, 159; in Over, 236–38, 243–44, 315n134; petroleum, 51; Puerto Rican, 159–61, 165, 173; racism and, 125–26, 151; rights of, 97, 196; Sandino and, 206; sugar, 133–34, 138–40, 224, 232–33, 243; tobacco, 160–61; United Fruit Company and, 224–25; US, 52, 88; West Indian, 108, 126, 225–26, 229, 238, 241–42, 244; white, 102–3, 113, 126, 229; in "Zafra-1934" (Pedroso), 139–40, 147. See also Black workers

Workers Party (WP), 47, 157, 260n8, 278n68

world-systems theory, 9–10

World War I, 16, 43, 110, 133, 157, 238

Yen, Huei Lan, 148–49

Yrigoyen, Hipólito, 208, 210

Zaldívar, Oliva, 178

Zepeda, Pedro José, 207, 209

Zumoff, Jacob, 241–42, 274n7, 312n49, 314n115

www.ingramcontent.com/pod-product-compliance
Lightning Source LLC
Chambersburg PA
CBHW020821270326
41928CB00006B/391